KU-627-742

REBELS ON THE AIR

Leeds Metropolitan University
17 0484924 9

JESSE WALKER

REBELS ON THE AIR

An Alternative History of Radio in America

New York University Press • *New York and London*

For Mom, Dad, and Andrew

NEW YORK UNIVERSITY PRESS
New York and London
www.nyupress.org

© 2001 by New York University
All rights reserved

First published in paperback in 2004.

Library of Congress Cataloging-in-Publication Data
Walker, Jesse, 1970–
Rebels on the air : an alternative history of radio in America /
Jesse Walker.
p. cm.
Includes index.
ISBN 0-8147-9381-9 (cloth : alk. paper)
ISBN 0-8147-9382-7 (pbk. : alk. paper)
1. Radio broadcasting—United States—History. 2. Radio
broadcasting policy—United States. 3. Amateur radio stations—
United States.   I. Title.
PN1991.3.U6 W35 2001
384.54'0973—dc21   2001003030

New York University Press books are printed on acid-free paper,
and their binding materials are chosen for strength and durability.

Manufactured in the United States of America

c 10 9 8 7 6 5 4 3 2 1
p 10 9 8 7 6 5 4 3 2 1

LEEDS METROPOLITAN
UNIVERSITY
LIBRARY
1704849249
KV - B
CC - 86457
00·6·03
384· 540973WAL

Contents

Acknowledgments

It's a funny thing about journalism: the more sources you have, the more they contradict one another. After a while, the parts of your book that seem the most solid are the ones you feel the least confident about. Somewhere out there, you tell yourself, are all the witnesses to history that you couldn't find, and once the book appears, they'll write to tell you everything you got wrong. (They can reach me at jwalker@reason.com.)

That said, it feels like I've met, spoken on the phone, and/or traded e-mails with virtually everyone ever involved with any kind of radio. My thanks to everyone who answered my questions: David Adelson, Don Agostino, Martin Allard, Angel Babudro, Michael Bader, Beverly Baker, Jack Balsley, Frank Bardacke, Harriet Bascus, Mara Beth Benjamin, Larry Bensky, Bob Bergstresser, Dana Berliner, Bob Bickford, Rasta Black, Jeff Blankfort, Bo the Lover, Mike Bracy, Ed Bremer, Doug Brewer, Willie Brown (not the mayor!), Steve Buckley, Scott Bullock, Jeannie Bunton, Brian Butler, Ted Byfield, Lynn Chadwick, Jerry Chamkis, Sue Cohen, Clare Conrad, Tad Cook, John Crigler, Ronald Davis, Frank Dean, Carol Denney, Jim Dingeman, Esty Dinur, Angel Dones, Kate Duncan, Stephen Dunifer, Marty Durlin, Laura Ellen, Jim Ellinger, Mac England, Lorenzo Ervin, Shawn Ewald, Eyebrow, Kathy Fennessy, Diane Fleming, Jim Foley, Chuck Forsberg, Peter Franck, Stephen Franco, Alan Freed (not the '50s DJ!), Ken Freedman, James Gattuso, Lyn Gerry, Maria Gilardin, Bruce Girard, Bill Goldsmith, Charley Goodman, Joshua Greenland, Paul Griffin, Doug Henwood, Paul Hernandez, Luke Hiken, Ray Hill, Penelope Houston, David Huff, Lisa Huff, Ace Humble, Mo Humble, Neva Humble, Amanda Huron, Thom Irwin, Vince Ivory, Jef Jaisun, Jonathan Jay, Double O Jones, David Josephson, Don Joyce, Vincent Kajunski, William Kennard, Mona Kennerson, Kelly Kombat, Alan Korn, Fred Krock, James Lane, Jeremy Lansman, David Leder, Michael Levier, Otis Maclay, Mike Malone, Bob Marston, R. Paul Martin, Cathy Melio, Lorenzo Milam, Morgan Miller, Phil Miller, Nicole Mones, Jim Moody, Chuck Munson, Allen Myers, Tom Ness, Joseph

Noonan, Mike O'Connor, Paul Odekirk, John Ohliger, Willy One Blood, Robbie Osman, Geov Parrish, Jeff Perlstein, John Perry, Frederick Phaneuf, Pirate Jim, Reverend Poppybreath, Adam Clayton Powell III, Ron Powell, Des Preston, Stephen Provizer, Joe Ptak, Paul Riismandel, Howard Rosenfeld, Wayne Roth, Greg Ruggiero, Steven Sandler, Paul Sawyer, Paul Schaffer, Danny Schechter, Don Schellhardt, Max Schmid, Tom Schreiner, Curt Schroell, Pat Scott, Ruth Seymour, Mike Shay, Mike Siegel, David Silberman, Melodie Silverwolf, Jim Simmons, Troy Skeels, Sam Smith, Norman Solomon, John Sommers, Peter Spagnuolo, Clare Spark, Bill Spry, Jerry Starr, Zeal Stefanoff, Cheryl Stopnick, Sue Supriano, Chris Sutherland, Jerry Szoka, Parry Teasdale, Tom Thomas, John Tirpack, Travesty, Pete triDish, Tony Truong, Phil Tymon, Uncle Sherman, Eduardo Vera, Dennis Wharton, Harvey Wheeler, Greg Whitcomb, Napoleon Williams, John Winston, Andy Wolcott, Jenny Wong, Mark Worth, Joni Wright, Larry Yurdin, Tom Zarecki, and Sara Zia-Ebrahimi, plus a few anonymous informants (on both sides of the law) and various people whose names now escape me or who answered e-mails I've foolishly forgotten.

Some of these people merely replied to a quick query or two. Others gave me hours of their time. Many became friends. One or two became the opposite, and a few more may decide they don't like me when they see what I've written about them. I appreciate their help, nonetheless.

Thanks also to several fellow writers on radio who generously shared their advice, their research, or the occasional lead: John Anderson, Jon Bekken, Tom Bell, Ted Coopman, Sarah Ferguson, Tom Hazlett, Benn Kobb, Richard Kostelanetz, Matthew Lasar, David MacFarland, Anita McCormick, Ron Sakolsky, Solveig Singleton, Tracy Jake Siska, John Whiting, and Andrew Yoder. Similar thanks are due my fellow editors at *Reason*, both for their help and for their patience: Brian Doherty, Charles Paul Freund, Nick Gillespie, Chris Hull, Michael Lynch, Virginia Postrel, Sara Rimensnyder, Jacob Sullum, and Jeff Taylor. Fellow staffers Mike Alissi, Barbara Burch, Robert Honrado, and Mary Toledo also offered some valuable assistance, as did our former colleagues RiShawn Biddle, Mariel Garza, Jennifer George, and Ryan Sager.

Yet more appreciation, less evenly distributed, is owed to the members of the Freepacifica, MRN, Pho, and Progressive Radio e-mail lists. And I offer a warm thank-you to my former colleagues at WCBN and KSER: it was DJing with you that started me on this particular road.

Several people read and gave me useful feedback on parts of the book: Bryan Alexander, Josey Ballenger, Alison Clark, Nathan Crow, Lyn Gerry, Michael A. Levine, Meredith McGhan, Virginia Postrel, Stacia Proefrock, Dave Rahbari, Timothy Virkkala, Jessamyn West, and John Whiting. Three more—Matthew Lasar, Lorenzo Milam, and Sara Ryan—read the whole blasted manuscript. Several publications allowed me to work out portions of the book in their pages: I owe thanks to the editors of the *Alternative Press Review,* the Cato Institute's *Policy Analysis* series, *Chronicles, Hobby Broadcasting, Inside.com, Liberty,* the *New Republic,* the *Portland Free Press,* the *Seattle Scroll,* and *Z*—and *Reason,* of course.

Then there's the broad "miscellaneous" category: from Mike Payson, who called me whenever radio-related material arrived in his bookstore, to Chad Williams, who helped me track down the lyrics to "Convoy." I couldn't possibly list everyone who rendered such timely kindnesses, but here are a few more: Matt Asher, Mary Beth Barber, Jonathan Chait, Bill Kauffman, Rona Kobell, Wendy McElroy, Hugh Morley, Michael Papadopoulos, Debbie Shamoon, and Martin Wooster.

I owe a great debt to many writers who came before me. The granddaddy of all the recent revisionist histories of radio is Erik Barnouw, whose three-volume *History of Broadcasting in the United States* is essential reading. The economic analysis of telecom policy has not been the same since Ronald Coase published his classic article, "The Federal Communications Commission," in 1959. And of the many good books about radio that have appeared since then, two deserve special mention here: Susan Douglas's *Inventing American Broadcasting* (1987), a strong influence on chapter 2 of this book, and Matthew Lasar's *Pacifica Radio* (1999), an equally strong influence on chapter 3.

Thank you to my editor, Eric Zinner, and to my agents, Lynn Chu and Glenn Hartley, for their help in bringing this book into print. Thank you to Despina Papazoglou Gimbel for supervising the editing and production and to Judy Kipp for compiling the index. Thank you to my old cohorts at Entity Haus, and to my fellow members of the *Liberty* diaspora. And thanks, finally, to my family: to my brother, Andrew, and my parents, David and Marjorie. I'm not sure what strange bug prompted me to write a book, but I know they had a role in infecting me with it.

Joe's Garage

The radio is hopeless, just a holding tank for miserable shits who don't want to offend or defy or speak the truth. They're too bland to even suck.   —Ben Hamper

JOE PTAK LIVES in a ranch house in Sunset Acres, a neighborhood just off the freeway in San Marcos, Texas. Joe is lanky, talkative, and often longhaired, though he keeps his crop short when he has to go to court. Up on Joe's roof, there's an antenna, about twenty-five or thirty feet tall. In his garage, there used to be a radio station: unwashed, unlicensed, and undoubtedly one of the best in the country. Then the government made him shut it down.

Fliers and graffiti covered its walls. Some days the studio would be littered with junk, only some of which was the station's aging equipment. Other days Joe's partner, Jeffrey "Zeal" Stefanoff, would sweep the place, gently scolding anyone he caught dropping litter. But even then, you wouldn't have to go far to find some trash: just outside, you'd find three big garbage pails filled with beer cans. And a wastepaper basket filled with beer cans. And a milk crate filled with beer cans. You might get the impression that the DJs at Kind Radio weren't always sober, a notion reinforced by the faint but sweet odor of cannabis lingering inside.

But Kind was more than a place to party. It may have been unlicensed—read illegal—but it was the only radio station in San Marcos, and it took it on itself to be the one medium in town that was truly open to local voices. It broadcast city council meetings. It interviewed city planners. It covered local politics with a patriotic passion—not the local patriotism of mindless boosterism and downtown cliques, but the kind that believes in digging up dirt, relieving human misery, and celebrating the lives that the locals really lead.

There were no commercials on Kind, no underwriting announcements, and no fund drives. DJs were supposed to pay a monthly subscription fee, but the station was often lax about collecting it. Kind subsisted on kindness, on volunteer labor and spontaneous gifts; it was a place where a DJ might vent on the air about broken equipment, then find himself accepting a replacement from a friendly listener.

The station played all sorts of music: country, metal, reggae, rap, Tejano, house, folk, jazz. Its talk shows stretched from the anti-authoritarian left to the libertarian right, and covered several places in between: feminism, on *The Estrogen Hour of Power*; patriotism, on *Liberty Call*; marijuana, on too many shows to mention. Some of the city's gangs had timeslots; Joe and Zeal claim this cut down on crime, with the gangsters channeling their rivalries into their fiercely competitive shows.[1] Even prisoners had programs, leaving their work-release jobs early so they could drop by the studio before returning to jail. ("There are some pretty cool bosses in town," a DJ explains.) There weren't any cops with shows, but when some of them wanted to organize a union, they went on Kind to make their case.

Kind had a genuine gospel show, and it had a fake one as well: *The Kneeling Drunkard's Plea,* named for the Louvin Brothers record that served as its theme. Its host called himself Reverend Poppybreath; his baseball cap sported the slogan "Jesus Christ, Superfly."[2] The Rev's occasional cohost, Willy One Blood, spoke with the deep, throaty tones of a man who's smoked several bales of hemp. "They come in here about eight in the morning and start drinking beer," their fellow DJ David Leder told me. "It's very Texas."[3]

Leder hosted *The Ombudsman Show,* a program he describes as "participatory journalism": people would call in with complaints or questions about events around town, and Leder would answer them by phoning public officials on the air. One June day in 1998, for example, several callers were curious about some mysterious construction by the San Marcos River. They seemed to be putting in a pipeline, but if so, they'd picked an odd place: the worksite was *below* the dam. Leder called a series of officials in the city government and at Southwest Texas State University (which owned the land in question), all the way up to the answering machine of Billy Moore, mayor of the city and PR director at the college. Moore returned the call: San Marcos is a small town (population 39,000), and Kind, outlaw or not, is its radio station. Eventually, the mystery was solved: they were indeed putting in a pipeline, thanks to an old pump station nearby. Kind had scooped the chain-owned *San Marcos Daily Record* by two days.

Leder himself ran for mayor in 1998, with a greenish platform. He got about 14 percent of the vote, forcing a runoff between the incumbent, Mr. Moore, and his Chamber of Commerce–backed challenger, Susan Clifford Narvaiz. A week before the second ballot, Narvaiz declared that she'd shut down the station her opponent had endorsed: she didn't like its staffers' foul language or their oft-professed fondness for pot. Moore turned mildly defensive—some of the programming, he told the *Austin American-Statesman*, "tends to give me a stomachache"— but he stood by his support.[4]

At the next mayoral debate, Narvaiz cut loose. "I turned on the station," she announced, "and I heard this person saying, 'I'm high! Call me if you're high! I'm a masturbator! Call and join me!'" It was time, she concluded, to close Kind's doors forever.

Unfortunately for Narvaiz, the debate was being broadcast on Kind, galvanizing the station's fans to vote against her. What's more, some of Kind's staff put their tape of the debate to mischievous use. Within a day, the local airwaves were filled with a carefully edited recording of Narvaiz's words. "I'm high!" her voice announced to listeners. "I'm a masturbator! Call and join me!"

She had received a plurality in the initial election, but she lost the runoff by thirty-nine votes. Kind Radio took credit for her defeat, and few dispute its right to do so.

Behind Kind stood Joe and Zeal. Joe does odd jobs and is a self-proclaimed mooch. Zeal's an unemployed veteran. They're both active proponents of legalizing marijuana, and they're both active smokers as well: a day with them is a day spent watching a series of joints and pipes passing from one hand to another, giving their political patter a spacy, stoned timbre. They're surely the only members of Earth First! to maintain cordial relations with Take Back Texas, a property-rights group that usually gobbles environmentalists for supper. The connection is localism, a shared interest in keeping their communities free of outside control.

Kind Radio's roots go back to 1989, when Joe and Zeal started a newspaper, the *Hays County Guardian*. Southwest Texas State University had told them they couldn't distribute it on college property, under a policy barring papers that carry ads. Joe and Zeal challenged the ban, and the fight ended up going to the Supreme Court, which ruled in favor of the *Guardian* and commercial speech. In the meantime, they and their cohorts started exploring other alternative media. They'd heard of something called *micro radio*—low-budget, low-power stations geared toward local communities and run, if need be, without the sanction of the government. Joe and Zeal reasoned that, since Texas allows oilmen and other entrepreneurs to own the natural resources they "capture," the same logic ought to apply to the electromagnetic spectrum. No one was using 105.9 FM, so on March 19, 1997, they staked their claim in the name of Kind Radio. Then they remade the *Guardian* as the station's schedule, fired up a transmitter, and invited anyone listening to apply for a show.

The station wasn't very popular at first. But as more volunteers joined, the programming began to diversify, and the DJs started shaking off that early thrill of going on the radio just to say "fuck." Their audience noticed the change. "When I first started listening," one of the townsfolk told the *San Antonio Express-News*, "it seemed like all they talked about was legalizing drugs. I wasn't real impressed. But now, you never know what you will hear. It could be interviews or jazz or Tejano music—lots of stuff you would never hear on any other station, that's for sure."[5]

Incidentally, no one was *supposed* to swear on the air at Kind. You could play a record with cuss words on it, since that would be "in an artistic context," but on-air personalities were told to follow a notice posted prominently in the station's makeshift studio:

Just because this is micro radio does not mean there are no rules.

Remember don't use obscene words that are not allowed on the air (ie. **fuck,** or any word with fuck in it, **shit,** or any word with it in it, **cocksucker, dickface, penis breath, twat, pussy, cum** and **any other words** that are obscene, swearing, cussing, vulgar, indecent, lewdness, salacious, foul, dirty and/or smutty)—well don't use them—help protect our right to be on the air—or **you** will not be on the air.

If any of you feel that you need to find a **loop hole** to this policy then just give up your show now.

The rules also prohibited broadcasting while drunk, with intoxication defined "according to Texas standards."

When it was young, Kind ran into some trouble with the local zoning authorities. The city said it was against the law to run a radio station in a residential neighborhood. The Kind crew prevailed, arguing that their project was more a hobby than a business. With time, Kind endeared itself to enough of the town to stop worrying about such attacks, despite the occasional left field challenge from the likes of Narvaiz. San Marcos was friendly territory; the enemies were in Washington. (Besides the government's usual distaste for unlicensed broadcasting, another issue was at play. In 1997, the Federal Communications Commission assigned Kind's frequency to a commercial station, forcing Joe and company to move to 103.9 FM. They did leave a residual, short-range signal at 105.9, though, as a reminder that the frequency was rightfully theirs.)

Besides their managerial duties, Joe and Zeal did some programs of their own. One was *Heads Up*, usually hosted by Joe, a wide-ranging talk show that covered politics, the environment, health, and pretty much anything else the host wanted to chat about. The program's dynamics changed a bit when Joe took to babysitting Madeline, some fellow DJs' infant daughter, while on the air. The baby would start crying at the most serendipitous times, punctuating reports of officials' evil deeds with bawling outbursts. Once, during an on-air discussion of hazardous wastes, Madeline produced some ill-disposed wastes of her own, provoking much merriment in the studio and much puzzlement among Joe's listeners, at least until he let them in on the joke. The moment summed up Kind better than any other: high-toned political analysis, homely family duties, and potty humor, all at once and all broadcast live on the radio.

It says a bit about Joe, too. He and Zeal are comic figures, endlessly remembering old escapades and planning new ones; they exude such an intricate combination of competence and stoned disorder that when you first meet them, it's hard to tell whether you should be paying them to teach you their secrets or offering them your spare change. They know this. Indeed, they play on it. Their laissez-faire personalities let them rule their station as absolute dictators without sparking much serious dissent. In Zeal's words, "Joe and I are tyrants."

Ah, I say; so you see yourself as a benign dictatorship?

"No," Zeal replies, "we're not benign."[6]

Once, some DJs started calling for a more democratic structure, with elected representatives and committees and the like. So Joe and

Zeal started calling programmers' meetings, just like the dissidents wanted, and then they turned them into parties. Pretty soon, most of the rebels were having too much fun to worry about fighting among themselves or establishing a formal sort of government.

All this fits well with the pair's political beliefs. Joe's a registered Democrat; Zeal's a registered Republican. They both hate big government. They don't like corporations either, but they don't knock them with the usual leftist language. The problem with corporations, they say, is that they're too socialist: they're legal fictions, special privileges, chartered by the government in an affront to free enterprise.

They sound like libertarians—well, like left-libertarians—but they insist they're really monarchists. "The king," says Joe, and stops; Zeal has handed him a pipe. Joe takes a deep toke and passes the grass along. "The king," he continues. "The king . . . should be the poorest man in the kingdom."

"That's us," chimes in Zeal. "We're the monarchs of San Marcos."

"Yeah," says Joe. "The king ensures everyone's well-being. Everyone ensures the king's well-being. He goes to your house, you fix him a meal. He needs some money, you give him some. Because he's the king."

"That's Joe," says Zeal.

"I haven't had a job in three years," says Joe. "I have no skills. I'm an idiot savant—that's what everyone tells me. But people take care of me, and I take care of the radio station. And I can't lock my door."

"If he locks it," adds Zeal, "someone just breaks the window and comes in."

"If I lock the door, it means something's cheesed me off, and people know enough to stay away for a couple of days and let me chill. And then it's back to normal."

"Either that," says Zeal, "or someone breaks the window."

"When my girlfriend's in town, she'll lock the door," Joe points out. His girlfriend lives in Mexico.

"That's true," admits Zeal, and huffs in some more marijuana.

"People just do things for us," Joe explains. "We're on the Internet, but we didn't do that. One of our listeners did. So we don't need—" He pauses for a second. "Some people," he says, "they want us to do fundraisers, make ourselves a 501(c)3, all that shit—"

"We've never done a fundraiser," interrupts Zeal. "If we need some money, people do fundraisers for us. And give us the money."

"People give *me* money," Joe interjects. "What keeps them from giving me too much is they figure I'll just squander it on pot. So they just give me the pot, so I won't spend any money on it."

"Pot and Pepsi," corrects Zeal.

"Right," says Joe. "Pot and Pepsi. Those are my vices."

What about all those beer cans outside your house? Aren't they yours?

"No," says Joe. "Those are the DJs'. And Zeal's."

"I drink a lot of beer," says Mr. Stefanoff.[7]

In the year 2000, Kind went off the air. This did not happen because its volunteers or listeners had drifted away, leaving no one to run the station or no one willing to pay attention to it. It happened because the government insisted that it happen. This act of repression is only a small part of a larger series of policies that have decimated the radio dial—policies that make projects like Kind all the more necessary.

Most radio today is boring and homogeneous, chains of clones controlled by an ever-dwindling handful of focus-group-driven corporations. There are very few exceptions. Talk radio—the one format that can't be automated—exploded in the early 1990s, allowing any opinionated populist with a phone to illuminate you with his observations or entertain you with his demented ramblings. In recent years, though, the talk boom has subsided. And the music stations haven't been getting better.

Still, if you're lucky, you may live within range of something special: a little black station that broadcasts manic musical sermons on Sunday mornings, or the frenetic Spanish surrealism of good border radio, or a scrappy freeform station run by local volunteers. And on a good night, if the air is clear and the feds aren't lurking, you might pick up something really unusual: an unlicensed pirate broadcast, here this evening and gone the next. Catching an unexpected, unlawful radio signal feels like stumbling across a book of secrets, published by an invisible college. Pirate radio has a *mystique*.

This is, on a deeper level, simply the mystique of radio itself. To a kid, every signal is like a pirate station, another hidden world he's never visited before. I was in grade school when I got my first clock-radio; I would excitedly twirl the dial in the middle of the night, unsure whether I was breaking some house rule by tuning in when I was supposed to be nodding off. I listened to old radio dramas on the local public station and midnight call-in shows on the commercial band; one night, I was surprised and pleased to hear a Top Forty jock giving away, not a record or a concert ticket, but a footlong sandwich. Years of late-night listening made me more familiar with the usual radio formulas, and I soon couldn't bear to hear anything but the nearby college station, WXYC, the voice of bohemian North Carolina. That and the soulful sermons I sometimes caught on Sundays on the AM band.

At age eighteen I entered the University of Michigan and joined its student-run station, WCBN, a rare place without playlists or prefabricated formats. There I could watch others inject imaginative, creative chaos into their shows, and, naturally, I could try to do the same myself. One of my colleagues lived in an apartment filled with obscure albums, reel-to-reel tape loops, sound-effects records, videotapes of UFO cranks, and cassettes of old programs he could re-edit and broadcast anew. Some nights he'd conclude his show with minutes of silence, interrupted occasionally by a recorded voice declaring, "There is no sound here at all."

Sometimes this was unlistenable. More often, it was brilliant. His show was a sound collage, with juxtapositions that could surprise, illuminate, excite. It was the exact opposite of formatted radio, of playlists devised by focus groups, payola merchants, and specialized software.

Once he brought a personal computer into the studio, hooked it to the console, and programmed it to replay a sound effect, over and over again. Then he started a record or two—he never liked to play only one thing at a time—and wandered out of the room.

A visitor entered and saw a Macintosh where a DJ would ordinarily be.

"What's that computer for?" he asked me.

"It's the DJ," I explained. "This is some new software we're trying out. The computer's been responsible for all the programming in the last hour. It's been doing a good job, don't you think?"

The stranger blinked a couple of times. "Yes," he finally said. "It certainly has."

"We're thinking about replacing a lot of the DJs with machines," I said. "This is sort of an experiment."

"It's amazing," said the stranger, "what they can do with computers these days."

"It is," I amiably agreed. "And this isn't even the best program. We're hoping to make enough money this pledge drive to get one of the newer models."

The DJ reentered the studio and got back to work.

"All right," I admitted. "I made all that stuff up." Our guest looked embarrassed, and a little disappointed. "Uh . . . yeah . . . I thought so," he lied.

So goes the mystique of radio. Combine that with another childhood obsession, the mystique of the pirate. Adventuring outside the boundaries of land and law, trafficking in dangerous booty, living freely in his republic of the waves—if you're of a certain cast of mind, an irresistibly romantic image emerges: *Radio pirates! Corsairs of the ether!*

Pirate radio has existed for as long as there have been radio regulations to defy. The most famous ethereal buccaneers were the jolly-roger entrepreneurs behind Radio Caroline, Radio London, and the other offshore AM stations of the 1960s that challenged the BBC's staid programming with the latest rock hits. Today, within the subculture of shortwave hobbyists, there is a sub-subculture of clandestine broadcasters whose unlicensed programming ranges from counterculture comedy to neo-Nazi rants.

But foreign shores and shortwave are ignored by most Americans. Now a new wave of pirates—the micro radio movement—has boarded the FM band, founding hundreds of illegal low-watt operations since the late 1980s. Ordinary people have taken the tools of radio into their own hands and set up their own stations, without the presence or sanction of the FCC.

I am aware that today's radio marketplace is open enough that the stations that survive in it are meeting somebody's needs. I wish such stations no ill. I have no desire to drive those two oxymorons, "classic rock" and "young country," from the air. I can coexist with "easy listening," with "adult contemporary," with even that unlistenable concoction called "smooth jazz." (That's like calling Scientology "smooth Judaism.") But what kind of musical desert contains *only* those brands of broadcasting?

A freer media landscape, shorn of such tight controls, is possible—one that would allow us greater freedom to choose, to create, and to escape.

Freedom to choose simply means more options: more radio formats, more TV channels, more film studios, more publishers. Market forces have already produced much media diversity, and were it not for the barriers erected by the FCC (among others), those forces would produce much more. Radio, in particular, is already very diverse, with more than eleven thousand AM and FM stations in the United States and dozens of formats for listeners to choose from. But for the most part, this is diversity without depth: an ether carved into a thousand niches, each only an inch deep.

Consider the state of country radio. Country is now the most popular format in the United States, with more than twenty-six hundred stations devoted to it. The most popular brand of country broadcasting is "young" country—that is, country divorced from its past. One typical outlet's TV commercials alternate grainy, black-and-white films of old folks square-dancing and playing hillbilly instruments (words on screen: "old country") with color footage of groups that look like rock bands (words on screen: "young country"). Most country stations won't play much traditional country music. By the mid-1990s, it had gotten to the point where Johnny Cash's albums had to be marketed as "alternative," even though anyone attending one of the Man in Black's concerts would see as many middle-aged moms in cowboy hats as grungy young dudes with goatees. In some towns, you're more likely to hear Merle Haggard or Willie Nelson on a punk-flavored college station than on the frequency theoretically devoted to country and western. And so country radio rules, but great reservoirs of excellent country music—new as well as old—are ignored or forgotten.

Freedom to create means more than that: not just the right to choose among five hundred TV stations instead of three, but fewer barriers to setting up a station of your own; not just greater ease in joining the licensed elite, but the right to operate outside it.

Like the freedom to choose, the freedom to create is being withheld by an alliance of policymakers and professionals. Since the mid-1980s, the technical cost of starting a low-power FM radio station has been within most Americans' reach—a couple hundred dollars plus the monthly power bill, which for low-watt stations isn't very high. The *legal* cost, however, is much higher: almost $3,000 for a license, plus $100,000 or more in startup costs. With very few exceptions, the FCC won't issue licenses to noncommercial stations of less than one hundred watts. Class A commercial stations require at least *six thousand* watts of power.

Note how the two freedoms dovetail: the effect of the hundred-watt and six-thousand-watt rules is not only to artificially restrict access to the airwaves, but also to ensure that those who do get on the air, having risked more money in the enterprise, will be less likely to try anything new.

Freedom to escape means being able to withdraw from the thick smoke of mediation and to interact more directly, more convivially, with others. It's not far from what the novelist Andrew Nelson Lytle had in mind when, in the '30s, he instructed his fellow southerners to "throw out the radio and take down the fiddle from the wall."[8] There have been times when doing free radio has meant evading the electromagnetic spectrum altogether, as with the Jamaican soundtrucks that played music beloved in the island's poor communities but absent from the official airwaves; or the street DJs who invented hip-hop, mixing disks with an eclectic ferocity that would have shocked even the most experimental freeform jockey of the hippie days.

Micro radio lets us speak for ourselves, lets us keep our radios on *and* take down those fiddles from the wall. By blurring the boundaries between mass media and face-to-face interaction, it puts the former at the disposal of the latter. A micro station based in a particular community—a housing project, a rural village, a bar, a church, a group of friends—isn't just a signal a solitary listener might catch on his stereo. It's a rallying point, a reason for people to gather both on and off the air.

In the early days of Steal This Radio, a pirate station in New York City, the broadcasters constantly moved from one location to another—"solemnly vigilant," an organizer later wrote, "against FCC-detection." *Solemnly* might not be the best word for the station. "Our weekly broadcasts quickly became the best floating party on the Lower East Side, and as thirty or forty people would inevitably arrive at every broadcast location, we often asked ourselves if anyone was home listening to the show."[9]

And if they weren't, would it matter?

I wrote this book to show how and why those three liberties have been constrained. I also wrote it to describe those times and places where innovators have managed to break through those constraints and create genuinely diverse, expressive, or immediate radio. From the 1930s on, radio has been streamlined, predictable, and regulated by people intent on keeping it that way. But there has always been a countertrend—pioneers with a different vision, a more open idea of what radio could be.

There were the amateurs who invented broadcasting at a time

when both the government and the big commercial interests assumed that the new medium would be used only for one-to-one conversation. There were the early, cheerfully slapdash stations of the '20s, the Mexican border blasters of the '30s, the independent black stations of the '40s and '50s. There was the Pacifica network (in at least some of its incarnations) and the "community" stations that imitated Pacifica's menu of diverse music, dissident views, and uncategorizable creativity. Even the Citizens Band made a contribution—and, more recently, there have been some exciting experiments in Internet radio. And, of course, there are unlicensed wildcat stations like Kind: rough-edged mini-stations that have always been around, squatting here and there, but congealed into a mass movement in the '90s.

Some of these broadcasters are essentially elitists, transmitting experimental or radical fare for limited audiences. Some are populists, less interested in advancing a particular artistic or political agenda than in opening the airwaves to popular participation. And some, paradox be damned, are both. Kind Radio existed so that everyday people could get on the air. But once those people got there, their listeners learned that the everyday can also be extraordinary.

2

The First Broadcasters

In attics, barns, garages, woodsheds, apparatus took shape.

—Erik Barnouw

ON JANUARY 2, 1909, five boys in New York City formed the Junior Wireless Club, Ltd. The group was the world's first amateur radio organization, a small affair run by an eleven-year-old and headquartered first at the Hotel Anson, then at the home of the group's corresponding secretary.

Barely a year later, the boys' club had taken the lead in lobbying against Senator Chauncey Depew's Wireless Bill, one of many congressional efforts to restrict amateur activity. It was a strange moment in history, a time when the defense of popular access to the airwaves could fall to a few boys on the cusp of adolescence. Stranger still, such boys were the radio innovators of the day, discovering uses for a technology the establishment had assumed would be employed only for point-to-point communication, ideally by licensed professionals. In 1911 or 1913—sources differ—two members of the New York club established one of the world's first broadcast stations, a crude, homemade apparatus whose arc chamber sometimes threatened to explode. The station was located at the corresponding secretary's house; its audience was in the Hudson River, aboard anchored battleships.[1]

Such groups were formed for mutual education and aid, not to advance an ideology. As apolitical as any other hobby clubs, they espoused, often inchoately, only one political idea: that the airwaves should be open to the public, not monopolized by a powerful few. Not everyone shared this vision. By the end of the 1920s, three nationally based advertising-supported networks—two of them owned by RCA, itself a direct creation of the government—dominated American broadcasting. The amateurs had been shunted aside to their own band, more than adequate for their own purposes but irrelevant to the casual listener. The only political challenge to the status quo came from a loose movement whose chief interest was public uplift, not public access. And, upon failing to prevent Congress from passing the Communications Act of 1934, even this opposition would wither away.

Radio was a scientific marvel at a time when Science was God. Born at the close of the nineteenth century, radio entered public consciousness at the dawn of the Progressive Era, a time when society was increasingly stratified and centralized.

The traditional account of the Progressive Era describes a time of popular protest, of trustbusting presidents taming oppressive monopolies. Richard Hofstadter espoused this notion in *The Age of Reform,* defining progressivism as

> that broader impulse toward criticism and change that was everywhere so conspicuous after 1900, when the already forceful stream of agrarian discontent was enlarged and redirected by the growing enthusiasm of middle-class people for social and economic reform. . . . Its general theme was the effort to restore a type of economic individualism and political democracy that was widely believed to have existed earlier in America and to have been destroyed by the great corporation and the political machine.[2]

That's a reasonably fair description of the Western and Midwestern progressives—at their most lucid, neopopulist insurgents who distrusted bigness in both business and government. But the Eastern progressives, the reformers who staffed the Roosevelt and Wilson administrations and actually drafted the new federal laws, were a different breed. Their progressivism was a philosophy of consolidation and corporatism, of partnership between giant enterprises and giant government, of "scientific" management. Their reforms were supported, and often initiated, by the largest corporations, which found that national regulation was a good way (a) to override the "inconsistent state regulation" (as John D. Rockefeller called it) the more populist reformers had passed, and (b) to stabilize their cartels, which had trouble surviving in a more competitive marketplace. And it was these progressives who were politically successful, while their inland kin, led by Wisconsin Senator

Robert LaFollette, were unable to attract the financial support necessary to win a national campaign.

The roots of the new régime could be found in the previous century. Compulsory schooling, professional policing, and centralized charity had already replaced less formal arrangements; subsidies, tariffs, and limits on liability had allowed businesses to attain previously unthinkable sizes. But with the Progressive Era, the country reached a turning point. The old liberal ideal of free competition, never fully realized and more distant by the year, was retired. A new ideology was ascendant: the technocratic ideal of elite management for the common good. "We are living in an age of organization," declared John Kirby, president of the National Association of Manufacturers, in 1911—"an age when little can be accomplished except through organization, an age when organization must cope with organization, an age when organization alone can preserve your freedom and mine."[3] Municipal reformers transferred control of local services from corrupt but neighborhood-based political machines to a corrupt but professionalized civil service. New licensing laws restricted entry to elite vocations. Public schooling was centralized. The autonomous and the local were out; the credentialed and the consolidated were in.

Into this social order entered radio. There is no need to recount here the invention's early history, a tale that has been told many times. Most interesting for our purposes are the amateur operators who took the new technology in hand and, armed with cheap crystal detectors, forged a new community in the ether. The hams, as they were called, were usually young and male, building their homemade sets in sheds, attics, and barn lofts with whatever materials were available, from tomato cans to rolling pins to tobacco tin foil, scaling trees and roofs to find the best spots for their antennas, insulating their aerials "with everything, from old pop bottles to porcelain cleats salvaged from somewhere."[4] An automobile ignition coil might serve as a transmitter; for a tuner, one might simply wrap an old Quaker Oats box in wire. The hams' hobby alternately impressed and annoyed the neighbors, whose approval was put to the test with every terrible mechanical noise that woke them at midnight.

Philosophically, the hams were a throwback to an earlier age, to the egalitarian optimism that had produced the lyceum movement in the 1830s and 1840s. The lycea were locally organized voluntary associations that sponsored scientific lectures and research; at their peak, eight hundred existed in different parts of the country. An 1831 pamphlet summed up the lyceum philosophy:

> Every rational man . . . is endowed with capabilities for improve-ment—wherever he is placed he is surrounded with materials for his improvement; . . . intellectual, moral and *social* faculties are confined to no favored few of our race; . . . science is confined to no favored spot under heaven; . . . intellects and affections are coexistent with the race of men, and . . . science is as boundless as the earth and the heaven.[5]

Every Man a Scientist—or, in the 1910 version, Every Boy an Engineer.
With time, the lycea withered, as scientists found it prudent to dis-tance themselves from mere amateurs and dabblers and to form more exclusive professional associations. This made sense at the time—American science had attracted more than its share of cranks and was crying out for some form of self-governance and peer review. But by the turn of the century, at least one field—radio—was being advanced pri-marily by men who worked outside those institutions: Guglielmo Mar-coni, Reginald Fessenden, Lee de Forest. And now it was the province of an informal community that stood outside both state and corporate structures, working without wages, building its own institutions from the ground up. In progressive America, this seemed archaic. Amateurs were craftsmen in an age of professionals, a loosely organized network in a time of consolidation, spontaneously evolving at a time when prog-ress was supposed to follow a plan. That, of course, was part of their ap-peal. Americans have always loved to think of themselves as individu-alists. At a time when this self-image was being battered on all sides, in-ventor-heroes such as Marconi and the amateurs were a welcome tonic.
The tradition of tinkering stretched back into the previous century, to the hobbyists who spent their spare time building mechanical de-vices and erecting neighborhood telegraph lines. Radio knit this scat-tered tribe into a grassroots subculture, as interested in interaction as in experiments. The number of active stations grew rapidly, from about 150 in 1905 to around 600 in 1910 to more than 10,000 in 1914. Electrical magazines began publishing radio columns. Periodicals devoted en-tirely to radio emerged, starting with Hugo Gernsback's *Modern Electrics* in 1908. Amateurs began to form organizations: first the Junior Wireless Club and then, less than a month later, Gernsback's short-lived

Wireless Association of America. Most important were the local clubs that began to sprout, from Albany to Fresno, meeting both in person and in the Morse Code cyberspace of the day. Such bodies allowed hams to share information, train newcomers, and regulate their craft.

Gernsback's group, by contrast, was hardly an organization at all. With no dues or obligations, it was easy to join; it soon claimed a membership of ten thousand, several times the number of active amateurs. It is notable not for its accomplishments but for its founder.

Few navigated the uneasy straits between progressivism and individualism more nimbly than Hugo Gernsback. Born in Luxembourg in 1884, Gernsback emigrated to the U.S. in 1904 after both France and Germany refused to grant him a patent for a layer battery he had invented. Upon arriving in America, he had to give up his plans to market his invention when he discovered that it could not be mass produced. He took a job with a New York battery manufacturer instead, and was fired within three hours. His boss had become convinced that Gernsback was an industrial spy. Gernsback, in turn, became convinced that he should never work for anyone but himself. He launched an array of business ventures, among them a radio-parts import company and a radio-parts catalog. The latter featured another Gernsback invention: the Telimco Wireless, the world's first ready-made home radio set, able to transmit Morse Code or ring a bell at a short distance. To the public, it was an almost unbelievable wonder—indeed, Gernsback once had to demonstrate his set to a skeptical cop to prove himself innocent of fraud.

Gernsback shared the optimism of the age, the faith in progress that others were using to justify new bureaucratic structures. Yet he was an independent, self-made entrepreneur who chafed under the restrictions of organization. If the scientific advances of the early twentieth century suited Gernsback's temperament, the social transformation did not. His response was not to protest the changes—or even consciously notice them—but to work outside the coalescing corporate state and to encourage such independence in others. Like the leaders of the lycea, Gernsback believed that knowledge should be diffused among the population, not monopolized by an elite. If people did not understand technology, he felt, they would fear and repress it. He founded *Modern Electrics*, he later declared, "to teach the young generation science, radio, and what was ahead of them."[6]

In part, of course, this was self-promotional shuck. As the critic Paul

Carter has noted, Gernsback's editorial style often "irritatingly blended the note of Chautauqua uplift with that of the hard sell."[7] The man was out to make a buck, and not every venture he launched improved the state of popular scientific knowledge. But Gernsback had a genuine love of invention, and he pursued those profit-making ventures that would also bring him personal satisfaction. That became clear when he took to writing what he called "scientifiction," serializing his seminal (and awful) science-fiction novel *Ralph 124C 41+* in *Modern Electrics* in 1911. No Mary Shelley or H. G. Wells, Gernsback extrapolated mechanical marvels in turgid prose, throwing style and characterization aside in favor of what he saw as science fiction's central purpose: technological prophecy. The closest the serial comes to literary invention is its title, a weak pun: "Ralph, one to foresee for one." Nonliterary inventions, on the other hand, litter *Ralph*'s pages: radar, television, and photovoltaic cells appear in the book, as do (lest the tale appear more prophetic than it was) antigravity, weather control, airborne "vacation cities," and travel through an "earth tube" buried deep underground.[8]

The hero is "one of the greatest living scientists and one of the ten men on the whole planet earth permitted to use the Plus sign after his name."[9] If the progressive ideal favored a credentialed scientific elite, this was progressivism taken to the nth degree. On the other hand, Ralph is not a bureaucrat "doing science" in a professional, institutional setting. He is a solo inventor in the Edison/Tesla/Marconi mode, only more so: rarely does Gernsback even suggest that Ralph is building on the work of others, except when it might buttress the author's contention that all his book's marvels are scientifically plausible. (We are thus told, again and again, that an idea was first proposed in the early twentieth century, only to sit dormant until revived by Ralph's fertile mind 760 years later.)

It's tempting to dismiss this as a power fantasy for adolescents—it *is* a power fantasy for adolescents—but it's also something more. It indicates that the author saw no contradiction between his adopted homeland's individualist values and the faith in scientific management that characterized his era. When Gernsback imagined a scientist, he thought of an independent inventor like himself. His ideal organization was a meritocracy, not a bureaucracy. And if he unconsciously imported some anti-individualist values of the day into his work, he also allowed many doomed nineteenth-century institutions to last another seven centuries.

The ham radio buff who read Gernsback's magazines was in a similar bind. He was trying to advance science and engineering, or at least enjoy those advances, in the decentralized, independent manner of a Jefferson or an Edison, at a time when political institutions increasingly favored a different arrangement. As the years passed, the amateurs and the professionals found themselves more and more at odds.

At this point, those professionals were concentrated in the U.S. Navy, which had an obvious interest in maintaining a reliable means of ship-to-ship and ship-to-shore communication. The soldiers of the sea had been slow to adopt radio at first, restrained by institutional inertia and a nationalist distrust of the British Marconi Company. By 1904, that reluctance had melted. That year, the Interdepartmental Board of Wireless Telegraphy—a government commission that included representatives from the navy, the Army Signal Corps, and the Weather Bureau—proposed that the navy should oversee the development of the wireless, that established naval communications stations should have priority over commercial operations, and that the Department of Commerce and Labor should license private stations. The recommendations were unpopular, and Congress failed to pass them. The navy was undeterred. It began building a coastal communication network in earnest, convinced that the airwaves should be military property.

Its chief rival was the commercial wireless industry—especially Marconi's company, which had monopolistic ambitions of its own. The hams initially escaped the navy's attention. By 1910, this had changed: there were more active amateurs than all the commercial and naval operators put together. Some weren't afraid to buzz their rivals, notes the historian Clinton DeSoto:

> If a commercial station wanted to do any work, it was usually necessary to make a polite request of the local amateurs to stand by for a while. If the request was not polite, or if an amateur-commercial feud happened to exist, the amateurs did not stand by and the commercials did not work. Times without number a commercial would call an amateur station and tell him to shut up. Equally often the reply would be, "Who the hell are you?" or "I've as much right to the air as you have."[10]

DeSoto was an amateur operator himself, and he wrote from that point of view. The hams were being selfish, he conceded. "And yet," he added, "the amateur *did* have equal right to the air with the commercial, from any legal or moral standpoint."

> He was seldom interrupting important traffic—contrary to accusations that have been made, there is no authoritative record that amateurs ever seriously interfered with any "SOS" or distress communication; on the contrary, there are instances when the constantly-watchful amateurs heard distress calls which were not picked up by the regular receiving points."[11]

In any event, the commercial operators weren't about to clamor for regulation, since they knew that sword could cut both ways. They regularly interfered with competing businesses themselves, though they often chose to foist blame for this on the most convenient scapegoat: the amateurs.

The navy, on the other hand, was ready to drive the interlopers off the air altogether. It too had received its share of amateur interference, pranks, and lip. (Once, in Boston, a naval operator told a ham to "butt out." The amateur replied, "Say, you navy people think you own the ether. Who ever heard of the navy anyway? Beat it, you, beat it.")[12] Like the commercials, the military had incentive to blame the amateurs for their own mistakes. Unlike the commercials, it had no incentive not to lobby for restrictive regulations. It didn't help that the amateurs were often better trained, even better equipped, than the sailors. The hams' anarchic meritocracy outperformed the navy's society of status, sometimes relaying rescue messages that the official radiomen had missed or mangled. This didn't exactly boost the seamen's self-image.

It was in this context that Congress considered a series of bills to govern the ether. At this point, almost no laws governed the airwaves; the only exception was the Wireless Ship Act of 1910, which simply required most oceangoing steamers to be equipped with "efficient apparatus for radio communication." Note: the ether was unregulated *by the government*. Self-regulation was widespread and growing, a rich spontaneous order nurtured by the amateur associations, from small college clubs and Boy Scout groups to large metropolitan federations.

For example: in 1910, the Chicago Wireless Club, a group devoted primarily to sharing technical information and training newbies, negotiated a complicated covenant among the area's amateur and commercial operators. *Electrical World* magazine described the arrangement:

The Chicago club has taken into its own hands the regulation of members' interference with commercial signals, a matter which has elsewhere recently echoed even to Congress. By agreement with the commercial operators, all club members having stations of over 1/2-kw capacity are limited to special times for sending, during which the commercial stations and low-powered amateur stations are not at liberty to work. The "big" amateurs thus have the ether to themselves the first 15 minutes of each hour from 6 to 11 p.m. weekdays, and all day Sunday. If a low-powered operator wants to talk to one of the high-powered stations, he is instructed to wait until 20 minutes after the hour, and then to put in his message, which will be answered during the first quarter of the next hour.[13]

Had the government imposed such a scheme, the protests would have been quick and angry. But when the operators imposed it on each other, it simply seemed like good sense—and not just in the Second City. The so-called Chicago Plan quickly inspired similar arrangements in other parts of the country.

The navy could conceivably have bargained its way into such arrangements instead of turning to Congress for redress. For that matter, it could have avoided many amateur pranks by encrypting its messages, a simple precaution that, unbelievably, it had not yet adopted. Instead, it continued to push for government intervention. In the wake of the *Titanic* disaster of April 1912, it got its wish. False reports had shot through the ether after the wreck, hoaxes that had probably issued from amateurs and sparked fury against the ham community as a whole. (Little public anger was directed toward the navy, even though Harold Bride, the one wireless operator to survive the iceberg, informed the *New York Times* that "the Navy operators aboard the scout cruisers were a great nuisance. I advise them all to learn the Continental Morse and learn to speed up if they ever expect to be worth their salt.")[14] The result was the Radio Act of 1912.

The new law strengthened the Wireless Ship Act's provisions, requiring, for example, that ships employ at least two radio operators and that one always be on duty. That was not controversial: it simply legislated measures that any sensible captain would adopt voluntarily. The law also gave distress calls priority over competing messages. This, too, hardly challenged the status quo.

The heart of the act, the watershed for regulation of radio, was the new licensing requirements. Henceforth, no one could legally operate a radio without a license from the Department of Commerce and Labor. (In 1913, Congress split this bureaucracy in two, with radio licensing falling to the new Commerce Department.) A heavy chunk of spectrum—all wavelengths between six hundred and sixteen hundred meters—was reserved for the government. Corporate stations were given the rest of the air, with the amateurs, in the historian Susan Douglas's words, "exiled to an ethereal reservation": confined to short waves of two hundred meters and less, a piece of spectrum then considered almost useless.[15] They were also limited to one kilowatt of power. The original bill—the legislation that passed the Senate in May—would have licensed receiving stations as well as transmitters, thus inadvertently closing off the prospects for broadcasting; it also would have allowed police to arrest errant amateurs without first issuing a warning. Those two provisions were eliminated after some strenuous lobbying by the Wireless Association of Pennsylvania, but the bill as a whole survived. President William Howard Taft signed it into law on August 17, 1912.

Enforcement of the new rules was spotty at first. Many hams—more than half in 1914—didn't bother to get licenses, thus becoming America's first radio pirates. Others applied for licenses but ignored the one-kilowatt and two-hundred-meter rules. As long as they were considerate of commercial and naval operators, they were usually left alone. Given its limited budget, the Department of Commerce simply couldn't afford a crackdown. According to DeSoto,

> It is almost a certainty that, had enforcement during the first years of the radio law been adequate, amateur radio would have been nearly extinct by the time of America's entry into the World War; and that after the war amateur stations would never have been allowed to reopen. But as it turned out, amateurs continued to do their operating as they had always done it . . . and by the time enforcement became sufficiently rigid to actually restrict them to two hundred meters, new technique and new apparatus had been developed to make the situation tenable."[16]

Order was kept, not by the government, but by the amateurs' increasingly successful efforts to police themselves. The organs of this self-regulation were, as before, the radio clubs. Club members approved and enforced complex rules of traffic, punishing miscreants with fines. These groups were strictly local affairs. Gernsback's putatively national Wireless Association of America, never more than a paper empire, had quickly dissolved. The Junior Wireless Club had renamed itself the Radio Club of America in 1911, but in practice its sphere was confined to Metro New York; what's more, it was less and less a ham association, becoming more of a scientific society. Amateurs did not have a truly national body until 1914, when the engineer-inventor Hiram Percy Maxim organized the American Radio Relay League, which remains the premier ham radio group in the United States. The ARRL was an ingenious path around the legal and natural limits to an amateur station's power. Its members built an intricate system for relaying messages across America, organizing routes from city to city and, eventually, from coast to coast.

After government control was established, this self-managing web would be forgotten or dismissed. Herbert Hoover, radio's chief regulator in the 1920s, later offered an interviewer this anecdote:

> The small boys in radio . . . had established an association of radio amateurs with whom we dealt constantly.
>
> One day I asked them how they were going to deal with enforcing the assignments of their wave band to prevent interference.
>
> The president of the association said, "Well, I don't think you'd like to know what we do."
>
> "Oh, yes," I said, "I would."
>
> He said, "Well we just take the fellow out and beat him up."[17]

As the historian Michele Hilmes has pointed out, Hoover was probably referring to either Maxim or Gernsback, both "well into middle age and hardly apt to behave in the 'boyish' manner described."[18] But it serves a clear rhetorical purpose to claim that the amateurs were all "small boys" whose idea of spectrum management was to punch people, especially if one also ignores the powerful systems of self-government that the amateurs actually built.

Broadcasting, too, began to emerge, as voice and phonograph joined Morse Code in the ether. The idea was not new. Decades earlier, before radio had been invented, many telephone retailers had promoted their product as a means of transmitting music and news to mass audiences. Foreshadowing today's cable systems, Paris, Budapest, and other European cities hosted experiments in "pleasure telephone" services throughout the 1880s. Some Americans took note. Speaking in Detroit in 1890, AT&T Vice President E. J. Hall excitedly proposed "providing music on tap at certain times every day, especially at meal times. The scheme is to have a fine band perform the choicest music, gather up the sound waves, and distribute them to any number of subscribers."[19] Another American, the socialist writer Edward Bellamy, included a similar idea in his utopian novel *Looking Backward*, in which "sound tubes" carry classical music to the citizens of his future society. In Budapest, in 1893, Theodore Puskas began broadcasting news, music, stock prices, and plays via phone to, by one count, six thousand subscribers. The pleasurephone proved to be a historical dead end, but it shouldn't have required much imagination to transfer the idea to the wireless.

Yet the founding fathers of radio developed the medium with only point-to-point communication in mind. As late as 1920, Marconi would predict that, when television finally arrived, its main use would be "the quick transmission of pictures for newspaper and police purposes."[20] The only one immune to this myopia was Lee de Forest, who was thinking about broadcasting as early as 1907 and was conducting actual broadcasts by 1910, though those were initially marred by a whining interference. In 1915, the inventor built a tower atop his factory and started delivering music, sportscasts, and—the following November—election coverage to whomever would listen. As a journalist, de Forest made a fine inventor: he incorrectly announced that the Republican nominee, Charles Evans Hughes, had been elected president.

Another inventor, Reginald Fessenden, is usually credited with producing the first non–Morse Code broadcast in 1900, using a primitive spark transmitter to fire a few words into the ether. On Christmas Eve, 1906, he offered a more elaborate program, broadcasting several pieces of music and a Bible reading from his wireless station in Brant Rock, Massachusetts. But the first true DJ was Charles "Doc" Herrold, a professor at the College of Engineering and Wireless in San Jose. A consummate tinkerer, Herrold was inspired by Bellamy's fictional sound tubes. A great idea, he decided—but why not broadcast with the wireless instead? In 1909, Herrold and some students began transmitting news, music, and banter from a local bank. By 1912, they were operating on a regular schedule. Their audience was not limited to amateurs, as Herrold had installed receiving sets in several San Jose hotel lobbies. He also pirated some power from the Santa Fe Railway's street-car lines.

Slowly but steadily, broadcasting caught on. Dozens of hams began playing phonograph records into their transmitters. 1910 brought the first sportscast, with live coverage of the Jeffries-Johnson fight; once more, hams were responsible. Outside the amateur world, a handful of university-operated stations began broadcasting weather, market, and news reports to rural audiences, usually in Morse Code. Meanwhile, across campus, amateur student clubs were airing material that was either more frivolous or more fun, depending on your point of view.

A decade later and an ocean away, Bertolt Brecht would declare that radio could be "the finest possible communication apparatus in public life," if only it "knew how to receive as well as transmit, how to let the listener speak as well as hear, how to bring him into a relationship instead of isolating him"—a system that would "step out of the supply business and organize its listeners as suppliers." He didn't realize it, but he was describing the world of the early hams. The one great difference was Brecht's belief that "only the State can organize this." The amateurs proved him wrong.[21]

In short, the new law barely hampered the hams. Their numbers swelled; their subculture grew; their technical skills became more adept. Business soon discovered that the amateurs knew their craft better than many professionals did, and some began hiring accordingly. "Do you suppose I could get a commercial operator to operate a radio telephone set?" asked Robert Gowen, chief engineer for the De Forest Company in the 1910s.

> I found they knew absolutely nothing about it and in every case I had to get a "ham," simply because the former was a man who knew only how to press the key and read code while the latter was a technician who had trained himself in the fundamentals of radio and knew how to analyze the circuit and keep it functioning properly in addition to his knowledge of key pressing. Likewise, every man I had in my laboratory was an amateur, not because I was one but purely because they were the only ones obtainable who could tackle the problems placed before them.[22]

When the U.S. entered World War I, the military made the same discovery. The Great War temporarily killed amateur radio. But it also ensured that once the war was over, the ham community, if not the ham dream of airwaves open to all, would survive.

World War I was the apotheosis of progressivism, a brief period in which the partnership between big government and big business blossomed into a full-scale authoritarian state. Dissidents were rounded up in the middle of the night, to be imprisoned or deported without trial. Men and women were arrested simply for speaking out against the war. The mail was censored. Radical newspapers were banned. A draft was imposed. And the economy was regulated by the War Industries Board, a central committee of political and industrial bureaucrats. This cartel of cartels fixed prices, ran the railroads, channeled contracts to favored interests, and kept labor in check. A separate Food Administration maintained an extensive and intrusive licensing system. From 1917 to 1918, the United States was a command economy.

Where the economy went, so went the ether. On April 7, 1917—one day after America entered the war—the navy nationalized the airwaves. Fifty-three commercial stations were taken over, along with the telegraph and telephone systems; the remainder were shut down.[23] The production and distribution of radio components also came under naval direction, though private ownership was preserved.

One consequence was government-guaranteed profits for those privileged corporations. Another was the near-disappearance of the independent inventor.

The government had ordered the amateurs to dismantle their stations, banning even experiments with dummy antennas. But it also discovered that it needed the hams, for the same reason that Robert Gowen preferred to hire them: they required little training. Douglas notes that

> In early January 1917, there were 979 navy radiomen; by November of 1918, that number had jumped to approximately 6,700, a large proportion of them from the ranks of the amateurs. The amateurs were no longer a source of competition and interference in the airwaves. Instead, the subculture of American men and boys who had previously fought with the navy over who owned the spectrum now supplied the armed services with thousands of willing, cooperative recruits. They were no longer outside the system, they were part of it.[24]

Indeed they were. While police were destroying stations run by hams unwilling to shut down, the leaders of the amateur movement were pledging their support to the war effort. The Radio Club of America surveyed itself for talent that might be useful to the military should the United States enter the war, then turned this information over to the government. The American Radio Relay League put its resources at the state's disposal, seeking out the best amateur stations so that the feds might convert them to military use. So the hams were militarized, and the military was invaded by hams.

After the war, the navy found it couldn't return to its old, categorically anti-amateur position. In 1921, the acting secretary of the navy acknowledged the new stance:

> It will be the desire of the Navy Department to further in every way practicable the interests of the amateur radio operators throughout the country, and with this principle established, it is hoped that the closest co-operation may be had between the Navy Department and the amateurs. My knowledge of the patriotic and valuable services rendered by the amateurs during the World War is sufficient to convince me that, as a factor in the national defense, the promotion of the amateurs is not only desirable, but necessary . . .[25]

By the same token, the amateur community was no longer its old anarchic self. Yes, the subculture reappeared; indeed, it flourished like never before. Old clubs were revived, and new ones begun; the technology continued to advance; the Knights of Columbus set up free radio schools for former servicemen. The self-organization, the self-regulation, the do-it-yourself energy were reborn. But the world they re-entered had been transformed. The airwaves were being policed as never before.

Julian Henney, a wireless operator aboard a civilian Great Lakes ship, discovered this not long after the war, when he encountered a radio inspector as his vessel prepared to depart Detroit:

> "What's your name? where's your license?" he demanded.
>
> I assumed an air of extreme civility. "The license hangs on the wall in front of your nose and my name is on it," I answered without cordiality, for I had looked over his shoulder and saw that he had already

copied my name, age and everything else in the way of information contained in the license.

He was not impressed with my independence. "'What is your name?' I said," he snapped. "Name of your captain? Where are you bound? Ever worked before? What are your call letters? Have you monkeyed with the connections? Are you red, or black, and if married state why?"—and so on.

He got all of this off in one breath, meanwhile working everything in sight from the spark to the auxiliary power plant.[26]

Henney's partner was less fortunate: he had forgotten his license and was therefore ordered to disembark when the boat reached Duluth. There would be no more careless flouting of the law—not by commercial operators, and not by amateurs. And, after a few years, there would be no more amateur broadcasts either.

In 1920, Warren Harding was elected president promising a "return to normalcy." Progressivism and prudery were out; peaceful trade and private pleasure were in. Old liberal values made a comeback in the 1920s. War gave way to isolationism. The White House was occupied not by activists like Roosevelt and Wilson, but by two relative libertarians, Harding and Coolidge. Neither man undid the new hierarchies imposed during the Progressive Era, and even Harding, remembered as a do-nothing president, occasionally intervened to protect a privileged group's position, as when he raised tariffs and when he sent federal troops to put down striking West Virginia miners. But compared to the Wilson years, the '20s were an era of freedom and prosperity, in radio as in almost everything else.[27] As the decade began, the number of Americans buying receivers took off; so, in response, did the number of broadcast stations.

Not that the industry lacked a privileged class. The chief beneficiaries of the radio boom were AT&T, General Electric, Westinghouse, and RCA, which, along with United Fruit, the Wireless Specialty Apparatus Company, and the Tropical Radio Telegraph Company, had formed a patent pool. The feds had in effect created RCA after World War I, once it became clear that the military would not be able to monopolize the airwaves anymore. The government still wanted the American airwaves to be in *American* hands, which meant trouble for the foreign-owned Marconi Company. The result was the Radio Corporation of America, which took over Marconi's American stations and patents while keeping most of the old corporate officers in place. The other members of the patent pool all held stock in RCA.

Several smaller firms were manufacturing radio products as well, but they were at a disadvantage, since the Radio Group controlled all the relevant patents. So radio manufacturing was a government-enforced cartel, fractured only by AT&T's rivalry with the other companies. (Until 1926, AT&T hoped to use its wire monopoly and its patents to establish a broadcast monopoly as well.)

The government hadn't given up all interest in the airwaves: it still kept about half the spectrum for itself, creating the Interdepartmental Radio Advisory Committee to allocate bandwidth among its different agencies. Despite this, private broadcasting, previously an amateur sidelight, became the activity people associated most closely with radio. Listeners carried on the ham tradition of "distance listening," searching for stations from as far away as possible. The stations, for their part, weren't sure what to put on the air. Or even, in many cases, why they were on the air in the first place.

The first professional station was KDKA in Pittsburgh—though WWJ, originally owned by the *Detroit News*, has also claimed that title.[28] Frank Conrad of Wilkinsburg, Pennsylvania, by day a Westinghouse engineer, had attracted a fair-sized audience transmitting from his garage-based station, 8XK. According to legend, Conrad originally became a ham after an argument over the correct time of day. He eventually concluded that the only way to be sure of his watch's accuracy would be to check it against the time signals transmitted from Washington. This meant building a receiving station, which led to further amateur experiments and finally, around 1920, to playing his old phonograph into the microphone on Saturday nights.

Eventually, his employers noticed that his broadcasts were stimulating demand for radio equipment. They struck a deal with the DJ, moving his transmitter to their factory roof and setting up regular broadcast hours as KDKA. Commercial radio was born—though in those days, it rarely carried commercials, and the advertising one did hear was more like an underwriting announcement on NPR than a modern ad.

Other businesses with an interest in drumming up consumer demand (e.g., department stores) launched stations. So did enterprises seeking publicity, such as newspapers. And so did a fair number of businessmen who simply thought it would be a gas to run a radio station. About a third of the stations were owned by nonprofit groups: universities, churches, in one case a labor union. Auto dealers, cabarets, YMCAs, flour mills, stockyards, factories, theaters, utilities, Bible institutes, even a poultry farm—anyone and everyone was going on the air.

Naturally, many amateurs expanded their operations into commercial outlets. Those hams who didn't make the change had to move out of broadcasting, thanks to a new regulation passed in January 1921. Hereafter, declared the Commerce Department, all licenses issued to amateurs would include this language: "This station is not licensed to broadcast weather reports, market reports, music, concerts, speeches, news, or similar information or entertainments." The ham subculture was set on its present course, and radio became a more passive medium.[29]

The change was not immediately obvious. The amateurs might have been pushed off the air, but look who was taking their place! If a marble factory or a chiropractic school could have its own station, how could anyone claim that broadcasting was becoming less open?

Indeed, stations were multiplying far faster than the number of slickly produced programs that could be put on the air. At first, broadcasting itself had been reason enough to turn on one's set. (As one of the first radio announcers, Hans von Kaltenborn, later recalled, "it was only the fact *that they heard you* that listeners reported. *What* you said was relatively unimportant.")[30] When the novelty started wearing off, station managers found themselves scrambling for material. "The first radio stations programmed randomly," notes the historian Susan Smulyan, "providing airtime for virtually anyone who showed up at the studio and wanted to play."[31] Opera here, country there, a lot of potted palm music and a little bit of jazz, even a weekly on-air meeting of a make-believe Keep Growing Wiser Order of Hoot Owls: early programming was energetic and diverse. The Hoot Owls, merry Masons of Portland, Oregon, sounded "as though there was a dandy party going on in the next room and somebody had left the door open," reported *The Wireless Age*. "The degree team is made up of the best wits in town, one merchant, one lawyer, a wholesaler, a piano dealer, the owner and manager of a booking service and an insurance man; also the manager of KGW and a goat that is always heard but never seen."[32]

Broadcasters had no quick means of getting feedback, other than the thanks and complaints that listeners volunteered. They were thus forced to rely on a slow, unreliable system of trial and error—which, with time, delivered results, producing schedules that were messy, improvisatory, and populist by default. "The same story happened time after time," Smulyan reports: "an old-time fiddler would take his turn in front of the microphone, and listeners would flood the station with letters and phone calls begging for more such music."[33] Station managers were surprised, but they adjusted their schedules accordingly.

So for all the state's encroachments, radio was still a freewheeling medium in the '20s. Traditional histories of the period describe it as a chaotic era: the Department of Commerce handed out licenses freely, the story goes, and the secretary of commerce (at the time, Herbert Hoover) was unable to hold the line against interference. With 1926 came the so-called Breakdown of the Law, in which the airwaves degenerated into complete chaos. Finally, Congress created the Federal Radio Commission, which undertook the long-overdue task of reducing the number of licenses to fit the available spectrum.

Recent scholarship has undermined this account. Since Ronald Coase's classic essay "The Federal Communications Commission" was published in 1959,[34] many economists have argued that a more rational solution to the Breakdown of the Law would have been to recognize property rights (or something like them) in the ether and to treat interference as a tort. Newer research, most notably by the economist Thomas Hazlett, has shown that such a common law–based order *did* emerge in the '20s, without federal direction. Broadcasters homesteaded particular frequencies at particular times of the day (twenty-four-hour stations were still rare). Spectrum rights were freely traded. Some areas adopted, without government prodding, the institution of "silent night," in which local stations shut down for an evening to let listeners tune in to long-distance signals.

As the demand for licenses began to exceed supply, some problems did develop. For some impenetrable reason, the Commerce Department required all "news, lectures, entertainment, etc."—in short, virtually all broadcasting—to take place at the same frequency: 360 meters, or 833.3 kHz. (Weather and government reports, however, had to be broadcast at 485 meters. "For bulletins," writes the historian Erik Barnouw, "the stations apparently swept back and forth across the dial, urging their listeners to tag along.")[35] Crammed onto the same channel, stations were obviously more likely to interfere with one another; broadcasters dealt with this by working out time-sharing agreements.

Eventually, Hoover declared that "the spectrum" (that is, the frequency devoted to broadcasting) was filled and that he would deny any further applications for licenses. This led to *Hoover v. Intercity Radio Co.*, in which a federal court ruled that Hoover did not have the legal right to deny an applicant a license but could assign the station particular hours and frequencies.

Established broadcasters, looking to reduce competition, wanted the government to limit the number of new licenses it would issue. They had a friend in Hoover. The secretary, who had spent World War I heading the Food Administration, was a strong supporter of business-government cooperation, of the reign of experts acting in "the public interest." And now he was the man with the most influence on American radio policy.

Every year from 1922 to 1925, Hoover hosted a national conference for the radio industry. The legal scholar Jonathan Emord, drawing on the conference records, has sketched a convincing theory of competition-fearing broadcasters and power-seeking government officials reaching a quid pro quo: "in exchange for regulatory controls on industry structure and programming content, industry leaders would be granted the restrictions on market entry that they wanted."[36] At the first conference, Hoover asserted that "the public—all of the people interested—are unanimously for an extension of regulatory powers on the part of the Government."[37] That certainly described the corporate interests represented at the conference. For L. R. Krumm of Westinghouse, for example, the problem facing the industry was that it was "perfectly possible to establish a so-called broadcasting station for about $500 or $1,000 initial investment." What's more, such outlets' "entertainment outlay represents nothing but phonograph records, and that sort of station can interfere very disastrously with such a station as we are trying to operate." (The phonograph reference was, among other things, a subtle swipe at jazz, which respectable opinion then disdained.) Krumm added, "I believe twelve good stations, certainly a maximum of fifteen, would supply most of the needs of the country."[38]

Hoover recognized that the interference problems that existed would be eased if the government would expand the spectrum available to the public. But on the whole, he opted for more regulation, not more space. In 1923, shortly after the *Intercity* decision, Hoover enlarged the broadcast band—and reallocated it, sorting his licensees into classes. The biggest broadcasters were granted clear channels. Others—

nonprofits, small entrepreneurs—were crammed together. Some licensees, it seemed, were more equal than others.

The groundwork for the so-called Breakdown of the Law was laid after the secretary decided, in November 1925, to stop issuing new licenses, arguing again that the spectrum was completely filled. He invited a court challenge, and one arrived in April: *United States v. Zenith Radio Corp.* Like *Intercity,* the *Zenith* decision denied Hoover the right to withhold a license. Unlike *Intercity,* it also denied him the right to assign times and wavelengths to particular broadcasters. Hoover did not appeal the case. Instead, he asked the acting attorney general, William Donovan, which District Court decision to follow. On July 8, Donovan came out for *Zenith,* asserting that the government had no authority to define spectrum rights. The effect was to eliminate *all* rights in the ether. "Faced with open entry into a scarce resource pool, a classic 'tragedy of the commons' ensued," writes Hazlett. "Stations had to be licensed by the secretary of commerce; once licensed, they were free to roam the dial, select their own transmitting location, choose their desired amplification level, and set their own hours."[39] Hoover had created a crisis, and Congress quickly passed the Radio Act of 1927 to remedy it. That law created the Federal Radio Commission, the forerunner of today's FCC.[40]

The Radio Act had its populist opponents. "This bill is fair to only one institution," declared an aggrieved Senator Key Pittman (D–Nevada). "It is fair to the monopoly that will be created under it."[41] But it had its populist supporters as well. Senator Clarence C. Dill (D–Washington), one of the law's chief authors, was also a leading critic of the radio trust, both before and after his bill passed. "The Radio Commission," he would later state, has "put the control of effective radio service in the hands of a few great corporations."[42] Yet he never took responsibility for his role in creating that state of affairs.

Arguing for the Radio Act in 1927, Dill made it clear that he was not concerned with "chaos in the air," which could no doubt "be righted as a matter of business." No, the law should be passed because "the Government must provide for the protection of the public interest as the numerous and urgent demands for the use of the air develop. That is the crux of the situation."[43] During the Progressive Era, business interests had found it useful to dress bills in the language of public-interest reform. However pure Dill's own motives may have been, he played this role in 1926, little realizing that it would not be his view of the public interest that would prevail.[44]

The courts upheld the radio commission's right to license broadcasters in 1929, when a station threatened to stay on the air after the government yanked its license. The definitive case came a year later, when George Fellowes, an Englishman in St. Louis, became the first person to be prosecuted under the Radio Act for unlicensed broadcasting. Fellowes, who was also charged with bootlegging other stations' shows, was ideologically opposed to any regulation of broadcasting; he admitted that his pirate station caused some interference but declared that this was technically unavoidable. He was sentenced to a year and a day in the federal pen.

Meanwhile, Congress was ignoring nonregulatory solutions. In November 1926, WGN-Chicago sued the Oak Leaves Radio Station, claiming that, by interfering with its signal, the latter had essentially committed trespass. Judge Francis Wilson ruled in WGN's favor, explicitly basing his ruling on the spectrum rights that had emerged over the past few years, a system he compared to the water rights that had evolved out West.[45] Bizarrely, Hoover would later cite this decision as a near-endorsement of the Radio Act. "One of our difficulties in securing legislation," he recalled, "was the very success of the voluntary system. Members of congressional committees kept telling me, 'It's working all right; why do you bother us?' . . . But finally a Chicago station broke away from our voluntary system. They preempted a wave length for themselves and established in the courts their contention against our weak legal authority. Then Congress woke up . . ."[46] In this manner, the victors rewrote history. The notion that there might have been an alternative to bureaucratic management was unthinkable, and so Hoover left the actual content of Wilson's decision on the proverbial ash heap.

Congress certainly knew of the WGN case—it was cited in the *Congressional Record*—but it had no use for the common-law approach.[47] Nor did it have any use for further enlarging the spectrum. This was technically feasible but politically unpalatable to the big broadcasters, who preferred to make room by eliminating their smaller rivals. The industry defeated spectrum expansion by arguing that it would require consumers to buy expensive new sets. Listeners might have preferred this, of course, to being completely unable to hear competing stations. No matter. Listeners weren't in charge.

■

During this time, RCA begat NBC, the first radio network. (Or, rather, the first *two* radio networks, the Red and the Blue. The latter would later spin off as ABC, following an antitrust suit.) A competitor, CBS, joined it not long afterward. Advertisers, initially wary of radio, began to enter it more readily. By the 1930s, it was advertisers, not listeners, who were paying the bills, and so—rhetoric to the contrary—it was advertisers, not listeners, whom programmers first aimed to please. Granted, the admen wanted to attract audiences with popular programming. But at this point, they had their eyes set on a national market, one with little room for diversity. It would be another two decades before niche advertising would arrive.

Standard histories tend to assume that the rise of advertising-based network radio was inevitable. Recently, revisionist historians such as Susan Smulyan and Robert McChesney have argued that it was actually a result of specific policy choices. Smulyan's book *Selling Radio* points out that broadcasters had to *sell* the idea of radio advertising to potential sponsors. She also notes that commercials were very unpopular with early listeners, even more so than today.

The revisionists are on the right track, though they sometimes overstate their case. It was natural for commercial interests, especially marginal ones, to look to radio as a way to sell their wares. And it was natural for at least some stations to seek sponsors, just to help pay the bills. After all, even some prewar amateurs, Doc Herrold and Lee de Forest among them, included ads in their primitive broadcasts. What was far from inevitable was the ad-saturated radio that took hold in the late 1920s, with nearly no noncommercial alternatives in sight.

In August 1928, the Federal Radio Commission announced its spectrum reallocation plan, called General Order 40. Its effect was to eliminate nonprofit stations and to nurture the networks. The commission favored "general public service" stations over "propaganda" stations, the latter defined, in McChesney's words, as broadcasters "more interested in spreading their particular viewpoint than in reaching the [broadest] possible audience with whatever programming was most attractive."[48] The commission argued that there simply wasn't enough "room in the broadcast band for every school of thought, religious, political, social, and economic, each to have its separate broadcasting station, its mouthpiece in the ether."[49] As we've already seen, this wasn't necessarily true—but then, the commission had an agenda to fulfill. The

National Association of Broadcasters, the commercial stations' lobby, was effectively under the control of CBS and NBC, and there was a revolving door between the association and the commission.

Radio had become a national medium. Early visionaries, seeing this potential, had spun elaborate collectivist fantasies of the new national or even global culture that might emerge in the radio age. In 1923, *Radio Broadcast* editorialized that since

> radio is destined, economically and politically, to bind us together more firmly, can it not accomplish, to some extent at least, unification of the religious ideas of the different creeds and cliques? Will it not do away with the "religious" squabbles which so frequently stir small communities? Is the self-sacrificing and penurious existence of the several ministers in the average small town really necessary?[50]

Ralph 124C 41+ would have been proud. Meanwhile, in *The Wireless Age,* advocates of different would-be international languages debated just *which* artificial tongue radio should deploy to wipe out the archaic linguistic divisions that plagued the world. Poor, misguided idealists—little did they realize that the Earth's many cultures would eventually be united, not by Esperanto, but by *Baywatch.*

Without federal meddling, the electromagnetic spectrum would no doubt have maintained common areas, collectively administered à la the Chicago Plan. The spontaneous evolution of spectrum rights in the 1920s suggests that individual proprietorship would have also emerged. The Radio Act of 1912, the wartime nationalization, the prohibition of amateur broadcasting, the creation of different classes of broadcast licenses, the Radio Act of 1927, and General Order 40 were a series of enclosures, in which the spectrum rights held by hams, nonprofit broadcasters, and small entrepreneurs were expropriated by powerful private interests and the state. This elite was not a united front, of course, especially after an antitrust settlement in 1932 divested GE and Westinghouse of their interests in RCA. But it was a recognizable set of institutions, with RCA atop the heap.

The Communications Act of 1934 codified the new order into law (and transformed the FRC into the FCC in the process). It's common to speak of today's broadcasting regime as a "perversion" of the Communications Act, and that makes sense if one examines only the rhetoric that accompanied the new law. But in its actual content, the bill was a triumph for the radio trust. As McChesney would later write, "Almost all the clauses objectionable to the commercial broadcasters were dropped in conference in exchange for keeping section 307(c)," a weak requirement that the feds "study" the notion of reserving channels for nonprofit stations.[51]

The spectrum shakedown sparked some protest, but it was the kind that suggested that the battle was already lost. One group—Levering Tyson's National Advisory Council on Radio in Education (NACRE), launched with Carnegie money in 1930—merely called for the networks to broadcast more educational programs. The other reformers tended to view the NACRE with suspicion, or even as collaborators; the group's main rival, Joy Elmer Morgan's National Committee on Education by Radio (NCER), offered the more radical (but still hardly earthshaking) demand that the feds reserve whole frequencies for educational use. One historian, Eugene Leach, has suggested that "the NACRE belonged to one wing of the progressive movement—the Eastern wing, long at odds with Midwestern protest, that proposed the efficiency and generosity of big business as the answer to the nation's problems."[52] In this view, the populist banner was held aloft by those reformers, such as the NCER, that were financed by the Ohio-based Payne Fund. Leach has the NACRE down cold, but the Payne crowd was hardly an heir to the LaFollette tradition. Their basic concern was that listeners were not getting enough spinach, and their basic demand was for government-guaranteed, educrat-run channels for the public's betterment.

For the most part, the so-called broadcast reform movement consisted of elitists, not populists, interested not so much in demanding popular access to the airwaves as in ensuring properly enlightened programming. Many (including Morgan) looked to the BBC as their model, and some privately hoped for outright nationalization of the industry. By and large, they did not challenge the *idea* of bureaucratic control. They simply thought they should be the bureaucrats in charge—or, more realistically, hoped the real power brokers would cut them a piece of the pie.[53]

There were exceptions. The American Civil Liberties Union searched for ways to ensure that diverse views were aired. (This eventually led them to oppose "public interest" content regulations as an infringement of the First Amendment, a position opposed by most of the era's other reformers.) And WCFL, the voice of the Chicago Federation of Labor, was trying to create a new kind of broadcasting. The station had been launched in 1926 by Edward Nockels, a diabetic Dubuque gas fitter who'd risen to become secretary of the CFL. It began as a member-supported nonprofit operation, mixing popular entertainment with a radical political perspective. Since it was run by organized labor, regulators deemed it a "propaganda station," an outlet judged less worthy than the presumably more universally appealing operations run by businessmen. So the Radio Commission moved it to a less advantageous portion of the band, then limited it to daylight hours. Needless to say, none of this helped it maintain its contribution base. When WCFL pushed for reform, it was a matter of self-defense. When reform failed, the station defended itself another way: it went commercial.

Nockels had dreamed of a different radio landscape, a diverse array of low-power stations run by and for ordinary people. It was the opposite of the emerging corporate order, and of other reformers' statist schemes as well. But it was not to be.

By 1934, the mystique of the wireless was waning; radio was a regular, predictable part of Americans' lives. True, there would still be moments when the airwaves would seem magical, even to adults. There were still some regional stations with their own exotic character; there was Mexican radio, with its crackpots and con artists and country musicians; and even the networks offered occasional creative delights, from the bizarre comedy of the vaudevillian called Colonel Stoopnagle to Orson Welles's infamous adaptation of *The War of the Worlds*.

But if radio could still convince people that Martian invaders had landed in New Jersey, the days were long gone when listeners could seriously discuss whether their receivers were picking up signals from the Red Planet itself. "We occasionally get very queer sounds and indications, which might come somewhere outside the earth," Marconi had told *The Wireless Age* in 1920. "We have had them both in England and America. The Morse signal letters occur with much greater frequency than others, but we have never yet picked up anything that could be translated into a definite message." A year before, Nikola Tesla had suggested that such signals might be coming from Mars, a hypothesis Marconi agreed was possible. RCA's chief engineer was less inclined to believe, arguing (not unreasonably) that "it is impossible for the people of Mars or any other planet to know the

Morse code." *The Wireless Age* was quick to note that this was merely the engineer's opinion.

A page later, the magazine displayed a photograph of a scientist, eyes alight with madness, earphones clasping his head, loose machinery all around him, touching a stethoscope to a globe. The caption: "Dr. James Harris Rogers, sponsor of an underground wireless system, hopes to receive signals from another planet."[54]

The mysterious signals *weren't* coming from Mars, of course—nor from Venus, the source one astronomer declared was more likely. They had many origins; in one typical case, they turned out to be the pulsating telegraph beat of nearby stock ticker wires. By 1922, Marconi was telling the public that reports of interplanetary signals were "bosh."[55] And he was right to do so. Tales of Martians would soon retreat to the fiction columns of Hugo Gernsback's magazines, not to bother radiomen again.

Yet there was a tragedy hidden in this triumph of common sense. Decades before, Mark Twain, piloting riverboats up and down the Mississippi, had to memorize every corner of the waterway, until all the river's majesty was diminished into the map he kept in his head. As men and women explored the ether, inevitably they demystified it. The result was progress, but also loss, as for Twain on his steamer:

> But as I have said, a day came when I began to cease from noting the glories and the charms which the moon and the sun and the twilight wrought upon the river's face; another day came when I ceased altogether to note them. Then, if that sunset had been repeated, I should have looked upon it without rapture, and should have commented on it, inwardly, after this fashion: "This sun means that we are going to have wind to-morrow; that floating log means that the river is rising, small thanks to it; that slanting mark on the water refers to a bluff reef which is going to kill somebody's steamboat one of these nights . . ."[56]

But radio is a human environment, with more potential surprises in store than the relatively predictable laws of nature can provide. America is a vast and diverse country; it should be home to a thousand and one kinds of broadcasting, with plenty to jolt and delight even the most jaded listener. Had they been allowed to flourish, the amateur broadcasters of the '10s and their scrappy successors of the '20s could have provided enough shocks, enough mystery, enough wild variety to keep

Americans tuned, if not to the Red Planet, then at least to the Martians the next town over.

And that was the final tragedy of the controls that took hold from 1912 to 1934. The experts, the managers, the military men, the politicians, the patent-poolers, the advertisers, the networks—together, they disenchanted radio.

3

Siberia

By adopting a licensed, advertiser-supported, limited-channel broadcasting system, America has penalized itself for half a century. It has
undermined its tradition of free communication, and it has limited
broadcasting to mass provision of the few most popular formats of
entertainment.   —Ithiel de Sola Pool

But the spectrum is as big as all outdoors—and there is a niche here,
a crack there, for those who care to squeeze some of the art back into
radio.   —Lorenzo Milam

IT IS WINTER on the eastern slopes of California's Sierra Mountains,
about a hundred miles south of Reno. It is freezing. A handful of men
are making sandwiches in the middle of the night. They are conscientious objectors, confined to distant barracks for their opposition to
World War II; they are preparing the next day's meals. There is no
power and no heat, but there is an electricity and a warmth in the air, as
the incarcerated pacifists talk about war and peace, poetry and freedom. And radio.

It is 1942. Another C.O., in another camp, would later recall the atmosphere of the times: "As we came into camp for the first time by
forestry truck," he said, "those of us who had read our Koestler and
Kropotkin concluded that we had finally reached Siberia. We could see
ourselves as a curiously American form of Narodniki, anarchist revolutionaries who would someday transform a society now given to war,
imperialism, and potential fascism."[1]

That particular year, such a transformation seemed inconceivably
distant. By 1942, the world had reached Siberia. It seems somehow inappropriate, even tasteless, to point out that the civil liberties horrors of
World War I—the censorship, the conscription, the command economy,

the suspension of due process—returned at full gale during World War II. Our enemy, after all, was a full-fledged totalitarian power (as was one of our allies). But if wartime America was freer than wartime Germany, that was small comfort to those whose commitment was to liberty itself, not to less slavery than was endured by the neighbors. And so the dissident faced a choice. He could swallow his distaste for the war state, convinced that defeating the greater evil of fascism justified organized violence abroad and incursions on freedom at home. Or he could resist. One man who chose resistance was Lewis Hill, a young poet and pacifist from Missouri.

Hill was a conscientious objector, despite an arthritic spine that could easily have exempted him from military service. When war came, he was shipped to the Sierras to do busywork for the state, clearing trails and making sandwiches near the isolated mountain town of Coleville. His stay would be relatively brief: his bad back grew worse, and he was given a medical discharge in October 1943, sixteen months after his arrival. But it was during his stay, as he and his friends worked late-night kitchen duty, that Hill started dreaming of a new kind of radio station. It would be independent. It would run few commercials. It would be a place for free discussion and constructive dialogue, a place true to his anarchist and pacifist ideals. It would be, one of his sandwich-making partners later recalled, "like a living room."[2]

A year later, Hill would be working for a radio station, but not one that resembled his Coleville fantasy. The station was WINX, an NBC affiliate in the Washington suburbs, for which Hill read and soon wrote the news. This, he soon discovered, was another sort of Siberia. Aging Americans remember the radio of the '30s and '40s with fond nostalgia: Jack Benny and Glenn Miller, Edward R. Murrow and the Ink Spots, Amos and Andy, Abbott and Costello, commercial jingles that rankled then but now rouse happy memories. Such nostalgia, the historian John Whiting has pointed out, is easy today, "now that the issues they didn't confront and the questions they didn't ask are well behind us."[3] There was pleasure here: real music, real comedy, real drama, even real journalism, albeit within tight confines of what could or could not be done or said. It may have been a vast wasteland, as someone would later call network TV, but this Siberia was far more comfortable than the Coleville camp.

It did not suit Hill at all.

Occasionally, in those days, someone would try to broadcast some-

LEEDS METROPOLITAN UNIVERSITY LIBRARY

thing different: more open, more textured, more interesting. There was WBKY, for example, an abortive effort to start a station for Kentucky's isolated hill people. Elmer G. Sulzer, director of radio at the University of Kentucky, had dreamed up the project in 1933 while installing receivers in the homes and shops of the mountains. With funds from the university and from the Lee County Board of Education, Sulzer and program director Ruth Foxx launched the station in 1940. Foxx, city bred and new to the hills, prepared for her job by practicing with a .22 caliber pistol. Just in case.

The station was based in Beattyville, the county seat: a tiny town in a little valley, where the north and south forks of the Kentucky River meet. It transmitted its shows from the village grade school (one of the county's largest, with a full staff of eight teachers and electricity to boot); Foxx solicited program ideas from the townspeople, drawing on the local Masons, the Beattyville Women's Club, the PTA, and other civic groups for volunteer help. "The new station will broadcast from noon until 2 a.m. daily," reported the Louisville *Courier-Journal*, "devoting its program to news, agriculture, health and safety for adults and an hour broadcast for children which will be planned in connection with the school curriculum."[4]

WBKY's shows ranged from a daily newscast written by a local English teacher to a weekly conservation program, from live coverage of PTA meetings to a Friday-night sermon. "It was an event in small-town life to appear in the studio, see the red light go on, the director's hand drop (indicating they were on the air), and then perform," recalls Foxx.

> Everyone was doing it. Judge Treadway talked about the law, Coach Wendell Boxley about sports, Mary Elizabeth Begley about hobbies, the Mountain Sky Liners played, the Sunshine Girls sang, Edna Porter talked about women in the news, and Mrs. Charles Beach gave an excellent talk on the importance of posture during National Posture Week.[5]

All commendable, and all futile: between the hill folk's weak, battery-operated receivers and the steep, signal-blocking mountains, hardly anyone could hear the broadcasts. The experiment quickly ended, nine months after it began.

Such localism was rare. In 1945, Charles Siepmann, formerly of the BBC, did a series of studies for the FCC. One, as he described it in his

1946 book *Radio's Second Chance*, took a look at broadcasting in Hibbing, Minnesota, a town best known today for being Bob Dylan's hometown and best known then for nothing in particular. Hibbing, Siepmann pointed out, was a place where one might expect the media to be more locally focused than usual. It had a station of its own—rare for a village of sixteen thousand—and many active civic groups that one might assume would appear on it: bands, professional organizations, labor unions, men's lodges, churches, a 4-H club, a medical association, a chamber of commerce, a book review club, and many amateur sports teams. Yet in a typical week, the station devoted only 2.3 percent of its schedule to live programs of local origin, and only one of those was broadcast after 6 P.M. No show was devoted to discussing local issues, and none to local music. Most of the town's civic organizations were shut out altogether.

And Hibbing was typical of the country. According to Siepmann's studies, local programming almost never took up more than two hours a day on average, and almost none of that was broadcast between 6 and 11 P.M.

It is too easy to blame the networks alone for this: local stations adopted those practices voluntarily, failing even to air many of the public-spirited or out-of-the-mainstream programs that the networks occasionally did create. Siepmann noted that in 1941, each network devoted several programs to debating the Lend-Lease Act, yet many of their affiliates—sometimes more than half—failed to carry them. And no, they weren't turning them down in favor of better, locally made shows on the same topic. (The Federal Radio Commission, of course, had already shut down most of the nonprofit stations that would have been likely to seek out such programming. And the Roosevelt administration's war on "unbalanced" broadcasting didn't help much.)

Radio, concluded Siepmann, was tipping dangerously "toward centralized direction and control," a trend he also saw absorbing government, industry, and culture. "Radio makes spectators of us all," he wrote: "passive recipients, through long hours, of impressions registered upon us by remote control."[6] The networks dominated the airwaves, and a rather small number of announcers, actors, and programmers dominated the networks.

Working at WINX, Lew Hill, who would soon read Siepmann avidly, learned of a test some of the networks required of announcers who aspired to join that elite. The applicant had to read a few paragraphs of meaningless gibberish several times, in different voices, each time inflecting the babble with a different flavor: sonorous sincerity, light humor, and so on. The test, Hill later wrote, measured the announcer's

> skill in simulating emotions, intentions, and beliefs which he does not possess. In fact the test was especially designed to assure that nothing in the announcer's mind except the sound of his voice—no comprehension, no value, no choice, and above all no sense of responsibility—could possibly enter into what he said or what he sounded like. This is the criterion of his job.[7]

So went the business of registering impressions by remote control. Surely, Hill reasoned, radio could be better than this.

Siepmann represented a new group of media critics, moderate reformers who had taken up the cudgel of the dormant broadcast reform movement. Generally speaking, these new dissidents were not interested in challenging the networks' power, as long as the commercial stations followed a sufficiently strict set of public-interest regulations.

Several such rules were eventually adopted, to many people's displeasure. To conservatives, they were unconstitutional assaults on free speech and private property, intrusive acts by a federal government that had no right to tell broadcasters what to do or say on the air. To radicals, they were a tepid substitute for real reform: as long as the big broadcasters followed a few general guidelines, their command of the ether would not be challenged. Both camps were right. The regulations abused broadcasters' rights but preserved their privileges, an arrangement the more "enlightened" industry leaders were happy to accept. Whatever small inconvenience such regs may have been, they knew they were benefiting from a much stronger set of interventions on their behalf.[8]

The government's latest favor involved a static-free method of transmission developed by the pride of Yonkers, New York: Edwin Howard Armstrong, nicknamed "the Major" after his service in World War I. Born in 1890, the young Armstrong had been an enthusiastic member of the early amateur subculture, tinkering with transmitters and quickly establishing himself as a leading light of the Yonkers ham community. He was also a loner, always secretive about his work, initially refusing even an invitation to join the Junior Wireless Club. In 1912, he devised the regenerative circuit, which used feedback to amplify and clarify signals; it was the first of many brilliant inventions to come. It also led to a lengthy patent dispute with Lee de Forest. That, too, foreshadowed the future.

As the 1920s progressed, the inventor became obsessed with the idea of eliminating static through a technology he called Frequency Modulation, or FM. Most engineers believed that this was impossible—in the mathematician John Renshaw Carson's then-famous words, that "static, like the poor, will always be with us."[9] In 1933, Armstrong unveiled his invention and proved Carson wrong. A few years later, GE's engineers discovered that two FM signals could coexist on the same wavelength without interfering with each other. The Major had unleashed a revolution.

And it stayed on the shelf. Armstrong tried to convince his old friend David Sarnoff, the head of RCA, to invest in his work, but Sarnoff believed the future of broadcasting lay in television, not FM. He also observed that FM receivers would initially cost more than AM sets, and feared that customers would not be willing to pay extra for superior fidelity—and that, if they did, they might not be willing to buy TV sets as well. Above all, he was aware that Armstrong, not RCA, controlled the patents for FM. Given that RCA was an empire built on patent monopolies, he was wary of investing in a technology that wasn't his company's intellectual property, especially since it would be competing with an older broadcast system that largely was—and particularly if he could instead be pushing television, a technology he hoped RCA *would* develop and own.

So he used his clout at the Federal Communications Commission to hinder Armstrong's invention. Siepmann and other critics denounced these protectionist tactics, but to little avail: the big broadcasters dominated the FCC as thoroughly as they had the Federal Radio Commission before it, and juicy jobs at RCA were available for powerful bureaucrats willing to toe the company's line. Federal regulators threw a series of obstacles in FM's way, using any argument, no matter how nakedly false, to justify themselves. Meanwhile, RCA's patent attorneys set to work trying to appropriate the Major's rights to his creation.

In 1936, the FCC reserved two small sections of the spectrum for FM broadcasting. (Not surprisingly, it granted considerably more space to experiments with television.) A few small stations, many run by amateurs, appeared in the new zone. Some institutions on the outs with the RCA-dominated radio establishment allied themselves with Armstrong as well. General Electric, anxious to compete with its former corporate partner, began to manufacture FM receivers. And the Yankee Network, a small would-be competitor with NBC and CBS, moved onto the FM band. Its fortunes received a boost in 1940, when it discovered that FM allowed it to relay its signals from station to station without losing tonal quality. This allowed it to bypass the costly telephone hookups an AM network required.

RCA eventually attempted a rapprochement with Armstrong, offering to purchase a nonexclusionary license to his patents for $1 million. He refused, arguing that RCA should accept the same deal he had made with other companies. A lengthy legal battle followed, breaking Armstrong both financially and emotionally. In 1954, he committed suicide.[10]

Nor did the networks cease their attempts to fend off competition from FM. In 1944, the FCC reassigned all FM broadcasting to a higher series of frequencies, instantly making every FM receiver obsolete and forcing anyone interested in broadcasting over FM, or in manufacturing FM sets, to redesign his equipment. The newly vacated frequencies were reassigned to TV. The government justified this move by arguing, falsely, that the change was needed to keep sunspots from interfering with FM signals. (Ironically, sunspots *did* interfere with some TV broadcasts.)

Was the commission willing to loosen *any* regulations related to FM? Yes. After buffeting FM broadcasters with restrictions and red tape, the commission announced that it would permit AM stations to duplicate their programming on FM. Initially, it planned to require each FM station to present at least two hours of original programming every day. In the face of industry pressure, it caved on even this modest demand.

So now listeners had little reason to buy an expensive new set, unless they were fidelity freaks; the same shows would be available on their old radios. What's more, the networks declared that anyone who bought ad time on their AM outlets would not be charged for the same advertising on the FM simulcasts. This further crippled independent FM stations, who found themselves asking potential advertisers to pony up for airtime they could acquire elsewhere for free. The FCC did create a new low-power FM service in 1948, licensing "Class D" outlets to go on the air cheaply and broadcast at a simple ten watts. But there

were few takers, at least at first: the program was initially open to educational institutions only, and the country's universities saw little future
in FM.

Siepmann had described FM as radio's second chance. It was starting to look like the medium's wasted chance instead: a giant empty
space that no one used.[11] But since no one cared much about the FM
band, no one cared to stop a young radical from going there to invent a
new kind of broadcasting. Re-enter Lewis Hill.

In 1946, Hill created the Pacifica Foundation. In 1949, Pacifica launched
a radio station in Berkeley, California, called KPFA. Hill's original plan
called for an AM station with few commercials. Necessity made KPFA
an FM station, with no commercials at all.

No station like KPFA existed anywhere else in America. Over the
next decades, its commentators would range from Trotskyists to Geor-
gists to Caspar Weinberger; its music would range from opera to jazz to
John Cage, along with the vast variety of styles that marketers today
lump together as "world music." It would air serious film and literary
criticism, from figures as notable as Kenneth Rexroth and Pauline Kael;
it would produce radio drama and children's shows. Poets would come
to its studios: Rexroth and Lawrence Ferlinghetti were there at the very
beginning, and were soon joined by the young Allen Ginsburg, the
young Gregory Corso, the young Michael McClure, and many more.
Alan Watts was a regular, too, bringing Buddhism to the Berkeley airwaves long before that faith was fashionable. "In short," John Whiting
would later write, "the last half-century of the San Francisco cultural
scene without KPFA is inconceivable. From the beginning Pacifica listeners were familiar with Artaud, Burroughs, Cage, Stockhausen, Berio,
Baldwin, Marcuse, McLuhan—and at first hand, not through a potted
synopsis in a Sunday supplement."[12] All this was presented in an open,
expansive way: the station did not squeeze ideas into soundbites or end
each interview on the hour. It did not organize its programs around its
schedule; it organized its schedule around its programs.

In those days, KPFA would take neither corporate nor government
funds, preferring the little-tried notion of turning to its listeners for
sponsorship. (It also sold FM sets to supporters at $40 apiece, so they
could hear what they were sponsoring.) With time, other outlets would
follow KPFA's example, often taking the medium in even more radical
directions. But in the Truman and Eisenhower eras, the station stood

alone. Writes Whiting: "The culture shock of tuning to KPFA in 1949 was like hearing an atheist sermon preached from the pulpit of Grace Cathedral."[13]

As he put together the station's first schedules, Hill was inspired by the BBC's Third Programme, a well-regarded radio service where ideas and art were allowed to flourish, to intellectuals' approval and other Britons' indifference. But the Third Programme was part of the British establishment. Early KPFA, by contrast, reflected the anarchist and pacifist ethos of 1940s Bay Area bohemia.[14] Kenneth Rexroth has attributed the anarchist revival of that place and time to the ongoing local interaction between avant-garde artists, disillusioned Reds, and conscientious objectors (like Hill) who came to San Francisco on their leaves. Rexroth's recollections are accurate, but there was more to Pacifican anarchism than his account suggests. Anarchism has traditionally appealed not just to bohemians and pacifists but to craftsmen, artisans, independent producers—those with what Paul Goodman called "a hankering . . . for craft guild self-management."[15] If radio had become a typical profession, more managerial than meritocratic, then any creative revolt of independent radio craftsmen was bound to be anarchist, in impulse if nothing else.

In this regard, it's worth noting that the six-year-old Lew Hill had been an enthusiastic ham, building a crystal set in a cigar box. The amateur subculture may have passed its frontier days by then, but its spirit of self-directed labor, free association, and mutual aid still looked a lot like anarchy in action. That memory may have been a faint influence on Hill two and a half decades later, as he launched his experiment in anarchist radio.[16]

Or maybe not. Hill's vision of Pacifica evolved from year to year—and, frankly, from audience to audience. At different times, the station was supposed to be populist or elitist, communitarian or individualist, specifically pacifist or ideologically open-ended. Hill told one story to the anarchists and pacifists who helped build KPFA, another to the FCC that licensed it, another to the Ford Foundation when the cash-poor station turned to it for financial aid. In an odd twist of fate, Hill's book *Voluntary Listener Sponsorship*, written in 1957 to squeeze more money from the Ford funders and posthumously published a year later, has gone down in history as the seminal document of Pacifica's early years. Notes the historian Matthew Lasar: "For several generations of community radio activists and scholars, Hill's book offered the definitive representation of the Pacifica Foundation. Few seemed to notice . . . that the text read primarily as a report to the biggest liberal megafund of its time."[17] In particular, the book ignored the entire topic of pacifism—the word "peace" never appears in it, Lasar observes—and drops the notion, always present in Hill's '40s work, of using radio to reach the average citizen. Instead, Pacifica was to be a haven for the intellectual elites, a radio realm of free speech and high culture.

Nonetheless, *Voluntary Listener Sponsorship* and its 1951 prototype, "The Theory of Listener-Sponsored Radio," offer a valuable glimpse at what listener sponsorship meant to the man who invented the term, even as the absence of sufficient listener-sponsors was forcing him to take money from a foundation. If "Theory" is Hill's most famous essay, that may be because so many subsequent stations, with little interest in the views or the cash of the Ford trustees, nonetheless found it an inspiring formula.

"The purpose of commercial radio is to induce mass sales," Hill wrote. "For mass sales there must be a mass norm, and the activity must be conducted as nearly as possible without risk of departure from the norm. . . . By suppressing the individual, the unique, the industry reduces the risk of failure (abnormality) and assures itself a standard product for mass consumption." Listener sponsorship, he proposed, was an alternative, a system that could "give the genuine artist and thinker a possible, even a desirable, place to work."[18] It did this by restoring responsibility for programming to those who actually created the programs and by handing the power of the purse to the listener. The admen who pay for commercial broadcasts were cut out of the picture entirely.

So: the individual listener pays directly for the programming, the advertiser is excluded, and KPFA evades the demands of cultural mass production. Wonderful. There was just one problem: anyone could listen to Pacifica, whether or not she paid to. There was, as economists put it, a free-rider problem.

For Hill, this could be an advantage. Subscribing would make the listener more than a passive consumer; it "implies the kind of cultural engagement . . . that is surely indispensable for the sake of the whole culture."[19] All the station needed was voluntary subscriptions from 2 percent of the FM audience in its area.

In part, Hill's essay was an effort to turn the policies he'd improvised over the past few years into a coherent theory. In part, it was an effort to present his station in a manner palatable to people like the Ford funders. And in part, it was wishful thinking: even 2 percent is a tall order. KPFA was popular within its sphere, but in 1951 it had never managed to bring in that many subscribers, a problem magnified by its initially weak signal.

Indeed, simply staying on the air was a struggle. On August 6, 1950, the station had to shut down. Or—in the more measured words of Eleanor McKinney, a young veteran of NBC Radio who had been one of Hill's first recruits—the Pacifica "Foundation decided to suspend broadcasting in order to make a full-time fund-raising effort."[20] By that point, Hill and McKinney were virtually the only staffers left: with no money for salaries, the others had exited, one by one.

But the listeners came through, quickly raising enough cash to pay off the station's debts, rehire its staff, and return KPFA to the airwaves. Hill then made his overtures to the Ford Foundation, which in 1952 kicked in a three-year grant of $150,000.

The early KPFA, thus, was not fully listener-sponsored, though as time passed and its audience grew it would come to merit that designation. It would be a long time before Pacifica again received assistance from an institution as establishmentarian as Ford. The Cold War was on, and Washington was suspicious of this left coast radio station, with its penchant for peace and its love of free speech, a love so strong it even let the dread Reds on the air.

Even as Hill was trying to plant good radio in FM's unkind soil, another revolution was erupting on the other broadcast band. America experienced an economic boom in the years after World War II, and AM radio enjoyed the ride. More consumers were buying receivers; more businesses were interested in advertising. The industry was in an entrepreneurial mood, more interested in making money off new stations than in protecting its existing outlets from competition, and the FCC, as always, was quick to oblige it. Before the war, applicants for new licenses had to prove that they wouldn't interfere with *any* existing stations, local or distant. Now, the regulators decreed, they had to demonstrate only that they wouldn't step on any signals in the same area.

Around the same time, would-be broadcasters started taking advantage of another policy shift. In 1940, the Supreme Court ruled that the FCC could not refuse to issue a license just because it might cause "economic injury to a rival station."[21] During the war this had little effect. After the war was another story. In the five years that followed 1945, the number of active outlets exploded, from a mere 950 to more than 2,000.

It may seem odd that the same government that did so much to squash FM broadcasting would open the doors to more competition on the AM dial. But there's no contradiction here. FM was a potential competitor, not just with existing AM stations, but with television: Sarnoff, you'll recall, was afraid the public wouldn't spend money on both FM sets and TVs. The boom in AM stations, on the other hand, meant more advertising dollars for NBC, which RCA then reinvested in television research and development. In the 1950s, as TV swept America, the company more than recouped its investment.

Radio itself fared somewhat less well. Its audience shrank, and so, more pointedly, did its profits. In 1945, the three major radio networks sold $134 million worth of spots to advertisers. In 1955, the figure was $64 million.

Television had arrived. Charles Siepmann had lauded FM as "a whole new continent," one "with room for all and opportunity for each."[22] Now it seemed that the new continent was TV. But the settlers were not the outcasts of the Old World, looking for virgin territory on which to plant their flags. They were the ruling classes of AM, abandoning their former domain to the outcasts. It was as though the king of England had declared *Britain* a penal colony and moved his court to Australia.

How could radio compete with radio-plus-pictures? It couldn't, went the conventional wisdom: one headline in *Look* declared that "Radio Is Doomed."[23] As far as traditional, network-style radio was concerned, the conventionally wise were completely correct. Dramas, sitcoms, and variety shows migrated from AM to TV, a few (such as *Our Miss Brooks*) uneasily existing in both media for a spell. Network radio withered; network television bloomed.

Yet radio did not die. You couldn't watch TV while driving, you couldn't watch TV at work, and you couldn't buy a clock-TV. Radios, on the other hand, were increasingly mobile and relatively cheap, and they didn't demand your full attention. A new form of programming emerged that took advantage of those qualities, programming that was more local, flexible, experimental, and spontaneous than the radio of the network era.

"I recall, as a kid glued to the radio in Detroit around 1955–1956, a show on WJR-AM," recounts Dave Dixon, who would one day glue another generation of listeners to their sets as a freeform DJ on Detroit's WABX.

> This deejay, Buck Matthews, mixed all kinds of music together in a pretty unrestricted, freeform way, and instead of using the familiar stilted announcer approach of the day, he spoke in a very conversational, laid-back style. He did this on an all-night show, which, I suppose, was considered by management to be the place to try something different.[24]

The sheer quantity of new stations had already opened the door to specialized fare. Black radio, for example, had finally emerged; the number of outlets with black-oriented programs grew from four in 1943 to 260 a decade later. In 1948, a floundering station in Memphis, WDIA, became the first station to go all-black. By 1949, at least one black-owned station—WERD, in Atlanta—was on the air. Other outlets brokered their schedules, letting blacks buy access to the airwaves. Even stations too conservative to hire DJs of color sometimes asked their white charges to program in the "black" mode, adopting faux-Negro accents, playing rhythm 'n' blues, and spinning stories in an African American style.

This happened as vast numbers of blacks moved from the rural South to the cities, particularly in the North. The new stations became the souls of the migrant black communities, places where old-fashioned modes of music and talk mixed with new urban concerns. In one historian's words, black radio "made the newcomers feel that some of what they had left had mysteriously reappeared with a familiar sound and nuance."[25] They might have moved to the city, but they could still listen to music—to quote the prototypical black Chicago DJ, Al Benson—"with a little chitlin juice on it."[26]

But if the black stations were links to the old traditions, they were something new, too. The old folkways were transformed by this new technology, and they, in turn, transformed that tech. The new black DJs were the first to turn down the music and talk over the records, the first to treat their consoles like musical instruments. In the '30s, DJing had scarcely existed: everyone from the network brass to the musicians' unions looked down on it, leaving only a handful of independently owned operations to embrace it. Now DJing was becoming a minor art form, with jocks choosing their own records, fiddling with the levers and dials in front of them, telling jokes, interacting with the music as it played. Some of the jocks paved the way for rap, improvising rhymes over and between the records they played. Lava Durst, who got his start as a rhyming P.A. announcer at Negro League ballgames, soon got a chance to bring his act to Austin's KVET:

> Jumpin' Jills and jivin' Cats,
> upstate Gates in Stetson hats,
> lace your boots and tighten your wig,
> here's some jive. Can you dig?
> I'm Doctor Hep Cat, on the scene,
> with a stack of shellac in my record machine.
> I'm hip to the tip, and bop to the top.
> I'm long time coming and I just won't stop.
> It's a real gone deal that I'm gonna reel,
> so stay tuned while I pad your skulls.[27]

To Martha Jean "The Queen" Steinberg, one of the biggest DJs in Memphis,

> We were the mayors back then. At that particular time, you have to understand that you didn't have any black politicians, no black judges, very few black lawyers . . . you didn't have any so-called black leaders. So we were the ones who spoke out. . . . We were shaping the minds and hearts of the people, and we did a good job. We encouraged them to go to school, to get degrees, to be educated. Told them about racial pride. We talked to young girls about not having babies. We kept our communities intact.[28]

In the course of turning the once-sterile AM band on its head, the DJs fueled the R&B revolution, bringing the new brew of blues, gospel, and swing to a radio dial dominated by pop and poppy jazz. Where older stations forswore the new wave of rhythm 'n' blues, rejecting the records for their gritty music and double-entendre-laced lyrics, the younger jocks embraced the new sound. So did their audience—an increasing portion of which was colored pale.

In North and South alike, young whites discovered the black stations, listening with fascination to this incredibly alien yet deeply

American music and humor and slang. One of those whites was future radio pioneer Lorenzo Wilson Milam, born in the deepest South—in Jacksonville, Florida—on August 2, 1933, the son of a speculator in real estate. "Some of my early inspirations," he recalled, years later,

> were the local AM stations in the south in the late '40s and early '50s. There were a number of characters I used to listen to in Florida and Georgia (where I lived). There was Daddy Rabbit "with the do-right habit" and Hank the night watchman and Pappy Schrappy ("makin' you happy"). They were true wits and originals—storytellers in the best southern tradition. . . . Hank and Daddy Rabbit and Pappy would tell stories (often rather lecherous ones)—would skirt the border between lurid and gross and hilarious, but always with a wit that made it impossible for those of us listening in to complain.
>
> We were spying on another culture, weren't we?—for in the segregated south, we knew nothing of the culture, the art, the exquisite music of the blacks because we never ventured into that part of town, what was so easily referred to as "niggertown." But we could eavesdrop by radio.[29]

Lorenzo listened to stations from Miami, from Nashville, from Charlotte, from New Orleans, each broadcasting either blacks or whites trying their best to sound black. From this fertile ground, this verge between the worlds of black and white, new ideas, arts, and music were born. It was these stations, and Mexico's equally mysterious border blasters, that allowed rock 'n' roll to blossom, turning it from a weird new movement at the social margins, a music for blacks and poor Southern whites, into a nationwide teen craze. And not just black stations, and not just white listeners: Milam would later ask a friend, KPFA host Robert Garfias, what it was that had launched him—"he, a poor Chicano, living in San Francisco"—on the road toward becoming an ethnomusicologist. "He said it was an AM station there, playing Chinese opera. It fascinated him. Tuning in on this absolute Other World of other culture, other music."[30]

One more thing about the black stations: they made money. Most of their audience couldn't afford televisions, and most of their advertisers didn't have anyplace else to go. Those other operations, the old-fashioned ones, kept plugging away, losing listeners and dollars by the month. To survive, they had to experiment. A lot of them didn't survive.

But many others did. They came up, between them, with something called *format*; it meant, more or less, that if you tuned to a station that you'd heard before, you'd have a pretty good idea of what you'd hear there again. People weren't going to sit in front of their radio sets in their living rooms anymore, listening to show after show; TV had usurped that role. So now there'd be stations for different demographics, each playing its own kind of programming 'round the clock.

Some of those stations were open and free: the DJs picked their own records, broke new acts, mixed musical genres, stirred up controversy. Others were more . . . restrictive. Two men proved that those tightly restricted formats could be profitable. One was a young Nebraskan named Robert Todd Storz. The other, the man Milam would one day call "the aether-rapist supreme,"[31] was Gordon McLendon.

McLendon was an artist of sorts, famous—like a few other broadcasters, most notably the young Ronald Reagan—for his evocative play-by-play coverage of baseball games he couldn't see. McLendon would sit in the basement of Dallas's Cliff Towers Hotel while a Western Union worker sat at the ballpark, entering shorthand descriptions of the game onto a teletype: a simple tally of strikes, balls, hits, errors. McLendon would watch the data scroll from the machine, then invent further details—what the umpire was doing, how the players looked, what the weather was like, the mood of the crowd. Meanwhile, he and his engineer would add sound effects: to indicate a hit, for instance, he'd strike the mike with his pencil. An entrepreneur as well as an artist, McLendon built a radio network over which to transmit his games. Then he and the major leagues had a falling out, and he had to find something new to play. That something was Storz's brainchild: Top Forty.

Storz was born and raised in Omaha, the son of a local brewer; as a teen, he was a ham radio operator. At age twenty-five, he and his father bought KOWH-AM from the local paper, the *World-Herald*. The younger Storz, enthroned as the station's general manager, started eliminating programs devoted to anything but popular music. Legend has it that Storz dreamed up Top Forty in an Omaha bar, blue over his station's mediocre fortunes. As one beer gave way to another, he noticed that the crowd kept playing the same songs on the jukebox, over and over again. And, at the end of the evening, when one of the waitresses picked a record, she played the hit that he'd already heard the most. An epiphany followed, and KOWH was soon operating on the same programming principle.

Sober historians will dismiss this account, or at least brand it apocryphal. The most likely scenario is that offered by the documentarian Richard Fatherley, one of Storz's former employees. Fatherley says his boss observed the jukebox phenomenon several times during the 1940s, and remembered it when new market research and format experiments around the country inspired him to invent Top Forty in the early '50s.[32]

It was McLendon, anyway, who gave the format its notoriety, even though Storz's outlet adopted it before McLendon's KLIF did in Dallas. Soon the repetition that is Top Forty had swept the country, with both Storz and McLendon buying new stations and with other operations imitating their success. Such stations rarely strayed from their ever-tightening playlists, and they usually used a regimented "clock" system to determine when each song would be played.[33] Remember what Lewis Hill wrote about ad-driven radio: "For mass sales there must be a mass norm, and [broadcasts] must be conducted as nearly as possible without risk of departure from the norm." Now there were several competing norms, representing more diversity, but some of those new niches were even more constrained than the national programming they replaced. It wasn't long before a number of the livelier stations started adopting tight formats as well, and the monologuists Milam admired so much began to disappear from the airwaves.

But not without a struggle. Most Top Forty stations actually existed in a sort of half-life, in theory hewing to a format, in practice showing some independence. Consider WWDC, an independently owned outlet in suburban Maryland. "Single format radio hadn't quite reached" WWDC in the late 1950s, according to Sam Smith, a cub reporter there from 1957 to 1960. "While WWDC was known as a top-40 station, emphasizing the two score most popular records of the day, it still pursued a relentless eclecticism ranging from singing canaries to the most modern radio news operation in town." They also had exclusive broadcast rights to the Washington Senators' baseball games.

Still, the irreal flavor of the new mainstream was beginning to filter into the station. Every morning, it greeted listeners with this bubbly ditty:

> *Good morning to you in the land of the free!*
> *This is Washington's Double U Double U D C . . .*
> *May your skies above all be sunny and blue:*

WWDC says good morning to you!
Good morning, good morning, good . . . [fade]

"The song," Smith recalls, "came from a jingle house, one of the new parasites of the business—a firm that provided stations with customized musical fillers. Knowing that the same jingle, slightly reworked, was being used by stations all over the country was a reminder of the illusions you could create in a medium where no one saw what you were doing."[34]

Behind those curtains, conflict was starting to simmer between the managers, who believed they could objectively discern what the public wanted to hear and thus limit their playlists to the most popular songs of the day, and the DJs, who jealously guarded their right to choose their own records. For management, this was a simple choice between finding a format that worked or keeping one that audiences clearly despised. As McLendon would later declare, in a speech in Detroit in 1969, "I have never bought a radio station for other than one reason: because I believed I could improve its programming and make it a success." He never bought successful stations, he explained; he looked for

> stations sick because of their sick programming, and because of their sick programming, sick in sales. . . . Our philosophy in deciding whether to buy a certain station in a certain market has always been: Is there some program service of utility to a large enough group here that is either (a) not now being provided or (b) not being provided as well as we can provide it?[35]

Fair enough: there were a lot of bad DJs out there, in the 1950s as today. It wasn't as though McLendon was out to homogenize the radio band. If anything, he was afraid the FCC was going to do that. "Any law forcing a *sameness* of radio," he told an audience in 1962, "forcing a programming common denominator, acts as a protection to the talentless, a shield for the lazy, a haven for the idea thief, *a legal shelter and sanction* for the mediocre."[36]

But several such laws were in place, and more were on the way. Nor was every manager as entrepreneurial as McLendon. Indeed, McLendon's self-justifications to the side, even he wasn't always willing to pay close attention to each city's needs—not when there was a preset formula ready for the taking. ("This was a big hit in Oakland! Why, it's sure to work wonders in Buffalo!") Many of McLendon's stations filled gaps in the market, not only with their music but with their lively contests (one announced it was going to give away a live baby, not mentioning that the prize was a live baby pig), their clever efforts to promote themselves (one parodied its own format by playing the same record for three hours in a row), and their commendable approach to news (McLendon's stations often had mobile news units, giving their reports a very immediate and local flavor). In other cities, the arrival of Top Forty didn't fill voids; it created them.

During the 1950s, *Billboard* magazine regularly polled station managers, asking such questions as "To what extent are your disk jockey programs supervised by station management?" and "Does station management exact more, less or about the same amount of control over disk jockey programs as a year ago?"[37] In 1953, 64.6 percent of the managers claimed to "partially" control their employees' freedom, and 17.7 percent claimed their control was "complete"; that left 17.7 percent giving their jockeys carte blanche. A simultaneous poll of DJs found that 94.5 percent of the jocks claimed to pick their own records, implying either that the on-air talent had a tendency to self-aggrandizement or that they often ignored management's orders—or, most likely, both.

What's most interesting is the trend across the rest of the decade. In 1956, 10 percent more managers at stations over five thousand watts said they gave their hosts complete freedom. At smaller stations, the trend was even stronger, with the figure more than doubling. But that was also the year KOWH introduced the first truly limited playlist, an innovation that quickly caught on. A year later, in the poll of DJs, the number who said that their program manager picked their records for them jumped from 1.3 percent to 7 percent. Further questions revealed that stations were playing more record sides per week but fewer new releases, suggesting a greater reliance on proven hits.

Around the same time, stations started bringing in outside monitors to critique their DJs' shows. Some outlets experimented with using no jocks at all, just prerecorded announcements between the records. By 1961, many "Top Forty" stations were unapologetically limiting themselves to thirty songs. "All it did was eliminate mistakes," one programmer later declared. "That's all you hope to do."[38] There was an optimal playlist out there, station managers told themselves—a plan that would maximize listeners—and any record that deviated from it was a "mistake." With time, a new class of consultants would emerge, a collection of self-declared experts in perpetual pursuit of the perfect playlist.

The new age called for a new breed of disc jockey. "It's a handicap to know anything about music," one Detroit jock confessed in 1957. "I can't let my personal taste come into it. I'd ruin myself and my audience would leave me."[39] Black radio was hit especially hard, with the Afro equivalent of Top Forty revoking not just the DJs' right to choose what they'd play but also their right to speak over and between the records.

But some of the old breed fought back. In 1958, at a Storz-sponsored convention of DJs, there were murmurs about starting an organization of their own, one that could assert the jocks' interests against management's demands. Some of the dissidents met again in Milwaukee, in July 1959, and formed the National Disc Jockey Association.

Alas: by the time the group held its first formal convention a year later, it was distracted by an uproar over payola. Record companies had taken to bribing DJs to play their releases, sometimes directly and sometimes through more subtle means. (Fans of Chuck Berry might want to look through their record collections and note how many of their hero's songs were allegedly cowritten by the host of *American Bandstand*. Dick Clark got a royalty check every time one of those tunes was played.) The practice was an old one: as far back as the nineteenth century, songwriters had been known to bribe bandleaders to play particular tunes, and rumors of radio payola were common throughout the 1950s. But in 1959 it became a scandal, complete with a congressional probe.

The American Society of Composers, Authors and Publishers had pushed hard for an investigation, since most of the payola-stained records were licensed through an upstart rival, Broadcast Music Inc. The established record companies could hardly object: by cutting off payola, they'd cut off one of the means independent companies had to get their wares aired. And in the public mind, the war on payola was a war on rock 'n' roll, a genre still disreputable in many circles—certainly in Washington.

The DJs thus became scapegoats: for the payola, for the music, for everything. In 1960, a gang of uplifters called the Listener's Lobby did a "study" of radio's effects on young people in and around Detroit. Its animus was obvious:

> It is clear that disk jockey programs are not designed to cultivate musical tastes, to set examples of vocabulary or diction, or in any other

way to educate their audience. It would appear that in the Detroit area radio's effects oppose the interests and politics of public education. As an institution the disk jockey tends to regulate the whole teen-age group to an inferior position in the social class structure—and then to keep them there. By sanctifying the relatively inferior tastes in music and the other arts, his emphasis upon sensation as opposed to analysis, and his limitation of his audience to an extremely narrow range of "favorite" material (all of these being characteristics of the lower social classes), the disk jockey confines teenagers within one of the better-designed, and one of the lowest, compartments of the social structure.[40]

The congressional hearings that followed were a lesson in Washington prejudices. Clean-cut Dick Clark, though obviously guilty, survived his trip before the tribunal; one inquisitor even lauded him as a "fine young man."[41] Alan Freed, whose sexually charged shows did more than almost anyone else's to bring black music to white audiences, had his career ruined; he lost his job, turned to drink, and died a few years later.

Legislatively, this led virtually nowhere: the bill that passed didn't give the FCC the power to suspend anyone's license for payola, and it didn't actually ban the practice. All it outlawed was taking bribes surreptitiously. If you announced your record's "sponsor," you were in the clear.

But the payola frenzy transformed radio. The National Disc Jockey Association had been formed to advance DJs' interests against program managers, but it was forced to devote its energies to defending the profession's image instead.[42] Within the stations, the threat of federal penalties provided the final excuse to revoke jocks' right to choose their own records. Some stations still gave their jocks a free hand, but not, generally speaking, in the larger markets. Naturally, this did not wipe out payola: if anything, it institutionalized it. Now, rather than bribing DJs to play their records on their shows, companies bribed program directors to add them to the playlist.

With the stakes higher, the cost of payola rose as well. By the early '80s, it was rarely a way for independent companies to break new records—the indies could never afford the prices. It was an exclusionary cartel, a way the biggest players could keep records *off* key stations. (By then the mob was involved, too, adding an element of direct violence.)[43]

At no point did anyone explain why payola itself should be

considered criminal, given that similar practices—for instance, paying a supermarket to display one's products—were an accepted part of American capitalism. Small-scale bribery may have put the occasional bad record on the air, but too much of that would hurt a station's ratings; surely it could be dealt with internally. Especially given how awful the alternative turned out to be.

DJ resistance didn't stop; it just turned into surreptitious sabotage. Witness the testimony of Bruce Morrow, a.k.a. "Cousin Brucie," of WABC-AM—one of the most popular Top Forty jocks in New York:

> Dan [Ingram] came to work one day and found a primitive system of clocks, lights, and alarms rigged up in the studio. [Rick] Sklar had just come back from one of his "fact-finding" missions and apparently had observed such a system in one of our sister stations. The idea was that whenever clock number-one tripped a red light, the jocks were to play the number-one song. Clock number two and the blue light were the cues for the number-two song, and so on. When I got to the studio that evening I found a memo detailing this Pavlovian exercise. "What are we—apes?!" I screamed.
>
> "Relax, man. There's an easy way to deal with this," Dan replied.
>
> He showed me how to turn the clocks back so the lights never went on. Sklar understood that the protest could turn into a mutinous situation and the clocks soon disappeared.[44]

Later, in another clueless moment, management tried to ban pre-Beatles records from the air, without regard for which oldies would still fit the station's format. Once more, sabotage saved the day, as Morrow and his confederates "gradually relabeled almost every oldie in the WABC collection,"[45] assigning late-'60s dates to their favorite hits of the '50s. In such ways, Top Forty radio remained true to itself. The problem was, it was still Top Forty.

Some stations never went through a period of being interesting before the format virus infected them. A few years before Storz invented Top Forty, Lorenzo Milam started work at the first of several distinctly unlively outlets. Like Lew Hill before him, he was entering Siberia.

When Milam entered Yale in 1951, he "heeled" at its student station. That meant he did a bit of everything: writing news, selling ads, engineering, announcing. (McLendon had done the same in his Yale days.) The outlet was run like a commercial station; its purpose was to introduce initiates to the mysteries of the radio profession. It did its job: after a year of college, Milam had enough experience to get hired at Jacksonville's WIVY, a tiny operation with a five-man staff, where everyone had to be a jack-of-all-trades. It, too, played conventional stuff; it was far from the nighttime world of Blind Gary Davis and Daddy Rabbit.

Milam dropped out of Yale. He stuck around WIVY for a year. And then polio got him, and he spent eighteen months in a series of hospitals, including a long, dreadful stretch at a North Florida torture palace called Hope Haven:

> The shock machine is an apparatus designed some fifty years ago whose main purpose is to keep muscles from atrophy, from loss of "tone." Two pads, one positive, one negative, are applied to the body. The muscle to be pulsated lies between these two moist pads. The operator can increase or decrease the amount of the current, or the rhythm of the shocks.
>
> It is a medieval torture machine. And I find out later, much later, that the efficacy of physical shock therapy is so limited as to make it useless. *Now* I find out. . . .
>
> After electrocuting me carefully (shoulders, thighs, stomach, back) Miss Bland stretches the muscles. With her hands she lifts my legs and forces them into certain positions which are as close to elaborate and exact fainting painfulness as possible.[46]

I suppose this was a faint, distorted echo of the wartime camp that had imprisoned Lewis Hill—that history was in some way repeating itself, first as tragedy and then as the theater of the absurd. Or, perhaps, the theater of cruelty. "I think there is some poignance to this as we realize that the pain I was privileged to attend was not the pain of a noble cause," Milam later wrote.

> I was not crucified for my god. . . . I was not tortured in some stony prison for freedom of the press. I was not martyred on some wheel for my pronouncements. . . . The country to which I was loyal, the country for which I experienced such torture was the country of my body. They tortured me for clinging to that. My God was the belief in American Medical Technology as practiced in 1952.[47]

After a year in that death house, Milam moved to the Warm Springs Foundation, in Meriwether County, Georgia, where the staff kept up with the appropriate research and treated the patients with genuine care. His condition improved. He found work again, as a switchboard operator at Jacksonville's Duval Medical Center. He returned to his studies, first at the University of Florida, where he took summer courses in engineering and chemistry, and then at Haverford College, a Quaker school in Pennsylvania. He returned to radio, working at Haverford's campus station and at commercial stations in Jacksonville Beach and in Philadelphia. The former was a black station without much of a budget. "The transmitter was always red hot," Milam later recalled. "I never knew from one minute to the next whether it would fall over."[48]

Then he moved to Berkeley, to work toward a master's degree in English. And one day, inevitably, he stumbled on KPFA, a station like none he'd ever heard, "a wonderful mix of music and talk and drama and high art."[49] Before long, he was volunteering there.

By this time, KPFA had already weathered several waves of growing pains. In 1952, Hill had proposed a new structure for the station, setting aside its original cooperative form so that he might have more "authority to organize the staff and operate the station." The staff responded by revolting, branding Hill, McKinney, and their ally Richard Moore a dictatorial "triumvirate." Hill resigned, then returned, then resigned again, flitting back and forth in a weaving effort to bring the station back under his control. Soon Wallace Hamilton, a more anarchistic anarchist than Hill, was in charge of the foundation, pledging to resign if Hill ever returned; the new regime declared Pacifica "an experiment in anarcho-syndicalism."[50] All this alarmed many in the station's audience: KPFA's inner circle may have been anarchist, but its listeners—and donors—were mostly liberals.

Hill, meanwhile, was trying to retake power from the outside. Hamilton's crew proposed that the two factions find a mediator, a suggestion that backfired when the mediation committee, made up entirely of wealthy liberals, endorsed Hill's plan to restructure the station. In the midst of this long battle—by now, it was 1954—KPFA broadcast a roundtable on marijuana. The show featured four *experts,* as it were, all of them obviously stoned; the police seized the tape and refused to return it. At least twenty-three liberals on the Pacifica board then resigned, protesting not the police but the program. In the wake of the controversy, Hill returned, retook the station, and ended the experiment in anarchy.[51]

The crises continued, with anti-Hill factions periodically emerging to protest the turn the foundation had taken. As the infighting alternately intensified and subsided, Hill grew seriously ill and increasingly withdrawn. On August 1, 1957, he committed suicide—"Not for anger or despair," he wrote, "but for peace and a kind of home."[52]

Nonetheless, the station persisted, maintaining its mixture of diverse, intellectually charged programs. Milam loved it, especially admiring Robert Garfias's programs of international music. There were sore spots, of course. Milam especially disliked the station's public affairs director, Elsa Knight Thompson, whom many revered but who struck Lorenzo as a Stalinist. Still, he liked the place. He was also, by now, a committed pacifist, a heresy he'd picked up at Haverford. That, too, fit snugly with the Pacifica vision, but eventually it would propel him back east.

In college, Milam later wrote with a note of sardonic self-mockery, he had learned two "perversions." One was pacifism, "an unyielding hate of war." The other was the notion "that I, personally, could do something to mitigate the drift of humanity towards World War III. Somehow, they taught me, I had enough power and passion to stop all wars of all mankind for all time. Of course, given my ineluctable narcissism, I helped the thought along; but they fired the madness." And so, he reasoned,

> if I started a broadcast station in Washington . . . when all those Senators and Representatives and Presidents and Generals and Civil Service Workers tuned in and heard a vigorous debate on our foreign policy, or when they heard a well-researched documentary on the hazards of radiation, and the history of human frailties—after a few months of this, they would be saying to themselves "We must be idiots to think that war is the answer to our problems." They would come to nod their heads sagely and think: "Maybe there are other, more peaceful, solutions . . . Something other than . . . than the Horror of Nuclear War. . . ." And the other Senators and Representatives and Presidents and Generals would nod their heads, and suddenly America and Belligerent will turn into America the Peaceful, and it will all be my doing.[53]

So he quit grad school and ventured back to Siberia—to Washington, D.C.—with the notion of starting a station of his own, one as engagingly intellectual as KPFA and as engagingly wild as those AM outlets he'd loved as a boy. Instead, he got two years of trouble: "two mind-wrenching, soul-crushing, nut-numbing years of chasing Radio Bigfoot through the halls of Congress, into the East Wing of the White House, down the dark halls of the Federal Communications Commission."[54] For he had gone to Washington in 1958, at the height of the Cold War, a time that did not look with favor on pacifists.

Milam did have one advantage: wealth. He had inherited a few hundred thousand dollars and thus didn't need much help raising the capital to put a new station on the air. It was the government that stood in his way, especially one John Harrington, described by one of Milam's attorneys as "a very diligent FCC investigator type"[55] and by Milam himself as "some flea-brain."[56] Harrington was suspicious of the would-be licensee: Milam, after all, had worked for Pacifica, and thus was probably a Communist, or a Communist sympathizer, or at the very least a Communist dupe.

Like I said: it was 1958.

Lorenzo rented an office on G Street for $25 a month, a little hole-in-the-wall he shared with a kindly old lawyer named Abraham Rockmore. He did some work for a consulting engineer. He haunted the FCC library, studying broadcast history and broadcast law. And he put a want ad in the *Post*, asking for help with "an incipient radio station." About a hundred people responded, among them Sam Smith of WWDC, the suburban station with the good-morning jingle. Smith doesn't remember much about his interview with Milam; what he does remember, vividly, is approaching Milam's office, hearing ever-louder shouts and screams, and suddenly seeing a great big man stalk out, his angry eyes afire. The man quickly brushed past Smith and disappeared, barely giving Sam time to recognize him as George Lincoln Rockwell, founder and führer of the American Nazi Party.

Milam doesn't recall any shouts and screams, just Rockwell's loud and vitriolic voice. The Nazi had made his appointment under an assumed name; when he arrived, looking ferocious and menacing, he launched into his ideas for a radio station, pacing around the tiny office in his big black boots as he talked. It was a one-sided conversation: Milam was too nervous to argue, even when Rockwell claimed, with a straight face, that some of his best friends were Jews.

"But I didn't fight with him," Lorenzo insists. "We left on an amiable enough note, but as soon as the door shut on his jack-booted back, I threw away his address and phone number. And I remember thinking, 'Jesus. If I get a station here, and if he comes in and asks for some air time—will I give it to him?'"[57]

Years later, after finally getting a station of his own, Milam would indeed give some airtime to members of the racist right; he did, after all, believe in Open Debate. But he never aired anything by Rockwell. He did interview the Nazi once, in Seattle in the '60s, but he threw the tape away. It simply wasn't a good interview, he decided—just "a devilish stomach-ache."[58]

Another bad interview: back in D.C., tired of waiting for the FCC to act, Milam decided to contact his congressman, Charles Bennett, who took him to lunch in the congressional dining room. Evidently, Representative Bennett had already spoken with someone at the FCC before he sat down with Lorenzo. "There are people who want to destroy the country," he told his constituent. "There are people who want to use the institutions of the country to wreck the country. These people have different political beliefs, and will use any agency of government or even the freedom of the press to wreck the United States of America. We have to be on the look-out for them. People go to colleges, liberal colleges. They get in the hands of the wrong kind of professors. These people take advantage of a youth's innocence. They fill their heads with dangerous propaganda, and the young people just can't handle it. They just haven't had enough experience in the world, they are overwhelmed. We simply have to protect ourselves against these . . . these traitors if you will. We have to be very careful, because our country, as good as it is, as strong as it is, is very fragile. Some people will take freedom of speech, and freedom of the press, and turn it against the very country that provides it. We have to be careful."

Milam tried to get a word in edgewise. He couldn't. "The country has to protect itself against those who will harm it," the congressman concluded. "That's our job."[59] And then he hobbled away. Slowly, Lorenzo realized that his congressman thought he was a subversive.

It was Washington. It was the Cold War. It was Siberia. "Those days weren't merely dark," Milam says; "they were like nightmare. Bleak, endless nightmare."[60]

After two years, he gave up. There was no way, he decided, that the government was going to let him start a station in the capital. So he submitted a new application, this time to broadcast in Seattle, because that was as far as you could get from D.C. and still be in the contiguous states. He asked for 107.7 FM, reasoning that it was the least desirable frequency: at the far edge of the dial, no one would stumble on his signal on the way to someplace else. Maybe then the government would let him have a radio station, he figured, if he'd stick to the far left side of the country and the far right side of the dial and keep his subversions far away from the Beltway's sensitive ears.

He hired a respected law firm, Haley, Bader & Potts, to fight for his application. And then he repaired, in despair, to Europe, to spend time in Spain and England and leave Washington and radio and Cold War politics behind.

4

The '60s

There were people doing things, both commercially and noncommercially, that were very exciting and wonderfully off the wall. And at times awful. But it was based on risk-taking, something that is antithetical to almost any radio now.   —Larry Yurdin

JUMP NOW TO Seattle, almost a decade down the road. A ramshackle little building sits behind a fence, old junk strewn in the yard. Once it was a donut shop. In 1968, it's a radio station.

A fifteen-year-old ham operator named Tad Cook walks past the station's tower—an antenna attached to a utility pole—and into the old shop. He passes the tiny control room and transmitter. To his left is a bathroom. To his right, an area that simultaneously serves as a broadcast studio, a record library, and (thanks to a desk pushed against a wall) an office. Old carpet samples cover the walls. A live mike hangs into the middle of the room. People are laughing, talking, trying to describe the pictures that flicker in front of them.

Someone has set up a movie projector and is attempting to broadcast his home movies. If you were in Seattle during that hour and tuned your radio dial to 107.7 FM, you would have heard a cacophony of chuckles and a projector's whirl, and a gang of voices trying to translate the camera's images into words.

You would have been listening to KRAB, an eccentric and eclectic station founded by the fellow with the movie projector. He is Lorenzo Milam. He's been back from Europe for seven years now. He liked his days at KPFA, but KRAB is something different. Weirder. Freer.

It is something new: a wide-ranging forum for more species of music and opinion than most listeners knew existed. It's a kind of radio that values independence, irreverence, and creative, risk-taking, volunteer-based programming. In the 1970s, it will come to be called *community radio*. But not quite yet. "Before that," Milam explains, "it wasn't community. The early KPFA . . . and KRAB were stations for the elite—those who wanted vigorous discussion, strong commentaries, shit-kicking interviews, and rich and controversial musical programming."[1]

Most historians point to KPFA as the nation's first community radio station, and there's something to be said for that point of view, even if the phrase is a little anachronistic. But if Lew Hill fathered the movement, Lorenzo Milam reared it. KRAB's varied schedule made Pacifica's look tame: a single day's lineup might include both a special report from the front lines of the civil rights struggle and a fifteen-minute program produced by the White Citizens' Council. Like Pacifica, KRAB broadcast music unlikely to be heard on other frequencies: medieval, Renaissance, and early Baroque composers; the experimental avantgarde; folk music from around the world. The station subsisted on listener contributions, Milam's inheritance, and the occasional grant.

In 1968, Milam left Seattle. Over the next ten years, he would lend his inspiration, experience, and money to help launch more outlets, the so-called KRAB Nebula, around the country. Some of those stations soon produced nebulae of their own. Other community stations emerged independently, inspired by what had gone on before them but without any old-timers' help. Some college broadcasters adopted KRABesque programming as well.

The new stations drew on the *Whole Earth Catalog* strain of the counterculture and its do-it-yourself ethic. It's difficult to define community radio; many contentious battles have been fought over just that issue, as we'll see. But basically, it represents a third model of broadcasting, different from both commercial and public outlets, though it overlaps in certain ways with each. In its ideal form, it is radio rooted in—forgive the expression—civil society, a phrase whose recent mutation into fatuous Beltway cliché should not blind us to the richness of the institutions it describes.

It was a long road, bent and treacherous, from Lewis Hill to the KRAB Nebula. At times it intersected with another path, one that led from the best AM stations of the 1950s to the "underground" FM of the '60s and '70s—a road that was popular, profit-driven, and otherwise distinct from the community broadcasters' narrow audiences and noncommercial style. When those routes crossed, something wonderful would appear: radio that was both eccentric and popular, that was spontaneous and diverse yet geared for mass appeal. A few characters managed to travel both roads, importing ideas from one to another, helping remake the radio dial—ever so briefly—as a place where eccentric creativity was welcome.

One of those characters was Larry Yurdin, a native of New Jersey. From the early '60s to the early '80s, Yurdin moved between both brands of radio, never quite fitting into either category but constantly reinvigorating each with the other's energy. "I was always regarded," he recalls, "as too commercial by the purists in noncommercial radio and too much of a noncommercial maverick by the commercial people." As far as Yurdin was concerned, he was being consistent. "My intuitive sense has always been populist," he explains: he wanted to do exciting, engaging, experimental radio, and he wanted to do it in a way that would appeal to a large audience.[2]

Larry got his start at Bard College's campus station, a tiny project in the back of the school gym. This was a carrier current operation, which means its signal was carried by wires, not broadcast through the air, and thus couldn't be heard outside the school's buildings. For a while, it had only one turntable. It was fun, but it wasn't much.

But better things were in the offing. Just across the Hudson River, Pacifica was putting down roots. It had already spent four years setting up KPFK, a second station in Los Angeles; the new outlet signed on in July 1959, with Terry Drinkwater, later a famed CBS correspondent, as its first general manager.[3] A few months later, an eccentric millionaire named Louis Schweitzer, owner of a mildly offbeat New York operation called WBAI, decided he would hand his station over to the Pacifica Foundation. Schweitzer had originally bought the station because he wanted to hear more classical music on the radio, picking WBAI—or so they say—because he could see its transmitting tower from his home at the Hotel Pierre. (Smart readers will take this story with as much salt as they apply to the one about the jukebox that spawned Top Forty.) Now he was tired of it, especially in the wake of a recent newspaper strike. With the papers gone, many New Yorkers had turned to BAI for their news, making it, for the first time, a money-maker. Unfortunately, the same ads that were making the station solvent were also making it unlistenable, at least to the ears of the man who owned it. "I realized right then, when we were most successful commercially, that was not what we wanted at all," Schweitzer later recalled. "I saw that if the station ever succeeded, it would be a failure."[4] So he gave Pacifica president

Harold Winkler a call. "If Pacifica wants a station in New York, I'll give you one," he said.

No transcript exists of the conversation that ensued, although much of it apparently consisted of Schweitzer's efforts to persuade Winkler that he wasn't a crank. (Or, at least, that he was a very rich crank who really did own a radio station.) In this way, WBAI became the third member of the Pacifica network. "Together," Winkler wrote in its first program guide, "we have to initiate a new sense of excitement in New York, a hopeful spirit dedicated to a rebirth of the responsible citizen in a large urban center. . . . This is a community station: We have no other objective but to serve the public interest in a completely public manner."[5]

Re-enter Yurdin, who had read about the changeover in the *New York Times*. Bard gave its students a two-and-a-half-month field period with no classes, so that they could get some career experience. So Yurdin asked WBAI whether it had any work for him to do, and on the basis of his collegiate "radio experience," they told him to start splicing tapes.

The job bored Yurdin, who was soon ready to quit. Then he fell into a conversation with another newcomer, an unemployed actor named Bob Fass.

Fass's most recent job had been in the cast of *The Threepenny Opera*. After the play closed, his friend Dick Ellman, a Pacifica staffer with an ear for good voices, suggested Fass try working as an announcer. He did, and was soon reading "miscellanies" over WBAI: little poems, stories, and mini-essays the station used to fill the gaps between programs. Before long, he had an idea for a show of his own.

In those days, WBAI signed off the air at midnight. Fass asked whether he could do an after-hours broadcast once a week. The managers agreed—perhaps, some have speculated, because they figured no one would be listening that late. Fass told Yurdin about his plans for the show and invited Larry to be his producer. Larry eagerly accepted.

In short order, Pacifica had a new style of radio on its hands. "When you undertook a radio show before or since," Yurdin recalls, "you didn't walk in at 12:30 at night to see in the main studio Ravi Shankar sitting on the floor doing a forty-five-minute raga live on the air. Or you didn't see a whole bunch of people crowded in the studio, sitting on the floor, with Phil Ochs standing up singing 'Love Me, I'm a Liberal.'"

The show aired each Friday from midnight to five, and even later if

Fass felt like sticking around. He played all kinds of records; he interviewed all kinds of people; he allowed musicians to jam, live, in the studio; he did news reports, took listener calls, and sometimes, his colleague Steve Post recalls, simply rambled, "free-associating from the innards of his complex mind."[6] Fass also pioneered the art of sound collage: he was surely the first DJ, and perhaps the last, to play a Hitler speech with a Buddhist chant in the background.

New York's New Left and counterculture embraced the new late-night circus, and Fass soon held a contest to name the show. He didn't like any of the suggestions that came in, so he branded it *Radio Unnameable*.

Fass's style owed little to the highbrow and sometimes dry mode of broadcasting that most listeners then associated with Pacifica. His precursors were more playful—and, befitting his former profession, more theatrical. The most famous was Jean Shepherd, whose broadcasts each evening on New York's WOR-AM featured funny, meandering stories that took long, strange digressions, plus the odd kazoo solo, novelty record, sour comment about his sponsors, or off-the-cuff social commentary of the kind one might associate with *Mad* magazine (to which he occasionally contributed). Marshall McLuhan called Shepherd's show "a new kind of novel that he writes nightly. The mike is his pen and paper. His audience and their knowledge of the daily events of the world provide his characters, his scenes, and moods."[7]

Another precursor was John Leonard, later a noted literary critic, whose *Nightsounds* occupied KPFA's late hours. By one listener's faint memory, the show was "a lot of sophomoric fooling around mixed with enough moments of zany brilliance to keep me listening many Saturday nights," with Leonard coming off as "an intellectual Steve Allen."[8] It was a long way from the BBC Third Programme that had inspired Lew Hill to Fass's anarchic antics. Leonard, whose show juxtaposed jazz with satire and poetry as well as other styles of music, was the bridge.

And Yurdin, in his first real radio job, got to witness it all. He was there with Fass when Bob Dylan first dropped by, back when Dylan's career was just starting. (Before long, Fass was the only radio figure Dylan would allow to interview him.) The satirist Paul Krassner, whose magazine *The Realist* was by some lights the first underground newspaper, was a frequent guest. So was an ex-beatnik stand-up comic named Hugh Romney, who would later don a clown's costume, change his name to Wavy Gravy, and inspire an ice cream flavor.

As the counterculture evolved into a mass movement, *Radio Unnameable* became its New York headquarters.

Fass had, in essence, discovered freeform radio: a spontaneous sort of broadcasting that ignores genre boundaries and allows the host's personality to pour freely over the air. He had his precursors, of course: not just Leonard and Shepherd, but the AM band's black DJs and the earliest rock 'n' roll jocks. Even staid old KPFA had been known to play classical pieces back to back with jazz and folk records. KRAB sometimes called itself a "free form" station, though it usually preferred the phrase "free forum." But Fass brought freeform into its classic period, and he helped introduce two innovations.

First, Fass was one of the first people to program music in *sets*. "I don't even know if we called them sets in those days," Yurdin recalls. "There was no precedent. But he was the first to do thematic, or mood-related, or musically related, beautifully segued combinations of music."

Second, Fass expanded the idea of what talk radio could be. The first call-in program had been launched in 1945, by Barry Gray of WOR-AM. But the idea didn't take off until the '50s, when it became one of the new formats that stations experimented with while trying to compete with TV.[9] There was a boomlet in talk stations in the early '60s, and, to an extent, Fass was riding that wave. But Fass's program was the only one where the local antiwar movement might organize a demonstration over the air, treating an FM signal like an enormous conference call. (This also ensured that Fass had a decent-sized listenership among the city's Red-baiters and cops.) No show had ever been so *participatory*.

This made the station's old guard a little nervous. Fass had joined the network at a time when most Pacificans wouldn't even call their shows *shows*; they did "programs"—or, better, *programmes*. Now their airwaves were adopting an earthier, more irreverent quality. Fass fought with management, leaving the air several times along the way.

Of course, this being Pacifica, *lots* of people were fighting with one another. One of the fiercest battles came in 1965, when program director Christopher Koch traveled illegally to North Vietnam and recorded the raw material for a series of one-hour shows on the then-nascent war. The series' stance was far friendlier to the Viet Cong than was ordinarily heard at that early date. At this point, bear in mind, WBAI had already run afoul of the national security state: in 1962, several people associated with Pacifica had been subpoenaed by the Senate Internal Se-

curity Subcommittee, which was investigating "possible communist in-
filtration or penetration of an important radio chain, the stations of the
Pacifica Foundation."[10] The subcommittee expressed an interest in several supposedly subversive programs, but the proximate cause of the
investigation was almost certainly an explosive exposé of the FBI that
had been broadcast on WBAI. (Pacifica had offered the FBI equal time
to rebut the charges but had been rebuffed. Evidently, the bureau was
more interested in silencing its critics than in debating them.)

After much debate, the foundation board agreed to appear before
the committee, a position that seems a mite less craven when one notes
that the FCC had been delaying each of the Pacifica outlets' license re-
newals. Notes Koch: "the FCC told us that it would not act on our licenses until [the subcommittee] completed its investigation. Although
FCC Chairman [Newton] Minow told Pacifica and reporters that there
was no connection between its delay and the substance of those hearings, they both asked similar questions."[11] The next FCC chair, E.
William Henry, was more direct: if the foundation cooperated with the
committee, its licenses would be renewed. The foundation agreed, and
the internal disputes that followed nearly ripped Pacifica apart, with
one man—vice president Jerry Shore—resigning from the network.

So now Koch was traveling illegally to Vietnam and making broadcasts that were bound to anger the government. Several board members got mad, both at the programs themselves and at the fact that
they had not been forewarned of (and, presumably, given a chance to
veto) Koch's unlawful sojourn. Some wanted to edit out parts of Koch's
programs. Louis Schweitzer—the station's landlord as well as its former owner, and a major donor as well—cast his lot with the censors. So
did the station manager, a nervous Chris Albertson. Koch refused to
soften his shows and eventually walked out, taking at least five more
staffers with him. A lot of angry listeners canceled their subscriptions,
too. When the dust cleared, Albertson was out and most of the staff
were back.

Fass was on every weeknight at 12, opening each show with the
same three words: "Good morning, cabal." Steve Post, one of Fass's occasional substitutes, was hosting another dose of freeform, *The Outside*,
on Saturday nights, centered around his proudly insecure persona. (He
also interviewed some of the oddest characters in New York City, including a blind transsexual, an enema fetishist, and various others who
would not ordinarily appear in the mass media in those days, though in

the Jerry Springer era they may seem ho-hum.) And Larry Josephson launched a freeform morning show, *In the Beginning . . .*, that showcased his early-rising grouchiness. In Post's words, Josephson's

> approach to his listeners was staggeringly different from any which had previously been heard over WBAI. He hated them. He hated getting up early in the morning, and whichever side of the bed he exited from, it was invariably the wrong one. His program, in its early days, reflected this wretched, hostile attitude, and . . . satirized the bright-eyed, cheery, smiling-voiced, "Isn't it great just to be alive?" morning radio personality prevalent on just about every other radio station in New York.[12]

The *New York Times* called him the "anti-morning disc jockey."[13]

The trio had its critics inside the network, and not just from the BBC-smitten old guard. There was, for example, Paul Schaffer, who was just twenty-two years old when he took over BAI's Vietnam coverage. Schaffer got a lot of attention for, in his words, "neglecting to operate within the parameters 'radio, subcategory left-wing.'" Instead, he "asked myself what sort of radar screen would best pick up Vietnam developments that weren't widely disseminated but ought to be." For instance,

> some of the time I'd try to think like an anthropologist looking for data. New York City soldiers rarely got obits, but the *Newark News* was conscientious about covering Vietnam deaths from the northern third of its state. A few brief obits in the course of a week provided an implicit social profile of the war's U.S. casualties.

Schaffer wasn't the only one at the station with an innovative approach to news. Dale Minor, for example, drew a lot of praise for his in-depth, intimate coverage of the southern civil rights movement. This sort of programming was as much a part of the new BAI as the freeform shows were.

Schaffer admired Fass's program, if only for its "cultural importance," but he drew the line at embracing Post and Josephson (an opinion colored, he admits, by some professional conflicts with them). "It's a major mistake to think of Pacifica as a subcategory within 'radio broadcasting,'" he explains. "You end up superimposing certain political and social agendas on paradigms taken from NPR and commercial radio. . . . There's a legitimate feelgood factor—now we have *our* equivalent of (fill in the blank)—but what you end up with is quite derivative." And Post and Josephson? "I don't think 'personality' programs should be a major element at Pacifica, unless the resources to do anything more important are absent. P&J took a WOR[-AM] talk-show paradigm and made it a bit funkier. So what?"[14]

The answer, I suppose, depends on how funky they made it—on whether their shows transcended the genre. At its best, freeform talk radio becomes great theater. Consider the episode of Post's show, aired shortly after student militants occupied Columbia University, in which Paul Krassner and fellow humorist Marshall Efron, while substituting for the absent host, declared that they were actually students "liberating" the station. "They read all the standard station announcements, carefully followed all FCC regulations, including station breaks on the hour and half hour, and made no attempt to disguise their voices, which, after years of guest appearances on my program, were as familiar to my audience as my own," Post later wrote. "Still, within an hour police arrived at the studios, having received reports of a student takeover and of my detention as a hostage in WBAI's bathroom."[15]

For many, Fass was becoming *the* voice of WBAI, a situation strengthened by the station's proximity to WOR-FM. The latter was the main commercial rock outlet in New York City; its advertising was aggressive, its DJs were obnoxious, and its signal was right next to Pacifica's. More than one young New Yorker stumbled on Fass while searching for his commercial neighbor, listened a while, and decided to stay.

Fass's love for lively stunts brought in new listeners, too. Early in 1967, in the era of New Left sit-ins and hippie be-ins, he called for a "fly-in." The phones started ringing, the callers started organizing, and on the appointed date a horde of hippies flocked to Kennedy Airport to greet the airplanes as they arrived. Later that year, when listeners started calling to complain about how dirty the city was, one caller suggested that the radio family should descend on one neighborhood and clean it up. Fass dubbed the project a "sweep-in," and the on-air organizers got to work. When the day arrived, thousands of listeners went to the Bowery, brooms and buckets in hand, to clean the designated block, only to discover that the New York City Sanitation Department, afraid of bad publicity, had arrived earlier that morning and swept the area already. Undissuaded, the throng moved to another dirty block nearby and, joined by the natives, scrubbed it clean.

Meanwhile, the overweight Post parodied his mentor by assembling a "fat-in" in Central Park, where chubbies took pride in their girth by gobbling junk food and burning Twiggy in effigy.

Such theater was also invading another Pacifica outlet's late-night hours. In Los Angeles, a quartet of comics called the Firesign Theatre was broadcasting strange, sometimes brilliant improvisations on KPFK.

David Ossman had worked for WBAI before it was a part of the Pacifica network, producing a series of interviews and documentaries on the Beat movement; he stayed with the station for a spell after Schweitzer gave it to Pacifica, then moved to L.A. Phil Austin's first job in radio had him reading the comics to listeners in Fresno; with that background, plus stints as a soldier, an actor, and a beatnik, he succeeded Ossman as KPFK's drama and literature director. Phil Proctor and Peter Bergman arrived with backgrounds in the theater; they had trod the boards together at Yale before going their separate ways, Proctor to New York and Bergman to England (where he worked with Spike Milligan of the legendary *Goon Show*). Both eventually ended up in Los Angeles, where Bergman and Paul J. Robbins started a show on KPFK called *Radio Free Oz*.

The first *Oz* aired on July 24, 1966, with four hours of phone-ins, music, and comedy. It aired five nights a week, starting at midnight; the station's general manager, Paul Dallas, felt that "hipsters, hippies, teenyboppers, swingers and hepcats had best be aired after hours."[16] At the end of the summer, KPFK devoted a special fundraising marathon to the program, a week-long, late-night-only pledge drive that proved the show had a substantial audience but also brought tensions between its hosts to a boil. Robbins quit soon afterward.

There was no shortage of substitute voices: *Oz* featured an array of semiregular guests, including Ossman, Proctor, and Austin (who had been serving as the show's producer). On November 17, for the first time, all four Firesigns found themselves in the studio at once. The result was the Oz Film Festival, a sequence of imaginary movies. "We all played various characters," Ossman explains, "who had come to show our movies on the radio. We described them . . . and totally improvised and then we took phone calls from the listeners."[17] A four-headed star was born.

Gradually, the comedy began to take over the show. "From my production standpoint," says Austin, "we really needed badly to fill three or four hours every night. There were only so many phone calls you take of people stuck on bad acid trips, or people who came in to read tarot cards, or various musicians."[18] But that comedy took a lot of work. "It was not as relaxed as it sounded, in the background," notes Don Mussell, who served as one of the show's producers at the tender age of sixteen.

> There was a lot of frenetic activity trying to keep the show going. . . .
> All we had in the way of sound effects were either on record or on tape. And so typically, during a Firesign Theatre show, I would have both turntables cued up with some sound effects records or some theme music that was [preselected], along with the three Ampex tape machines that had tapes of various sounds loaded up to go at a moment's notice.[19]

Sometimes someone played the wrong recording. Sometimes the Firesigns improvised a response to the mistake that was even funnier than the original plan.

Radio Free Oz jumped to KRLA-AM, a relatively conventional commercial station, in March 1967. The Firesigns were still loosely associated with Pacifica, though—they performed their first stage piece, *Freak for a Week,* at a KPFK benefit in Santa Monica—and after spells at KMET and KPPC, outlets to be discussed later, they returned to the station that birthed them. Their new show, launched in September 1970 and called *Dear Friends,* was syndicated to other alternative stations around the country.

From its Fass-like beginnings, the Firesign Theatre had evolved into something unique, rather like someone had crossed an old-time radio serial with the Tibetan Book of the Dead. It didn't always work. "What you hear on records from that era are the best tidbits," warns Mussell, referring not to their intricate studio albums but to collections of their radio work. "Out of an hour of amazingly awful things, you'd get maybe five minutes of amazing things." Many would dispute that ratio, but few would deny the point. The same freedom that allows for eccentric triumphs also allows for eccentric failures.

Still, when it managed to cohere, it was magic. One Firesign might start reciting mass. Another chimes in with a simultaneous "translation," taken from another text: "He is saying that at a determined time, the command module, now all alone, glowing because of air friction like a shooting star, enters the Earth's atmosphere. . . ." Another interjects an Indian legend. Someone starts reciting a list of extinct animals. "No," a clerk says apologetically, "we're out of those. No, I'm sorry. They're all gone." The list of dead beasts gradually melts into something else: "California condor, southern sea otter . . . pink and black socks, charcoal gray suits . . . Nikola Tesla, Charlie Chaplin. . . ."[20]

The Firesigns soon moved almost exclusively into the recording studio, where they created some of the finest albums ever made.[21] They were the first comedy group—arguably the only one—to take full advantage of multitracking and other new recording technologies widely used in the music world, fusing them with more old-fashioned audio traditions. "The way we wanted to produce the records," Proctor later said, "was as if radio had continued into the modern era with the full force of energy it had during its golden age. We thought of them as being 'movies for the mind.'"[22] The four have periodically returned, individually and collectively, to the medium that gave them their start. In the '80s, they even did some work for NPR.

Further up the coast, Milam was bringing a different kind of playfulness to Seattle. He had returned from Europe in autumn 1961, when his lawyers sent him word that the FCC had finally approved his radio station.

The lawyers in question were Andrew Haley and Michael Bader of Haley, Bader & Potts, one of those ancient law firms that haunt the halls of the regulatory state. Haley had helped draft the Communications Act of 1934 for Senator Dill and was the FCC's staff attorney the day the commission opened for business; he started his firm in 1939 and rapidly attracted an impressive list of clients. The commissioners respected him and tolerated his mild eccentricities—his interest in space law, for instance, and his willingness to go to bat for odd characters like Lorenzo. Before Haley, Bader & Potts entered the picture, the FCC associated Milam with Pacifica. Now they associated him with his lawyers. In Bader's words (pronounced, I should stress, with a strong accent of irony), "People on the commission staff thought that Lorenzo could be a flaming commie pinko bastard." He adds: "I think he bugged the commission. Here's this guy walking around on crutches, he's in the reference room of the FCC and he's all over the place; almost a gadfly." Haley, Bader & Potts, by contrast, presented "a little bit of respectability."

Besides its respectability, the firm brought stamina and patience. The commission couldn't simply deny Milam a license because it suspected him of being a Communist: aside from the obvious constitutional questions, he *wasn't* a Communist. But it could hold him off with red tape. With the D.C. application, Bader recalls, "They had kind of ground away at Lorenzo and nothing ever happened, and he finally gave up, and I think that was kind of the hope in [the Seattle] case: that he'd just go away. But we served notice that we weren't going to go away." The D.C. application had simply drifted; with Seattle, the FCC felt some pressure.

So Milam came back to America and put a classified ad in *Broadcasting* magazine: "Be daring. Help our poverty-stricken operation start from nothing. KRAB (FM) 9029 Roosevelt, Seattle 15, Washington."[23] A few responses trickled in.

One was from Jeremy Lansman, a Los Angeles native who'd grown up in St. Louis. Just nineteen years old, Lansman had been fascinated with electronics and radio since he was seven. Stuck in the hospital for some forgotten ailment, he'd received a diverting gift: "a breadboard, upon which had been placed several lights, several knife switches, a rheostat, a telegraph key, and a buzzer. This was all powered by a bell transformer. The board was supplied with a myriad of little wires, at each end of which there was an alligator clip."[24] Lansman spent hours with the toy, then started making gadgets of his own; over the next few years, he put together two crystal radio kits, a tube radio, and an FM receiver. He also tried, apparently unsuccessfully, to build a transmitter.

Lansman's parents separated when he was a teenager, and he moved to San Francisco, where he followed in Milam's footsteps and became a volunteer at KPFA. He soon dropped out of school—he never did well at formal studies but seemed good at learning on his own—and got a job in commercial radio. Again like Milam, he found the experience less than thrilling, disliking both the stations and the work they had him do. ("Threading tapes into the blinking automation machine," he later declared, "made me feel as though I was little more than an automaton myself.")[25] He eventually became chief engineer at KHOE, in Truckee, California, where he helped start a rock 'n' roll show. The owner then sent him to Honolulu, where, at age eighteen, he took charge of building a new station. He stayed in Hawaii a while, then quit his job and started traveling back on the mainland.

He was visiting a friend in Yakima, Washington, when he stumbled on Lorenzo's ad in *Broadcasting* and decided to scoot over to Seattle to answer it. Lorenzo hired him as an engineer, and Jeremy set to building KRAB. Their first effort to fire up the transmitter was a dismal failure, but the second was more successful, and on December 12, 1962, the new outlet went on the air, inaugurating itself with two hours of East Indian music by Ali Akbar Khan.

KRAB was a diverse family. Robert Garfias, whose Pacifica programs had so impressed Milam in Berkeley, had moved to Seattle to set up an ethnomusicology department at the University of Washington; he quickly became KRAB's music director as well. Gary Margason, another ethnomusicologist, was also a musician; he liked to spend his spare time playing Japanese court music. On KRAB, he could share that passion with anyone around the Puget Sound with an FM receiver. The station's commentators ranged from the Bircher radiologist Frederick B. Exner, a tireless opponent of fluoridation, to Frank Krasnowsky of the Socialist Workers Party. (Those two shared a timeslot, alternating from week to week.)

KRAB played a lot of classical music, but it consciously avoided the warhorses that dominated the classical stations' playlists. (For Milam, "the symphonies of Tchaikovsky may have been invented to keep middle-class turnips safely in the concert halls, and off the backs of the rest of us who care for some guts and meaning to life.")[26] It also played blues, country, and the occasional Bulgarian brass band and a daily show for children and readings from Ezra Pound, and Antonin Artaud, and *Dr. Dolittle*. In fact, it played almost everything. On one night—November 18, 1964—the station presented these four programs in a row:

9:15 PM ASSORTED TROUBLE WITH HENRY JACOBS. Mr. Jacobs creates sounds and words and trouble with tape machines and appallingly unintelligible but quite correct logic. This program cannot be explained, much less heard.

9:45 PM A KU KLUX KLAN ENLISTMENT RECORDING. A talk with interviews by Wally Butterworth of the Atlanta branch of the Klan; it's rather strong, and tries to show how civil rights workers violate property rights for their own ends; it is followed by the Klan's view of history of the United States since the civil war—and how domination by Jews and Catholics has caused most of our present-day problems.

10:30 PM KENNETH REXROTH DISCUSSES DOPE AND MEDICAL-LEGAL RESTRAINT THEREOF. One of the series broadcast each Saturday evening on KRAB, the San Francisco poet and critic discusses with appropriate humphs and grumps the books that have come to him in the mail.

11:00 PM THE BLUEGRASS REVOLUTION. A talk, with examples, by Ron Ginther of Turkey Plucker Fame, of the socio-economic forces invading the once proletariat field of country music. A bi-weekly program.[27]

The Klan record was something of a mainstay, and whenever the station played it, the staff "received many requests to replay it. And to burn it."[28] Once, they sandwiched it between a Folkways album of Somali freedom songs and a Folkways album of freedom songs from Angola, an unusual sequence even for KRAB.

In the midst of this, there were silences. "Lorenzo thought it was a good idea to have dead air between programs," one of the station's early volunteers recalls. That way, listeners could have "time to absorb what was going on and think about it."[29]

Yet for all this, KRAB was not cacophonous—except, that is, when it devoted a program explicitly to cacophony. The station had a definable flavor, even if it didn't have a homogeneous sound. There was a connecting vision to the schedule, a whimsical logic that harmonized all those contradictions. KRAB was large. It contained multitudes.

On October 8, 1964, it broadcast a speech by Barry Goldwater at 8:30 in the evening and another by Lyndon Johnson at 9:30. Sandwiched between them was "a campaign concert":

Lucy Stewart: "Two Pretty Boys"
Robert Johnson: "Hellhound on My Trail"
Big Joe Williams: "I Want My Crown"
Thelonious Monk: "Nice Work If You Can Get It"
Mercy Dee Walton: "After the Fight"
Juan Onatibia: "Txankarrenku (Dance of the Victor)"
Ornette Coleman: "Tomorrow Is the Question"[30]

That single show was suffused with the young KRAB's sensibility. So, for that matter, was Milam's goofy description, quoted earlier, of *The Bluegrass Revolution*—which, in case any readers feared otherwise, was a music show, not a neo-Marxist lecture. It was this playful impulse, more than anything else, that separated KRAB from KPFA.

Another difference: as Pacifica drifted steadily to the left, KRAB remained an open forum. Granted, not all of its listeners saw it that way. "KRAB exists," an exasperated Milam wrote in 1964, "for the sake of and in the shadow of the human spectrum, and yet the frantic efforts of some to color us a livid red are beginning to cramp our style." If this kept up, Milam concluded, "We will be allotted a color on the spectrum, our rainbow will disappear and so will our reason for being here."[31] The station thus found room on its schedule for talks by the seminal conservative intellectual Russell Kirk, the free-market economist Douglass North, and the firebreathing antileft pedant Eric von Kuehnelt-Leddihn, along with an array of socialists, anarchists, and psychedelic revolutionaries.

There was some disagreement, in those Cold War days, as to whether KRAB should identify its commentators' political affiliations before they spoke from its microphone. Milam wrote to his lawyers in 1964, asking them to clarify the relevant laws and adding that he felt "strongly that I am not in the business of investigating for the government, and therefore" had "avoided any identification up to this point."[32] Haley replied:

> Your absolute legal obligation is clear: Unless you have reason to know that a person is a member of an organization registered or required to register under the Subversive Activities Control Act . . . as a Communist, Communist-action, or Communist-front organization, there is no law which requires that you must identify him as to political viewpoints. (You are undoubtedly aware that if he is sponsoring the program, his sponsorship must be announced.) . . .
>
> It may be well for you to extend the practice beyond the bare legal requirements. KRAB has always existed in a regulatory "goldfish bowl". It is likely to remain in this position. I realize it is never pleasant to compromise a strongly held position, but, at least where the commentator has no objection, I do not see any position that is compromised if you require identification.[33]

KRAB also faced a possible threat from the misnamed Fairness Doctrine, the government's policy (abandoned in 1987) of demanding that views espoused on the radio be "balanced" by opposing opinions. In theory, this promoted the free exchange of ideas and open access to the airwaves. In practice, it was a way for politicians and interest groups to harass anyone who aired a view they disliked. The Kennedy administration was infamous for using it against its critics, as was Nixon's regime; during the intense antiwar demonstrations of October 1969, President Nixon told his staff to take "specific action relating to what could be considered unfair network news coverage"—not once, but twenty-one times.[34] The very possibility of such persecution chilled broadcasters' willingness to speak freely. (In the 1980s, the mayor of Milwaukee attacked WTMJ-TV under the Fairness Doctrine for an editorial it aired. The courts actually ruled in the station's favor, but not before it ran up a legal bill of $17,000 defending itself.)

You'd think KRAB would be immune to a fairness-based attack, given its open microphone. Milam, in fact, was a strong supporter of the Doctrine: with the airwaves monopolized by such boring crud, he reasoned, any rule that might force an eccentric opinion onto the ether was good. Nonetheless, some local conservatives complained that the station was unbalanced, and threatened to file a report with the FCC. It was a weird and inaccurate charge, but it made a cynical sort of sense if you assume the complainants were less interested in spreading their ideas than in suppressing the ideas of others.

That said, the station faced few political challenges in its early years —largely, one suspects, because it had so few listeners. In Milam's words, "I think in the first few years we had between five hundred and a thousand subscribers. People really didn't pay much attention to us. Which was very fortunate, because it gave us an opportunity to do pretty much what we wanted to, and there just wasn't much criticism of our programming. In fact, when criticism did begin to happen, in the late '60s, it was a surprise to us that people were taking us seriously."[35]

The new station did make waves in some sectors of Seattle. The same month it went on the air, its founder was among seven individuals and organizations cited by the Seattle ACLU for their support of civil liberties—in Milam's case, for establishing KRAB as a free-speech zone. Columnist Emmett Watson praised KRAB in the *Seattle Post-Intelligencer* for "delivering some of the liveliest radio programming in the city."[36]

The *Catholic Northwest-Progress* called the station "pretty much everything that we could ask for in a contemporary communication device."[37] Even the *New York Times* noticed it, in a brief item published before the station was a year old:

> Latin, sometimes called a dead language, has died again. A Seattle radio station, after briefly broadcasting a weekly half hour in classical Latin, has had to revert to all-English programming.
>
> The station, KRAB-FM, is a small subscriber-supported enterprise founded less than a year ago. In addition to carrying the Latin program—a unique feature, according to the 1963 yearbook of *Broadcasting* magazine—KRAB-FM also broadcast 30 minutes in classical Greek. But, a station spokesman said yesterday, the two fluent gentlemen who had volunteered to do the programs were unable to continue. And summer replacements in classical Latin and Greek are hard to find.[38]

All this was done on a shoestring, with neither government grants nor commercials to pay the bills.[39] It was in this cash-poor context that KRAB invented, or stumbled on, that most obnoxious of fundraising tools: the pledge drive.

Originally, the station raised most of its money the way KPFA did—for a minimal subscription, one became a member and received a program guide. It wasn't afraid of taking the odd grant as well, but it drew the line at commercial sponsorship. "The idealism of radio's early stations of the 20's was the inspiration for KRAB," Lorenzo explained to one reporter. "That 55 people can come to our studios, to say 55 different things about as many subjects, means that KRAB is beginning to move towards filling the responsibility abdicated by the commercial broadcasters. We have no sponsors, and we will never have any—even if it means ceasing to exist."[40] Unfortunately, the station's volunteer base wasn't very big, once you excluded those whose volunteering was limited to producing programs. As the reporter observed: "The fence surrounding the station needs painting, so Milam has planned a paint party for this Saturday. He has been announcing it over the air, and confidently expects that about 10 people will show up to get the job done, as they have in the past for previous urgent projects."[41] Ten may be enough to paint a fence, but you need more than that to keep a station afloat.

The result was a perpetual deficit, most of which came out of Milam's pocket—about $3,000 a year. To absorb the financial blow, Milam moved to his pal Jonathan Gallant's houseboat on Lake Union, limited his personal spending to about $150 a month, and took no salary for his more-than-full-time work. He didn't like asking for money, and he didn't like many of the people who did enjoy it; as he eventually confessed, "we refuse to go through the boorish act of fund raising except on the most superficial level; yet we refrain from hiring a professional because we tend to regard them with the same affection as we do a process-server, a coral snake, or a mortician."[42] Soon the station was next to broke.

The situation called for desperate measures, and in 1963, desperation came calling:

SATURDAY, NOVEMBER 9, 1963. Starting at 12:01 AM, KRAB (Seattle) will conduct its first gigantic marathon in order to raise $1000 for the station. Most of the regular programming will be suspended, and for 42 hours we will play music and parts of the most unusual lectures, discussion, concerts, commentaries that were heard over the station for the past year. Pledges will be solicited at disarmingly frequent intervals, and we will have a squad of motorcyclists (to be identified by hearts and "KRAB" tattooed on their arms) ready to go out and pick up the pledges. The money is needed to buy essential tubes, tapes, and to pay a bad assortment of bills that have collected in our TO BE PAID file. The Marathon will extend until 6 PM on Sunday.[43]

It worked. It also worried Milam; writing in the marathon's wake, he noted that those forty-two hours were "as close to commercial radio as KRAB has ever come. Every half hour, religiously, sometimes for as long as five minutes, there was a heavy appeal for funds."[44] By the 1970s, Lorenzo would be apologizing, sort of, for the innovation: "The sad fact is that the Marathon is no longer a stop-gap emergency money-raise for the community stations. Rather, it has come to be a method whereby those stations can budget ahead of time an extra $20,000 or $80,000—knowing that a month's beggary will raise some sum like that."[45] As the practice spread to the more professional quarters of public radio and public TV, with pitches from legions of Cats fans and grown men dressed as Doctor Who, Milam could at least take comfort in the fact that WBAI had stumbled on the same fundraising technique, apparently independently. So even if KRAB had kept quiet that November, the precedent would still have been set.

For the New Yorkers, the financial crisis hit in the summer of 1965. BAI was behind on its bills, its taxes, and its payroll; the staff was angry and hungry, and Ma Bell, Con Edison, and the IRS were yapping at the doors. At an emergency meeting, the staff decided—in Steve Post's words—to "suspend all programming and turn to the audience, twenty-four hours a day, until either we raised the money necessary to stay alive or the plug was pulled." Not everyone liked the idea: "This marathon thing more than smacked of Jerry Lewis selling diseased children to the highest bidder of guilt."[46] But they did it anyway, pleading around the clock until the money they needed was there. It was completely disorganized, a sprawling, open-ended panhandling spree, with celebrities ranging from Pete Seeger to Tony Randall dropping by to beg. It was successful enough to become institutionalized—since 1965, not a year has gone by at BAI without at least one (and, lately, many more) on-air pledgefests. The practice was quickly imitated at the other Pacifica stations, then at more outlets around the nation.

Back in the northwest, KRAB's influence was spreading. In Portland, Oregon, the city's only classical music station, KPFM, switched to a more commercial format, leaving its listeners with no place to go. A number of them formed a group called Portland Listener Supported Radio, hoping to buy the station and return it to its old ways. When that plan failed, and when they found themselves unable to persuade any other local outlets to adopt a classical lineup, they asked KRAB if it might help them start a new station. The result was a grant from Milam —via the Jack Straw Memorial Foundation, which formally owned the Seattle operation—and a mass mailing. The Portlanders sent between four thousand and five thousand booklets and questionnaires to potential supporters in early 1965, explaining the sort of radio KRAB was doing in Seattle, asking whether the recipients would be interested in contributing money and/or labor to such a station in their own town, and requesting donations. About 250 people responded, enough for the organizers to call a meeting at a local college, where forty-five Oregonians spent four hours debating how the operation would work. ("This is getting really silly," Milam wryly wrote to his attorney; "those guys are so well organized that they have meetings. Without booze.")[47]

The prospective broadcasters agreed to start small, with the Jack Straw Foundation applying for a low-power repeater station in Portland. The outlet would initially limit itself to rebroadcasting KRAB's signal. Gradually, it would bring more locals into the operation, boost the transmitter's power, and ease away from the Seattle mother ship. On Halloween, Lorenzo and friends dubbed the fledgling station KBOO—not after the holiday, as some sanitized histories have suggested, but after Berkeley Boo, a strain of marijuana.

The task of setting up the station fell to David Calhoun, a big, red-haired monk-turned-medical-student from KRAB. Calhoun loaded a transmitter into his Volkswagen and drove to Portland, where he slept on couches, bummed meals, and gradually pulled together the people and equipment required to start a radio station. The new outlet set up shop in some donated space downtown, a cramped and dirty basement room that soon served as Calhoun's home and office as well as a broadcast studio. KBOO signed on the air in June 1968, a ten-watt signal that aired local voices only when it took a break for station identification. But Portland-based programming soon emerged.

In the meantime, the KRAB crowd was plotting yet another spinoff. Jeremy Lansman had long wanted a station of his own. In 1963, he discovered that a frequency was open in his former home, St. Louis, and he applied for a license to broadcast over it. Unbeknownst to him, Milam had applied for the same channel; upon discovering that they were pursuing the same prize, they combined their applications. Lansman surveyed a selection of St. Louis citizens, asking them what they felt was absent from the airwaves; he compiled their comments, which decried everything from the absence of folk music to the other stations' poor "technical quality of music reproduction," and sent them to the FCC.[48]

There were two other applicants, one of which quickly dropped out. The other was the Christian Fundamental Church, a temple that proudly proclaimed, on a sign out front, that it was racially segregated. The FCC held a hearing in Washington, D.C., to determine which would-be broadcaster would better serve the public interest. The churchmen took the opportunity to fire every volley they could at the Lansman-Milam application. They complained about some minor technical differences between the rival claimants' applications. They argued that the KRABites' station would not be "balanced." They claimed that Jeremy did not intend to move back to St. Louis. They even asked whether the commission could trust a broadcast license to men who had been known to *wear beards*.

Lorenzo and Jeremy fought back as best they could, with the law squad from Haley, Bader & Potts providing advice, legal and otherwise. ("There is no room for frivolity at this stage," Haley wrote Milam before the hearing, "so please restrain your refreshing sense of humor. Try to do the same with Mr. Lansman's.")[49] It was tough going. By November, Lansman was almost "willing to concede the case to the church"—but only "if their program proposals become more interesting."[50] They did not.

In April 1965, the FCC examiner made his initial ruling in favor of the church, giving it a "minute preference" for being based in St. Louis already and for having a coverage area that would include about 2 percent more potential listeners. Lansman and Milam objected and took the matter to court. It was an odd conflict, made odder by the administrative law judge who handled the case, an old government hand named Jay Kyle. Kyle was so well connected in military circles that he had Q clearance, the Pentagon's highest access credential—or so it was rumored in the Lansman-Milam camp. Some suspected Kyle had been picked to judge the case for fear that Lorenzo and Jeremy were subversives.

In the meantime, the attorneys from Haley, Bader & Potts kept flashing their picture of the racist sign outside the Christian Fundamental Church. The church itself scrambled to adjust its image to the authorities' evolving views on race, but with little success. "We have been accused of being hard-core segregationists," its pastor told the *St. Louis Post-Dispatch*. "That's not true. Why, we had a Negro family living in the church a few years ago. The father was a custodian. And there are a few Negroes who attend church services although they are not members of the church."[51] Uh-huh. The church also officially revoked its policy of segregation at its affiliated school, but it did not match this formal change by actually admitting any black children.

Indeed, the closer the Seattleites looked at the church, the sorrier it seemed. Its school was unaccredited; its pastor called himself "Doctor" Autenreith but had never been awarded a doctorate. (He claimed to have an "honorary" degree conferred by his own church in "about 1949"—one presumes the diploma wasn't dated.) Finally, in 1967, the FCC ruled against the Christians, and Lansman prepared to return to Missouri.

By the summer of '68, Milam, too, was preparing to leave. He had stepped down from his perch atop KRAB and would soon buy a com-

mercial station in Los Gatos, California, revamping it as an ad-free outlet called KTAO. Lansman spent the summer building his station in St.
Louis, drywalling in the terrible summer heat. And in the streets of
Chicago, cops were beating protesters outside the Democratic Party
convention. Many of those marchers would not have been there had it
not been for yet another broadcaster—Bob Fass.

Radio Unnameable's marriage of the counterculture and the New
Left had caught the ears of Abbie Hoffman, Jerry Rubin, Ed Sanders,
and the aforementioned Paul Krassner, all of whom walked the same
line between radicalism and hippiedom and all of whom soon became
part of the *Unnameable* family. Together with Fass, they invented the
yippies, a playful group as devoted to media pranks as it was to traditional demonstrations; they spent the first half of 1968 encouraging people to go to Chicago to protest the Vietnam War, using BAI, as always,
as their central communications system. Along the way, they promoted
themselves with events such as the Grand Central Yip-In, in which
Hoffman and Rubin asked the radical and the hip to descend on Grand
Central Station on March 21, 1968, to celebrate their countercultural
identity. Some people feared this would provoke a police riot, and sure
enough, it did; the crowds were thick, a few yippies engaged in some
vandalism, and suddenly the cops were charging. The entire event was
covered, via telephone, on Fass's show. It was a sad moment—Alta-
mont to the sweep-in's Woodstock—but it showed, starkly, the power
and potential of radio.

It also foreshadowed the Chicago convention, site of another police
riot, with cops clubbing reporters and bystanders as well as marchers.
After Chicago, the government indicted Hoffman, Rubin, and six others—the so-called "Chicago Eight," later reduced to Seven after Black
Panther leader Bobby Seale was removed from the group and tried separately—for "crossing state lines with intent to incite a riot." When the
charges came down, Fass, Krassner, and Sanders formed a conga line on
Hoffman's roof, singing, "We weren't indicted! We weren't indicted!"[52]

They weren't the only ones left out. "Hell," one of Fass's listeners
later said, "the whole Chicago Democratic Convention was organized
on BAI. You sat there and you listened to it. We should have all gone
to Chicago and have been tried as conspirators instead of just the
Chicago Seven . . . because we were all in on it. Everybody made
phone calls, everybody made suggestions. That whole thing was
planned on Bob's show."[53]

The listener I just quoted is Vin Scelsa, who was making some trouble of his own that summer at WFMU, in East Orange, New Jersey. Before relating that adventure, though, we should note an uprising on the other coast.

In San Francisco in 1968, there was a strike at KMPX, a once-modest outlet that had in a matter of months become *the* station for the Bay Area's bohemian community. It was a commercial station, but it was unformatted, unpredictable, and underground—part creative, part sleazy, and part hip.

KMPX was a small-scale, low-budget operation—at one point, it had been based in a hotel room. Now it was in a refurbished warehouse on the waterfront. It had changed styles several times over the years, turning in 1966 to a foreign-language format, a place where the local Armenians, Chinese, and others could rent a few hours of airtime a day. Few noticed it before a Detroit DJ named Larry Miller came calling in 1967. Miller figured the hippies were as legitimate a minority as the Armenians; he couldn't see any reason why he couldn't buy some late-night hours for himself, recoup the investment by selling airtime to advertisers, and play a freeform mix of folk music, classical music, jazz, and acid rock. He convinced the station's owner, Leon Crosby, to give it a shot—Miller's dollars were as green as anyone's else's—and went on the air in February. He quickly found an appreciative audience, to Crosby's surprise and initial disbelief.

Then Tom "Big Daddy" Donahue entered the picture. Donahue had been involved with radio since 1949, working at a couple of small stations (including a short spell at WINX in Rockville, Maryland, the same station that had briefly employed Lewis Hill) before landing a job in 1951 at WIBG, in Philadelphia. This had originally been a Christian station—the call letters stood for "I Believe In God"—but in the 1950s it embraced rock 'n' roll. And from his perch as host of *Danceland*, Donahue established himself as Philly's biggest rock DJ. (When I say *biggest*, I don't merely mean that he was the most influential and popular. Big Daddy was a giant, more than three hundred pounds, with a voice that was deep and rich.) The payola scandals ended his career there, so he headed west in 1961 for a four-year stint at KYA, a Top Forty operation in San Francisco, where he became one of the first DJs in northern California to play black music for a white audience. Then he briefly left broadcasting to work as a studio producer and concert promoter.

According to legend, the notion of commercial freeform came to Donahue in the early months of 1967, as he and his wife-to-be, Raechel Hamilton, listened to the Doors' song "The End" and bemoaned the fact that no station in town was willing to play that kind of music. It's likely, though, that he was familiar with one earlier, albeit abortive, attempt to do freeform in a commercial context: New York's WOR-FM had tried to turn away from its Top Forty heritage in 1966, adopting a freer ethos for a few months—then quickly retreated when it became clear that the new approach was incompatible with the station's corporate ethos. Donahue probably knew about Miller's late-night show, too, for it was Leon Crosby and KMPX that he approached in March 1967, proposition in hand.[54]

He had some trouble getting hold of Crosby—the station phone had been disconnected—but he finally managed to set up a meeting. His initial proposal was modest: a timeslot, like Miller had, but earlier in the day, from eight to midnight, Monday to Friday, starting on April 7. Crosby hired him, and within three weeks he had established himself; listeners were sending him beads and posters to decorate the studio, advertisers were asking for airtime, and he'd fired his engineer, announcing that he'd rather work with a woman. Thus began KMPX's tradition of the "chick engineer," cueing up records and answering the phones while their male DJ partners spoke to the listening masses. Donahue brought more people on board, and, gradually, the hippies took over KMPX.

For listeners, this meant a heady dose of freeform. But it was not the same freeform that Bob Fass had developed in New York. For one thing, there were commercials: low-key ads often produced, or even improvised live, by the on-air talent. More important, most of the staff came from a background in commercial radio, and as much as they hated the Top Forty style they were rebelling against—the jingles, the screaming DJs, the clocks, the narrow playlists—that very rebellion affected them in ways that had never touched Fass. Fass's freeform was an extension of his background in theater; if you asked him to name an influence in the radio world, he'd probably mention Jean Shepherd or John Leonard. Donahue's freeform harkened back to Al Benson and Wolfman Jack, to the best AM jocks of the 1950s, remade for the white '60s counterculture—except that KMPX's musical palate stretched from the psychedelic to the baroque, in every sense of both words.

As Donahue rose within the station, his business sense proved as important, and as eccentric, as his programming philosophy. There was, for example, the matter of hiring a sales manager, someone who could combine some capitalistic smarts with an appreciation for what hippie listeners would abide—someone who could get ad accounts from head shops. Who better, reasoned Donahue, than his dope dealer? And so the job went to Milan Melvin, who was soon dragging Donahue to a Contra Costa County jail to bail out his buddy Chandler Laughlin so he could hire him for the sales staff.

Meanwhile, Crosby bought a second station in the Los Angeles area—KPPC, originally owned by the Pasadena Presbyterian Church—and let Tom and Raechel try to remake it as the KMPX of the South. But relations between Crosby and the staff were getting tense, partly because he was nervous about the station's cultural politics (all those on-air drug references might mean trouble with the FCC), partly because he was jealous of Donahue's power, and partly because his management style left a bit to be desired. Paychecks were bouncing, Crosby's lawyer was trying to impose ridiculous rules on the staff (even a dress code!), and Crosby himself was increasingly paranoid, convinced that Donahue and the others were trying to squeeze him out.

In March 1968, everything fell apart. Crosby told Donahue that the business couldn't afford to have him constantly flying between San Francisco and Pasadena; he'd have to work at either KPPC or KMPX, not both. Donahue responded by quitting. Melvin followed suit, and a few days later the rest of the staff decided to join them, voting unanimously to strike. They formed a new union—the Amalgamated American Federation of International FM Workers of the World, Ltd., North Beach Local No. 1—and walked out at 3:00 in the morning, Monday, March 18, with DJ Edward Bear announcing the protest on his late-night show. "This is now Radio Free San Francisco," a striker's voice in the background added. "Everybody is free to do as they please."[55]

Outside, a crowd gathered to support the walkout, complete with a light show and a free concert by the Grateful Dead, Creedence Clearwater Revival, and others. The strikers' demands, if adopted, would have essentially booted Crosby and his lawyer from any oversight at all, extending the freeform ideal of DJ decision making to station management. Donahue and Melvin would be reinstated and given absolute control over programming and sales, respectively; other staffers would be assured of autonomy in their departments; profit sharing would be introduced; wages would rise. Above all, Crosby and his attorney would no longer be allowed to saddle the staff with any new rules. Down in Pasadena, the staff of KPPC walked out in sympathy.

Larry Yurdin was in San Francisco around this time, staying with some friends. He got home one night, tuned his radio to KMPX, and heard nothing but dead air. Puzzled, he switched to KPFA—and there were the strikers. Pacifica had given them their late-night hours as an act of "community support."

Larry immediately called Bob Fass, who deputized him to cover the walkout for *Radio Unnameable*, editing his tapes at KPFA's studios. He also started working for the strike fund. He did his best to draw his two radio worlds together, and one night he managed to get Fass and Donahue—who'd never met—on the air together, live, on both KPFA and WBAI. It felt like a puzzle falling into place: the king of noncommercial freeform and the king of the commercial kind, meeting on Pacifica. The strangest thing was, it was the commercial jock who seemed more adventurous. Pacifica was having its usual troubles with the FCC, so when Donahue casually used the phrase "get laid," Fass fretted that such language might enrage the feds.

KPFA's late-night shift was becoming a study in cultural collision, as Pacifica's upright radicals rubbed shoulders warily with their down-and-dirty colleagues from across the Bay. "These were old commercial Top Forty people," Yurdin explains, "who had been swept up in the counterculture and the Vietnam War and been radicalized and evolved, and yet came from a completely different culture than the people who were at Pacifica." Different DJs and engineers came in each night to play their records, do their shticks, and talk up the strike. Then morning would come, and it would be back to the BBC dramas and Marxist roundtables.

Crosby tried to keep KMPX running, hiring scab DJs (including Larry Miller) and keeping a brave face. But the community was pretty solidly behind the strikers, with rock bands asking the station not to play their music (surely a first) and businesses pulling their ad accounts. A twenty-four-hour picket formed outside the studios, the marchers demonstrating their displeasure in ways ranging from the theatrical (going topless) to the threatening (hurling insults at scabs). The strike lasted eight weeks, petering out finally with a few staffers returning to Crosby's station, a few disappearing, and many finding a new home downtown. Donahue had negotiated a deal to take over KSAN, a heretofore classical station recently bought by the corporate giant Metromedia. There weren't enough positions for all the old staff to fill, prompting some bitterness among the rank and file, and some wondered whether an empire like Metromedia would really be a more permissive overlord than Crosby had been. Nonetheless, on Tuesday, May 21, they settled in at their new home, hoping for the best and ready for the worst.

As it happened, Metromedia was desperate for ideas. There was a youth market out there that it wanted to reach, and it didn't have any idea how. What's more, the FCC had just passed a troublesome new rule. Back in 1965, the commission had decided that companies that owned stations on both the AM and the FM bands could no longer play the exact same programs on each all the time; at least 50 percent of the FM schedule would have to be different. The rule didn't go into effect until 1967, but a lot of station owners still found themselves scrambling to fill those hours, on an FM band that they weren't sure anyone really listened to anyway. In New York, Metromedia hired a band of veterans from WOR-FM's short-lived experiment in freeform to remake its WNEW-FM as a quasi-freeform outlet. The new NEW was, in Steve Post's words, "more hype than hip,"[56] much as you'd expect from an operation that referred to itself as "The New Groove." But it was a lot freer than almost everything else on America's commercial airwaves. And now the same company was ready to turn its San Francisco signal over to a group with an even more radical programming philosophy.

There were some would-be meddlers in Metromedia, of course, but for the most part Donahue and company were able to fend them off. The format was fairly free and certainly wasn't limited to rock; one account of the period describes a DJ moving from a Buffalo Springfield song to a Mozart sonata, "which he then mixed in and out of a Balinese gamelan piece—the counterpoints cross-culturally counterpointing with each other—and then resolved the whole set with some blues from John Lee Hooker."[57] The new KSAN was a quick commercial success, becoming the number one FM station in the San Francisco Bay within two months. Other outlets across the country started trying to copy its success. Soon all the major markets had a "progressive" FM station, as did several smaller spots, from Glendive, Montana, to Utica, New York.

In some cases, that meant hiring creative people and giving them the same freedom Donahue allowed his staff in San Francisco. Other times, it meant granting somewhat less freedom to somewhat less creative programmers. Often, it meant a tense balance between the two approaches.

A few forward-looking entrepreneurs had started imitating Donahue even before he left KMPX. On March 15, 1968, WBCN—a Boston classical station that had never turned a profit—handed its night hours, and then its day hours too, to a freeform crew headed by Ray Riepen, a self-styled hip capitalist who admired what Donahue had done in San Francisco and who figured he could replicate Donahue's success in the Northeast. He recruited a staff from the nearest student-run stations, told them to focus on folk and rock, and found an audience almost immediately. He called the new format "the American Revolution," but it wasn't as revolutionary as another *putsch* being launched just a little further south.

That summer, Yurdin helped spark a coup d'état at WFMU, an obscure outlet licensed to a tiny Lutheran college. "The Radio Voice of Upsala College" had been on the air since 1958, broadcasting sermons, lectures, and "serious" music; it was, in Yurdin's words, "thoroughly undistinguished." It wasn't even on the air all day. But Saturdays at midnight, Vin Scelsa would come on, playing folk, blues, and rock and speaking freely until six A.M. Shortly before he left for California, Yurdin had stumbled on Scelsa's show and liked it; the music was good, and Scelsa's on-air style reminded him of Steve Post's. (Even the show's title, *The Closet*, seemed to echo Post's *The Outside*.) When he returned to New York, he had a proposal for Scelsa and the station manager, Ransom Bullard.

"Why aren't you on twenty-four hours?" he asked.

Bullard said he didn't think the station's license would allow that.

Not so, said Yurdin. FM licenses aren't limited by time. And listen, I just got back from California, and you won't *believe* what they're doing on the radio out there.

The men considered their options. It was summer; the college was closed; no one was around. The time seemed right for a coup. And Yurdin had a pretty good idea as to how they could pull one off.

"Drop the name Upsala College," he told the station manager. "Call this 'Freeform Radio—WFMU.' . . . Let's find some outrageous people in New York who are doing really interesting things. You don't have many college kids on the air anyway; it's just whoever wanders in. There's no reason not to recruit amazing people. They'll work for free—

they'll take the public service bus out to Jersey—because they can build a following for whatever it is they're doing."

And so they did. On May 31, they started a marathon; for a week they begged for money, trying to raise the $3,000 they needed to move to a full-time schedule. The listeners came through, and the station went 24/7; Scelsa started doing his show every night. Each DJ brought his own personality to his show. Danny Fields, for instance, often played the music that would eventually be known as punk—Iggy Pop, the Velvet Underground, the MC5—and frequently had Lou Reed on as a guest. Other timeslots played the acid rock more commonly associated with the era; still others played scarcely any rock at all, preferring jazz, classical music, novelty records, and/or folk. The station had its share of experimental comedy as well, with Lou D'Antonio—an old-timer, since he'd been on FMU since 1962—mixing good music, wonderfully bad music, doctored public service announcements, and cheerful non sequiturs on a show called *Hour of the Duck*. It was esoteric, but it was accessible; in Yurdin's words, it was "freeform for the masses."[58] The New York counterculture opened its arms, ears, and wallets to the newcomer, donating thousands when the station held another marathon in October.

Finally, the Upsala administration noticed what was going on under its nose. Apparently, none of the administrators actually listened to their radio station; instead, a trustee had apparently stumbled on a DJ on a TV talk show, bragging about how his crew had "liberated" Upsala's station. The college tried to crack down, prompting a ton of telegrams from angry listeners. After much sniping back and forth, Scelsa himself turned off the transmitter on August 31, 1969. When the station returned ten months later, only D'Antonio was still doing freeform.

Right would eventually reassert itself—today WFMU is one of the best stations in the country. But it would take it many years to recover the spirit that had infected it, and so many other outlets, in 1968.

5

Into the '70s

I like disc jockeys that are essentially groupies, who love their music
and take it home with them and are involved with it to a degree that
approaches fanaticism.   —Tom Donahue

FEW FREEFORM DJs liked Richard Nixon, and Nixon, in turn, cared
little for them. The relationship hit its nadir in 1971, when the FCC
started rumbling about the evils of drug songs—a category that, in
those paranoid days, some stretched to include "Puff the Magic
Dragon" and "Hey Jude" (for the phrase "let her under your skin").
Perhaps, the commission suggested, stations should rein in their DJs,
lest they turn their listeners into pill-popping zombies. The FCC never
punished anyone for playing songs with real or alleged drug lyrics, but
its public ruminations had an undeniable chilling effect—and gave
some uncomfortable companies a reason to end their outlets' experiments in freeform.

The FCC was pushed into this stance by the White House and the
Defense Department—not the agency you might expect to lead a war
on domestic psychedelia, but then, drugs weren't the only issue at play.
"It is not surprising that the Nixon Administration and the Defense Department, two primary targets of the youth culture, should try to strike
back," noted Nicholas Johnson, at that point the FCC's only commissioner with a dissident streak. "But it is revealing and somewhat fright-
ening that many of the song lyrics singled out as objectionably pro-
drug-use . . . turn out, in fact, to have nothing whatsoever to do with
drugs. They relate instead to social commentary."[1] The Pentagon, for instance, was distressed at a song that proclaimed, "War is out—peace is
the new thing."

But for all their contentiousness and repressiveness, those were
good years for radio. It was under Nixon's unfriendly administration

that the community radio movement really began to grow, and it was on his watch that freeform swept across the FM dial. And if those were days of conflict as well, that was hardly unique to the Nixon years: the turmoil would only increase as the '70s wore on and the '80s began.

It was in 1969, year one of the Nixon era, that Lansman and Milam finally started their St. Louis station. Surprisingly, given their background, the station—dubbed KDNA—ran commercials. Jeremy had planned on this approach long before the outlet's first broadcasts; were it not for that long battle with the Christian Fundamental Church, KDNA could have become the country's first commercial freeform station, beating KMPX and the others by a hair. But that would have been an almost meaningless title, since it didn't stay commercial for long. The sort of people who wanted to work at a community radio station tended to dislike the task of seeking sponsors, and most of the city's potential advertisers didn't quite understand the station.

So the station had two options. It could go head-to-head with the local KSAN clone, a not-quite-freeform outlet called KSHE, and make money by bringing better rock radio to St. Louis. (The main thing Lansman remembers about KSHE is that it played Arlo Guthrie's "Alice's Restaurant" to death.) Or it could drop the commercial trappings, rely on its listeners for financial support, and go its own way. After about a year and a half of commercial failure, it dropped the ads.

With no advertisers, and no government support, the station subsisted on next to nothing, keeping the utilities barely at bay. One morning, just two days before a fundraising marathon was to begin, DJs Tom Thomas and Terry Clifford received an anxious phone call: "There's a guy from the electric company climbing the pole behind the station, and he's got a really big pair of pliers."[2] Evidently, the electric bill had been left unpaid for too long.

Fortunately, the transmitter wasn't in the same building as the studios. The antenna was atop an office tower on the crest of a hill; in an artful move of guerrilla engineering, Lansman had wired the transmitter directly into the building's power supply, sparing the station the cost of the electricity. So Terry, Tom, and Jeremy grabbed some equipment and made for the tower, where they climbed to the roof, threw a long cable over the side of the building, pulled the wire into the transmitter room, and plugged it in.

That morning they woke up St. Louis broadcasting directly from the top of the Continental Building. They started the fund drive right then and there, vowing to remain on the roof until they'd raised enough to pay their bills. "We did the weather report looking up and we did the traffic report looking down," Thomas recalls, "and we interviewed pigeons that dropped by. As the morning went on, people heard what we were doing and musicians and poets started coming by. We broadcast all that day from the rooftop. Then we set some tents up, it started raining, and we broadcast overnight."

The station's remote unit was battery powered, so while the core group remained on the rooftop, another crew roamed St. Louis, transmitting live from every corner of the city. In two days, they raised more than they'd ever gotten before. The electric company got its money, the broadcasters returned to the studios, and the station didn't die.

"On one hand," says Thomas, "it was *really stupid* that we didn't have the electric bill paid. We never should have been in that kind of hole. On the other hand, the kind of creativity that backed against the wall said, 'They're not going to get us down, there's one more fight to fight,' the rallying of the community, the outpouring of support . . . that was an enormous, renewing, emotionally inspiring thing for us who worked at the station, for our supporters, and, I think, for the community."

Or communities. The station's primary audience was urban, young, and hip. Its bluegrass shows cast a wider net, drawing in an older, more rural crowd. The bluegrass DJs didn't have long hair, and they didn't share all of the core group's values. But their music fit well with the station's other shows, and there weren't any other outlets in St. Louis that would play it. Before long, the bluegrass hosts started doing their own benefits for the station, sometimes not bothering to tell Lansman and company until afterwards. ("Here's $500 we raised last weekend.")

Relations between blacks and whites were more strained. The DJs at DNA were committed to civil rights, but they couldn't always escape the era's conflicts, surrounded as they were by a black population less interested in having young white people "provide" them with "opportunities" than in having a broadcasting base of their own. Nonetheless, even that barrier sometimes broke down. There weren't—and aren't— a lot of radio stations that broadcast both black and white voices, but KDNA did. It was also one of the few stations in those days that would play both Caucasian folk music and black jazz.

KDNA's style turned out to be as different from the KRAB model as it was from commercial radio. While the Seattle station broke its schedule into distinct blocks—French jazz one hour, Bircher chat the next—the Missourians blended their ingredients into a more consistent (if no less eclectic) sound. In part, this reflected its commercial origins. From the start, KDNA's core staff, about a dozen people in their twenties or early thirties, was paid—though not very much, and sometimes just in shares of ownership. They were on the air most of the time, and their constant presence gave their station what Thomas would later call "a consistency of attitude, if not of genre."

If you tuned to KDNA in the morning, you'd hear classical music, mostly from the baroque or Renaissance eras. As the morning aged and people arrived at work, the DJs would gradually insert traditional music into the mix. One style would slowly flow into the other, until the folk records dominated the air.[3] Toward midday, the music would get more contemporary; works by modern singer-songwriters rubbed shoulders with older Irish instrumentals. Around noon you'd start to hear drums and electric guitars. The afternoons were the most eclectic time, with the sound shaped by whichever DJ was at the boards. Leonard Slatkin, for example, was a young assistant conductor at the St. Louis Symphony; he stuck to classical music. (These days he conducts the National Symphony Orchestra.) Another afternoon was hosted by Trebor Tichenor, one of the country's premier scholars, collectors, and performers of ragtime.

Then came a late-afternoon news block. Evenings and overnights were geared more toward jazz, rock, and blues, plus the odd call-in show. Then it was back to classical in the morning. Across the week, the station would drop in longer public-affairs shows, one of the few times they'd use programs from outside sources.[4] Weekends featured more specialized fare, including the huge bluegrass block.

It sounds a little like NPR—funkier, more radical, but not too distant from what an above-average public station might play today. In fact, it was very different. For one thing, it was more locally focused, with its own low-budget mobile unit. For another, it was more varied. Few public radio schedules today have room for a documentary on metropolitan towing, or live coverage of a welfare hearing, or a commentary called *The Voice of Americanism*.

But the biggest difference had to do with the station's culture, organization, and setting. KDNA operated on the edge of chaos, allowing both more creativity and more misery than public radio provides today.

Its studios were in the St. Louis ghetto, at the end of the old Gaslight Square—what one DJ called a "really terrible but sort of romantic" part of town.[5] The romance wore off pretty quickly. The station was surrounded by abandoned buildings, one of which housed some squatters. "The streets," Milam wrote after a visit, "are filled with pimps and whores and angry Blacks and drunks and kids in rags playing and forty-five-year-old bohemians and junkies: right outside the window you can see them laughing and talking and running and falling down."[6] During the station's brief life, three buildings within two blocks of it were burned down. Some of the neighbors refused to believe that they lived near a radio station and asked if the DJs weren't really running a whorehouse. People would try to break into the station, prompting the staff to board up the first-floor windows. Stuff was stolen from programmers' cars. One woman was raped.

Inside the station, things were a bit less threatening. The station proper was on the first floor; with time, it started spilling into the basement and onto the second floor as well. The rest of the second floor, and all of the third, were residential. Staffers received room, board, and about $80 a month; they bought food together, and cooked for one another in a communal kitchen. When the group got a little too big for the building, the station rented a somewhat dilapidated house nearby where the extra workers could live. In both buildings, the DJs suffered and enjoyed all the tensions and affections you'd expect under the circumstances, from love affairs to fierce disputes. It was stressful, it was exciting, and it changed people's lives. To quote Thomas, it was "a little like combat, a little like college."

Final decision-making power lay with Jeremy: he owned the license, after all, so he bore ultimate responsibility for what went on there. (Lorenzo was an equal co-owner, but in practice that merely made him an investor and adviser. Living in faraway Los Gatos, he had little say in how the station was run from day to day.) Lansman rarely invoked his power, governing instead in a manner Thomas fondly describes as "surrealist" and "chaotic." When he did step in to issue an ironclad decree, it was usually in response to a specific crisis. For instance, when St. Louis detectives arrested eleven staffers on suspicion of drug violations, Jeremy banned narcotics from the station's property. The alternative, after all, was to risk losing KDNA altogether.

Lansman also enforced the station's eclectic parameters, recognizing that sometimes this required more than managerial laissez faire.

Otherwise, the station was governed collectively, with the housemates-cum-DJs making most of the decisions. (There was a board of directors, too, with members drawn from the city's cultural and political life. It was much more conservative than the staff, and it often was outraged by what went over the air. But it had little power to change things.)

The core staff was a varied bunch. There was Thomas, for instance, who'd grown up across the river from St. Louis. At age twenty-three, he'd hoped to start a national news service for alternative papers. His brother Bill told him he should talk to radio stations as well, starting with the one in his hometown. Before he knew it, he was devoting all his energies to KDNA, drawing on his newspaper experience to fashion its program guide.

There was Laura Hopper, a runaway teen who'd drifted into Gaslight Square and started dropping by KDNA to use its washer and dryer. One thing led to another, and soon she was pressed into service as an audio engineer, ambitiously attempting to edit all the "fuck"s out of an Eldridge Cleaver speech. Before long, she was part of the informal collective; for several years, she and Lansman would be wed.

There was Elizabeth Gips, Jeremy's mom, a middle-aged hippie who decided to stop by the station en route from Haight-Ashbury to The Farm, a Tennessee commune to which she didn't really want to return. Her son and his friends invited her to stay, and soon she was rooming with a young engineer, with a cornmeal line down the middle of the room to separate his space from hers. It took her a while to learn radio, but soon she was doing the same tasks as the rest of the collective—that is, a bit of everything.

KDNA trained many more people in the art and craft of radio, some of whom left to start new stations in other cities. Many listeners did the same. If KRAB's offshoots were dubbed the KRAB Nebula, these outlets might be called the DNA Spiral, a cousinly set of stations across the country—from Telluride to Pittsburgh to Grand Rapids, Minnesota—but especially in the Midwest.

Many of those offspring are still active. KDNA is not. As FM licenses became more valuable, Lansman and Milam realized that if they sold the station, they'd make an incredible profit—enough to pay off their debts with enough left over to start several more stations. Furthermore, life in Gaslight Square was becoming intolerable. "St. Louis at that time was one of the fastest-decaying cities in the United States," Lansman explains. "By the time we sold the station, we were concerned for our lives. Looking out the window was more exciting than watching TV. We certainly had as much violence as TV."[7]

So the owners started searching for a buyer, and the station became a lame duck. As Lansman withdrew from managing KDNA, some staffers, volunteers, and listeners started a group called the Double Helix Foundation, both to take over day-to-day management and to try to raise enough funds to buy the station's license. It was a tough pitch to make: few listeners were willing to buy something that they felt they already had. Lorenzo and Jeremy held off selling for a while, hoping the Double Helix group would be able to match their best offer. But the market price kept spiraling upward: they originally thought they'd be lucky to get $400,000, but when they finally sold the license in 1973, it was for $1.1 million.[8] So Double Helix turned to Plan B: find an open frequency on the noncommercial part of the band, then start anew there.

The city school board controlled a full-power channel that it was using only about half the time; Double Helix asked whether the board would let the former KDNA staffers take over the unused hours. The board refused, so the Helixers went to the FCC, arguing that since the school board hadn't used those hours in twenty-five years, it had in effect abandoned them, and the government should simply license them to Double Helix. The commission mulled this over, but ruled that it would not impose a shared-time arrangement unless both parties agreed to it.

Then they spotted another frequency, where a ten-watt high school station was broadcasting for just three hours a day, and only on school days. When the station's license came up for renewal, the Helixers filed a competing application, arguing that they could put the frequency to better use. The FCC sat on the application for years before finally holding a hearing—which Double Helix won. And so, in 1987, community radio returned to St. Louis, this time with the call letters KDHX. I've listened to the station, and it's a good one. It's a shame they had to resort to expropriation to get it.[9]

The commercial and noncommercial wings of the new radio finally met at Goddard College in Vermont, where Yurdin was doing some graduate work. Upon earning his master's, Yurdin persuaded the president to hire him to teach a mass media class, for room and board plus $50 a month. At his course's first session, Professor Yurdin announced that he didn't want his students just to *read* about the media. They'd get more, he figured, out of a hands-on project, and he listed several such activities that they might pursue. The class opted to sponsor an alternative media conference.

Larry exploited his connections, persuading both Fass and Donahue to endorse the gathering. "My concept—with radio as a prototype and then extending into other media—was to ignore distinctions of whether people were doing things for money or out of pure passion," he explains, "and just bring together people who were posing a threat to the normal way things had been done." Donahue couldn't make it, but many others from KSAN and kindred stations did. On the noncommercial side, there were Milam, Lansman, Fass, much of the top Pacifica brass, and a horde of people from the stations they ran or had founded. Outside the broadcasting world, participants of note included Paul Krassner, pop-guru Baba Rama Das (who was accused of being a CIA agent), *Mad* founder Harvey Kurtzman, radical journalist Andrew Kopkind, rock star Dr. John, nutty "Dylanologist" A. J. Weberman, representatives of the Newsreel film collective, and Gilbert Shelton, the cartoonist behind *The Fabulous Furry Freak Brothers*, who penned a special comic strip for the conference newsletter. In it, the Freak Brothers started a pirate radio station. ("It's a tiny radio transmitter! Cost $6.95! Just plug it into your cigarette lighter, and you have a mobile radio station!") Another participant claimed to be involved in a real-life mobile pirate station, dubbed KRAP, in Chicago; he led a workshop on "Guerrilla Radio." In all, about 1,700 people came to the gathering.

The convention caught the eye of ABC Radio, which was looking for a way to improve its FM stations' ratings. In 1968, it had aimed for the youth market with a widely derided format called "LOVE Radio," mixing a tight playlist of rock album cuts with recordings of "Brother John," whose preachments on behalf of LOVE were repeated ad nauseam throughout the day. The old format had been devised by Allen Shaw, a young man who had rebelled against Top Forty but evidently lacked the imagination to come up with something better.

In 1967, Shaw had mildly stretched the format of Chicago's WCFL-AM, the station started by the Chicago Federation of Labor forty years before, by convincing his boss to give a DJ of his choosing one hour a week to play album cuts instead of the usual 45 rpm singles. When he heard what had been happening at KMPX and WNEW, he decided that Chicago was ready for something more. For Shaw, the "single most important and long-lasting aspect of what was happening" was "the music, album rock, played in stereo high fidelity on FM." He wasn't very interested, though, in bending genre distinctions or stretching the conventions of format radio. Indeed, he "had difficulty with the undisciplined, rambling, and often boring product of the so-called freeform, underground stations that had begun to spring up around the country."[10]

A lot of those freeform DJs could indeed be boring, playing the same old acid-rock chestnuts and droning endlessly about matters that could seem important, or even coherent, only to someone smoking the same weed. Any format that's open to experimentation is also open to failure, and some people just aren't good DJs. There are several sensible ways to address those problems. Shaw's approach—to toss out experimentation altogether and adopt a contrived, prefabricated format—is not one of them.

Nonetheless, when Shaw shopped his idea around the country, WABC-FM in New York City took the bait. Soon Brother John's loving commentary could be heard not just in New York but on ABC affiliates in six other cities as well, each of which transmitted tapes of the mother station's programs. By 1970, it was clear that LOVE wasn't getting the audiences that the freer-formatted stations were getting, and the network decided to make a change. One of its staffers, David Herman, had just gone to the Goddard conference; he suggested they hire Larry Yurdin as their production director. Shaw agreed, perhaps unaware of what Yurdin-style radio would entail. And Larry jumped at the chance, if only to see how much he could get away with in such a buttoned-down environment. "We knew it wasn't going to last," he says, "so we went as far as we could for as long as we could."[11]

To mark its new identity, the station dropped its establishment-reeking call letters, redubbing itself WPLJ after an old R&B song recently covered by Frank Zappa, "White Port and Lemon Juice." Yurdin decked his room at ABC headquarters with East Indian blankets, to the point where it seemed more like a tent than an office. He abolished the playlist, hired DJs from freeform and community stations around the country, and arranged some cooperative ventures with WBAI (Pacifica working with ABC!). The ratings were respectable, though the disc jockeys suffered from two terrible handicaps.

First of all, there were those ABC newscasts. At other stations, the news was getting progressively more, well, progressive, in both style and content. In Boston, WBCN billed Danny Schechter not as a news-caster but as a "news dissecter." ("I believed in explaining news, not just reciting it," he later wrote. "That meant that sometimes my newscasting would resemble storytelling, with a beginning, middle, and end.")[12] In California, Scoop Nisker came to radio from a theatrical background—he had passed up a job at the famous San Francisco Mime Troupe to take over KSAN's news department—and he imbued his journalism with showmanship as well as radicalism. In a typical program, he later re-called, he might mix street interviews with pieces of political speeches, "throw in lines from a few cartoon characters and some sound effects, and put it all together over a rock song or Indian raga." He kept his ukulele in the newsroom, too, for those moments when the headlines just demanded some Hawaiian strings. Nisker's newscasts were billed as "the only news you can dance to."

"I often reedited politicians' speeches to make them say ludicrous things," he adds. "Sometimes, of course, the speeches needed no edit-ing." Once he made a tape loop of Nixon intoning, "No power on Earth is stronger than the United States today, and none will ever be stronger than the United States in the future," punctuated by the sound of thun-der.[13] On WPLJ, by contrast, underground music sat side-by-side with the straightest, dullest newscasts imaginable—produced, of course, by ABC News. The results made the DJs cringe.

But there was an even bigger problem. The engineers' union had a contract with the network that allowed them—and only them—to cue up the records. And most of the ABC engineers hated rock music. So they miscued songs, left dead air between records, and otherwise sabo-taged the shows, sometimes cluelessly and sometimes out of malice.

Yurdin soon grew bored and took off for another gig. WPLJ per-sisted but grew increasingly formatted: freeform and ABC proved a less than stable combination. Unfortunately, the same dynamic would soon repeat itself in other commercial stations around the country.

But for a moment, FM was vibrant, with lots of local variety. In Detroit, for example, freeform had a harder edge: a factory-belt sound with more metal than was kosher on the coasts, though it had room for quiet, folky records as well. WABX "was a pure Midwest product," one DJ re-calls, "created by the natives."[14] It was radical commercial radio in the Donahue tradition: onetime Top 40 jocks who'd been swept up in the Michigan counterculture.

Other well-regarded stations emerged in Cincinnati, in Baltimore, even in Lake Tahoe, where KSML (the call letters stood for "Secret Mountain Laboratory") attracted a loyal fan base with its wild, creative programming—and alienated a lot of people with its owner's wild, destructive behavior. Most of these outlets suffered some turbulence. (A Denver station was saddled for a while with two rival staffs.) Some prospered; some didn't.

Naturally, all this influenced noncommercial community radio. On the plus side, it loosened up a lot of stations, making them more willing to be playful and popular. There's a thin line, though, between popularity and pandering, and occasionally a manager would have to remind his volunteers of the difference. Jeremy Lansman once locked up all of KDNA's rock records, telling his DJs that they'd have to explore the rest of the library for a week. In the late '70s, at a Dallas station called KCHU, Milam felt compelled to write a memo on the topic and hang it directly in front of the studio console. "KCHU is licensed as a noncommercial radio station," it announced. "This means that we are not here just to be a juke-box, or to feed the egos of people who want to go on the air and play. . . . We are here to enlighten, instruct, delight—and, in general, fill the gap left by other radio stations in the area."[15]

In L.A., the staff of KPPC had drifted back to work after its sympathy strike with KMPX fizzled. They no longer worked for Leon Crosby, though—in 1969, their erstwhile owner's finances diminished to the point where he had to sell both of his stations to survive, passing them along to something called the National Science Network. Among KPPC's most impressive personalities were the members of the Credibility Gap, a comedy troupe that had first read its satiric newscasts over another Pasadena station, KRLA, before moving to its new soapbox in 1970. The Credibility Gap's most famous graduates are Michael McKean and Harry Shearer, who went on to cowrite and costar in *This Is Spinal Tap*, among other films and TV series. Shearer has maintained his interest in the audio arts, hosting *Le Show* on Santa Monica's public station KCRW and providing more than a dozen voices for *The Simpsons*.

And KPPC had a competitor. Metromedia had entered the L.A. rock market with KMET, a freeform station that soon hired Yurdin as its news director, telling him to do "something between the Credibility Gap and conventional news." Larry adopted a collage style, broadcasting as "the Kapusta Kid" (a name he'd borrowed from an Ernie Kovacs character). He was joined by Chandler Laughlin, who'd held several on- and off-air radio jobs since his days selling ads for KMPX and was now calling himself Travus T. Hipp. Laughlin-Hipp espoused a sort of psychedelic populism; in the words of Susan Krieger, who interviewed him for her book *Hip Capitalism,* "He was against big government, against big business, an individualist," and "more conservative, he felt, than his father."[16] He also had a healthy sense of humor, and he worked well with Larry.[17]

Yurdin continued to jump from job to job: he didn't like to stay in one place for too long, and he liked starting new projects more than maintaining old ones. Out of the blue, in 1972, he got a call from his old friend Willis Duff. Duff had worked in stations everywhere from Boston to Los Angeles; now he was back in his native Texas, and he had a proposition for Yurdin. He had gotten to complaining about the state of Austin radio with Eddie Wilson and Mike Tolleson, owners of a local club called the Armadillo World Headquarters. The trio ended up walking into the local FM rock station—KRMH, which had been on the air for about a year—and telling them they'd get a lot more listeners if they'd open up their format, play more of the new music that was coming out of the city, and hire someone like, say, Larry Yurdin as program director. The station agreed, and now Duff was offering Yurdin a job.

To most California hippies, Texas was Klan country, a place where they shot liberal presidents and strung up uppity blacks. "At that point," Yurdin recalls, "nobody on the two coasts would even go into Texas." But he did, and he discovered something amazing there: "the Texas version, in 1972, of what happened in San Francisco in '67. In a good ol' boy, Wild West context, it was the Summer of Love. With guns." Thus began one of the weirdest, most fruitful chapters in the history of alternative radio, a momentary marriage between the spirits of Lewis Hill and Willie Nelson.

Austin in the early '70s was one of the country's most creative cities. Its alternative culture had always been rooted in the American grain: the local New Left was a stronghold of the "prairie power" wing of Students for a Democratic Society, a faction more interested in anarchism and populism than in Marxist-Leninist imports from the Old World. Now its hippies were starting to romanticize their traditional enemy, the redneck, and were mixing country music with their diet of rock, folk, and blues. Around the same time, Willie Nelson, Jerry Jeff Walker, and other country "outlaws" were opening their ears to rock music. The result was a new counterculture figure, the *cosmic cowboy,* and a new playlist of local favorites: Kinky Friedman, Michael Murphy, Waylon Jennings, Ray Wylie Hubbard, and more, all of them either based in Austin or frequent visitors to the city.

Yet none of this was visible on the local airwaves. KRMH was trying desperately to be hip, a surefire formula for phoniness and failure. Its programming, one reporter wrote,

> was limited to Dylan oldies and *Billboard*-approved rock, and at first, the advertising spots were enough to send even the most avid listener into the great outdoors. They were the standard pleas to purchase this product or that service, only they were couched in quasi-hip lingo, which made them more obnoxious.[18]

It was the sort of place that thought it was a clever play on words to pronounce KRMH as "karma," and the managers never understood Yurdin when he told them it would be much funnier and cooler to call themselves "the mighty krum-ha!" Yurdin's tenure there didn't last very long.

But while he was there, he recruited a staff capable of combining the spirit of freeform radio, circa 1968, with the shit-kicking stoner spirit of early-'70s Austin. Yurdin announced his presence with a day-long Texas Special, described by the journalist Jan Reid as an "assembly of rambling interviews interspersed with music that tried to acquaint the audience with Texas' surprisingly rich musical tradition."[19] The station's owner found this unsettling, and a mass firing followed.

Across town, though, a mainstream country station called KOKE was reaching out to the longhaired rednecks. Its AM operation had done all right with the standard Nashville sound, but its FM outlet was floundering. Then, around the same time Yurdin and his staff got fired, a local DJ named Rusty Bell approached KOKE with an idea for a format that ended up with the unlikely moniker "progressive country."

It was one of those formulas that seems obvious—once someone else has thought it up. "If anything remotely country could be discerned in a recording, it qualified," explains Reid. "George Harrison was sometimes accompanied by a bottleneck guitar, which sounded almost like a steel, and even Paul Simon's 'Baker Duncan' song about a youth driving down the upper New England coast toward a first piece of ass was fair game."[20] It took a while for the style to congeal—for the first few months, it felt like an old-fashioned country station that merely played an above-average number of Willie Nelson records—but as more DJs joined, including several refugees from Yurdin's brief stay at KRMH, the station improved. Soon it was a hit.

And Yurdin got to stick around Texas a bit longer. In 1970, Larry Lee had put a Pacifica station on the air in Houston. It needed a new general manager, and Yurdin needed a job. With Fass's endorsement, he soon found himself in charge of KPFT, the youngest and grungiest station in the Pacifica network.

At that point, KPFT was best known for having been bombed by Klansmen three months after it went on the air, an event that probably did the station more good than ill: no one was hurt, it brought in tons of free publicity, and the station was suddenly awash in donations from liberals and radicals of means. By the time Yurdin got there, that brief burst of notoriety had long passed. "KPFT, at that point, wasn't like the other" Pacifica stations, he explains. "It was people wandering off the streets and going on the air. There was no record library. During the day they would play ancient tapes from the Pacifica archives. It was just amateur hour." The schedule was divided into narrow blocks, few of which tried to relate themselves to life as Houstonians lived it. The operation subsisted mostly on money from the De Menils, a wealthy family that seemed more interested in funding a bad copy of KPFA than in backing anything in the Texas grain. (Ironically, Lee had originally planned for KPFT to be an independent station, not a Pacifica outpost.)

Yurdin called a station meeting. "I'm not going to make any changes right away," he told them. "We have a period of time to see what's worth saving. It is quite possible that everyone in this room will stay on the air. It is equally possible that no one in this room will stay on the air. It depends entirely on you. If you're able to rise to the occasion and do exciting, interesting programming that builds an audience and gives this radio station a reason for existence, everybody will be here. I'm not here with a hatchet. On the other hand, I am determined to have one of the most exciting and amazing radio stations in the country, and if you guys aren't able to do it, there are people who can."

Jerry Chamkis was an engineer at the station when Yurdin arrived. "It was the sort of thing that now would start a revolution," he recalls. "He basically became the god; he became the king. He made it real clear that, all right, there were going to be some changes made, and I'm the boss. And not everybody's going to come out the other end." How did the staff react? "The ones who got their shows cut were kind of bummed, but, I don't know, people were just more understanding in those days."[21] The biggest flare-up came when Larry canned some Latino DJs for taking payola. They organized some protests, claiming they were victims of racism. But they obviously weren't, and the charge soon fizzled. And in the meantime, the station was taking off.

Yurdin dropped about half the shows and brought in friends from other alternative stations to fill the gaps. He didn't drive out all the amateurish DJs, but he made sure the ones who stayed gave the station *character*. (Thus, he kept Liselotte Babin, the heavily accented matron whose *Musical Trot with Liselotte,* a weekly dose of German music, was authentically, artlessly weird in a way no one could ever emulate self-consciously.)[22] He got one country outlaw, Michael Murphy, to serve on the station board, and he established good relationships with Willie Nelson and Jerry Jeff Walker. (He asked them to sit on the board too, but Willie and Jerry Jeff didn't care for meetings.)

Once the new schedule was finalized, Yurdin took everything off the air. For a week, KPFT played nothing but music—all kinds of music, without any interruptions or announcers except an hourly station identification. In the second week, it did the same thing, only this time, at the top of the hour, listeners were told to tune in next week for "the new KPFT." It was an unorthodox attempt to stir up rumors, get people worried, and start a buzz. When listeners tuned in on the appointed date, they were greeted by twenty-four hours of live music.

"We tried to take the Pacifica First Amendment spirit and give it a real Texas flavor," Yurdin recalls. "It was the most fun I ever had in radio."

There was lots of country, lots of blues, lots of rock, and not a little of almost everything else, from Liselotte's foxtrots to the folksongs of Peru. Willie Nelson came by one morning and played just about every song he'd ever recorded, all day, from six in the morning until midnight. Then he went out back and hosted a free concert starring all of his musical heroes that he could gather. KPFT broadcast it live.

The staffers were a varied lot. Lawrence Jones was a wounded vet, a black man who'd lost both his legs and parts of his hands in Vietnam, who was passionate about music, especially contemporary soul and R&B. The station wanted to play more of those genres, and Jones obviously knew them well. There was a problem, though. In the words of Nicole Mones, a young woman Yurdin had hired away from KRMH,

"Lawrence had a speech impediment so thick it was difficult to under-stand him. He talked like he had a mouthful of rocks."

So Yurdin said, "Okay. You have the job. Two A.M. to six A.M., five nights a week. But for the first six months, you don't speak. Only recorded IDs and spots. You start talking slowly, when you're ready."

Lawrence left, excited to be a DJ. Nicole turned to Larry. "Are you sure?" she asked.

"Are you kidding?" Larry replied. "He's gonna be great!"[23]

Sure enough, Jones's speech cleared up, and he drew in a devoted listenership, especially in the black community. After he left Pacifica, he became a commercial DJ.

KPFT's most memorable staffer was probably Huey Purvis Meaux, a legend in Gulf Coast music. An energetic Cajun reared on the Louisiana prairie, Meaux's unlikely musical career had begun in the 1950s in Winnie, Texas, where he had owned a barbershop. Once a week, he'd do a remote broadcast from his shop, via KPAC in nearby Port Arthur. "It was a wild affair," according to one reporter, "that fea-tured live music and Meaux's infectious, nonstop, mush-mouthed ban-ter."[24] Before long, Meaux had made the back of his shop into a make-shift recording studio. After setting his first few hits to vinyl, he moved to some less modest digs in Houston and launched a small web of in-dependent labels, discovering and recording such legends as Freddie Fender and Doug Sahm. His acts played blues, country, rock 'n' roll, Tex-Mex, Cajun, southern soul, swamp pop, Tejano, R&B, and just about every conceivable combination of the above. In Meaux's studio, the cultures of the Gulf Coast met, mingled, and made stunning music.

He was a terrible man: not just tyrannical and sleazy, as so many producers are, but a molester who assaulted his stepdaughters and pro-duced child pornography. None of this came to light until 1996, when it earned Meaux a prison term. When Yurdin asked Meaux to do a show on KPFT, the only hint of Huey's ugliest side was the fourteen months he'd served in a Texarkana pen, fallout from an encounter at a Nashville music convention with a sixteen-year-old prostitute. No one dreamed that Meaux's tastes might run to still younger girls or that he'd ever force someone into sex.

And so it merely seemed colorful when Meaux told Yurdin and Mones why he'd entered the music business. They had come to Meaux's Sugar Hill Recording Studios to ask him if he'd join their sta-tion. Meaux didn't just agree; he elaborated.

"Some people get into show business for the money," he announced, his voice thick with Cajun inflections. "I don't care about money. Some people get into show business for the fame. I don't care about fame. There's only one reason why I'm in show business." A sly pause. "*Black pussy.*"

But his show—ah, his show. By all accounts, *The Crazy Cajun Show* was brilliant radio. It was filled with rootsy music, with a constant stream of friends dropping by to tell jokes and drink bourbon. Meaux, says Yurdin, "was what Wolfman Jack tried to be."[25] He played great, obscure records and told strange, funny stories about them; he read letters from his buddies in prison; he screamed over the records when he felt like it and was that rare species of DJ who could make that work. "Give it to me good, Houston," he'd yell. "Unh, you sure betta b'lieve it. Come close to the radio and give your papa some sugar, sweet cher ami."[26] It was wild, earthy radio. According to Chamkis, "By the end of the show, man, that transmitter was *smokin'*. If you were tuning across the dial, it didn't matter what your tastes were"—you listened. As Larry took KPFT apart and reassembled it, he used Meaux as his road marker. "I'm going to take this station away from the De Menils," he'd say, "and give it to the Huey P. Meauxs."

Interspersed with this was far more free speech than most Texans were used to. Yurdin's approach—and, by his account, it "horrified" some members of the Pacifica board—was to figure that if someone was willing to sit through ten minutes of ads each hour on a commercial station, the same listener would be willing to put up with ten minutes of controversial ideas instead. "If you really want to raise the consciousness of a large variety of people," he explains, "you play music they can relate to. You forget about these block programs. You create an *environment,* and you stick in produced public affairs and things that will raise people's indignation and radicalize them, and you use a lot of humor and creativity and production and wit to do it—you don't preach in this dry, doctrinaire way. I was out to compete with commercial stations in the market, not for dollars but for audience, because if I could take their audience, we could open their heads and really have an enormous effect." What separates that from mere pandering is the commitment to do the programming really *well*—not to "aim" for a "youth" "demographic" but to hire people who are excited about great music and know how to communicate that excitement. And to do public affairs shows with the same spirit.

So while KPFT set aside some time for talk shows, it preferred to take a little piece of talk—maybe produced locally, maybe culled from a longer show in the Pacifica archives—and stick it in the same hour as the latest record by Waylon Jennings (or the oldest one by Howlin' Wolf). There were long stretches of satire as well, perhaps none so amusing as the seven-day stretch dubbed Cult Week, in which representatives of different cults, broadly defined to include everyone from Eastern and Christian sects to Leninist fringe parties and even Weight Watchers, were invited to bring along their favorite records and each sit in with a DJ for a four-hour shift. (The Weight Watchers walked out when they saw what they'd been roped into.) With that precedent, KPFT later offered week-long gavel-to-gavel (or "bliss-to-bliss") coverage of a convention at the Astrodome, featuring the followers of the boy-guru Maharaj Ji. The week included floor reports from Paul Krassner and Jerry Rubin, a debate between Krassner and Rennie Davis (a Chicago Seven defendant who had adopted the Maharaj faith), and special guest appearances by everyone from Wavy Gravy to Louden Wainwright III. At first the conventioneers didn't realize they were being mocked. They knew they were being covered by a local radio station with ties to the counterculture, they were delighted to have the exposure, and after four days they decided to pipe the station's signal everywhere in the building, so all the boy-god's followers could enjoy their moment of local fame. At that point, relations between the station and the Maharaj fans turned suddenly sour.

The ratings didn't track noncommercial stations back then, so if you listened to an outlet like KPFT, you didn't show up on the charts. Soon, the radio ratings displayed a strange trend: in the Houston market, eighteen-to-thirty-four-year-olds were . . . disappearing. The station's staff wasn't surprised: they already knew they were a hit. "After the first couple of months," Mones recalls, "there was a definite sense that people were listening—the phones were ringing all the time and there was an almost electric charge in the air—but who was listening? Who were they? We had no idea." Halloween was approaching, so someone suggested they throw a costume party for their listeners.

According to Mones,

when I walked in the party was already howling. And I remember having the breath knocked out of me at the sight when I opened the door. There was an enormous crunch of people, but that was not what was so shattering. It was the costumes. They were brilliant, people had masks, people had headdresses. There were masterful cross-dressers, incredible tricks with makeup. That all these people were here—that they existed in Houston, people this offbeat and this creative—and that they had all come together from their different corners for a night—this really gave us our audience. We got to see them for one night. (Masked—which was perfect. It was radio.)

The party, she concludes, "was like a collaborative improv, the masked meeting with the audience. They really rolled with it. It was always a pleasure to play to them after that."[27]

Before long, Yurdin was chafing to move on. Not everyone was sorry to see him go. Some of Pacifica's national leaders didn't care for the Houston experiment—Yurdin claims KPFK chief Ruth Hirschman even sent spies to make sure his operation was "Pacifica enough."[28] (Hirschman says she has no recollection of this.) Within the station, too, some of Yurdin's habits sometimes rubbed people the wrong way. Chamkis had a lot of respect for Larry, whom he credited with kick-starting a station that had seriously stalled, bringing in a lot more listeners and donations. "But then he started being Larry Yurdin. I mean, there is a kind of problem with leaving a big stack of uncleaned records all over the floor and candy wrappers and spilled Coke. . . . Everybody hated being the next air shift." Yurdin didn't have a dark side, says Chamkis. "But he had a wild side."

Laura Hopper would later work with Yurdin at a Gilroy, California, station called KFAT. When I spoke with her, she called Larry "a very disturbing genius."[29] And then she laughed a knowing sort of laugh, the kind that suggests she wasn't disturbed by Yurdin so much as respectfully bewildered.

I should say a thing or two about KFAT, though it's a hard station to describe. It was a commercial operation, but it was owned—for a while—by Lorenzo Milam and Jeremy Lansman. It was a hippie station in the KMPX mold, but its focus wasn't rock; it was country. It was, in many ways, the logical successor to what Yurdin and company did at KPFT, but in a completely different social and economic context. If the Summer of Love had taken place in a garlic-growing country town, if Berkeley's longhaired rebels had preferred George Jones to the Jefferson Airplane, if Jerry Garcia had joined Bill Monroe's bluegrass band—well, then it would have been a very different world, and KFAT would have been a commercial triumph. Instead, it was a financial failure, a strange tributary of '70s radio that didn't lead anywhere in particular but sure took an interesting route.

To understand KFAT, you might start with the night some visitors stopped by while a DJ called Uncle Sherman was doing his show. He heard a banging at the door downstairs, and after he cued up a record he trotted out to see who it was. Apparently, the last jock had left the door unlocked, because some big cowboy types were already climbing the stairs, carrying a keg of beer. "So they came in," Sherman remembers, "and they introduced themselves, and they said, 'We thought we'd bring you a beer. You sounded thirsty on the radio.'"[30] Then they asked if Sherman would play some Willie Nelson.

So Sherman dug out a Willie album, and the group set to talking. About the second beer in, one of the cowboys said, "Well, listen, you know, we got a little problem with some of the music you guys play here."

"What's that?" asked Sherman.

"Well," said the cowboy, "you guys play that nigger music. And especially that guy John Lee Hooker."

Hooker, one of the all-time great bluesmen, lived nearby. He was a friend of the station, and Sherman didn't just like his music; he liked him personally. "What do you *mean*?" he shouted. "John Lee's a friend of mine. I'll tell you what, you guys, I don't want to hear that shit, you guys just take your beer and get the hell on out of here."

So the cowboys got up and left, but before they did, each one gave the DJ a card from his wallet. All of them were members of the local Klan.

KFAT was a country music station, but it wasn't like any other commercial country operation. It was a *freeform* country station run by hippies and hip rednecks. The Klansmen obviously didn't know what to make of it: it played music they loved and couldn't hear anywhere else, but then it miscegenated it with a lot of other stuff—stuff that sounded great together if you loved good music but not if your first loyalty was to the White Race. Then there were those weird promos it ran, like the station identification announcements that featured "famous people sneezing." The Kluxers probably didn't care for the tape of Angela Davis's achoo.

On top of that, there were all those hippies on the staff, starting with

Uncle Sherman himself—who, granted, wasn't exactly an ordinary hippie. Another jockey once described him as a "young coot."

Sherman had been involved with radio since his childhood in Fayetteville, Arkansas. His mother was a preacher, his dad sang in a gospel quartet, and the two of them did a Sunday afternoon show on a little station called KHOG. They brought their boy to the studio with them each week, and since Sherman, in his words, "wasn't interested in that shit hardly at all," he spent that time hanging out with the engineer, learning how to operate the station's equipment. "I did it for a couple years as a kid," he recalls, "and then I discovered girls and beer." As a grown-up, he tried his hand at acting, selling shoes, and the navy, but he never lost his taste for broadcasting; he did a little Armed Forces Radio while he was in the service, and in the early 1970s he worked at several stations along the West Coast.

"I had a couple of real bad radio experiences," he reports, "and I had moved back to San Jose and was going to go back to selling shoes, and then I heard about KFAT." Suddenly he was working for a weird station in Gilroy, an isolated town in northern California where the biggest industry was growing garlic.

It was September 1975; KFAT had been born just a month before. The station itself was older than that—Lorenzo and Jeremy had simply bought it and changed the call letters. Lansman claims he didn't have any special plans for it: "I started out thinking we'd do nothing creative whatsoever, and try to make a buck. . . . What could be further from what we had done before than a country music station?"[31]

Then Yurdin intervened. He had met Lansman and Milam at his Goddard conference, and they later heard about the work he'd done in Houston. They asked him whether he had any idea how to program a country music station, and he told them he'd think about it. Not long afterward, he found himself sitting on some stairs with Jeremy at the National Alternative Radio Konference in Madison, Wisconsin, telling him what he'd come up with.

"You know what?" he said. "We could create a radio station that, masquerading as a country station, is like a twenty-four-hour-a-day lampoon of country music. But in the process, it's playing folk music, it's playing music with a living-in-the-country feel, whether it's the Grateful Dead or George Jones. And mixed in is inventive production, and mixed in is satire and engaging, interesting characters who have funny names." He loved the call letters Lorenzo had come up with, but he figured they could take the idea further. "Not only do we want to call it KFAT—we want to call it *The Fat One*. We want to give it that image, to have a big fat cowboy logo." KFAT, Yurdin suggested, should feel like something vaguely forbidden—like an old Mexican border blaster or a distant black station in the 1950s South. It should be unusual, eclectic, and *exciting*.

So it was. KFAT played classic honky-tonk, bluegrass, and western swing; it played folk music with a country edge (Woody Guthrie usually fit the bill, Pete Seeger usually didn't); it played countryish songs by rock bands—the Kinks, the Dead, the Stones. It played blues, Hawaiian music, and just about anything with a steel or slide guitar. It played Cajun music, and it played rockabilly. It played the new brand of country coming out of Austin, and it played the more soulful side of California country-rock. It played a lot of novelty songs: everything from Utah Phillips's "Moose Turd Pie" to Toots and the Maytalls' reggae rendition of "Take Me Home, Country Roads" to an ancient and obscene-sounding western swing tune called "Here, Pussy, Pussy." And it hired Travus T. Hipp as a commentator.

It may have been the only commercial station, a listener later declared, where you could hear Slim Pickens introduce a Dead Kennedys record. There was a joke a lot of the DJs liked: "It's *all* country music. It just depends on what country you come from."

Yurdin didn't stay long—he didn't care for how the station was being run, and he had a new project in the offing, a syndicated interview series called *The Daily Planet*.[32] The station kept going, with Jeremy Lansman and Laura Hopper in charge. (Lorenzo still owned his share of it, but he was busy setting up a station in Dallas.) Over the next several years, it would go through several owners, each with a slightly different style; some played more ads than others, and some were better tuned to the FAT sensibility. Yurdin returned to the station in 1981, and was so intent on enforcing his vision of the KFAT sound that he instituted a Top Forty–style pie chart and card file—which, granted, many jocks ignored with no repercussions. Different DJs vied to play different kinds of music: Bill Goldsmith, for instance, thought the station relied too much on hardcore country. It could attract more listeners, he felt, if it mixed in more southern rock, and maybe a little punk: the Clash, say, in their rockabilly moments, or perhaps some country-flavored tracks by Elvis Costello.

Goldsmith, a veteran of several freeform stations, had first tried out for a slot on KFAT in 1975; he still remembers the chagrin he felt when Yurdin told him his audition tape was "too normal." (Too *normal*! For a *country* station!) A Gilroy native—his dad owned a local flower seed company—Goldsmith came back to KFAT in 1980, after an unhappy stint at an automated Top Forty station in Salinas. The day John Lennon was shot, he decided he wanted to do something special in the Beatle's honor, but the Salinas station didn't have a music library. So he headed over to KFAT, which let him spend most of the night taping songs from its Lennon and Beatles collections, then returned to Salinas, where he did "what, I gather from the feedback I got, was a pretty cool little tribute to John Lennon."[33] The station manager didn't see it that way, and he burst into the studio to complain. "What was that all about?" he yelled. "What are you doing? You're breaking format! You weren't playing the hits! You were playing all this John Lennon stuff!"

The choice seemed pretty clear. Besides, he was in mortal fear that the station's automation system would play Lennon's "Just Like Starting Over" back to back with another song in rotation: Queen's "Another One Bites the Dust." So Goldsmith moved to KFAT—right after Lorenzo and Jeremy sold it. Fortunately, the new owner was a fan of the station, a longtime listener who'd bought it in hopes of preserving it. He figured that might mean toning it down a bit—but then, Goldsmith came from a rock background, and he didn't mind moving closer to the FM mainstream.

The station never did become a financial success, and small wonder: even at its most money-grubbing moments, it didn't have a very commercial attitude. It didn't just produce a lot of the ads it ran; it made *fake* ads and mixed them with the real ones, to many a sponsor's chagrin. The comedian behind the commercials was a Gilroy native named Frisco, a heavy-drinking fellow who'd show up around midnight with a six-pack of beer, a quart of whiskey, and some cocaine. "And he'd sit back there, man," says Sherman; "he'd sit in the chair, turn the microphone on, and just get shit-faced, but everything he turned out was beautiful. That was the only way he could work. I'd sit there on the air and watch him through the glass, and he'd be weaving in that chair. But he would turn out some of the funniest stuff. And he could do straight commercials for people too." (Frisco's drug habit grew steadily worse, and, after an awful period of paranoid delusions, he sobered up and got a straight job in Dallas.)

Not content to make fake ads, the station also made some fake beer.

One of its promotional gimmicks was a sticker you could attach to a beer can, identifying the brew as "Gilroy Brand FAT Beer," the beer "for a fatter bladder." Originally, the station was actually going to produce its own brew, but when it found out how much that would cost, it just gave away the labels instead. Under Yurdin's stewardship, the station did yet more outrageous stunts: it was OK, Yurdin figured, to sponsor contests, as long as they parodied every ridiculous radio contest in history. The point was to be creative, funny, and always, always tongue-in-cheek. (Larry may have had a stricter approach to the music than Jeremy and Laura did, but when it came to managing people, he was much looser. Sherman compares Laura, fondly, to Victoria Barkley, Barbara Stanwyck's character in *The Big Valley*: "She was with all these rowdy young 'uns that were grown, and she sorta rode herd on them." And Yurdin? "Oh, Larry's crazy. He was just fun." He was a good teacher, but he wasn't exactly the type who kept people in line.)

The money kept getting tighter, and in 1983 the station finally went under. Yet even then, bits of it continued to float around. The most significant of those is KPIG, in Watsonville, California, launched by some FAT vets in the late 1980s. It suffered a lot in the early years, especially during its experiments with a bland pop-country format and with a Top Forty service beamed in via satellite. Laura Hopper, now split from Jeremy and named Laura Ellen, decided that if the station was going to go broke, the staff might as well have fun along the way. So they returned to the FAT sound, or a slightly more pop version of it: there was more rock and less hardcore country, and a somewhat more organized (though still DJ-driven) approach to choosing which records to play. Suddenly, the station was a hit: the audiences took off, lots of advertisers signed on, and it became—and remains—the region's top music station.[34]

Still, if stations like KRAB and KMPX are notable for the influence they had, KFAT is notable for the influence it should have had but didn't. It was born too late, and it came of age as commercial freeform was dying.

Commercial freeform did die, gradually, even if a few stations kept some of the old ideals afloat. It was a child of fortunate circumstances, of companies that didn't expect to make money from their FM outlets and weren't sure how to reach a young audience. Once FM started turning a profit, a new generation of consultants decided they could hold those younger demographics far more tightly than any hippie DJ could. They fancied themselves scientists, talked incessantly of "research," and brought back all those clocks and pie charts that Tom Donahue thought he'd escaped forever when he abandoned Top Forty.

The key player here was Lee Abrams, a young consultant from Chicago who hadn't even reached his teens when Top Forty was born. When he did reach his teens, in 1965, he was already managing fledgling rock bands and, foreshadowing his later career, distributing questionnaires after each show to find out which songs the audiences didn't like.

In this way, he discovered that a lot of listeners didn't care for everything they heard on FM radio. In 1971, he dreamed up a format that took this into account, and sold it to WQDR in Raleigh, North Carolina. The station would play the rock monsters of FM—Hendrix, the Stones, etc.—and maintain the new DJs' laid-back style. But it would shy from freeform's headier excursions, and would limit the jocks' right to choose which records they'd play.

Meanwhile, those stations that did have free or semi-free formats were looking for something "safe" to call themselves. *Freeform* and *underground* scared investors. *Progressive* sounded a bit less threatening, and it dominated the discourse for a while. Then came the ultimate neutral label: *AOR*, for Album-Oriented Radio. (Or, sometimes, Album-Oriented Rock.) Gradually, AOR stopped being a code word for freeform and started denoting the format that was replacing it.

This delighted Abrams. People like Donahue "opened the door" for AOR, he concedes,[35] but their approach was "self-serving, elitist, and ultimately destructive."[36] Freeform, he argues, was just waiting for a better approach to beat it in the marketplace.

A lot of the old freeform DJs *were* self-indulgent, of course, and there were a lot of listeners who *did* prefer a more packaged, hits-oriented approach. And heaven knows, a lot of the stations that tried to imitate KSAN didn't attract staffs that were remotely as talented as Donahue's. Bill Goldsmith of KFAT—no apologist for the Abrams approach—thinks that it was this, more than anything else, that did in commercial freeform. "The biggest thing that killed off that style of radio was the way that the stations were run internally," he suggests.

Most of the stations that I had contact with—which would have been the San Jose and San Francisco stations—were run by people who were much more interested in impressing their little clique of friends and coworkers than they were with actually entertaining anyone outside that circle. It was run by people who had some pretty heavy ego things going, and who were extremely impressed with themselves and consequently less concerned with entertainment. And people who did way, way, way too many drugs.

But this scarcely begins to explain why commercial freeform was, in effect, exterminated. Nor does it account for the near-abolition of DJ autonomy. KMET in Los Angeles, the station Donahue started for Metromedia, struggled through the early 1970s, holding a small freeform audience but never doing very well. Halfway through the decade, it decided to adopt a more restricted format, repositioning itself as the home of Real Rock Radio. But within those not-yet-clichéd boundaries, it trusted its staffers to program their own shows. "There is nothing inherently wrong with using call-out research, or focus groups, or statistical trends, or any of the rest of it," argues Jim Ladd, who hosted a show there for several years. "The key is what you *do* with that information. . . . We provided a staff of highly creative professionals with the information, and it was their job to *interpret* the data and transform it into a living breathing radio show."[37]

The consultant-driven stations, by contrast, often seemed to think that their research would interpret itself. With their self-consciously "scientific" approach, they forgot that their measurements weren't neutral. "All research does is give you answers to questions you ask," one of the smarter consultants once told *Mediaweek* magazine. "It's up to you to know that you're asking the right questions. . . . Far too often, research is used to be noncreative."[38] Small wonder that KMET outran its rivals, holding the number-one slot in L.A. for several years.

It seems like the best solution. Some hardcore freeform stations for adventurous music-lovers, some heavily formatted stations for those who crave familiarity, and a slew of semi-freeform outlets like KMET's: for the country audience, the jazz audience, the various immigrant audiences—a thousand mutations, each with a distinct sound but none tightly constrained by the artificial divisions of genre, format, marketing category. Niches needn't always be narrow.

That wasn't what we got. By the 1980s, AOR was one of the most restrictive, conservative, and boring formats ever, a style of radio dominated by rock's most formulaic bands. You hardly ever heard a new artist on an AOR station. You hardly ever heard anyone black, either. There were other formats, of course, but they tended to be terrible, too.

The last gasp of the old FM came in 1979. On the West Coast, KSAN finally abandoned freeform, moving to a pop-country format. And in the East, Infinity Broadcasting bought Boston's WBCN and fired nineteen staffers, prompting an intense three-week strike. Newsman Danny Schechter headed the union's negotiating team. "In the end," he remembers,

> I helped convince the new management that it was in their interest to settle on our terms since the station's uniqueness was its biggest asset. They did. We won the strike. I wrote separate victory statements for both the union and management. Impressed, the company hired our strike leaders as their managers. It was the most successful broadcast strike I've ever heard of.[39]

Yet in the next few years, the format still grew tighter, the news was scaled back, and the station's flavor faded away.

By then, commercial freeform was surviving only in a few out-of-the-way towns (Annapolis, Watsonville) and special programs (Vin Scelsa, co-commander of the FMU coup in '68, has hosted an open-format show called *Idiot's Delight* on a series of New York stations since 1985). Across the rest of the spectrum, the consultants ruled.

KMET finally fell, not because it was too radical, but because it was too conservative: new wave blindsided the station, its DJs' tastes failed to evolve with the times, and after it fell a few slots in the ratings—no longer the town's top broadcaster, but still maintaining a respectable share—management hired a consultant to boost it up again. "From Chuck Berry to Bruce Springsteen, the Jefferson Airplane to U2, anything that wasn't a national Top 40 hit was eliminated," Ladd writes.[40] Audiences fled. In 1987, the station switched to an automated format without any DJs at all.[41]

What killed freeform? A lot of things. There were the problems Goldsmith observed: the big egos, the big drug habits. Some DJs just burned out. Some died. (The biggest loss was Tom Donahue, who was killed by a heart attack in 1975.) Some station owners were afraid of freeform, and the FCC wasn't filled with good will either.

There was another problem: progressive radio had never really broken with the mass counterculture that had spawned it. The nation's small handful of freeform country stations (KFAT, KOKE) were still run, basically, by hippies. And though there was a brief revival of free black radio, of the community-oriented and DJ-driven style of the '40s and '50s, it never took hold the way the hip white stations did.[42]

But you don't have to be a hippie to be a good DJ. Indeed, it can be a disadvantage. Good radio requires an aesthetic sense, something not every child of the '60s possessed. (Thirty years after Woodstock, few will still make grand artistic claims for the seventeen excruciating minutes of "Inna Gadda-Da-Vida.") A real radio revolution would have spread beyond the bounds of Haight-Ashbury and its psychogeographical neighbors.

Why didn't it? Mostly because of the financial speculation that set in after the first wave of FM entrepreneurs proved that one could make money outside the AM band. As more investors entered the marketplace, the price of the stations was bid further and further up, an inflationary frenzy fueled in part by the artificial scarcity imposed by the FCC. Smaller players who were more willing to take risks were squeezed out of the market. The moneymen who stayed wanted a quick return for their investment. It wasn't enough to be a respectable fourth place in the ratings; you had to jump quickly to number one, increasing the value of the station's ad time and, thus, the investors' stock. And the quickest road to a sudden ratings boost was to switch to a format that was doing well for someone else.

In an environment like that, it's no wonder the consultants took command: they were the kings of the prefab format. And if you wanted to compete against them with a different approach, with a new station that cut against the conventional wisdom, you were out of luck. With the FCC keeping the supply of licenses tight, the cost of starting a station went through the roof.[43]

Freeform may have been disappearing from commercial radio, but it survived in two other places. One was noncommercial radio, especially those college stations that embraced the punk revolution. Even this brand of freeform wasn't pure: for much of the '80s, many student outlets weren't much more than a junior league for the commercial rock operations, a place where new artists could build an audience before moving on to the majors. But around 1991, when "alternative" rock became the mainstream, such stations began to sound less distinctive. If they wanted to seem adventurous, freeform became a more enticing prospect.

Even before then, several college stations devoted specialty shows to jazz, bluegrass, and the like. In the late '80s, stung by charges of racism, many added rap to their playlists. And some adopted completely free formats. The most famous of these was WFMU. The Upsala College outlet had gravitated toward AOR in the early '70s, but Lou d'Antonio still did his freeform *Hour of the Duck,* and soon other DJs were following his lead. In 1985, Ken Freedman took over the station and pushed it back into radio's avant garde.[44] It was WFMU that spearheaded the revival in "cocktail" music, emphasizing the weirdest out-of-print recordings; it was WFMU that revived interest in the French rock/jazz crooner Serge Gainsbourg and the otherworldy Peruvian chanteuse Yma Sumac. Upsala went bankrupt in 1995, but FMU's volunteers bought the station and kept it alive. In 1998, it moved from East Orange to Jersey City, and it supports itself today through listener donations, special events, and sales of unusual books and recordings. It runs no commercials and receives no support from the government. As one of the first stations to simulcast its programs over the Web, it is well-equipped to survive in the digital age; with its unique programs and talented hosts, it's drawn in new fans from around the country.

That's great if you live in northern New Jersey or have a decent Internet hookup. In most places, to find the real spirit of freeform, one must leave the boundaries of broadcasting altogether. Much has been written about the street DJs of the South Bronx who invented hip-hop in the '70s, mixing records while rappers recited rhymes. But it's rarely recognized that these jocks were reinventing the black radio of the '40s and '50s.[45] Like the original black DJs, they used their mixing boards as instruments and spouted sometimes silly couplets. But the new music was harsher, less melodic—and, after a minimalist, funk-driven start, its components were increasingly varied. By the '80s, dance DJs were sampling snippets of everything from heavy metal to TV theme songs, mixing genres that even Bob Fass wouldn't dare play side-by-side.

Far from alienating listeners, this excited them. The DJs' mixes circulated first on homemade tapes, then on independent records, and finally as major-label releases. They became hits, and, in some cities, street and club DJs became the kind of community leaders their forebears in black radio had been three decades before. In inner-city Miami in the early 1990s, the city police commissioned a survey to find out who young people looked up to the most. To their surprise, DJs led the list. (This led to a series of cooperative events called—I am not making this up—Jammin' with the Man.)

But while some of those hip-hop records made it onto the radio, few stations allowed their DJs to do the same sort of mixes live in the studio. If the consultants couldn't control it, it was out of bounds.

In Seattle, KRAB was undergoing near-permanent turbulence. In 1970, when the station's license was up for reapproval, the FCC objected to some putatively obscene material it had broadcast. Rather than issue a standard renewal, the commission extended KRAB's license by just one year. The government had taken offense at a number of programs, most notably a sexually graphic twenty-three-hour "autobiographical novel" written and recorded in 1967 by Paul Sawyer, a Unitarian minister-hippie recently fired from a congregation just north of Seattle. (Or, rather, it had objected to *part* of Sawyer's novel: Milam, aware of the program's possible legal repercussions, stopped the tape before it finished.) The station took the FCC to court, where the hearing examiner, Ernie Nash, ruled in the broadcasters' favor, declaring that "KRAB seeks and most often attains those standards of taste and decency in programming that we should like to see reflected more often in our broadcast media."[46] It was an impressive victory for free speech.

But KRAB had other problems. It found itself floundering for money after Milam left, a problem it eventually dealt with by finding another rich man to run it. The new manager, Robert Friede, was a wealthy scion of the Annenberg family; his life thus far had included stops at an exclusive Connecticut prep school, at Dartmouth, and at Sing Sing. On February 7, 1966, the New York police had found the corpse of nineteen-year-old Celeste Crenshaw in the trunk of a red Chevrolet Impala, with Friede at the wheel. Celeste—Friede's girlfriend—had been dead for thirteen days; Friede had injected a fatal combination of drugs into her bloodstream. He was convicted of manslaughter, possession, and—thanks to a subsequent trip to Illinois—violating probation. The first two sentences were suspended, but the last landed him in prison. When he got out, his family banished him to Seattle.

Like Milam, Friede had a vision for the station and an appreciation for interesting radio. Unlike Milam, he was always throwing temper tantrums, abusing and intimidating any staffers or volunteers who raised his ire. "Friede was, for all his brilliance as a programmer, an unmitigated asshole," comments Jef Jaisun, a KRAB DJ from 1973 to 1976. "And most people knew that. So they walked this very thin line between being intimidated by him and wanting to stick around and do radio."[47] Another DJ, Greg Whitcomb, was even blunter: "He didn't seem to have any social skills."[48] Relationships within the station frayed.

Friede was a complicated character. A short, intense man with nicotine moss on his teeth, he was a creative but cruel fellow who loved modern art, hated country music, and sometimes called DJs during their shows to heckle what they were playing. Most people at the station disliked him, but whenever the Jack Straw Foundation made noises about reducing the volunteers' power, he'd stand up for the staff.

KRAB still had a distinctive flavor—not exactly the sensibility Lorenzo had given it, but not an entirely different one either. The DJs were playing more rock, though even here they tended to prefer the outré; you were more likely to hear a Kinks rock opera than a Grand Funk Railroad hit. The few shows specifically devoted to rock 'n' roll took oddball approaches: Whitcomb's oldies show, for instance, deliberately avoided schticky '50s revivalists like Sha Na Na, preferring rare rockabilly, surf, and R&B records. The station prided itself on playing what the city's other outlets were ignoring, and if that meant rock, so be it. When Seattle's "progressive" station, KOL-FM, adopted a more restrictive format, the music it stopped playing started to show up more often on KRAB. When punk emerged, it turned up on a program called *Live Elsewhere*.[49]

The station broadcast city council meetings in the afternoons, and it did live remotes from concerts around the city. As before, there were talk shows in other languages, international music, ancient field recordings, commentaries from Birchers and Panthers, and the rest of the free-forum melange. Some of this was good, some was bad, and some was actually technically incompetent. The station continued to hold fundraisers, and sometimes it sponsored special events. The most fondly remembered of those took place in the interregnum between Milam's and Friede's tenures: two DJs in an airplane dropped a piano to the ground, while onlookers gawked.

Yet KRAB never really caught on with the larger community, and it almost always had to rely on outside sources of income: first Milam's money, then Friede's money, then the taxpayers' money. As the internal bickering increased—first under Friede, and then, even more so, under the Jack Straw board's bureaucratic reign—potential volunteers were turned off, further separating the station from the city. After Friede was finally fired in 1975, rumors of corruption and mismanagement began to make the rounds, especially as the station started taking federal grants.

Some volunteers argued for a more accountable system. Most just avoided the issue of governance altogether, coming in to do their show and ignoring the station's argumentative core as best they could. The amazing thing was that good material continued to slip onto the air, even if this was more a function of luck and politics than of any guiding vision.

One of the most intriguing '70s shows was *The Ham Radio Hours*, Seattle's answer to the Firesign Theatre. It was hosted by Danny Eskenazi (a.k.a Captain Kilocycle), Homer Spence (a.k.a. Homer Heterodyne), Phil Miller (a.k.a. Phil Harmonic), Leila Gorbman (a.k.a. Guda Cremora), and sundry guests, from the famous (Pat Paulsen dropped by once) to the obscure. Danny, Homer, and Phil knew one another from the amateur radio world—hence the show's name—and from a band they all played in, the Hedy Lamarr Harrington Review. (According to Miller, the Review mixed straightforward rock with "free jazz, or our impression of it. . . . We could clear an auditorium in five minutes.")[50]

Their program—an eclectic and frequently scatological assortment of music, comedy, and call-ins—probably cleared some rooms as well, but it also attracted a fascinated fan community. It was kicked off the air several times, usually for episodes that would make Howard Stern blush. In the most infamous incident, Phil got the show suspended for describing, in clinical detail, a sexual encounter he'd allegedly had with a dog.

There were several regular callers, some of whom could dish it out as well as the hosts could. A teenage Penelope Houston—later the lead singer of one of the best West Coast punk bands, the Avengers, and still later a notable singer-songwriter—started calling in claiming to be a twelve-year-old named Jennifer and describing what she insisted were her sexual fantasies. "I was pranking the station," she recalls, "because they had a sort of call-in lonely hearts thing for weirdos. I wanted to see if people would call an underage pervert. Seems they did."[51] She eventually dropped by the station in person, crammed into a Brownie uniform.

In short, the program was spontaneous, disgusting, sometimes hilarious, sometimes unlistenable, and out of anyone's control. That is, it was a lot like KRAB itself.

The station was an increasingly unpleasant place to work, and the Jack Straw Foundation was becoming a self-perpetuating bureaucracy. Between the internal disputes and the increasingly uneven quality of the programming—itself both a product and a cause of many disputes—KRAB wasn't attracting the money it needed. It didn't help that, in Jaisun's words, "There was this faction at the station that thought, 'Oh, we don't want to be too popular.' . . . It really seemed like a bizarre power play of some sort. To keep the station at the mercy of certain other people who had more power and more influence."

KRAB did own one very valuable property, though: its license. It was located, after all, in the commercial band, and the value of 107.7 FM had inflated considerably over the years. At some point in the early '80s, someone suggested that the foundation should sell the station and use the proceeds to buy another, smaller space in the noncommercial section of the dial. The plan hit its first snag when the Jack Straws discovered that Seattle's educational band was completely filled. Undeterred, they approached KNHC, a station run by Nathan Hale High School, and asked to share its frequency. When it refused, the Straws asked the FCC to *force* the Nathan Hale station to share, on the grounds that it had operated for less than the minimum hours required of stations per day.

That was in December 1983. Three months later, the foundation sold KRAB to Sunbelt Broadcasting. The Nathan Hale fight dragged on for several more years, with a federal court ruling for the high school in 1988.

By that point, the Jack Straw Foundation had become one of the most unpopular organizations in Seattle. Most of KRAB's volunteers had opposed the sale, and some had tried to block it in court, arguing that the then-ruling board had violated a slew of rules in the course of establishing its reign. After the sale went through, no one was entirely sure what happened to all the money the foundation made; to this day, many Seattleites believe someone pocketed a lot of it, though there is some disagreement as to just who that someone is. (The hypotheses I've heard range from the relatively benign notion that the foundation simply squandered its profits to an elaborate if vague conspiracy theory that seemed to involve virtually every lawyer in the city.) Even Lorenzo Milam, who came to Seattle to sign off on the sale in 1984, later regretted his involvement, feeling that he'd been misled about Jack Straw's plans and cheated out of money the foundation owed him.

The fight with Nathan Hale only further soiled Jack Straw's reputation, and not just because for once it found itself playing Goliath rather than David. KNHC had been around since the end of 1969, though for its first thirteen months it was a minuscule operation—just one hundred milliwatts—on the AM band. KRAB claimed to be offering it a good deal: the students could still broadcast for part of the day, the Straws argued, and the foundation would be happy to help give them radio training. But NHC already intended to move to twenty-four hours on its own, and it didn't like the schedule Jack Straw was proposing. Nor was it interested in having someone else train its volunteers. "Why in the world would we, as a training institution, who do this and had built a curriculum, need to go outside to people who are not professional educators to get their supposed quasi-expertise to build a curriculum?" asks NHC manager Gregg Neilson. "It was transparent that their motive was not what they could give us, but what they wanted from us."[52]

KNHC went on to prosper. Now nicknamed C-89, it may be the only high school station in the country that has frequently broken hits. Jack Straw finally got another station, KSER, in the nearby city of Everett,[53] with a signal that didn't reach most of Seattle. As the station began to establish itself as a community resource for the suburbs north of Seattle and the rural area west of the Puget Sound, its relations with Jack Straw grew tense, as the foundation still hoped to boost the station's power and remake it as a Seattle operation. Finally, in 1995, the station seceded from the foundation. It has continued to do good radio—though I'm a little biased, since I used to be a volunteer there— while the Jack Straw Foundation has dabbled in several activities, most related either to studio production or to seeking grants.

Seattle wasn't the only city whose stations were infected by turmoil in the '70s and '80s. Turmoil, indeed, seemed built into the very structure of community radio. Two Pacifica stations faced full-fledged uprisings. In Berkeley, a 1974 strike ushered in a Third World Department with full control of minority hiring and a guaranteed ten hours of airtime each week. In New York, staffers locked themselves in WBAI's studios for six weeks in 1977, ultimately winning recognition for their union and fend-ing off a proposal to reorganize their schedule. Meanwhile, in Portland, KBOO contended with a faction that wanted to aim for a more upscale audience with NPR-style programs. The gentrifiers lost, but not before saddling the station with a considerable debt.

And then there was the saga of KCHU—pronounced like a sneeze —in Dallas, the station that drove Milam out of radio.[54]

Dennis Gross, a veteran of KDNA, had spent the better part of the early '70s trying to bring community radio to Dallas. When Milam sold his Los Gatos station and joined Gross's project, he hoped the station would become "a center for informality and reason and thought and ideas and ideals which so far, because of artifice, or fear, or greed, or pettiness—have eluded the air, and thus our ears."[55] Instead, it became a center for ferocious infighting. "Those people were beleaguered down there," Milam recalls. "Their lives were miserable. They were actually meaner than the people that we ran into in Seattle or in Los Gatos or even in St. Louis."[56] The natives noticed his dismay. ("He didn't seem to get along with us younger Hippies very well," one engineer recalls.)[57]

KCHU signed onto the airwaves on September 1, 1975, and signed off exactly two years later. "We always like to think of ourselves as friendly anarchists," Milam explained, "but street tactics came to infest the halls of that beautiful broadcast castle on Maple Avenue, and the station just wasn't old enough and strong enough to absorb it. And the people in the city didn't give a good goddamn."[58]

Well, most of them didn't. The local branch of ACORN, a leftist group that had considered taking over KCHU during the station's death throes, started a new community station, KNON, five years later. That outlet is still there today. But Milam left Dallas—and left radio. The cost of liquidating the station nearly bankrupted him, though he slowly managed to pay off its debts, in part by selling the building and land that had housed it. But he was on the verge of a nervous breakdown, was convinced that he no longer knew what he was doing when it came to radio, and was ready to try something different. He moved into new areas—traveling, writing, editing a literary journal called *The Fessenden Review*[59]—and, aside from a brief, unprofitable foray into low-power television in the 1980s, he did not dip his toes in broadcasting again.

6

Money from Washington

They all listen to the same radio station, no matter what part of the country they're in, because even if the call letters are different, it's still the *same* radio station.   —J. R. "Bob" Dobbs

EVEN AS ONE set of freewheeling DJs found themselves working for the country's biggest media conglomerates, their noncommercial counterparts discovered an even unlikelier partner: the federal government. Credit for that improbable marriage belongs to the Carnegie Commission on Educational Television, a nominally independent group that was in fact largely directed from the Johnson White House. As the commission's name suggests, the Carnegie philanthropists weren't really interested in radio. When Congress, at their recommendation, passed the Public Broadcasting Act of 1967, only some last-minute lobbying by the National Association of Educational Broadcasters led the feds to fund radio at all, and it was another three years before the new Corporation for Public Broadcasting established National Public Radio.

Some hoped, in those early days, that NPR would be something radically new, a network close to the experimental spirit of Milam and Hill. When William Siemering, the innovative manager of SUNY-Buffalo's WBFO, conceived of the new network, his plan for its flagship show, *All Things Considered,* called for news reports from public stations around the country, with the Washington offices serving more as a clearinghouse than a command center. Instead, NPR became yet another centralized institution run by political appointees, especially after Siemering was fired as program director in 1972. Like the Corporation for Public Broadcasting, NPR was supposed to be shielded from government influence. In practice, both institutions are as susceptible to political pressure as any other part of official Washington. By 1993, things had gotten to the point where the head of the CPB could seriously call for merging NPR with the Voice of America. The idea was rebuffed, but the two talent pools started combining nonetheless. In 1997, a former deputy director of the Voice of America, Robert Coonrod, became head of the CPB. A year later, Kevin Klose—a former director of the International Broadcasting Bureau, which oversees the VOA—became president of National Public Radio. And in 1999, another veteran of the International Broadcasting Bureau, Kenneth Stern, became NPR's executive vice president.

Competition from a rival network—American Public Radio, later renamed Public Radio International—hasn't reversed the trend toward centralization. In 1987, 60 percent of the country's public radio programs were locally produced. Ten years later, the ratio tipped the other way.[1] Nor was the programming getting better. In the early days, *All Things Considered* and other shows experimented with sound collage, an evocative approach in some ways similar to Scoop Nisker's reports on KSAN. Sound collage is still an element on NPR news today, but it's been reduced to a limited vocabulary of clichés, a problem noted even by some of its staff. In the early 1990s, the journalist Glenn Garvin reports, "when NPR was running a long, long, *long* series of stories on local people shunted aside by development in Latin America, several reporters formed a pool. Recalls one: 'We bet on how long each story would go before it cued a strumming guitar, followed by a grandfather mourning his lost son, then singing long-forgotten revolutionary songs.'"[2]

Public radio isn't inherently dull, and there are some decent NPR stations out there. Consider Santa Monica's KCRW, a community college outlet that was taken over, in the late '70s, by ousted KPFK program director Ruth Hirschman, who built it into the most powerful and profitable public station in southern California.[3] It isn't governed like a community station—there's no pretense of democracy, and there's a large paid staff—and many of its programs emit a strong yuppie scent; meanwhile, student brodcasters complain that they've been squeezed out. On the other hand, KCRW isn't afraid to ignore conventional public-radio formulas: it plays an eclectic range of music, produces its own talk shows, and even records radio plays, drawing on the nearby Hollywood talent pool. Hirschman clearly learned a lot at Pacifica. It's sometimes said that her station got where it is by positioning itself as a "safe" KPFK.[4]

But most public radio is upscale and middlebrow, offering hour after hour of candy-coated brie. It's hard to see how one can call this arrangement "public," unless one's only criterion is an influx of public dollars.

From the beginning, there was some crossover between the new style of radio and the old community stations, as reporters and administrators from Pacifica and smaller outlets moved on to positions at National Public Radio. Many community stations ran some NPR programs—KRAB, for instance, carried the network's coverage of the Watergate hearings—and a few landed in a hazy zone between the two camps. WYSO, licensed to Antioch College in Yellow Springs, Ohio, gave its volunteers copies of Milam's book *Sex and Broadcasting* and sent students to do internships at KRAB and other stations like it; until the early '80s, it was clearly a station in the Milam mold. Yet it also became a full-fledged member of National Public Radio. KUSP, in Santa Cruz, was built—for just $700!—by Milam protégé David Freedman in 1972. It is still eclectic, unusual, volunteer based, and otherwise imbued with the community-radio spirit. And it, too, is part of NPR.

But for the most part, the groups remained distinct, and their relationship has always been uneasy. Milam had denounced the older educational stations as "a terrible waste," calling them "bores" that "have yet to issue one interesting, controversial, meaningful program in their entire sordid (and expensive) history." NPR was "somewhat less dull," he conceded, but it still had problems: "The people who run those stations are scared. You don't have to be. They are imitative. You don't have to be."[5] The Pacifica stations joined NPR when it was established—and quickly left, convinced that the two networks were pursuing different missions.

Over the years, whatever commitment NPR had to airing eccentric or innovative fare has largely disintegrated. The poverty of modern public broadcasting is symbolized best by *StarDate,* an expensive daily feature—$597 for the first year, $769 after that—that tells stargazers which celestial bodies will be visible each evening. It's a pretty superficial program, partly because of its length (only two minutes) but mostly because of its national scope. Any station that carries it could both save money and improve itself by airing a local astronomer instead. He'd probably do it for free—certainly for less than *StarDate* costs. He'd be able to go into much more detail. And he'd be able to say what will be visible that night *in the station's listening area.*

This institutional aversion to exploiting the most obvious local re-sources is matched by many programmers' timid refusal to give audi-ences anything that might challenge their assumptions, or even—to judge from a tale told by the artist and critic Richard Kostelanetz—their existing store of knowledge:

> When Glenn Gould died several years ago, National Public Radio, which then had a Sunday arts show, asked me to talk about him as a pianist. Since I have a private rule as a commentator never to do any-thing that somebody else could do better, I recommended two other critics, one of whom spoke to NPR about Gould the pianist. As it hap-pened, this NPR Sunday arts show was at the time celebrating Radio Art Month, mostly, if I remember correctly, by playing Bob and Ray; and since Gould had also produced some of the most extraordinary radio programs ever made in North America—hour-long composi-tions of interwoven speech and sound—I proposed to do a feature on those, "to any length you wish," as I told the man from NPR. Oh yes, he said, he knew of those Gould programs, but he hadn't actually heard them because they hadn't been broadcast too often south of the border. He said he would need to discuss my proposal with his col-leagues. On my answering machine two days later was a message telling me that they couldn't commission my proposed feature, be-cause, as the voice told me, "We can only feature things that every-body knows."[6]

When Congress created the CPB, many community stations refused to take its money, fearing that federal aid would bring federal depend-ence.[7] Others accepted government subsidies in the same spirit that they might take a grant from a private foundation: nice dough if you can get it, but nothing to rely on.[8]

Shortly after the CPB released its Public Radio Plan in 1972, KBOO manager John Ross sent it a wire. "The Public Radio Plan describes a station operating on an average current budget of more than $120,000," he argued. "KBOO operated last year on less than $500 a month. . . . The plan's recommendations for financial support of qualified stations seems to be geared to allow the already large station to grow larger while the small station has to stay where it is."[9] Within the station, meanwhile, a lot of staffers and volunteers were upset that Ross was applying for federal grants at all. "He was well-intentioned," one DJ recalls, "but he bought a lot of really high-quality, like recording-studio-quality, equipment, and it put us on this time schedule for burning so much money. Otherwise, there was a good chance that it could put the station under."[10] In other words, by accepting the government's money, the station might be making itself unsustainable. And indeed, its debts nearly drove it out of business.

But times were changing. As the community-radio universe grew larger, it started organizing. And as it organized, it started looking for friends in Washington.

In 1974, about twenty-five people came to Madison, Wisconsin, for the National Alternative Radio Konvention, a.k.a. NARK. It was a contentious and exhilarating meeting, with broadcasters swapping stories over cheap beer and wine, trading tips, making plans, and trying to figure out just what "community radio" means. The word "community," Jeff Lange of Madison's WORT later remarked, "was picked by a huge committee . . . and was a compromise between political ideologues, radio experimentalists, media-philosophers and total greenhorns—all of whom could feel that the rubric 'community broadcaster' would suit their image of themselves."[11] It was tough enough just to bring together those outlets that had evolved in close contact with one another: the Pacifica stations, the stations around KRAB, the stations around KDNA, the stations around Antioch College's WYSO. Some at Pacifica, for example, weren't sure whether they wanted to participate: the ethos seemed a little too midwestern, and maybe a bit un-P.C. But those fissures were nothing compared to the trouble the attendees would face when they tried to integrate some entirely different radio traditions, outlets that in the words of one activist—Frederick Phaneuf, who'd spent time at both WYSO and KRAB—weren't "white hippie stations."[12]

Like San Francisco's KPOO, which had once been part of the KRAB Nebula but had, in effect, splintered away. A fellow named Meyer Gottesman had been awarded an open frequency several years before, then despaired of ever getting the station built and funded. In 1971, he turned the construction permit over to Milam, who figured the Bay Area could use a noncommercial station that avoided both "the educate-'em-dead school of institutional broadcasting," represented locally by KQED, and "the political babble-rabble school of radio," which he feared was overtaking KPFA.[13] It went on the air in 1972, and, says Milam, it was a good station—a good KTAO or KRAB type station. But then the black radicals moved in, and began to raise hell. . . . They didn't think it was black enough, or giving enough time to black issues. Which wouldn't have been an issue, except it turned out one of my board members was on their side. And that really blew everything; that was too bad. So, instead of having yet another internecine battle in the operation, we went to a meeting with the black radicals and I said to them, "Well, shit, why don't you guys just take over the station. I'm tired of it." So we gave it to them.[14]

The displaced staff was not pleased. But the deed was done, and KPOO had become the West's first black-owned and -operated noncommercial radio station. And it was there at the conference in Madison, looking askance at the folks from KAXE in Grand Rapids, Minnesota, wondering why it didn't have any black volunteers. (Turns out Grand Rapids didn't have many blacks to begin with.)

From NARK, an organization grew. The founders played with several names (including "the League of Stations") before settling on the bland but direct National Federation of Community Broadcasters. The new group formally organized itself at another meeting—in Cincinnati, in 1975—and embraced several more radio traditions over the years. There were the Hispanic operations, such as Radio Bilingüe, a five-station, two-language network in California. And there were the American Indian stations, several of which had been launched in the early 1970s. (KTDB in Pine Hill, New Mexico, is usually credited as the first, though other outlets have also claimed that distinction).[15]

The Natives faced challenges most urban broadcasters never imagined. (Few city stations have had to consider whether their listeners had electricity.) They also tended to be dependent on the federal government, a relationship that generally worsened with time. The Indigenous Communications Association, the country's only alliance of Indian stations, would not even exist were it not for a 1990 grant from the CPB. On the other hand, many Natives have long contended that their sovereign status ought to exempt them from the FCC's regulations, and several Indians embraced the unlicensed micro radio movement of the '90s.

The Indians weren't the only ones starting community stations in the countryside. "Since most broadcast frequencies in or near major cities have long been taken," the historian David Armstrong noted in

1981, "the growth of community radio has been chiefly in small towns and rural areas," mixing shows by local radicals with shows by local Rotarians.[16] The conventional wisdom had assumed that community radio couldn't find an audience in the world beyond big cities, college towns, and hippie enclaves. With rural stations appearing in such spots as Eugene Springs, Arkansas, and Grand Rapids, Minnesota, the conventional wisdom gradually changed.

Then there was the new wave of college stations. Some of these had adopted the Milam mode of broadcasting, more or less: WYSO may have been based in a drab, institutional college building, but its programming was far from drab or institutional, and it wasn't always collegiate either. (The Saturday-night bluegrass show was far more popular with the farmers outside town than with anyone connected to Antioch.) KAOS, at Evergreen State University, was also part of the community-radio network.

Other school stations were not. Student broadcasting had been around since the amateur radio clubs of the 1910s, and its social role hadn't really changed: it was a way for undergrads to talk to one another, and, while those conversations could be useful, enjoyable, or lively, they were rarely relevant to the world outside their campus. There were exceptions, of course. Harvard's WHRB had a campus role: it was, in the 1950s, "a counter-fraternity, a *salon des refusés* for all those who, because of ethnicity, class or inclination, did not fit the mold of Harvard."[17] (The alum speaking is Sam Smith, who would later be employed, you'll recall, by a bubbly-jingled outlet in suburban Washington.) But because it was based at Harvard, it attracted some impressive guests:

> Duke Ellington had once played the upright in Studio B, Eleanor Roosevelt had visited for an interview and Leadbelly had performed for four hours while being plied with Scotch. Once a staffer was sent to try to entice Robert Frost to tape an interview, a seemingly futile task since Frost had always refused to appear on radio. The student went to Frost's home and started discussing poetry, never daring to broach the invitation. Frost enjoyed the talk and invited the student back. On the third visit, he finally asked what had brought the student over the first time. The student explained, Frost accepted, and [he] subsequently made his first radio broadcast ever on WHRB.[18]

Even so, WHRB was a campus station, not a community station and even with the occasional hijinks you'd expect from college kids, it mostly maintained a professional sound. The first student operation to radically break with this kind of radio was probably WFMU, and it never joined the National Federation of Community Broadcasters. But another outlet—Georgetown's WGTB—did.

Founded in 1960, WGTB was unremarkable at first, playing pop songs, Catholic sermons, and little else. But in 1970, a cabal of campus radicals took it over, and the old programs were replaced with leftist politics and avant-garde classical, jazz, and rock music. The campus authorities didn't like this, and they soon saddled the station with a new manager. He made the station less amateurish, but no less radical; indeed, after a while, he went native.

By this time, a lot of the on-air personalities weren't even students, just members of the local left, some of whom let their political passions get in the way of good radio. Once a newscaster fabricated a story claiming the United States had bombed Libya. Confronted by the station's angry manager, the offender offered a defense as defiant as it was pathetic: "If Nixon could have his way, he would have done it."[19]

Despite such sophomoria, the broadcasters built a big audience: after a power boost in 1974, its signal reached all the way to Pennsylvania. When the university cut back its subsidy to the station, the listeners filled in the gaps with contributions. The administrators tried sterner measures, firing the manager they'd hired and, when the staff still proved defiant, sending in campus cops to shut down the station altogether. They hired a new manager from another college station, where he'd helped put down another unruly staff, and he tried to tone things down. He failed. Finally, the university threw up its hands and decided it would be better off without a radio station. In 1979 it gave its license, gratis, to the University of the District of Columbia. R.I.P., WGTB.[20]

The station wasn't beloved by every community broadcaster either. Milam didn't care for it; he once wrote Sleeman that "the main failing of WGTB right now is that you think commercial radio. This makes the station the outhouse of 50 or so doubtful egos. . . . If you did honorable manful radio, instead of jack-off dj stuff, the University would *have* to defend you."[21] During one of its tussles with the administration, Milam even asked Georgetown if it would turn the frequency over to him.

Other observers found the operation more admirable, and more than one of its programs later graduated to Pacifica. In any event, it was an early member of the NFCB, adding yet another style of broadcasting to the stew.

NPR had sent some agents to NARK as well. They weren't entirely welcome there. "We Mau Maued them," recalls Phaneuf. "They sent out some really straight-looking people, and we were *very* scruffy hippie-looking people." But the connection was there, and soon there would be more ties between the community radio movement and the public radio establishment. While Bill Thomas, the prime mover behind the Konference, started a program service for the NFCB in Champagne, Illinois, Tom Thomas and Terry Clifford set up a national office in Washington, D.C. The latter outpost helped stations and would-be stations navigate through the government's red tape—not just FCC paperwork, but applications for federal subsidies.

Gradually, across the mid- to late '70s, community stations started seeking CPB money in earnest. At about the same time, the NFCB convinced the government's Public Telecommunications Facilities Program to pay for independent outlets' equipment purchases and upgrades. And many stations, some of which had previously subsisted entirely on volunteer labor, began paying staff with funds available under the Comprehensive Employment and Training Act.

One can certainly understand the lure of federal lucre. Most of these stations operated on the edge of bankruptcy, and they could do some pretty desperate things to get by. In Los Gatos, Lorenzo even sublet some of KTAO's hours to a supercommercial religious broadcaster, a culture-clashing arrangement that quickly fell apart.

But the government's money wasn't free. To receive a Community Service Grant from the CPB, stations had to follow certain rules. Strict from the start, those regulations have gotten only tighter with time; these days, besides meeting reasonable requirements of programming and equipment quality, a station seeking handouts must have at least five full-time paid staff and must operate at one hundred or more watts of power (250 watts for AM stations), at least eighteen hours a day, seven days a week. In addition, it must receive $195,000 or more from nonfederal sources. Starting in 1998, there was a new requirement: qualifying stations must demonstrate a minimum level of either listenership (as measured by the Arbitron rating service) or local financial support.[22] (The second option was added only after several small stations protested the change. The committee that made the original recommendations included two figures, Lynn Chadwick and Patricia Scott, who play significant roles later in this book.)

All those rules may seem reasonable—after all, one can hardly expect the government to give money to just anyone who asks for it. But they have created a perverse set of incentives. Community stations that previously got by on listener pledges and local underwriting might be eligible for thousands more—*if* they hire more full-time staff, increase their broadcast hours, seek more funds, and, under the later rules, make their programming more mainstream in pursuit of higher ratings. The result, as *Democratic Communiqué* editor Jon Bekken has noted, has been to encourage "ambitious expansion programs" that foster professionalization and centralization.[23] It is possible to receive less in government assistance than you spend making yourself eligible for that support.

So there is an innate tension here. The limited amount of money the state has to offer requires it to discriminate on some rational basis: if the CPB dispensed funds to every small community station in America, it would have to divide its budget so finely that no station could receive enough money to justify the corporation's existence. So the CPB strives to direct its money to the stations with the most powerful signals and the largest measured audiences, and prefers not to finance more than one outlet in a single market. But the corporation's requirements encourage stations to grow and to adopt a high-priced professional style, putting further pressure on the CPB's budget and forcing it to further restrict the flow of money, refueling the cycle. If the budget is expanding anyway—as it did during the Carter years, for example—the cycle can be slowed and the problem concealed. If the budget is contracting, as it did through much of the '80s and '90s, the problem only gets worse. Under any circumstances, the cycle of professionalization and expansion is built into the federal subsidies; it cannot be eliminated by minor reforms or by putting a friendlier group of bureaucrats in charge.

It takes more than government money to demoralize a radio station, of course. A station united by a particular broadcasting vision can survive—can prosper—with state funds coming in. But the CPB's subversion of community radio didn't stop with the strings it attached to its subsidies.

As we've already noted, the FCC began issuing Class D licenses in 1948, allowing noncommercial groups—at first just colleges but later community stations as well—to broadcast at ten watts. It cost less money to put small stations on the air, so the Class D license did a lot to open the airwaves to the public. But as those stations multiplied, they began to crowd the dial, blocking the expansion of the new public radio network. The CPB—which, you will remember, had already refused to fund low-watt stations—began pressuring the commission to reconsider its rules. NPR agreed: it saw the ten-watters as an impediment to growth, cluttering frequencies where it might instead bring *All Things Considered* to the benighted masses.

Community broadcasters were less enthusiastic. In 1972, when the CPB first asked the FCC to do something about the small stations, the *Alternative Radio Exchange* raised an eyebrow, and then a fist: "The CPB proposal represents the classic conflict between the well-funded, expensive, heavily bureaucratized, heavily narcotized institutions—and the rowdy, slightly seedy, mostly poverty-stricken non-institutional community stations."[24] Within a few years, however, the NFCB had joined the anti-low-power chorus, even though many of its members were ten-watters. The federation's rationale was the same as NPR's: all those ten-watt outlets were preventing larger community stations from entering the spectrum and keeping smaller ones from expanding. Tom Thomas recalls the debate within the organization:

> There was a kind of knee-jerk reaction within community radio groups that said, "Oh my God, this is going to close off one of the options that's been effective in getting groups on the air." But . . . groups that were trying to get on the air were finding themselves blocked, right, left, and center, by large numbers of high school stations, community college stations, and so forth that were basically just being run as adjuncts to school radio clubs and things of that sort but who just wouldn't budge.[25]

As you might expect, Thomas's position owed a lot to the Double Helix Foundation's struggle to find a space for a new KDNA, its path blocked by a part-time, ten-watt high school station.[26] The same experience led Jeremy Lansman to take the anti–Class D side of the debate. Eventually, the rest of the group fell in line. Surely, it declared, spectrum space could be used more efficiently: "Were it not for existing Class D stations, at least 40–45 new high-power noncommercial FM stations in the top

100 markets could be established and . . . significant power increases could be obtained for another 25–30 existing stations."[27]

The Intercollegiate Broadcast System—an association of student stations, most of which held Class D licenses—disagreed. In its petition to the FCC, it noted that "the industry" (that is, National Public Radio and the Corporation for Public Broadcasting) had devised the proposed rule change without asking any Class D stations for their input. "At least this conception of the 'industry' as excluding half the present educational FM licensees unmistakably demonstrates that diversity would suffer if the educational band were given over to the clique," the petition noted. "At most it may demonstrate an anti-competitive combination with the intent to eliminate competition."[28] The big stations' collusion sometimes inspired darker theories. One college broadcaster of the day remembers hearing rumors that "some fairly heavy pressure was brought by CPB for [NFCB] to toe the line. The message was that they all ought to be 'professional,' and forcing the ten-watters out would make better radio somehow."[29]

There may be some truth to that. Still, those in the NFCB who favored the change almost certainly believed that they were doing what was best. Thomas had become closely associated with D.C.'s public broadcasting establishment in the 1970s and had helped many community stations acquire federal grants. His group was, among other things, a lobby playing the interest-group game, competing for a piece of a finite electromagnetic pie. Once it accepted the idea that spectrum space should be allocated politically, and once it became convinced that the ten-watters were standing in its members' way, its position was a foregone conclusion.

The CPB insisted it didn't want to drive the ten-watters off the air, but that is, in effect, what happened. The FCC announced that it would no longer issue licenses to stations of ten watts or less.[30] Existing Class D stations had until 1980 either to relocate to the commercial spectrum (if room could be found there) or to upgrade to one hundred watts. And ten-watt operations would no longer be protected against interference from larger stations' signals—though they themselves still weren't permitted to interfere with other transmissions. That rule effectively allowed any neighboring station to seize a ten-watt outfit's frequency.[31]

Only a few outlets continue to broadcast at less than one hundred watts of power. Yet many of the old stations survived. They expanded to one hundred watts before the FCC's 1980 deadline, leading some people to argue that the new rule has backfired and only further cluttered the spectrum. The NFCB's prediction that community groups could establish "at least 40–45 new high-power noncommercial FM stations in the top 100 markets" turned out to be a substantial exaggeration.[32]

In 1979, KBOO manager Michael Wells suggested that "CPB and NPR are plotting to have an American BBC by 1984." This "isn't a bad thing," he continued, "but it means that community stations are going to have to scramble to avoid being co-opted, crushed or swallowed."[33] As we all know, there was no American BBC in 1984: the Reagan administration was less than enthusiastic about public radio, and stations found themselves scrambling for money instead. By the 1990s, when something like One Big Radio Network really was in place, it bore little resemblance to the BBC, except to the extent that the BBC had been commercializing itself. But the community stations still had to contend with the risk of being coopted, crushed, or swallowed.

Clearly, community radio can survive without the CPB helping to pay the bills. But would that actually be good for community radio? And what would become of those stations that rely on the corporation for a significant slice of their budget yet have avoided the money's many pitfalls? Wouldn't killing the program only hurt them?

The first question is easy to answer. The CPB has financed some good stations and some good programs, and if it were to disappear, many of those stations and shows would undergo difficulties. Some might die. Yet federal aid has brought with it incentives to professionalize, to centralize, to homogenize. Whatever its effect on individual stations, its net effect on community radio has been poor.

The second question is trickier. Past experience shows that the sudden withdrawal of federal funds has damaged stations, particularly stations with mostly low-income listeners. When Congress abolished the Comprehensive Employment and Training Act in 1981, several stations were hurt, some badly. KUBO, a bilingual station in California, went into debt and, eventually, off the air. WVSP, a black-oriented station in rural North Carolina, relocated to an urban, more upscale location.[34] That hardly means that CETA shouldn't have died, but it does show that the loss of federal support can hurt.

The best solution is to cut off the CPB from tax funding, and thus from federal interference, by making it into an independent trust fund, with seed money from the government's spectrum auctions. Ideally, the trust would have a decentralized, democratic structure, so that power would rest with the member stations rather than with a self-perpetuating national board. Even then, most stations might find it best to wean themselves from the fund, given that it would probably be dominated by public television and its upscale urban and suburban audiences. But at least they'd have a transition period.

The NFCB had been formed, among other reasons, to lobby for community radio's interests within the Beltway. By the 1990s, it sometimes seemed to be lobbying for the Beltway's interests within community radio.[35] (By this time, many of the NFCB's founders had moved on to other jobs. Thomas and Clifford, for example, had become public radio consultants.) In the new era, it was not unusual to hear an NFCB administrator denounce the "old hippie paradigm" of diverse programs and volunteer-based management. Paid staff, they suggested, should call the shots. Community radio, in theory a domain for volunteers, now had to contend with a homegrown professional class.

This conflict became obvious in the late 1980s, when the NFCB and American Public Radio launched the Blueprint Project, a CPB-financed "consulting initiative." When American Public Radio dropped out, the NFCB rechristened its efforts the Healthy Station Project. The program's coordinator, David LePage, wrote that it was simply "a curriculum designed to support and create successful local stations," a "method of facilitation and training." It "brings no hidden plan or agenda, no magic wands, no predetermined programming answers," he added, but merely "evaluates a station's health based on its behavior and performance in relation to achieving its mission, not in relation to any particular program format or organizational structure."[36]

That was a half-truth. The NFCB's advice did vary from place to place, depending on what content it felt would build audiences in a particular locale. But the form that content would take was distressingly— well, blueprintish. LePage and his associates (most notably his then-wife, NFCB president Lynn Chadwick) consistently called for reducing volunteers' power over both station management and the content of their shows. "Healthy" stations were to embrace predictable "strip" programming. Their music would be more homogeneous, more "consistent." Oddball shows that didn't immediately fit the new format would be dropped, no matter how popular they might be.

The idea, derived from the research of programming consultants George Bailey and David Giovannoni, was that listeners like predictability—that if they tune to a station Monday and hear some rap, then try again Tuesday and get a Gregorian chant, they won't come back again. Obviously, there is some truth to that, and many community stations have gained listeners without losing their eclectic identity by arranging a more logical flow from program to program. But variety can also be a station's selling point, its niche, especially if those varied shows are hosted by talented, knowledgeable DJs. Wipe out that variety and fire those hosts, and you're headed for trouble.

One of the first testing grounds for the Healthy Station Project was WERU in rural Maine. Founded on May Day in 1988, WERU had only six full-time and one part-time paid employees, plus about 150 volunteers. Important decisions were made by all: one person, one vote. Most of its funding came from local sources, although it also accepted federal subsidies.

In 1993, it collided with the Healthy Station philosophy, represented by LePage, Bailey, and a handful of local staffers. It didn't take long for the new vision to wear out its welcome. According to Cathy Melio, later the station's manager, "their advice was that in homogenizing your programming, you'll have a lot more listeners and thus you'll be more 'healthy.' And we challenged that. We said diversity is the strength of community radio. Your community is not homogeneous, and thus your programming shouldn't be."[37]

In that case, the interlopers were eventually ousted; the station has continued to prosper, recently moving to new quarters. Less fortunate was KOPN, in Columbia, Missouri. In the early '90s, KOPN faced some financial hard times, thanks largely to problems that had beset its former cash cow, a fundraising bingo game. Change was definitely needed. But what kind of change?

The station had operated without any paid staff for its first two years; it then hired one manager. Then, from 1976 to 1980, the number of paid workers jumped to twenty-five, with 23.5 of their salaries paid out of grants.[38] They weren't necessarily overpaid, but there were far more of them than a community station would traditionally maintain. When the bingo crisis hit, KOPN volunteer Jay Teutenberg pointed out that during the previous year, "the staff's salaries amounted to $145,000, approximately half our budget. This year the station will carry forward a debt note of $20,000, in addition to the other accounts payable. . . . [I]t has been their salaries and their decisions that have created this dire situation."[39]

That was not LePage's diagnosis. According to Teutenberg, the Healthy Station cadre offered the station a choice between drastically enlarging its budget with federal money or running with no paid staff at all: "David LePage has laid it out in black and white terms, either we can lift the budget to $400,000, or we can run at $100,000 with no paid staff or CPB . . . funding. No one has talked much about what it would be like to run without paid staff, just left it as sort of an 'unspeakable horror.'"[40] And so KOPN took the Healthy Station road.

Different stations reacted to the Healthy Station Project in different ways. Back when the invader was called the Blueprint Project, WRFG in Atlanta was told to throw its blues shows off the air—to become more "multicultural"! The Blueprinters also advised it to replace its volunteers with paid DJs and to streamline its programming. Those changes were unpopular with the listener-subscribers, prompting the station to reverse some of the changes. The consultants then withdrew, declaring the outlet "wasn't serious" about becoming healthy.[41]

Several broadcasters have praised particular aspects of the Healthy Station approach, especially the notion that stations should figure out what exactly their missions are.[42] But as a whole, the program met resistance in almost every outlet it invaded. Several stations protested the project by reducing their involvement with the NFCB. Many joined the Grassroots Radio Coalition, a fledgling group cofounded by Cathy Melio of WERU and Marty Durlin of Boulder's KGNU. Some broadcasters abandoned their "healthy" homes and moved into micro radio.

Today, the Healthy Station Project is dead. Yet the ideas that animated it have survived, and similar efforts are underway around the country. The most infamous is taking place at Pacifica, whose listeners and volunteers finally erupted in rebellion in 1999. It wasn't Pacifica's first civil war, of course. But more than usual was at stake this time: the network wasn't simply evolving in a new direction, but was taking on characteristics that threatened to change it on some fundamental, existential level—to make it something that no longer deserved to be called Pacifica.

By the mid-1990s, Pacifica bore little resemblance to the project launched by Lew Hill fifty years before. The five-station network—the fifth, Washington's jazz-oriented WPFW, had gone on the air in 1977—

soaked up about a million dollars in federal subsidies each year, applied to the Pew Charitable Trust and other corporate foundations for yet more outside money, fired volunteers for criticizing station policy on the air, and occupied a predictable political niche, self-righteously P.C. but almost as averse to the genuinely radical as it was to the right-of-center. (Long gone were the days when a DJ could read the John Birch Society's *Blue Book* over the air, sans tut-tutting commentary, so that listeners might simply learn what all the fuss was about.) Interesting, unusual shows were being dropped, to make way for what former KPFK shop steward Lyn Gerry calls "annoying clusters of soundbites interrupted by little blurbs of music."[43] Critics charged the larger network with an intense effort to centralize power, water down programming, and break any force that might block the path to NPRification—even if that meant traversing its professed progressive politics by trying to bust its staffers' unions.

Needless to say, that is not how Pacifica's managers preferred to describe the changes under way. "I hear all these stories," complained Patricia Scott, the network's executive director from 1994 to 1998. "I read the Internet, and I listen to questions from people like you writing about this stuff, and it's so far removed from reality. . . . What you're doing," she told me, "is you're taking statements from a small group of people that have been fired. And they represent no mass movement of people in Pacifica stations."[44]

That was in 1997. Two years later, no one could make such a claim: throngs of listeners were protesting outside KPFA, denouncing the new Pacifica. But even when I spoke to her, Scott was clearly wrong. I had already encountered several Pacifica workers—not just former workers—who didn't like the way the network was being run, and I'd talked to many concerned listeners as well. What's more, several of the former programmers I spoke with had been let go only *after* they protested the turn their stations were taking. Others had left voluntarily, without being fired.

Furthermore, different dissidents offered different complaints, some radically opposed to the others, further undermining the thesis that the network's critics were a single "small group." (One listener, for instance, preferred KPFA's revamped schedule. It was, he said, "the Byzantine in-fighting and secrecy, and refusal to figure out a way to incorporate member participation and communication, that I deplore.")[45]

And most of the dissidents conceded that the network needed some sort of change—just not the kind it had gotten.

For management's side of the story, one might turn to the foundation's former development director, Dick Bunce, and his contribution to the network's 1996 "strategic five-year plan," titled *A Vision for Pacifica Radio: Creating a Network for the 21st Century*. Anyone who doubts the essentially bureaucratic mindset of the new Pacifica should reflect a while on that title—and then, if she can stomach it, on the prose that follows:

> In the half century since the Pacifica Foundation was incorporated, the worlds of public radio, broadcasting, and the media have been through multiple transformations. The present and onrushing future is no less dynamic in opportunities and risks for Pacifica Radio. Patricia Scott, Executive Director of Pacifica, believes that we stand at an "unmarked crossroads" in the life of our network, "where a failure of the will necessary to make investments in our franchise could trigger the beginning of our demise. Imagination and a new sense of purpose in Pacifica can make us a national force, defining the course of electronic journalism, not being defined by it." Challenging the network to address improved methods of impacting political discourse and culture, Scott and Pacifica's leadership committed extensive time, energy and resources in 1996 to strategic planning.[46]

There you have it. The Pacifica of Kenneth Rexroth has given way to the Pacifica of an "onrushing future" that is "dynamic in opportunities and risks," of "impacting political discourse and culture," of "multiple transformations" and "strategic planning" and "investments in our franchise." These aren't phrases; they're wordclots. Former KPFA volunteer Maria Gilardin, already disillusioned with Pacifica, nonetheless found Bunce's language disturbing. "What muddled thinking is hiding behind these words?" she asked. "What obfuscation? . . . They should get their money back. It is just a boilerplate that some consultant sold them."[47]

A shrinking cartel of trusts controls the media, the plan complains, and the Republican Hordes want to destroy the Corporation for Public Broadcasting.[48] "If public funding is eliminated," Bunce writes, "chances are the dominant players in public radio—NPR, PRI and their satellite-driven franchise stations—will replace federal support with commercial support." That leaves Pacifica to rescue listeners starved for intelligent, critical analysis. "The opportunity is ours."[49]

And how would Pacifica exploit this opportunity? It's hard to tell, if all you have to go by is the five-year plan. As Gilardin says, this is boilerplate stuff—"so vague it could apply to anything."[50] Among its recommendations:

> Maximize the use of Pacifica's resources.
> Stay abreast of new developments in technology of potential significance to Pacifica.
> Establish and maintain a healthy work culture.
> Exploit economies of scale.
> Establish local readiness criteria and basic minimum standards.[51]

Shovel through the mush, though, and you'll discover that Pacifica had decided to adopt the very practice Bunce bemoans in NPR and PRI: to become a network of satellite-driven franchise stations. As Gerry put it, Pacifica's managers "see a vacuum created as NPR goes more corporate, and intend to fill it."[52]

Some trace the network's latest troubles back to the 1960s, when the governing board transformed itself—illegally, some say—from a democratic body elected from below into a largely self-perpetuating institution. Others point to the mid-'70s, when Pacifica started accepting government subsidies. As we've seen, the '70s also saw staff revolts at several stations, leading the network in a Third Worldist direction that some see as its glory days but others regard as the beginning of the end. By their account, the revolts launched a period of inconsistent patchwork-quilt programming, inadvertently paving the way for reformers to move too far in the other direction—and inadvertently introducing the poisonous language of multicultural one-upmanship, a game the Scott regime would prove itself all too able to play, even as it wiped out actual signs of cultural diversity.

For John Whiting, the key date is 1985. Prior to that year, noncommercial stations were not allowed to rent out their subcarriers— "sideband" frequencies that don't interfere with the primary signal. After that year's broadcast deregulation, they could. The result, writes Whiting, was a windfall: "Having got into FM on the ground floor, [Pacifica] now owned half-a-dozen high-output transmitters on elevated sites in big urban centers, whose by-products were suddenly worth a small fortune."

That much was fine. The catch: "In order to guarantee that the bonanza would not be frittered away on running expenses, the national board quickly staked its claim to the sub carriers of all the stations."[53] Suddenly, the board had access to money that didn't percolate from below. The dynamic of power shifted from the individual station managers to the network's executive director. And the opportunists and centralists who'd long circulated through Pacifica had a new incentive to capture the national board.

Over the course of the '80s and '90s, they did just that. At KPFA, Scott became general manager and began cleaning house, eliminating departments that lay outside her control and moving the station to more upscale facilities. Dissidents began calling her a "Yuppie Stalinist"—the second word as much for her P.C. bludgeon and her Communist Party past as for her autocratic style. From KPFA, Scott advanced to become executive director of the foundation and the person most responsible for changing the network's off-air management and on-air sound.

Other stations went through transformations of their own. When some black programmers aired some anti-Semitic material on KPFK, for instance, management could have reacted to the public outcry in a way consistent with the network's history of free speech and open discussion: by inviting the outraged listeners onto the air to make their case, express their views, and engage the people they'd been protesting. Instead, faced with public criticism—some from the floor of Congress— the station purged the offending broadcasters from its staff and imposed new restrictions on on-air speech.

Few would dispute that Pacifica required reform. Many of its programmers were overly cozy with the left political establishment, particularly in Berkeley, a city where socialists have wielded substantial power at City Hall. Furthermore, on a radio spectrum already carved into extremely finely tuned niches, its stations' schedules sometimes seemed like yet another patchwork. The problem wasn't the diversity— indeed, that was a strength. It was the feeling that a lot of the hosts weren't listening to anyone else's shows. The result could sound more like coalition radio than community radio.

But Pacifica's ties to the left establishment grew only tighter under the new order. And though the new guard understood that balkanization was a problem, it seemed less interested in weaving the little communities together than in snuffing them out. Listeners began complaining of a blander, more homogeneous sound, as radical and oddball programs disappeared and more streamlined fare took their place. Not all the cuts were ill advised, as anyone who'd suffered through KPFT's *American Atheist Hour* can attest. But something more than clearing the driftwood is afoot when KPFA cans a commentator as important as William Mandel, its longtime analyst of Russian affairs. (It's not Mandel's frequently pro-Soviet views that I'm praising, mind you. It's his ability to enunciate a significant perspective that's rarely heard on American shores.)

In the meantime, here's a quick rundown of the results of Scott's reforms:

• *Labor troubles*. Until 1997, the United Electrical, Radio, and Machine Workers of America represented both paid and unpaid workers at Pacifica's New York and Berkeley stations and paid workers alone in Los Angeles. (In 1997, the Berkeley staff shifted to the Communications Workers of America.) One wouldn't expect a network that most associate with the political left to have a serious dispute with its union, any more than one would expect Jimmy Swaggart to hire prostitutes or Pat Buchanan to drive a foreign car. So more than a few eyebrows were raised in 1996 when dissidents charged Pacifica with hiring the American Consulting Group as its labor relations firm. The ACG is on the AFL-CIO's roster of union busters, and the contract it was advancing would decertify Pacifica's volunteer staff—nine-tenths of the union. Of course, the less a station relies on its volunteers, the more positions are filled by people who depend on management's good will to pay the rent. It was this that prompted the network's labor troubles, and not, as many assumed, a substantial dispute over wages and benefits.

Pacifica initially denied that ACG was a union-busting company. Scott then minimized the amount the network paid the group, claiming that the contract was for only $1,000—not for more than $30,000, as her critics had claimed. Union activists replied that this was entirely inconsistent with the amounts other companies had paid ACG for its services.

While it's difficult to discern what exactly went on between Pacifica and ACG, it's clear that the network's managers had trouble keeping their stories straight. Thus, Scott told me that "we hired a lawyer that we subsequently found out was associated with this same organization. And the minute we found out this lawyer was associated with ACG, we terminated his relationship with our organization too." Yet, after *Current* magazine published an article about Pacifica's labor troubles, Scott wrote a letter to the editor describing ACG as "a *firm* that was advising us on labor law and other matters" (emphasis added).[54] The *Current* feature itself described some more contradictions. For example: "[WBAI General Manager Valerie] Van Isler says Pacifica hired ACG to 'help review and consolidate the three contracts.' But Scott says ACG has only advised Pacifica on labor law and that she herself drew up the contract."[55]

Eventually, under the glare of bad P.R., Pacifica broke its ties with ACG. The labor dispute, however, has continued. In February 1997, the National Labor Relations Board ruled that WBAI could not decertify its volunteers. Pacifica appealed the decision, and received a ruling more favorable to management in late 1999. Meanwhile, shortly after changing unions, KPFA adopted a contract that excluded the station's unpaid staff.

Late in 1999, labor troubles flared again when Pacifica fired Dan Coughlin, executive producer of the network's nightly newscast, apparently for his coverage of the turmoil within Pacifica. (He was told that he was being made a "consultant" instead, and was asked to prepare a report on "Developing a Plan for Pacifica Network News in the Year 2001.") In January 2000, news anchor Verna Avery-Brown resigned in protest, and the show's stringers went on strike. The strikers created a weekly newscast of their own, *Free Speech Radio News*, which was soon picked up by forty stations across the continent.

With fewer reporters to rely on, the Pacifica Network News began taking an increasing number of reports from Feature Story News, a corporation whose faceless reports—or "ready-to-air television and radio news material, tailored to individual on-air styles," to quote its website[56]—also appeared on such radical alternative outlets as the Voice of America, ABC Radio, NBC/Mutual, *The News Hour with Jim Lehrer,* and the British Forces Broadcasting Service. The strikers noted the change: "Lest FSN's clients worry about broadcasting the equivalent of spoken wire copy, FSN's web site assures them that 'every story we supply is different: produced and edited to suit your program's on-air style, delivered by your deadline, and complete with your sign-off.' But how different can they be? Reporters drawing on mainstream sources and filing for clients like Voice of America or the Wall Street Journal do not cultivate alternative sources and cannot provide the kind of independent, critical reporting that Pacifica listeners expect."[57]

• *Blander, less locally derived programming.* On February 27, 1995, the Pacifica stations' program directors and general managers met in Albuquerque. The radio consultant David Giovannoni was there, too, to tell them how they might increase their ratings and income. His conclusions were recorded in the minutes:

> David suggested that Pacifica begin to pool programming because centralizing programming lowers the cost of producing it by 80%. It needs to define a national community to which it can appeal—it should re-think its concept of community—toward communities of interest and program to these interests. . . . He also thinks that the national office should mandate a schedule—sharing programs should not be optional.[58]

Giovannoni's idea of a mandated schedule was not new. In 1993, Pacifica central had begun pushing a regimen of national programming on its stations, which would in turn have had to drop local (and often better) shows to make room for the satellite feed. A national program adopted by three Pacifica stations was to become a "must carry" for the other two. Furthermore, decreed the board, "The National Program Director has the authority to declare a program a must carry based on . . . news value and urgency."[59]

That time bomb exploded when WBAI stopped airing *The Julianne Malveaux Show*, a slick and expensive gabfest hosted by the leftist *USA Today* columnist. WBAI staff complained that Malveaux's program was dumbed down and soundbite driven, and that they could fill that time better on their own. Dissidents at other stations agreed. The program was eventually canceled, not because staffers opposed it but for lack of funds. Sources differ as to whether it was a must-carry or simply a show that the national office pushed hard. Either way, its death in effect pushed the must-carry idea aside.

The flip side of more national programming is less local programming. In the early 1990s, for example, Houston's KPFT dumped most of its locally produced talk shows in favor of syndicated news and "Adult Album Alternative" music. Much of the latter is also syndicated: it's produced in Pennsylvania and beamed to Texas via satellite. Pacifica eventually cut back on national programming after the Malveaux debacle, but with such syndicated shows available, KPFT avoided a renaissance of localism.

Managers at Pacifica have long complained, with cause, that on-air volunteers had an improperly proprietary attitude toward their timeslots. In the words of Peter Franck, a former president of the Pacifica Foundation and no friend to the current regime, "There's a tacit, very strong agreement amongst the staff, 'You don't challenge my lock on this half-hour, I won't challenge your competence.'"[60] Unfortunately, when the new guard started cleaning house, their decisions seemed to have less to do with competence than with preppifying Pacifica's image. Longstanding programs devoted to unusual music or radical commentary were axed, making room for bad imitations of NPR, bad imitations of commercial radio, and—of course—those satellite feeds.

• *An increasingly top-heavy bureaucracy.* In 1989, the Pacifica National Office consisted of one half-time and three full-time workers. In February 1999, staffer Larry Bensky informed the foundation board that there were "no fewer than 13 employees. Moreover, the longest term of employment of anyone in this office is a year and a half. Everyone else is new, or there are vacant positions waiting to be hired."[61]

The number of national programming employees, meanwhile, jumped from three and a half to ten. But after the Malveaux affair, the amount of national programming declined: what was half a day in 1989 was just 105 minutes when Bensky spoke to the board—and fell still further later that year, after Bensky's own show was canceled.

"For the Pacifica national programming staff, our product is our justification," Bensky argued. "But what is the justification for the proliferation of Pacifica's expensive, secretive administrative bureaucracy? Aside from empire-building, there is none. Moreover, this useless administration is organized in a top-down, one-way manner [that is] completely inappropriate for a progressive organization founded on anti-authoritarian ideals."[62]

This authoritarian structure replicated itself in the individual stations, with managers Mark Schubb of KPFK, Garland Ganter of KPFT, and Valerie Van Isler of WBAI getting particularly low marks for their dictatorial styles. In New York, this was offset by a strong union. The Los Angeles and Houston stations were not so lucky.

• *Secretive management.* Pacifica refused to open its books to serious public scrutiny, even as it began taking more money from foundations

and spending more on consultants. At the same time, its finance committee—and its national board—took to meeting behind closed doors.

In 1995, Brian McConville of the CPB started to investigate whether
the board's closed "retreats" violated the open-meetings requirement
imposed on stations that receive federal funds. A few weeks later, he
was fired. In 1996, Take Back KPFA, a group of concerned listeners and
former programmers, asked the CPB to reopen the inquiry, and, after a
period of inactivity, agent Mike Donovan did so. In February 1997, before he could complete his audit, he, too, was dismissed.

Finally, on April 9, Inspector General Armando Arvizu released a
report. Arvizu decided that, for the most part, Pacifica personnel did
not deliberate on foundation business at their retreats; therefore, he concluded, those were legal. Otherwise, he came down hard on the network, declaring that its closed board meetings violated the law. "The
public was not being offered the opportunity to observe Board of Directors deliberations," wrote Arvizu, "as all board sessions were being
held in closed session, with the exception of one hour for Public Comments." Pacifica was also judged guilty of giving insufficient advance
notice of the meetings. Furthermore, the network's local advisory
boards "were not being provided with the autonomy they needed to
perform their functions."[63]

Vindication? Morally, yes; legally, no. On May 19, 1997, the CPB
board held a public meeting, putatively to determine how it would
react to its auditor's report. Jack O'Dell spoke on behalf of Pacifica;
Jeffrey Blankfort spoke on behalf of Take Back KPFA. But the CPB had
already decided what it would do: in a statement drafted *before* the
meeting, it declared that it saw no reason to reduce or eliminate KPFA's
subsidy. Rather than accept that the network's board meetings were improper, it would produce new open-meetings guidelines. In effect, the
CPB rejected its inspector general's report.

It added that it "wishes to commend Pacifica for actions taken in recent years to strengthen and improve operations and programming."[64]

This all came to a head in 1999, just as the network was preparing to celebrate its fiftieth anniversary. On February 28, the national board met in
Berkeley and approved a change to its bylaws that, by banning members of stations' local advisory boards from serving on the national
board, in effect removed the lower rungs from any role in guiding net-

work policy. Pacifica's governing directorate was now a completely self-selecting body.

Here again, one could see the hand of the Corporation for Public Broadcasting. The centralists had already tried to push this change through once, and they knew the network's dissidents would oppose them on the next attempt. So, late in 1998, just before her reign atop the network was scheduled to end, Pat Scott wrote to CPB president Robert Coonrod, asking him whether Pacifica's internal organization violated any regulations. Thus prompted, he replied that it "appears to be at variance" with the rules.[65] It wasn't clear that this was actually the case—the rules in question were in fact partly modeled on Pacifica's structure—and in any event, there were several alternate systems that would have fit the CPB's strictures without giving more power to the national board. Nonetheless, the network treated Coonrod's letter as gospel.

The dissidents spread the word about what was happening, and many of them came to the board meeting in Berkeley to speak against the change. At that point, several board members still weren't sure whether the new bylaw was a good idea; many felt that they should table the motion and look for other ways to bring the board within the law, if indeed it was violating federal rules. But the centralists had another card to play. At the last minute, the CPB sent Pacifica another letter. The new missive suggested that the government might have to cut off all subsidies to Pacifica in mid-March (that is, almost immediately) if it didn't change its structure before then (that is, at that very meeting). *That* scared the doubters into line.

It was a surreal atmosphere: Pacifica insisted on an intense police presence, and the board chair, Mary Frances Berry, was constantly accompanied by an armed bodyguard. The board approved the rule change, voting before it listened to public comments on what to do. Berry left the room well before the comment session was done. The coup seemed complete.

But was it? In New York, WBAI's staff spoke constantly about the changes and asked listeners to protest the takeover. And on March 31, 1999, the network's new executive director—Healthy Station Project cofounder Lynn Chadwick—fired KPFA manager Nicole Sawaya, sparking a revolt in Berkeley.

Sawaya was, by all accounts, KPFA's most popular manager in a long time. A veteran of National Public Radio, Sawaya had come to a station riven by purges and infighting and had somehow put herself on good terms with all the splintered factions. Staff morale improved dramatically, and so, according to many listeners' testimony, did the quality of the station's programming. Sawaya was also, however, an *independent* manager, one willing to defy orders from Pacifica central.

Chadwick consistently refused to discuss why Nicole was terminated. (Indeed, she wouldn't even admit that she had fired the woman, preferring the sophistry that Sawaya's "contract was not renewed.") But Errol Maitland, a member of WBAI's local advisory board, claims to have inadvertently walked in on Pacifica's executive committee during the board's February meeting in Berkeley. According to Maitland, Chadwick was demanding that Sawaya be fired for criticizing the network's management; the others present, including Berry, seemed to agree. At this point, Maitland says, someone noticed him, and Berry's bodyguard escorted him from the room. He immediately told this story to several dissident activists, one of whom later relayed it to me. It is thus unlikely that he made up the tale, since he was telling it before Sawaya was actually fired.

In any event, KPFA responded to the dismissal angrily and immediately, and constantly protested it over the air. The sleeping staff had awakened: virtually every host demanded that Sawaya be reinstated, and several devoted their shows to more indepth discussions of Pacifica's ongoing decay. Chadwick and Berry initially allowed the protests to persist, then began firing hosts, starting with Larry Bensky. Chadwick sent armed guards to occupy the station, where they promptly took to overbearing, intimidating, and sometimes foolish behavior. (At one point they barred two members of the singing group SoVoSó, who had been scheduled to perform live on the air, from entering the studio. Evidently, it would have broken security to host more than one guest at once.) Network spokeswoman Ellen Fabbri asserted that the guards were there to protect the managers, whom she claimed had received death threats; she also noted—constantly—that shots had been fired into Chadwick's office the night Nicole Sawaya was dismissed. The dissidents (and most outside observers) were skeptical, noting that the guards seemed more interested in intimidation than in protection.

The staff enjoyed tremendous local support, and protesters set up camp outside the station. Soon, Chadwick was demanding that the Berkeley police arrest the demonstrators—and when the cops initially proved reluctant, she forced the issue with a citizen's arrest. Later that week, Joe Brann, a high-ranking officer at the Justice Department, called Berkeley Police Chief D. E. Butler to ask why his force wasn't pursuing the arrests more aggressively. Brann also mentioned that Attorney General Janet Reno had asked him to make the inquiry.

We never learned, incidentally, who fired those shots at Chadwick's office. It could have been one of the dissidents: as with any large radical movement, the Pacifica protests attracted its share of hotheads and flaky fringe characters. It also could have been a random passerby, and, for all anyone knew, it could have been Chadwick herself. The network brass never missed a chance to mention the gunshots, and for all their use of the passive voice ("shots were fired"), they were clearly implying that a dissident was responsible, that the dissident movement was filled with violent nuts, and that management, by contrast, was the stable, responsible side of the dispute. Fabbri repeatedly claimed that the police were investigating the incident as an attempted homicide, even after the cops denied this.

Sawaya's dismissal came right before one of the station's regular fund drives, prompting a crisis of conscience among the staffers. They finally decided to go ahead with the drive but to ask listeners to make their pledges "under protest," as a sign that the larger community stood with KPFA and against Pacifica. The result was one of the station's most profitable fundraisers ever, taking in around $605,000. Over six-sevenths of the pledges came with protests attached.

Then Pacifica changed the access code to a phone extension the station had set up to answer questions about pledging, erased the staff's message, and inserted one of its own. The new recording told callers that "we cannot accept any contributions that require specific operational demands be met" and that "if you would like to request a refund of your contribution at this time, please leave your name, your address, the amount of your pledge, and your member identification number. . . . That will provide us the opportunity to refund your money as quickly as possible."[66] A Pacifica press release of May 23 underlined the point, claiming that "since its inception" the foundation had always "refused sponsorships and funding to which any conditions are attached" and that this category would include a "pledge under protest."[67]

This was a baldfaced lie. There is a substantial difference between a general protest and a "specific operational demand." Furthermore, Pacifica *has* accepted funds with conditions attached. As Matthew Lasar noted, "KPFA would not exist if it weren't for conditional funds. In 1946 the Pacifica Foundation established a 'radio establishment fund' that solicited donations that would become active only after the foundation received a . . . license." He adds: "One does not have to go back 50 years to question Pacifica's historical claim of refusing conditional funds. Did the Foundation not just reorganize its governing board structure based on the claim that it was out of sync with the Corporation for Public Broadcasting's conditions for funding?"[68]

Odder still: even as it encouraged its listener-sponsors to withhold their pledges, the foundation was hemorrhaging money—about $397,000 in "security" costs, and, later, about $58,000 for Fineman and Associates, the top-end P.R. firm it hired after it became clear that Fabbri had lost all her credibility. Was Pacifica *trying* to bankrupt itself?

Some thought it was. A popular conspiracy theory noted that both KPFA and WBAI were located on the commercial band and that their licenses were very valuable. Those two stations also had the network's most recalcitrant staffs. Selling one or both stations would bring the board a lot of money, and would cut a lot of dissidents loose, too. But it would be very hard to get away with selling either outlet, politically speaking—unless, perhaps, the foundation faced a financial crisis so severe that such a sale was the only way to survive.

Well, there were a lot of conspiracy theories floating around the dissident movement, some of them reasonable and some of them ridiculous. As time passed, this one sounded less silly: in July, it became clear that, whatever else might be going on, Pacifica was considering a station sale. On July 9, Michael Palmer, a Houston real estate developer who for some reason sat on the national board, wrote a memo to Mary Frances Berry. In a stroke of strange luck, he then sent it accidentally to Andrea Buffa, a critic of Pacifica whose electronic address happens to be similar to Berry's. I reprint the e-mail in full:

> Hello Dr. Berry,
>
> I salute your fortitude in scheduling a news conference opportunity in the beloved Bay Area regarding one of the most pressing issues of our time. . . . .
>
> But seriously, I was under the impression there was support in the proper quarters, and a definite majority, for shutting down that unit and re-programming immediately. Has that changed? Is there consensus among the national staff that anything other than that is

acceptable/bearable? I recall Cheryl saying that the national staff wanted to know with certitude that they supported 100% by the Board in whatever direction was taken; what direction is being taken?

As an update for you and Lynn I spoke with the only radio broker I know last week and his research shows $750,000–$1.25m for KPFB [a "repeater" station that rebroadcasts KPFA's signal]. There would be a very "shallow pool" of buyers for a repeater signal such as this and it would be difficult to do a marketing effort quietly due to the shortage of buyers. So there is no profound latent value to that asset. The primary signal [i.e., KPFA] would lend itself to a quiet marketing scenario of discreet presentation to logical and qualified buyers. This is the best radio market in history and while public companies may see a dilutive effect from a sale (due to the approximate 12 month repositioning effort needed), they would still be aggressive for such a signal. Private media companies would be the most aggressive in terms of price, which he thinks could be in the $65–75m range depending on various aspects of a deal. It would be possible to acquire other signals in the area, possibly more than one, to re-establish operations, but it could take a few years to complete if we want to maximize proceeds from the initial license transfer, or leave only $10–20m in arbitrage gain when purchase(s) is complete. None of this reflects tax consequences. This broker, just like any other that would undertake such an effort, would need certain agreements in place prior to starting.

Mary I think any such transfer we would ever consider requires significant analysis, not so much regarding a decision to go forward, but how to best undertake the effort and to deploy the resulting capital with the least amount of tax, legal and social disruption. I believe the Finance Committee will undertake a close review of the Audigraphics data provided recently to determine what it is costing us per listener, per subscriber, per market, per hour of programming . . . in order give [sic] the Executive Director and the General Managers benchmarks for improvement. Even with that data my feeling is that a more beneficial disposition would be of the New York signal as there is a smaller subscriber base without the long and emotional history as the Bay Area, far more associated value, a similarly dysfunctional staff though far less effective and an overall better opportunity to redefine Pacifica going forward. It is simply the more strategic asset.

With this in mind I would encourage frank description of the realities of the media environment we operate in and of Pacifica's available resources to participate and have impact in the evolving media world. The Executive Committee, at a minimum, should have access to experts (whether from Wall Street, NPR/CPB, Microsoft or otherwise) to get a strong reality check (me included) about radio and Pacifica's position in it so that informed decisions can be made. My feeling is that we are experiencing a slow financial death which is having the normal emotional outbursts commensurate with such a disease. We will continually experience similar events, in fact we have been experiencing similar events over the past several years, primarily because we are not self supporting through subscriber contributions and have a self imposed constraint on asset redeployment that leaves us cash starved at a time when our industry is being propelled in new directions, each requiring capital outlays of consequence. We're boxed in at our own will. This board needs to be educated, quickly, and to take action that will be far more controversial that [sic] the KPFA situation. How can we get there?

So, now I've exhaled more than I should, but you know where I'm at. Let's do something.

MDP[69]

Buffa released the intercepted e-mail to the world, and, after an embarrassed silence, Fabbri confirmed that Michael Palmer had written it. She quickly added that Palmer spoke only for himself, that he had investigated the possible sales at his own initiative, and that Pacifica would not sell any stations. Readers can decide for themselves whether Palmer's letter feels like the words of a man acting entirely on his own. Or they can examine the testimony of Pete Bramson, a member of the national board, who held a press conference in Berkeley on July 28, 1999.

"Pacifica Board Chair Mary Frances Berry has repeatedly said during these past several weeks that she has no intention of selling KPFA," Bramson told the crowd.

That's not true. During a telephone conference call yesterday, Pacifica Board Vice Chair David Acosta . . . proposed taking out a five million dollar loan against the value of the KPFA license. That could happen quickly. He proposed selling the KPFA frequency, which has an estimated value of 65 to 75 million dollars. That would take longer to accomplish. With a small portion of the proceeds of the sale of KPFA, Acosta proposed that Pacifica set up another Northern California station—perhaps in Palo Alto, which Mary Berry said might be a friendlier city than Berkeley.[70]

Then there's the testimony of Mimi Rosenberg, who'd worked at WBAI since the 1960s. About a month after Bramson's press conference, Mimi stopped by her station to drop off a tape and was surprised to find Berry there, engaged in a bizarre discussion with a roomful of staffers. Berry was making a terrible impression—at one point she self-righteously asked whether the others in the room were "aware of the diversity of populations that exist in the New York area,"[71] apparently oblivious to the fact that about 90 percent of the people present were not white. (Berry had taken to insisting, against all standards of logic and evidence, that the conflict's underlying issue was her alleged effort to "diversify" Pacifica's audience.) But the strangest moment came when Berry asked what people thought of selling KPFA, or WBAI, or both, and using the proceeds to buy a string of black stations in the South. ("A kind of black NPR," another New York staffer told the online magazine *Salon*. "Laudable, but to cannibalize Pacifica with its own 50-year history and listeners? She should go out and build that network on her own and see how hard it is!")[72]

What about Palmer's "impression" that there was "support in the proper quarters" for "shutting down" KPFA "and re-programming immediately"? Jump to July 13, when KPFA reporter Dennis Bernstein played parts of a press conference about the conflict on his show. Garland Ganter—the manager of the Houston station, whom Berry and company had temporarily brought to Berkeley—stopped the tape, replaced it with a recording of an old speech, and told Bernstein to leave the building. Dennis instead walked to the station newsroom, on the grounds that such censorship was a legitimate story; the guards pursued him, and news anchor Mark Mericle turned on the studio mikes, letting listeners hear Bernstein yelling fearfully and getting dragged away. Then the guards took over the station altogether, and KPFA's entire staff was put on "administrative leave" and locked out of the building. This wasn't a spontaneous response to the day's events: Pacifica had changed the door codes several days before, had sent for the tapes it played in place of the regular programming, and had already changed its official mailing address to a post office box. After several days of playing old speeches, some by people who fiercely objected to being used as unwitting scabs, Pacifica replaced the tapes with a live signal beamed in from a studio at one of its other outlets, apparently KPFT.[73] Meanwhile, the protesters did their own broadcasts via micro radio and the Internet. A lockout had begun.

It took seveteen days of escalating protests and escalating costs before Pacifica changed its tactics. It reopened the station and withdrew the guards, thus removing the focus of the media's attention, and told the staff they'd have six to twelve months to increase the station's ratings (and its audience's "diversity") before management might have to clamp down again. It ignored the protesters' other demands—to rehire Sawaya, for example—and it made this "offer" directly to the press, bypassing the staff's negotiating team.

The guards had wrecked the station, and it took several days to put the studios back in order before the staffers could return to the air. Pacifica had employed IPSA International, a security firm run by and filled with former agents of the FBI and other federal agencies; to this day, many of the station's reporters are concerned about what those former cops might have gleaned from the station's files, which included, among other things, information about reporters' confidential sources.

Meanwhile, members of three local advisory boards sued the network over the bylaw change passed back in February, making a strong case that the board had violated the California Corporations Code. (Pacifica, they argued, was supposed to let the local boards vote on the change, too.) While that case remains pending, more and more dissidents are demanding that Pacifica devolve its power, replace its board, and stop taking money from the Corporation for Public Broadcasting.

Chadwick and Berry resigned the next year, but the network remained in the hands of the centralizers. When the board met again, in February 2000, it listened once more to a report from David Giovannoni. The consultant told them that, though "several enlightened leaders within Pacifica have attempted to rejuvenate its grand mission by applying proven broadcasting practices," they had been just "sporadically successful," a result he blamed on the rebellion within the network. Pacifica, he reported, had "lost its influence"; whatever the Scotts and Chadwicks and Berrys had accomplished was "too little too late." If they wanted to make an impact, he concluded, they might think about getting into the Internet.[74]

From management's point of view, Giovannoni's pessimism may have made sense. Pacifica's plans to centralize the network's programming had failed completely, with fewer hours of national programs being aired each week than ten years before. The Berkeley station, once apparently pacified by Pat Scott, was now united in—if nothing else— its distrust for and disaffection from the national network. New York's outlet also seemed uncontrollable. The coup had been a failure.

And yet: the coup had been a success. The national board had managed to change its bylaws and was now immune to local interference; thus shielded, it was busy packing itself with Michael Palmer–style corporate executives. The only real challenge to its power were three lawsuits protesting the bylaw changes, one filed by listeners, one by the disenfranchised local advisory boards, and one by dissident members of the national board. They were a real threat, but they were the final threat. No other lawful force could break the new guard's rule.

Meanwhile, the reporters' strike dragged on. The network brass started harassing Amy Goodman, the BAI-based host of the nationally distributed *Democracy Now!*, Pacifica's best-known, most respected, and most visibly radical program—demanding, for example, that she clear her show topics with management a week before production. And late in 2000, Pacifica fired WBAI chief Valerie Van Isler. Many were glad to see her go: she was a terrible manager, and had played a significant role in fighting the station's union. But many were also concerned that the network was stepping on the station's autonomy, especially when the new interim manager, Utrice Leid, fired some of Van Isler's supporters, changed the station locks, launched her own attacks on Amy Goodman, and then, as the station's battles spilled into the public, told the staff that they weren't allowed to talk about the changes on the air.

The war arguably reached its nadir in February 2001, when the network founded by anarchists and raised by civil libertarians threatened to call on the government—the *government*—to censor its opponents. Sounding more like hired mouthpieces for a *Fortune* 500 firm than like attorneys for an alternative radio network, Pacifica's lawyers wrote to four dissident websites—freewpfw.org, wbaifree.org, wbai.net, and savepacifica.net—accusing them of appropriating the network's trademarks (as though anyone could mistake the rebel pages for official Pacifica sites) and telling them to abandon their domain names or face legal action.

And that's where things stand as this book goes to press. The battle is not yet over, and one can only hope that ten years from now there will still be a Pacifica worth fighting over.

If nothing else, the Pacifica fracas should remind us of the importance of structure, of building a sound foundation that will allow free-spirited radio to thrive. In the short history of community broadcasting, there have been as many station structures as there have been stations—even more, really, since those stations inevitably change form over time. Yet most of these can be fit, if not always easily, into six rough categories:

The Benign Dictatorship. KRAB fit this model for its first six years. Lorenzo Milam founded the station with a particular vision in mind, and he enforced that vision. Few objected, because (a) he'd started the station, after all; (b) he kept it afloat financially; and (c) he had a tolerant and diverse concept of what it should broadcast, generally trusting talented programmers to make their own decisions. Milam may have scolded his volunteers from time to time, but he knew better than to govern with a sledgehammer.

The trouble with benign dictatorships is that they can degenerate into category two:

The Malign Dictatorship. If the benign dictator governs like a Taoist sage, the malign dictator governs like Idi Amin. Put another way: if the benign dictator governs like Lorenzo Milam, the malign dictator governs like Robert Friede.

Friede was, for all his faults, a man who believed in volunteer-driven radio. When he left KRAB and power shifted to the Jack Straw board, the station adopted our third structural form:

The Monstrous Bureaucracy. Typical features include a preference for day-to-day governance by paid staff over governance by volunteers, an overreliance on grant money, and, often, a canned style of programming. The CPB has traditionally pushed this model, much of the NFCB has embraced it, and Pacifica's national board is firmly wedded to it. Many would dispute that such stations are community-radio outlets at all; I mention them here only because they usually contain at least some shows that maintain their former spirit, and because they are often embroiled in conflicts with listeners and volunteers who want to bring them back to their roots.

It is possible, by the way, to rescue a station from this fate. Both Madison's WORT and Portland's KBOO, among others, have fended off the bureaucracy bug. WORT, in particular, exemplifies our next genus:

The Benign Democracy. These stations are governed by elected bodies; the voting community consists of the volunteers, the listener-sponsors, or some combination thereof. Besides WORT and other legal outlets, this model is in place at many pirate stations.

Unfortunately, a benign democracy can sometimes devolve into our fifth category:

The Malign Democracy. This group can be further divided into two subcategories, *The Time-Brokered Snoozefest* and *The Civil War.*

In commercial radio, time brokering is the practice of selling pieces of one's programming schedule, resulting in an operation that sounds like a gaggle of separate stations sharing the same frequency. In the community-radio equivalent, there's one hour for the Spanish-speaking Trotskyists and one for the Episcopalian lesbians and one for the left-handed triskaidekaphobes, but little sense that anyone listens to anyone else and little sense that tired shows will ever be removed from the air.

As for civil wars, a recent example (but not, alas, the only one) is Austin's KOOP, formerly a shining model for radio's small-d democrats. The problem here, I stress, was not an excess of democracy, but rather an excess of internal problems that democracy was not sufficient to cure.

It is the fear of becoming a malign democracy that often prompts a station to take the bureaucratic or dictatorial route. Consider KRAB's successor, KSER. During my time as a volunteer there, the station was governed on the benign-dictatorship model. My boss didn't dislike democracy, but he did have some pragmatic fears of it: he often recounted to me the tale of a station where some people were so protective of their timeslots that, during one tense meeting, someone pulled a knife.

Let us conclude on a happier note:

The Anarchic Meritocracy. This term was coined by Des Preston, a colleague at my college station. It is more an ideal form than a living example, but one can find elements of it in various stations of the present and past. KDNA was basically a benign dictatorship: Lansman owned the station and therefore reserved the right to step in and ban drugs from the premises. But it was mostly governed, you'll recall, by an informal collective. How did one become a part of this group? By being at the studios almost every day. How did one make one's opinions count? By doing a good job.

Kind Radio was another dictatorship in theory that tended toward anarcho-meritocracy in practice. Joe Ptak and Zeal Stefanoff set the schedule and ultimately called the shots, but they gave their hosts wide latitude on the air, and they preferred to defuse conflicts by buying the troublemakers some beer than by cracking down. Kind was a community station in the most literal sense: it was an almost organic expression of much of the San Marcos community, with order maintained through informal checks and balances rather than a formal constitution.

At my college station, we had our share of internal conflicts, would-be homogenizers, self-inflicted injustices, and, of course, interference from the university administration. But we also had two great checks on any empire builder's ambitions. One was the simple fact that most staffers were students and thus would be gone in a few years—a somewhat solid bulwark against reformers with overly grand designs. The other was the presence of knowledgeable nonstudents—not college officials, but community volunteers. These people didn't govern the organization (though some took on administrative jobs). They served as elders, a living memory of the outlet's past. This was especially useful whenever the university tried to assert more control over the station's structure or programming. With other campus groups, the college could afford to bide its time, aware that the next generation of students would be unaware of the administration's goals and methods. Our nonstudents, however, kept us apprised of the station's past battles. (Not surprisingly, one of the administration's favorite demands was that we get rid of our nonstudent DJs.)

A great community radio station eschews bureaucracy, gives its volunteers wide latitude, and relies on its listeners for most of its funds. Its shows are neither standardized into a predictable sound nor rigidly balkanized from one another. Instead, a day's programs sound like an enormous conversation, where hosts comment on one another's shows, DJs mix musical genres, and listeners feel like they're part of the family. It is radio as diverse, messy, and alive as the community it reflects.

There is no easy formula for creating such a place. The best guarantee I know is simply open entry—for the government to stop reserving most of its radio licenses for corporate giants and NPR, and instead allow more small, locally based operations to enter the airwaves, to experiment with different forms, to find what works for them, and, if need be, to let dissidents split off and start their own stations.

As for Pacifica, the most important demand—more necessary even than disentangling it from the federal purse—is to stop its march toward rule by a centralized, self-selecting board and to devolve power from the national network back to its five constituent stations. Community radio, after all, should be rooted in actual communities.

7

Free Radio Abroad

Dirty communists, we're going to make you pay dearly for this radio station. We know who you are.

—Anonymous caller to Radio Alice

THE INSURRECTION ERUPTED on March 2, 1977.

It had actually begun a few months before, a low-key campaign against a plan to overhaul Italy's system of higher education. Gradually, it had acquired a strange momentum, as though it were searching for excuses to explode. Protesters occupied the University of Rome, then campuses in Palermo, Naples, Florence, Torino, Bologna. Student radicals mingled with full- and part-time workers, with the unemployed, even with juvenile delinquents. The original pretexts for the occupations grew foggy. Anyone could be protesting anything, and some were protesting everything.

In Bologna, the police closed in. The atmosphere tensed. On March 2, a cop shot a demonstrator. The occupation became a riot, spreading quickly into the city's streets and alleyways. Windows were broken, restaurants ransacked, a gunshop looted.

For many Italians, the oddest thing about the riots was where they took place. Bologna was Communist territory, governed by a solidly Red set; it had been the party's showcase city since 1945. By the mid-'70s, its leaders' rhetoric had taken stock of the New Left's anti-authoritarian streak: urban officials now invoked cooperatives and self-management and dismantling institutions, not bureaucracy and planning and statism. But in practice, they had rejected the new decentralism as well as the old Stalinism. The local Communists had developed a cozy relationship with the employers to whom they were allegedly opposed; more and more, their role seemed to be to discipline labor, not to rouse it. Young radicals, in turn, dismissed the traditional left, turning instead

172

to direct action: wildcat strikes, squatting in abandoned buildings, even mass shoplifting. They soon developed their own media as well, including a very strange station in Bologna called Radio Alice.

Alice took its name from the heroine of *Through the Looking Glass*, and often patterned its programming on Lewis Carroll's world as well. "Let's allow holes to grow," the station collective once announced; "let's not fear orifices, let's fall into them and pass on elsewhere. *Wonderland*."[1] Like Lorenzo Milam, Alice was fascinated by dead air, broadcasting silence so that listeners might "pass beyond the mirror of language."[2] Less esoteric but no less radical were its live telephone reports from street demonstrations, programs that kicked down the boundaries between listener and broadcaster, medium and experience.

Which brings us to that riot in March 1977. Alice was there, covering the melee—or, perhaps, allowing the melee to cover itself. Wherever police attacked, someone would grab a phone, call the studio, and go on the air. Alice became the protesters' communication system, a giant revolutionary Citizens Band, a portal open to any listener who wanted to join the revolt. The station was an extension of the demonstration, and the demonstration an extension of the station—a rhizomatic beast that slid in and out of the streets and ether of Red Bologna, tangling with the authorities and always getting away.

As the smoke cleared, the Communists charged the station with inciting the riot. Armed officers smashed into the studio to shut it down. Alice broadcast that, too. "They are pointing machine guns at us," listeners heard, heavy footsteps in the background. "Our hands are in the air. . . ."[3]

Needless to say, the United States and Italy have very different histories in radio as in other areas. In America, the state socialized the airwaves on behalf of big business. In Italy, and most other countries, the state took the more direct route of socializing the airwaves on behalf of itself.

The British government, for example, seized that nation's spectrum in 1922, defending its policy with the eccentric argument that a broadcast was basically a telegram, and the telegraph system, after all, was already run by the state. As usual, a more direct motive lurked behind the official rhetoric. The British establishment had seen the "chaos" (that is, freedom) of the early American ether, and it didn't want anything like that taking root in fair Albion.

Some countries did pass through a phase akin to America's early years. In Switzerland, as in the United States, the first broadcasters were hams. By 1922, the loose network of amateurs had evolved into a more complex web of radio clubs and radio societies, member-financed associations that ran local stations. But the central government gradually invaded the airwaves, and soon the amateur tradition was forgotten. In 1922, the state started licensing stations. In 1924, it started subsidizing them. In 1931, it formed the centralized Swiss Broadcasting Corporation. By the '60s, despite Switzerland's long tradition of local direct democracy, the SBC's schedule was overwhelmingly devoted to national and international programs. Local radio simply wasn't part of the plan—and *private* radio was unthinkable.

Similar stories unfolded all over Europe; indeed, all over the world. Nation after nation adopted a tightly centralized broadcasting system, with private or community-based competition tightly regulated, if not banned outright. But in the '60s and '70s, two rebellious waves crashed across Western Europe, cracking the state's monopoly. First there were the offshore broadcasters, pirates pursuing profits. Then came the *radios libres*, anarchists pursuing revolution.

The first pirate to broadcast from international waters was actually an American operation, more or less. RXKR—licensed, like the floating casino from which it transmitted, by the Republic of Panama—started pumping popular music and commercials into southern California in May 1933. And not just to California: blessed with a high-powered transmitter and unconcerned with the spectrum rights of others, the ship's shows could be heard everywhere from Hawaii to northeastern Canada, running roughshod over other stations' signals in the process. The U.S. government did little to stop the violations, and even after Panama yanked its license, RXKR continued to operate, telling mainland stations that it would stop interfering with their signals only if they ponied up a substantial ransom. That proved too much for Washington. Ignoring the rule of law, ripping off small stations' frequencies, demanding heavy fees from anyone who wished to broadcast unmolested . . . *those* were the Federal Radio Commission's jobs! In August 1933, the Coast Guard towed RXKR into Los Angeles Harbor, shutting the station down for good.

The story of offshore radio properly begins with Per Jansen and Borge Agerskov, two Danes who defied their nation's post office (which regulated such things) and began broadcasting from a small fishing boat in 1958 under the name Radio Mercur. The station was financed by a Danish silverware merchant; its ship was registered, like RXKR's, in Panama, though that nation soon withdrew its sanction. Mercur's programs proved popular, and it soon could be heard in southern Sweden as well as Denmark. Other aquatic stations—Radio Veronica, Radio Nord, Radio Syd—soon followed its example, transmitting illicit signals to Holland, Belgium, Denmark, Sweden, and, eventually, the United Kingdom. The affected governments, stung not only by the threat to their monopolies but by the fact that so many listeners obviously preferred the pirates' programs, started searching for ways to shut the ocean broadcasters down. In 1962, the Danish government found one. International waters lay outside its jurisdiction, it conceded, but Danish citizens did not. Henceforth, it decreed, no resident of Denmark could work for—or advertise on—an unlicensed offshore station.

That same year, Denmark and Sweden agreed to restrict pirate vessels' access to fuel and provisions. Denmark began pressuring countries not to license the broadcasters' ships. And an onboard murder gave the Danish police an opportunity to board Radio Mercur and shut that particular pirate down directly.

For the English-speaking world, the new era began on Easter Sunday 1964, when a twenty-three-year-old Irishman named Ronan O'Rahilly launched Radio Caroline. In July, O'Rahilly merged his operation with a rival's, Allan Crawford's Radio Atlanta.[4] The Gael's outfit became Radio Caroline North; the former Radio Atlanta became Radio Caroline South. Between them, they bombarded Britain with the pop music the BBC had been doing its best to ignore. They also observed the cozy relations that had developed between the big record companies and the broadcast monopolists, and went out of their way to play music from independent labels. More stations soon followed the Carolines into northern European waters, transmitting not just rock 'n' roll but middle-of-the-road pop, classical music, and talk shows. Some of the pirates were rather eccentric: the infamous Radio Sutch, for example, was run by the lavender-caped Screaming Lord Sutch, a singing ex-plumber who never appeared in public unless bedecked in tights and a Viking helmet, a cutlass in his hand. But most were relatively sedate, and many were almost as tightly formatted as American radio. Radio Nord, in fact, was owned in part by Gordon McLendon. Two typically restrictive stations broadcast from aboard the *Olga Patricia,* rechristened the *Laissez Faire*: Radio England, which had a Top Forty format, and Britain Radio, which offered easy listening.

Yet even the most formatted pirates were offering things that couldn't be found elsewhere on the British dial, and many Britons who came of age in the 1960s look back to the offshore era as a golden age. Also pleased, though for different reasons, were several evangelical Christians, particularly the Seventh-Day Adventists: the official broadcasters weren't willing to sell them airtime, but the pirates were. Many musicians also appreciated the exposure: the Who's 1967 album *The Who Sell Out* was, among other things, a tribute to the pirates. (The record companies were less sanguine, as the offshore stations paid nothing for the songs they broadcast. Some, however, saw the airplay as free advertising, and adopted the Who's more enlightened attitude.)

The government increased its broadcast hours and began playing more recorded music, transparent efforts to compete with the privateers. Then it began looking for more forcible ways to drive its competitors from the air. Behind closed doors, officials considered jamming the pirates' signals; the Ministry of Defence even proposed to "blow them up"—or, rather, to blow up some aquatic platforms the pirates were using. It also suggested putting "noxious substances on the platforms to render them uninhabitable."[5] But the offshore stations were growing steadily more popular: a 1966 survey showed that about one in five people had listened to Radio London in the past week and one in six to Radio Caroline—and that one in two Scots had tuned to Radio Scotland.[6] And so, as one postmaster-general after another called for action against the pirates, the politicians held them back uneasily. Anger was growing in Westminster, a rage stoked by many pirates' overt antipathy to the Labour government. But the prime minister, Harold Wilson, feared the public reaction a war on the broadcasters would bring, and the state held off acting until after the 1966 elections.

Labour's opponents took advantage of the impasse. Some Tories and Scottish Nationalists even bought ads on offshore programs, and Radio Caroline regularly attacked the governing party. Not that the pirates lacked enemies among the Tories. When one Conservative MP accused the broadcasters of "providing what people want," he didn't mean it as a compliment. "To some members of this House that is sound democracy," he warned. "It is not. It is pandering to populism."[7]

Finally, in 1967, Parliament passed the Marine Broadcasting Offenses Act. Like the Danish decrees of 1962, this law enjoined British citizens from aiding or abetting offshore broadcasters. Advertisers were emphatically included.

Most of the stations went off the air soon afterward. Radio Caroline South hobbled along, surviving in lesser form until 1980, when its ocean base, the *Mi Amigo,* sank in a storm. Even then, it managed to return to the air in 1983, helped along by mostly American advertisers recruited by Wolfman Jack. The new Caroline could be heard on shortwave as well as AM, and, even after its main transmitter went off the air in the early 1990s, it continued to broadcast via various European satellites. These days it's located on the Isle of Sheppey and can be caught locally—and legally—on the AM band. But that is a far cry from the seafaring powerhouse of earlier days.

Like any gray market, offshore broadcasting attracted its share of shady characters. The Radio Mercur murder was not an isolated crime; the writer Erwin Strauss notes that at least five deaths can be connected to offshore broadcasting in the '50s and '60s, "ranging from fairly clear-cut murder to circumstances that might be described as 'mysterious,'" along with several "acts of vandalism, armed invasion, and the like."[8] That does not justify the government's crackdown, of course: the authorities could have resolved the problem much more easily by simply establishing a legal market. The majority of pirates were not murderers or thieves, and those who were might not have been if faced with different legal incentives. Furthermore, as time passed, the ships began to reach agreements with one another, and even with onshore stations; the violence consequently declined. With no overarching authority, the Dutch pirates worked out a reasonable set of turf rights. War simply turned out to be less profitable than peace.

About a decade later, the second wave of pirates arrived. Land based and devoted to radical politics, these broadcasters emerged not from the commercial sector but from the Italian left.

The '70s were to Italy as the '60s were to the United States, only more so. In the U.S., many may have thought the nation lay on the verge of revolution, but that was a delusion, believed only by those who most desperately wanted (or desperately didn't want) an uprising to take place. In Italy, by contrast, the forces let loose in 1968 seemed, for a decade, to seize the entire country. There were wildcat strikes in the factories, demonstrations on the campuses, backyard rebellions in the neighborhoods, feminist revolts everywhere—and, alarmingly, a sudden rise in terrorism, not just on the left but on the right.[9] Right-wing terror seemed to provoke little official hysteria, perhaps because it was harder to link it to the more peaceful dissenters; only one Italian neofascist was ever imprisoned for any terrorist crime. But left-wing terror, or the specter of it, would eventually bring the revolt to an end. After the ferment reached a peak in '77 and '78, the state retaliated with a massive crackdown in 1979, arresting more than fifteen hundred dissidents and, without credible evidence, charging them all with responsibility for the terrorist campaign. Coupled with a long string of police abuses, those arrests reveal that the grandest terrorist organization in Italy was the Italian state.

With the arrests of 1979, the rebellious decade finally quieted. The clampdown targeted Autonomy, a diffuse archipelago of radicals whose skepticism toward labor relations had evolved into a skepticism toward labor itself. Government prosecutors and propagandists painted Autonomy as the mass wing of the Red Brigades—in one British journalist's words, "the principal recruiting ground for the armed struggle."[10] This was clearly false. The autonomists were never a firm, unified organization, and they often differed radically among themselves (though almost all denounced the Red Brigades). Some were little more than thugs, enforcing their political will with blunt instruments and heavy sacks. Autonomy also included its share of bombastic, jargon-spewing Leninist ideologues.

But the movement's general thrust was anarchistic. Its prime theorist was Antonio Negri, a maverick Marxist who believed that the working class was no longer confined to the factory. Society itself, he proposed, was becoming a "factory without walls," in which every kind of labor, from service jobs to housework, was a part of the circuits of capital. Everyday life—health, shelter, recreation, culture—was coming under capital's control; industrial rules were intruding into every sphere, replacing the "mass worker" of the factory with a "socialized worker" who labored in all places, at all times. The autonomists eschewed traditional socialist demands for nationalization. Instead, they called for "autovalorization," Negri's favorite term for collective self-organization. Such activity, he argued, already takes place: workers naturally tend to resist the discipline that is imposed on them, and to carve out space and time in which to act independently.

This is not the place to examine the autonomists' specific claims or their often torturous efforts to fit their ideas into Marxist economic theory. I am not a Marxist, and I don't really care whether or how any of this fits the arguments in *Das Kapital*. What's interesting to me is how much the hyperrational order the autonomists denounced—a bureaucratic world in which informal arrangements are transformed into professional services and industrial commodities—resembles the technocratic dreams of the Progressive Era. Autovalorization, meanwhile, brings to mind the original network of ham operators. The amateurs built their web on their own, outside the corporation and the state. It grew out of their own experiences, and it was theirs, until the government expropriated it. Fifty years later, stations such as Radio Alice would try to construct consciously what came naturally to the hams: a medium with no strict line between producers and consumers.

At this point, Italy's broadcast media were the sole domain of RAI, a government-run network. RAI was born after World War II, but its roots go back to 1924 and Mussolini's Italian Radio Union. The Italian courts defended the government's monopoly even after fascism's fall, declaring in 1960 that "the State as monopoly-holder is placed institutionally in a more favorable position of objectivity and impartiality."[11] In practice, this "objectivity and impartiality" was a joke: RAI's bias toward the Christian Democrats was well known.

Naturally, the new dissidents were drawn to pirate radio, launching wildcat stations around the country. One, Radio Popolare, operated from a sparsely furnished row house in Milan, but its listenership extended well beyond the ghetto of radical activists.[12] From its dingy studios, it offered programming so diverse that relatively few other pirates, of any political stripe, took to the Milanese airwaves. Why bother, when they knew there'd be room for them on Radio Popolare?

Elsewhere, there was Controradio, governed by a collective of Florentine radicals. In the ferment of 1977 and 1978, the station was an open microphone for the left; after the Italian state's blitzkrieg against dissent, it began drifting toward music shows and a cleaner on-air sound, though its political side did not disappear. Controradio found itself in conflict with the Communists almost as much as with the Christian Democrats, raising Red ire for its support for the squatters' movement and the decriminalization of heroin, and its opposition to the Soviet invasion of Afghanistan.[13]

Rome's Radio Città Futura ("Radio City of the Future") took a more formal—and, some argued, less successful—approach to political speech, organizing lengthy on-air assemblies that often bogged down in factional in-fighting. More interesting were its book-review call-ins, an experiment in listener-driven cultural criticism; and its fake news stories, such as a prank report of a leftist coup d'etat, complete with phony sightings of tanks in the streets of Rome. Other programs ranged from live call-in songwriting sessions to in-depth documentaries. On a couple of occasions, police dropped by the station to dissuade its volunteers from organizing an antifascist march. Unbeknownst to the constables, their visits were broadcast for all of Rome to hear.

And then, of course, there was Radio Alice, born in February 1976. Alice, the brainchild of the philosopher-activist Franco "Bifo" Berardi, was radically populist in intent: it tried to open itself completely to popular participation, to merge itself with its listeners, to reflect them like a looking-glass—a looking-glass that, like the mirror in Carroll's book, was also a portal any listener could enter. In practice, it could be far more elitist. "It is dada," its governing collective once proclaimed, "that terrorizes the gray, the obtuse, the dangerous."[14] Faced with proles who didn't appreciate audio dadaism, the station sometimes turned contemptuous.

Alice, as we've seen, was shut down for its role in the March '77 riots. By that time, such clampdowns were rare. In an extraordinary turn of events, the Italian government had legalized unlicensed broadcasting.

As the radicals took to the airwaves and to the streets, apolitical entrepreneurs started illicit cable TV systems. The first of these was Tele Biella, established in the textile town of Biella in 1971; many others quickly followed. When the government tried to shut Tele Biella down, the pirates took the authorities to court. Surprisingly, the pirates won. In 1974, the Constitutional Court ruled that local private cable and broadcast systems were legal, provided they did not interfere with other signals.

It couldn't have happened at a more opportune time. Suddenly, it wasn't just the radical left that had a political stake in autonomous broadcasting: with the Socialist and Communist parties' power growing, the conservatives' stranglehold on RAI was no longer guaranteed. Private TV and radio started to look more appealing.

So in April 1975, the legislature legalized private cablevision. RAI retained its monopoly on wireless broadcasting, but after some conservative magistrates applied a little pressure on the Constitutional Court, even that unevenly enforced restriction fell. On July 28, 1976, the court restricted RAI's monopoly to national programs. Local broadcasters could do as they pleased, as long as they did not establish networks. Licenses weren't required.

The airwaves were thus opened to stations of every conceivable hue, from the Catholic to the feminist. There were big commercial stations, financed by heavy advertising, and there were tiny micro stations, described by one observer as "three or four young people, a transmitter and a pile of records."[15] One outlet, Radio Sicilia, narrowcast to Sicilian migrants in Rome. Another offered round-the-clock Hare Krishna chants. Some stations were Marxist in the dullest possible way, devoting all their energies to their particular "correct line." Others ignored the spoken word almost entirely, playing nothing but music. By mid-1978, there were about 2,275 independent radio stations in the country, plus 503 independent TV stations; the former claimed about a quarter of the country's radio audience.[16]

Broadcasters soon found ways around the antinetwork rule. The court had banned only interconnected systems, allowing "soft" networks to emerge. Further national regulation did not stem this trend, and in some ways fostered it. From 1979 on, the once-anarchic Italian spectrum began to centralize, leading to the rise of such media moguls as Silvio Berlusconi, who for a short time in the early 1990s would serve as his nation's head of state. Nonetheless, the most heavy centralization took place in television. Quirky, nonprofessional radio continued to percolate at the local level, encouraged by easy entry, low capital costs, and the general lack of regulation.

In 1990, the government tried to reassert its authority. A new law called the Legge Mammi gave local stations two years to keep operating while regulators prepared a frequency plan and assigned licenses. The government missed its own deadline, but it eventually finished the job. By February 1994, about four-fifths of the FM stations in operation were licensed. The state tried to shut the other 20 percent down, though some successfully appealed to the courts for a stay of execution. In 1996, the authorities imposed an annual tax of $20,000 on private stations, further calming the once-stormy ether.

Despite these recent developments, Italy still has the world's freest radio spectrum. (Shortwave, for example, is virtually unregulated.)[17] And in the 1970s, it was a constant inspiration to other would-be broadcasters, particularly in France. French radio was homogenous: the government network had only two legal competitors, and both were essentially indistinguishable from it. Piracy existed, but until 1977 it was rare.

That year, during a nationally televised political debate, the Green candidate said nothing at his turn to speak. Instead, he pulled a radio from his pocket and tuned it to a new unlicensed station, Radio Verte. A horde of guerrilla stations—*radios libres*—were soon broadcasting, inspired not only by the Italian free radios but by the offshore pirates, by community radio in Quebec, and by America's then-blossoming Citizens Band. By September, there were enough pirates to form a federation. Some were basically propaganda outlets; some were fledgling commercial stations; and some were rather experimental. Radio Ici et Maintenant, for example, sometimes invited listeners to hook their stereos to their telephones, call in, and play DJ for a while.

As in Italy, the major parties' reaction to all this generally depended on their relationship to the state broadcasting monopoly. The governing conservative coalition, led by President Giscard d'Estaing's Republican Party, felt no need to give up its control of the broadcast media. True, a free-market contingent within the Republicans had pushed through a moderate reform package in 1975, decentralizing the broadcast agency into seven separate (though still government-controlled) corporations. But the Gaullist tradition of centralized state authority remained strong. The balance began shifting toward the free-marketeers only after it started looking like the left might do well in the 1978 elections and thus claim a share of Radio France. To prepare for that contingency, the Republicans launched a pirate station of their own, Radio Fil Bleu, in the Mediterranean town of Montpellier. When the right-wing parties won the election, the pendulum swung back, and the state started eliminating the *radios libres*. The government imposed severe penalties for radio piracy, jammed illegal stations, and dispatched police raiders to seize the pirates' equipment. All but the most committed illicit stations quickly left the air.

Meanwhile, the left was dancing a similar do-si-do. The dominant wing of the Socialist Party, like the Gaullists, wanted a powerful, centralized state; naturally, it favored a national broadcast monopoly. But there was another tradition, a "second left," that preferred the anarchistic ideals of decentralization, civil society, and *autogestion* (self-management).[18] This tendency was stronger outside the Socialist Party than inside it, particularly among the Greens who started Radio Verte and similar projects and in the syndicalist wing of the labor movement, which also launched some stations. But some Socialists were sympathetic (Michel Rocard, a future prime minister, had espoused *autogestionnaire* ideals in his youth), just as some Republicans preferred free markets to Gaullist statism. And so, though the Socialist Party had chosen not to launch a pirate station in 1975, it changed its collective mind in 1979, when it became clear that Radio France would not be falling into its grasp.

On June 28, the Socialists launched Radio Riposte. The party inaugurated its new station with a vitriolic attack on Radio France, read by the party's first secretary, François Mitterrand. Mitterrand was among those arrested later that day, when the police raided the station's studios. The Socialist leader was unrepentant, declaring, "In the history of France, there have always been times where men have had to take risks in the name of freedom. Today is such a time. The audiovisual monopoly has been hijacked. Freedom of the press is under attack."[19]

Mitterrand's choice of words—"The audiovisual monopoly has been hijacked" rather than "The airwaves have been hijacked,"—should have been sufficient warning to those who assumed that a Socialist government would embrace the *radios libres*. Elected president in 1981, Mitterrand did declare an amnesty for those arrested during the earlier crackdown—hardly a surprising development, since he was among the indicted. But he did not legalize the pirates, instead enacting a moderate plan to permit state-subsidized local stations. In 1984, his government chose to allow on-air advertising, opening the way for commercial networks as well.

Meanwhile, after a brief thaw, the crackdown against the *radios libres* resumed. In 1983, French soldiers joined the police in a concerted military operation against the pirates. Some outlaw outlets nonetheless survived. For example, Paris's anarchist Radio Libertaire, mounted in 1981 with a budget of 15,000 francs (less than $200), continues to broadcast its mix of ethnic music, punk rock, reggae, jazz, and radical politics, despite constant government harassment.

The successes of the Italian and French *radios libres* inspired others around the continent. Pirate radio and TV stations sprouted behind the Iron Curtain, playing an important role in bringing down Communist dictatorships. The revolutions of 1989 ended Marxist rule, but the piracy only continued. In 1990, an unlicensed Prague station began transmitting from the basement labyrinths beneath a razed monument to a particularly odious foreign dictator; in honor of their location, the young ironists christened their operation Radio Stalin. In a broadcast coup, the pirates scored an interview with Czech president Vaclav Havel, who apparently did not realize the station was illegal.

When the authorities figured out what was going on, their first reaction was to crack down. The police soon raided the station and seized its equipment. But public opinion, shared by the tolerant Havel, favored the young broadcasters. The police returned the equipment, and independent radio was legalized. Radio Stalin renamed itself, becoming first Radio Ultra and then, to honor its status as Czechoslovakia's first free station since the brief Prague Spring of 1968, Radio One.

Other *radios libres* emerged in Belgium, Holland, West Germany, Spain, Portugal—pretty much everywhere. When one nation's movement seemed to falter, another country would pick up the slack. Thus, as the French stations disappeared in the late 1970s, a new wave of piracy rose among the squatters of Amsterdam, espousing yet another brand of anarchy; by the early '80s, by one estimate, more than ten thousand unlicensed stations were on the Dutch airwaves.[20] Besides the radical operations—"action stations" with names like The Free Emperor—there were ad-driven capitalist pirates, some of them thoroughly commercialized. "Anyone who has a commercial slot every ten minutes is a pirate, because the official government radio (and television) only has commercials on the hour," the squatter Ronald van Wechem of Radio X told a reporter in 1986. "There are some pirates who make I think two million guilders profit a year."[21]

Holland gradually eliminated *its* pirates by alternately shutting them down and granting them licenses. Only a few have persisted, with one—the café-based Radio 100—actually refusing the authorities' offer to license it. Waxing libertarian, it argued that the state had no business regulating the air and that legalization would just mean a new set of rules to follow anyway; better to put up with the occasional police raid.

Some states preferred repression: in West Germany, which didn't even permit private commercial radio until the late '80s, police were known to punish people caught listening to pirates by confiscating their radios.[22] Other nations—Belgium, for instance—followed the Dutch path and allowed limited legalization. None went as far as the Italians.

But on the other side of the world, one country came close, albeit by accident. In 1981, a group of Japanese artists and activists interested in the Italian experience found an intriguing loophole in the law: in order to allow for TV remote controls, garage-door openers, and the like, unlicensed broadcasts "below 15 microvolts per meter at the distance of 100 meters from the transmitter" were legal. They built an FM transmitter to those specs and discovered that it could reach a .3-mile radius. Not very far—except that in Japan's densely populated cities, it meant a potential audience of twenty thousand.

Soon, hundreds of "Mini FM" stations were on the air, some conventional and commercial, others wildly experimental. (Radio Komedia Suginami, for example, was based in a coffeehouse; anyone in the shop was welcome to join the on-air discussion.) Nor was the boom limited to businessmen and bohemians. Women working at home set up what amounted to family stations. Other stations became community centers where any neighbor might drop by—the electric equivalent of a front porch or pub. Mini FM became a fad, much like CB in the United States; and, like CB, it attracted at least as much pointless, egotistical babble as good radio. By the mid-'80s, the Japanese ether was host to a fair number of eccentric lone ranters, some interesting and some merely immature.

Eventually, like all fads, Mini FM began to fade. In 1985, there were more than a hundred mini-stations in Tokyo alone; by the early '90s, the city could boast of no more than ten. There is more to this story than a simple change in fashion. The Japanese government looked on the Mini FM explosion with distaste, if not terror. Low-power broadcasts might be legal, it decided, but most low-power *transmitters* were not. Using this rationale, it forced one well-publicized station to shut down, and that act cowed a lot of other projects into submission as well.

But in 1993, the government turned around, easing the licensing requirement for one- to ten-watt stations. Surveying the results, *Radio World* reported, "Unlike established radio stations that try to please all tastes, the low-wattage FM stations are doing all sorts of things the large stations would never dream of."[23] Sony and other companies began selling relatively inexpensive community FM sets, with all the equipment you need to start broadcasting.

In the wake of the Kobe earthquake of January 17, 1995, ethnic stations started springing up to coordinate relief efforts and to pass along important news. FM Yoboseyo appeared on January 30, broadcasting to Koreans in the city of Nagata. FM Yeu Men appeared on April 16, based in a Catholic church and sponsored by the Vietnamese Evacuee Relief Council; it broadcast in Tagalog, English, and Spanish as well as Japanese and Vietnamese. "After the earthquake," one of the relief workers

explained, "we handed out written translations of various relief information to Vietnamese survivors in shelters and parks. But that had limitations in terms of timeliness and number of people we can reach. . . .
What kind of means is available? We found radio."[24] The stations were
unlicensed, but under the circumstances, the government felt it would
be wise to let them be.

In July, the two outlets merged into a bigger operation, FM-YY. The
station still exists, is now licensed, and has branched into Netcasting. It
also inspired other stations to go on the air, a movement helped by the
government's increasingly tolerant regulations. By 1999, there were 116
licensed low-power stations in Japan. Mini FM was back.

In the Western Hemisphere, community broadcasting took root in
Canada's frozen far north. Distant Indian communities had been experimenting with low-power radio since 1958, if not earlier, scavenging
equipment from white bureaucrats and Mounties. Those first stations
were unlicensed, and their programming bore little resemblance to the
radio of the south. They were more like village centers, informal places
where neighbors could share information, be it local gossip or an emergency announcement. Nor were all the broadcasts in English or French.
Where native languages were spoken off the air, they were spoken on
the air as well.

For years, the Canadian government didn't realize this was going
on; word didn't get out until the late 1960s, when two pilots stumbled
on an unlicensed Indian signal. To its credit, Ottawa did not crack down
on the aboriginal operators. After all, they weren't competing, let alone
interfering, with anyone else. In most of the north, there *were no* other
broadcasters with whom to compete, with the sometime exception of
the Accelerated Coverage Plan, a satellite service subsidized by the
state. So the authorities made it easy to establish a community station.
To this day, instead of the U.S.'s expensive, delay-ridden licensing process, northern Canadians need only fill out a simple form.

The government also offered funds to the stations. Readers persuaded by my earlier screed against the Corporation for Public Broadcasting should note that, for the most part, similar problems did not
take root in northern Canada. While some operations did (arguably)
overexpand and thus became more vulnerable to budget cuts, most did
not. The stations are generally governed by elected boards and operated by volunteers, and they usually supplement the Canadian Broad-

casting Corporation's dollars with other means of support. (The Wawatay Radio Network, based in the tiny village of Muskrat Dam, has sponsored bingo games. It's also been known to charge listeners a fee when they request dedications.) The broadcast license is typically held by an independent, nonprofit organization, often organized as a cooperative.[25] In the bureaucratic world of Canadian "social democracy," northern radio is remarkably free, perhaps because it springs from local initiative.

That comes through in one of the classic accounts of Indian radio, Paulette Jiles's essay "Community Radio in Big Trout Lake":

> This is the country above the Canadian Shield where rivers run north to Hudson's Bay. To the newcomer it seems incredibly empty. As the newcomer becomes less new, he finds it is a jungle of government bureaucracies desperately grasping for water, for mines, for cheap Cree labor and for gold. Indian Affairs employees try to keep their jobs by proposing programs the Indians don't want; the Indians try to fend off the worst programs and suggest more intelligent ones. The radio station was one of the more intelligent ones; a small victory, and perhaps not preferable to a laundromat or to electricity to Indian homes, but a win nevertheless.[26]

The station, founded in 1973, was a simple affair, a minimal collection of equipment in a three-room building. "The young volunteers went in every morning," Jiles later wrote, "and turned on the transmitter, and the mikes, and began to broadcast." And what did they broadcast?

> They told jokes and stories, read announcements, played country-and-western music. They went home at noon to cut wood for their wives and mothers. They came back, eating sandwiches, and turned the mikes on again.
>
> "Nancy Fiddler, come home. Your mother wants you. Tell your husband she wants to borrow the ax. Be careful of the ice. Come the way you came yesterday."[27]

The Big Trout Lake station, CFTL, inspired many similar projects. More than three hundred broadcast today, among northern whites as well as Inuit and Cree. The confederal government offers them funds but doesn't demand much control; typically, the CBC sends out a technician or two to train the locals and then move on. In the United States, this would be almost unthinkable.[28]

Not every government in the New World has proved as tolerant as Canada's. In Argentina, more than two thousand small FM stations have sprung up in shantytowns and poor rural areas since 1986, offering neighborhood-oriented programming from virtually all points of view. Thanks to ambiguities in Argentine radio law, the shantytown stations were neither legal nor illegal; the larger outlets, displeased with the competition, called for the government to "clarify" its regulations by suppressing the microbroadcasters. At their behest, the government proposed a bill that would have outlawed stations of less than a thousand watts. Arguing for the law, broadcast regulator Pedro Sán-chez denounced the micro stations as "acts of institutional subversion." His "principal wish," he announced, "is that Argentina will be rid of this plague of underground radio stations."[29] But the bill did not pass, and, despite sporadic police harassment, the variety continues.

Community radio has also proved a force in Brazil, in Bolivia, in Mexico, in El Salvador, and, most notably, in Haiti. In 1991, after a military coup deposed the island's leftist president, Jean-Bertrand Aristide, illegal micro stations became focus points for the resistance, transmitting radical editorials, international news, even clandestine talk shows from headquarters hidden in shantytowns and the countryside. Unlike the official stations, which broadcast in French, the pirates programmed in Creole, the language of the people; they were therefore assured of a loyal audience.

Aristide eventually returned to power, assisted by the bayonets of the U.S. military. Thus restored, he generally pursued policies congenial to Washington. But he wasn't about to shut the pirates down. Indeed, his successor, Rene Preval, seriously mulled a proposal to reserve 50 percent of the Haitian spectrum for microbroadcasting. This led to the unlikely spectacle of the American pirate Stephen Dunifer—self-proclaimed anarchist and perpetual thorn in the FCC's side—getting invited to Port-au-Prince in 1997 to advise the Haitian government on telecommunications policy.

Haitian stations continue to sprout, in thatched huts and shanties and little stone houses around the isle. Even where no electricity is available, transmitters have bloomed, powered by solar panels. And they haven't lost their dissident bite. When Radio VKM first signed on the air on May 1, 1996, it wasted no time celebrating the end of the old military dictatorship. Instead, it turned its rhetorical guns on the government, demanding land reform and denouncing the president's economic policies.

I could go on, describing the illegal and semilegal stations of Taiwan, Turkey, Greece, Indonesia, Israel, Martinique—nearly every nation seems to have hosted at least one radio revolution. One could write a whole book about Ireland's pirates. It would start with the Dublin revolutionaries who independently invented broadcasting on April 25, 1916, declaring the birth of the Irish Republic in a Morse Code message beamed from their Sackville Street base to anyone who happened to tune in; it would climax the mid-1980s, when for six years a legal loophole unleashed a wave of unlicensed stations; it would have many contemporary stations to describe as well. But enough is enough. The important point to glean is that a lot of people in a lot of places have used transmitters to spread sedition, talk to their neighbors, and play funky music.

So I turn instead to a related subject: the governments that have responded to these rebellions by actually trying to foster community radio, or at least some facsimile thereof. For example: the United Kingdom's response to the offshore pirates was not merely to add more pop songs to its broadcasts—though it did do that, even hiring onetime pirates to host the new shows.[30] It also created some local channels, adding a taste of decentralization to British broadcasting for the first time. The BBC started planning the new stations in 1967, the same year it cracked down on the pirates; in 1972, it allowed the Independent Television Authority to enter the local radio business as well.

But this was not community radio as we know it. Bureaucratic, afraid of controversy, parochial in the worst way, the local stations could be incredibly restrictive; one on-air host has said flatly that she faced more censorship at BBC Radio Manchester than she would have on a national program. "The problem was that this was local radio, and Manchester local radio at that. Local vested interests had to be appeased," she recalled. "And that was in the days before Thatcher, when local radio stations were expected to encourage diversity."[31] She was eventually axed.

In short, Great Britain's self-proclaimed "local radio" is unadventurous, unautonomous, and unconcerned with the real color and flavor of the island's towns and regions. Small wonder that pirate radio has returned to the United Kingdom—not the offshore variety, though that too has seen a mild revival, but the noncommercial micro kind. In 1977, some activists formed the Community Communications Group, an informal association eclipsed in 1983 by the Community Radio Coalition; both groups encouraged unlicensed low-power radio and lobbied the government to permit nonprofit local broadcasting. As lobbyists, they had little luck: for all the prime minister's rhetoric about liberty and deregulation, the Thatcher administration proved somewhat less pleased with free speech and local initiative in practice.

With or without Thatcher's blessing, England was entering what some have called the second golden age of British pirate radio. About fifty underground stations with names like Horizon and the Dread Broadcasting Corporation could be heard in the London area alone, many of them black operations devoted to reggae, funk, or soul. Uncomfortably aware that it was having trouble enforcing the law, the government finally acted. In 1985, the authorities agreed to allow an "experiment" in community radio. As intended, this announcement reduced the number of active pirates, who saw no reason to risk their necks presenting a service that they might soon offer legally.

At that point, the authorities canceled the project before it even began.

The gambit worked only briefly: within months, pirates were returning to their high-rise studios and turning their transmitters back on. By 1990, there were more than six hundred illegal stations in the country, a tenth of them in London.[32] Things seemed to brighten a little with the Broadcasting Act of 1990, a post-Thatcher measure that cleared some space on the dial for independent nonprofit outlets; some of the new licenses went to onetime pirates. The same law, alas, caused yet more trouble for the remaining unlicensed operators by imposing further restrictions on advertisers and others who might help the privateers from the outside. At one point, the Department of Trade and Industry threatened a magazine with prosecution for merely printing unlicensed stations' program listings.

Today there are a handful of legal community stations in the U.K., as well as the much-beleaguered array of illegal ones. British blacks have particularly taken to piracy. "Most pirate radio is black because nearly all mainstream radio is white," one pirate told the London *Independent* in 1998. "There is no legitimate voice for black culture. I have applied for a licence in the past and been turned down. Now it would be too expensive."[33] So much for the vaunted inclusiveness of Britain's legal local radio.

In France, meanwhile, independent radio was quickly commercialized. Consider NRJ (pronounced "energy"), the nation's most profitable private network:[34]

> NRJ transforms sound by using special effects (equalizers, compressors, limiters) to give listeners "unreal" audio perception. NRJ homogenizes sound and creates a structure in which music, voice, advertising and news intermingle. NRJ abhors live broadcasting, which interrupts its sound pattern; it despises on-the-air telephone calls from listeners, which localize the programming; and it eliminates disc jockeys, who tend to personify programming. NRJ is everywhere and nowhere. . . . It is like a hearing aid for people who want to stay within their own protective shells.[35]

You could see this as the antithesis of local, participatory, non-professional broadcasting, and you'd be right. You could also view it as a unique and popular option that should be available to anyone who wants to hear it. You'd still be right. Love it or hate it, NRJ has succeeded in the marketplace, turning a profit without aid from the state. And it has a large following, demonstrated by the thousands of young people who demonstrated in Paris in 1983 when regulators refused to grant it a power increase. The trouble is, the same government that backed down then never backed down in its war on the anarcho-pirates. There's room for both NRJ and Radio Libertaire on the French airwaves, but the thought of such diversity makes the authorities quake.

The same story has recurred across Europe. Faced with pirate broadcasters, or perhaps just a restless listenership, governments have permitted limited local radio services that, while not necessarily awful in themselves, are no substitute for actually opening the airwaves. The Swiss, aware that citizens were tuning both to domestic pirates and to unlicensed broadcasts from across the Italian border, created a radio system that drew kudos for much of its programming but jeers for pretending to be local. In Norway, regional radio exists, but it's run by the central government and allows little local access. From Scotland to the Balkans, "local radio" has remained a province of the professionals.

There are exceptions. In Catalonia, an initial wave of Italian-inspired *radios libres* evolved into a semilegal set of "municipal" radio stations. (Despite their name, most of these are operated by nonprofit civic groups, not by city governments.) And in Sweden, neighborhood radio—*närradio*—has brought something like public-access TV to the Scandinavian air. The state broadcast system, Sverigas Radio, is supposed to be impartial on public issues. The *närradio*, by contrast, are a place for people to espouse anything they please, provided they set up their own studios and pay a fee for the use of the government's transmitters.

The result is different not just from professional radio but from most community broadcasting as well. Unlike, say, Pacifica or Radio Alice, a *närradio* frequency has no unifying vision. It is a place where diverse visions collide, visions far more different than even the most radically opposed programs on the old KRAB.

Outside Europe, the difference between free and government-sanctioned local radio is even clearer. Consider the rural radio movement in Africa, a motley array of provincial radio services that began to emerge in the 1960s. The rural stations are neither autonomous nor self-managed, nor otherwise opposed to professional control; they are financed by African governments, and many shut out dissident points of view. Despite this, some have adopted the rhetoric of community broadcasters. In Mali, Kayes Rural Radio has tried to open its doors to peasant participation, seeking inspiration and advice from the Montreal-based World Association of Community Broadcasters (AMARC), a federation founded in 1983. But even though it is relatively free of government control—state money helped launch it, but it is nominally independent—Kayes really isn't a community-based project. Founded and financed by Terra Nueva and Gao, two Italian charities, Kayes has a foreign agenda to fulfill. If the locals invaded the studio to proclaim the wonders of, say, traditional African patriarchy, it's hard to believe the station's owners wouldn't run them out, or even pull the plug.[36]

Homa Bay Community Radio, in Kenya, was more authentically autonomous. The station was founded in 1981 by Jake Mills, the former chief engineer of the Ghana Broadcasting Corporation, and Martin Allard, a Radio Caroline fan who worked for a digital video company. The two engineers designed a small, self-powered transmitter and taught some Kenyan technicians to use and maintain it. Then they and the Kenyans erected the station in a building owned by the National Union of Teachers, a small, white structure on a brown hillside overlooking Lake Victoria. This station didn't cost much to build and run (just $25,000) and could boast of real local participation—too much, in fact, for the national government, which abruptly shut it down in 1983.

Mills and Allard formed Mallard Constructs, a company that builds small, cheap, easy-to-use FM transmitters and helps set up community-radio stations in the Third World. While their projects are certainly more autonomous than, say, Kayes, some are freer than others. The company's close association with UNESCO—the United Nations Educational, Scientific, and Cultural Organization, a partner since the Homa Bay days—certainly raises some uncomfortable questions. While it's nice to see the United Nations doing something for local sovereignty for a change, centralist habits are hard to break, and it's easy to wonder whether its efforts for local radio really lend themselves to community control.

Granted, when the *UNESCO Courier* devoted its February 1997 issue to "self-reliant low-cost radio stations," its rhetoric sounded appealing:

> In this kind of project, the initiative comes from the communities. The local folk build the radio station, and after group discussions, they set the guidelines for the broadcasters. They organize the radio team, drawing on all sectors of the village. There is no lack of volunteers. At Banga [a small town in the Philippines], Lyn Villasis, a beautician turned broadcaster, reads fairy tales to children over Radio Manduyong, modulating her voice to evoke the characters in each story. A health programme is hosted by a midwife.[37]

But sometimes there were hints of something darker. The same magazine mentioned a Sri Lankan project that came bundled with a vast, publicly funded development scheme:

> When the valleys were flooded, some one million settlers would have to move downstream to the drylands which would eventually be watered by the new canals. One could imagine the anguish of farming families at having to uproot their homes, farm implements,

and religious shrines and settle in some unknown dry region down-
stream. Whole villages with their sacred temples would soon be un-
derwater. . . . [UNESCO] aimed to create and train a team of mobile
radio producers who would visit the villages both before and after
resettlement and would produce programmes to smooth the transition to their new homes.

The Guirandurokotte Community Radio, Sri Lanka's first permanent FM station, was a key feature of this project.[38]

You'd expect a station that really spoke for the community to be a focus
for protest against this giant land-grab, not a therapeutic device for easing the pain of transition. Nonetheless, the *UNESCO Courier* reels off a
couple of anecdotes about Sri Lankan volunteers, just as it did describing the Philippine stations, and concludes that "Guirandurokotte has
been eminently a people's station."[39] Sure, but *which* people?

Not that there's been no popular participation in the station. When
the radio producers came to town, more than a hundred villagers sometimes showed up to play music, recite poetry, and perform plays for the
microphone. The shows that resulted might last as long as eight hours.
Yet this sounds more like an anthropology project than a community
event; the villagers, after all, can play music, recite poetry, and perform
plays whenever they please, microphone or no microphone. If listening
to another village do those things takes the place of actually doing
them, this "community radio" is merely a pre-industrial oldies station.
The villagers themselves may be involved in creating the programs, but
the station is not a village project.

Neither are the other outlets that have come to the country in its
wake. When Evelyn Foy of AMARC visited Sri Lanka, she found "a
number of problems: the difficulty of keeping resources intended for
MCR [Mahaweli Community Radio] within the project, a general lack
of local resources, and centralization of decision-making in the capital
and in the head offices of the Sri Lanka Broadcasting System."[40] And the
national government is not the only outside force that interferes: UN-
ESCO and a Danish development agency have poured money into Mahaweli Community Radio, bringing to mind an old saying about pay-
ments and pipers and tunes. Furthermore, some have argued that the
UNESCO money led to overexpansion. While some within MCR claim
that they will soon be able to get by without foreign aid, the fact remains
that, as one participant put it,

> After ten years the MCR project had come to operate as if the funding would always be there, and had not developed an appropriate plan for the withdrawal of international support. . . . At the end of the final phase of the project there were only some sketchy proposals to create an autonomous, institutional structure for community radio. Nothing solid had materialized and MCR was in a very vulnerable position.[41]

In all, there is no reason to suppose that foreign stations heavily subsidized by governments and aid agencies will be able to avoid the problems that have beset American stations heavily subsidized by the CPB. The two great counterexamples, Sweden and Canada, each enjoy special circumstances. In Sweden, *närradio* exists only because a moderate-conservative coalition briefly took power in 1976. The Social Democrats, committed to the bureaucratic management of everything except young people's sex lives, hated the idea of independent broadcasts.[42] The conservatives knew they couldn't eliminate Sverigas altogether, and public-access radio seemed like a reasonable compromise. So they opened the door to the kind of scrappy, volunteer-based broadcasting that most other governments were doing their best to destroy.

When the socialists returned to power, they found the neighborhood-radio system had become too popular to dismantle. And neither party wanted to interfere with the *närradios'* freedom of speech, fearing the precedent that would set. So the stations survive to this day. (The national government did intervene when a far-right group began broadcasting extremely racist programs in 1981, but even this was done carefully. Instead of kicking the bigots off the air, the legislature passed a neutrally worded law decreeing that the *närradio* system was open only to groups involved in more than just broadcasting. This eliminated the racists in the short term, but it did not prevent them from reorganizing and successfully reapplying for a broadcast license.)

Canadian community radio is a trickier case. Why have these stations avoided the problems that have befallen so many other publicly funded outlets, from Sri Lanka to California?

Five reasons jump to mind:

1. The stations are launched by members of the communities themselves, not imposed from the outside.
2. The circumstances encourage community control. A station run by outsiders would lose local support and would therefore fail,

since the CBC does not provide enough money or personnel to run a full-fledged professional operation.

3. The government's money has mostly bought equipment, not programming, although outlets can transmit CBC programs if they want to.[43] The stations therefore don't depend on subsidies for day-to-day operations.

4. The northern stations exist in areas where few others want to broadcast. Thus spared from serious competition, they don't have to worry about special-interest pressures from rival operations.

5. As low-power, low-cost, nonprofessional outlets, the northern stations are not expensive to start or run; a private foundation could easily step into the CBC's sugar-daddy shoes. It therefore wouldn't be *that* hard for the stations to survive if government support were to disappear. All they would need would be a reasonable transition period in which to seek other sources of money—or, better, to pool their own resources.

It's worth noting that southern Canada has community broadcasters as well, many modeled on the KRABish stations to their south. College radio also thrives. Heaven knows, the Canadian system is far from perfect: this is a nation where Howard Stern can't make a few on-air jokes about French speakers without prompting Quebec's justice minister to demand the shock jock be brought to court. But in many ways, broadcasters enjoy more liberties in Canada than in the United States.

And they aren't alone. From Italy to Haiti to the Cree Nation to Japan, many lands could teach the United States a few lessons in broadcast liberty.

8

American Pirates

I've been searching for you on my radio
This time your station really must have gone underground

—Ray Davies

PIRATE RADIO IN the classic sense—offshore signals broadcast to the mainland—never took hold in the United States, probably because any American entrepreneur interested in unofficial broadcasting had an alternative that was cheaper and not quite as questionably legal. Not long after the feds started regulating radio, Mexico's megawatt border blasters—high-powered stations planted just south of Texas and California—started beckoning. The FCC couldn't control them, and Mexico's left-leaning government wasn't about to do Washington any favors. One of the first people busted by the fledgling Federal Radio Commission—a Kansas quack named John R. Brinkley, who claimed he could cure ailments by transplanting goat glands into human bodies—responded to the American authorities' enmity by retreating to Del Rio. He might have been banned from the Kansas airwaves, but he could still broadcast from XER's three-hundred-foot towers. So could a lively array of preachers, DJs, and budding country stars.

Eventually, that option was closed. As the U.S. government grew closer politically to its southern neighbor, the border stations were gradually tamed; treaty followed treaty, culminating with the North American Regional Broadcasting Agreement of 1986, which seriously cut back the blasters' legally protected range. That same year, the Mexican government revised its radio licensing law, drastically reducing the X stations' autonomy.

But that is recent history. For most of the century, border broadcasting made offshore radio unnecessary for Americans. After the Federal Radio Commission drove RXKR off the air in 1933—this was the station licensed in Panama and operated off the California coast—no one would attempt to broadcast from American waters until 1973. And that effort, a right-wing Christian station called Radio Free America, was quickly felled by technical troubles, dying after a mere ten hours on the air. Housed on the *Oceanic,* a minesweeper anchored just off the Jersey coast, the outlet was owned by the Reverend Carl McIntire, a wealthy fundamentalist who had launched a legal station, WXUR, in 1965. In 1970, the FCC had revoked WXUR's license, on the grounds that its ultraconservative programs violated the Fairness Doctrine. Thus barred from the mainland airwaves, Reverend McIntire turned to piracy.[1] The only other offshore station in American history was the short-lived Radio New York International, a late-'80s project of which I'll say more later.[2]

This thin history hardly means that Americans were denied the sound of unlicensed radio. For decades, offbeat broadcasters have seized small parcels of the airwaves from their rooftops and garages, usually just as a hobby but sometimes as something more. The practice stretches back to the beginning of the century—recall those early amateurs with their primitive ham broadcasts—and it didn't stop when Congress created the FCC. In 1998, when the FCC asked for public comments on whether it should create a legal microbroadcasting service, one of the most interesting letters it received came from Harold Parshall, the general manager of a public radio station in West Carrollton, Ohio. Parshall explained that he and a friend had built an unlicensed, low-power AM station back in the 1940s, when both were in their teens, and kept it running until the FCC intervened. Fifty years later, he was a respected mainstream broadcaster, but he hadn't forgotten how he'd gotten into the business, and he supported the right of others to do the same.

Parshall is hardly the only former pirate to move into the broadcasting mainstream. In the summer of 1961, thirteen-year-old Robert Meuser of Hickory, North Carolina, built his own mixer and transmitter and went on the air. He convinced some record companies to send him some music, and he sold commercial time to two stores. Unfortunately, both shops were on his paper route, and "when the second store came on, the first cancelled the radio *and* the newspaper delivery."[3] Like Parshall, Meuser is still in the business today; I mention him not because his station was significant but because it was typical. A more prominent former pirate is Art Bell, whose late-night interviews with saucer nuts, survivalists, and others from the apocalyptic fringe have made him one of the country's most popular radio personalities. Bell has confessed to having operated several unlicensed stations in his younger years, on the AM and FM bands, on shortwave, and even on TV.

And so on. High school students ran hobby stations. Hams did unlicensed AM broadcasts on the side. One backyard operation, Delaware's WTFC, broadcast intermittently for twenty-four years—from 1964 to 1988—without ever getting caught. Even a military school tolerated an illegal station in its barracks. In the 1950s, some teens at the Western Military Academy, in Alton, Illinois, built a transmitter and started broadcasting at 590 AM, as WMAS; in 1961, they started simulcasting on FM. The kids "didn't even have a licensed ham around, much less a[n] FM or AM license," one of the participants later recalled. "To be exact, we were pirates."[4] The station played pop, jazz, and folk music and covered school sports; it also offered two *Mad*-influenced satirical shows, *Radio Free Moscow* and *Wisdom on the Loose*. Before it went dark in 1961, WMAS spurred some students to start a rival station: WVMC, for "Western Venezuela Mexico Cuba," with programs geared toward Latino students.

None of this had much impact outside Alton and the academy, which closed its doors roughly a decade later. "We weren't trying to change the world," one of the military pirates recalls. "We were just a bunch of teenagers having fun and trying to impress chicks. WMAS and Radio Free Moscow gave vent to our creative energies."[5]

A few years after the Western Military Academy lost its stations, a slightly older group of boys in uniform would start one of the best-known pirate operations in American history, though it wasn't actually based in the U.S. In Saigon, a soldier called Dave Rabbit—not his real name, of course—preached the virtues of drugs, blow jobs, and acid rock over Radio First Termer. A night with Rabbit might feature music from Steppenwolf, Jimi Hendrix, Vanilla Fudge, and the Who, plus a lot of raunch, a warning about an upcoming M.P. raid, and some drug news ("If you're going by the Magic Finger lounge tonight, stay away from the Korean at the door; he's pushing some bad H").[6] First Termer was the most famous of many clandestine G.I. stations, tapes of which still circulate among connoisseurs of radio piracy and Vietnam kitsch.

By this time, some stateside stations were ready to move beyond the hobby stage and actually seek regular audiences and community support. As Radio First Termer's signal was fading overseas, a young

Yonkers hippie named Allan Weiner was spearheading several unlicensed stations, dubbed the Falling Star Network. Weiner was an electronics whiz, a kid who at age six was already taking radio and TV sets apart, figuring out how they worked, and putting them back together. Before he had even reached his teens, he was a full-fledged junk collector, scavenging the old gadgets and parts that his neighbors had tossed away, dragging the loot home, and unlocking their mysteries—all over the protests of his father, who appreciated his son's hobby but didn't care to see his basement filled with "everyone else's trash."

Weiner soon wondered whether he could rebuild a radio receiver as a transmitter. He couldn't. Still, he later wrote, "the idea of transmitting had occurred to me, and putting my own radio station on the air just seemed to be the natural course of action."[7] One step at a time, Weiner and a shifting collection of accomplices crept onto the ether.

Step one: Allan and his friend Kenny Sofer pool their pennies and buy a Lafayette Broadcaster, an AM transmitter with a signal so weak—it reaches roughly half a block—that it's actually legal to operate it without a license.[8] Allan and Kenny are still in elementary school at this point, no older than the kids who'd formed the Junior Wireless Club half a century before. Together with another kid, Paul Rosenberg, they declare themselves the staff of KPSR-Yonkers and play their parents' records for anyone who happens to be both tuned to their frequency and within about five hundred feet—that is, for no one.

Step two: Weiner, now fourteen, discovers the world of government surplus electronics. By this time, he's tired of broadcasting music he doesn't like to an audience of zero. He's also grown interested in the art of broadcasting, as opposed to the fun of making machines work, and has started to wonder why Yonkers—a city of two hundred thousand people, a city rich in radio history, the city that gave Major Edwin Armstrong to the world—has no radio station of its own. Over the course of many visits to a surplus store in New York City, he gathers the gadgets necessary to launch a pirate shortwave station, and, in the summer of 1968, from a basement studio on Kneeland Avenue, WRAD goes on the air. The audience remains small (just those friends of Weiner's who have shortwave receivers), the programming remains simple (just Dad's classical collection and Mom's easy-listening albums), the technology remains rudimentary (Weiner built a primitive mixing board inside a cigar box), and the sound quality remains poor. But they're reaching a mile or two of Yonkers: not a lot, but more than half a block.

Step three: a couple of months later, Weiner convinces his parents to pay $125 for a World War II military transmitter, a four-hundred-pound behemoth that required six people to haul it inside. After much work, Weiner gets the monster running, makes up some fliers with his friends ("A NEW AND DIFFERENT KIND OF RADIO BROADCASTING WILL BE PRESENTED"), and starts broadcasting just above 1600 AM. For three days in October, Weiner and two others transmit light music, weather reports, and high school gossip. Then one of the local hams tattles to the FCC, and WRAD goes dark once more.

Step four: now more wary of the law, the station changes its name to WWJ and adopts a more sporadic schedule. With this lower profile, its programming begins to evolve, as Weiner and the other DJs soak up both the rebellious spirit of the age and the contrarianism of adolescence. The talk starts turning to high school life—not idle chatter but increasingly critical complaints. The principal of Lincoln High School doesn't care for this turn of events but is too scared to do anything about it: between his mechanical talents and his recent run-in with the feds, Weiner has inadvertently acquired a fearsome reputation. And with his friends embracing rock music, the counterculture, and the antiwar movement, he's ready to turn his little station into something more than a hobby. "We would have political discussions about what was going on," he later wrote, "and we would talk about the unrest. Our radio station would be the loudspeaker for our friends at school and in the neighborhood."[9]

Weiner, Sofer, and the others recruited some kindred spirits, assembled a hipper music library, and beefed up the studio to let more people be on the air at once. They rechristened the station one more time, changing the call letters to WKOV. "They didn't really mean anything," Weiner later recalled; "they just sounded good. And they looked good when you wrote them down."[10]

On September 23, 1969, WKOV made its debut. It set aside the easy-listening sounds featured on its predecessors—no more Montovani or Herb Alpert—in favor of Hendrix, Dylan, and other rockers. It started criticizing the Vietnam War, giving peace activists their only local media platform. In fact, WKOV was the only local media platform that *anyone* had; Yonkers, you'll recall, had no other radio station of its own. When WKOV started taking calls live on the air, it was virtually the only phone-in forum in the area, and certainly the only one without a seven-second delay. Callers debated the war, denounced the draft, announced meetings, threw parties. "We encouraged our listeners to call in anytime during the broadcasts," Weiner reports, "and if there was anything they wanted to discuss, we would do it between records."[11] For Yonkers, this was radically new.

But I'm getting ahead of myself. Early in 1970, long before his little station had become a community center, Weiner got a phone call from a listener named Joseph Paul Ferraro. Ferraro was a longhaired student at a nearby community college who lived down the street from Edwin Armstrong's old house; he had stumbled on Weiner's station by accident, figured out where the signal was coming from, and decided he wanted to get involved. The two became fast friends, and before long they were setting up a second station at Ferraro's house, building a twenty-foot tower by hand and erecting it atop his roof. Weiner lent him some spare equipment, and Ferraro scavenged some more from his dad's old workshop; by spring's end, the new operation was transmitting at 1620 AM. Ferraro named his station WFSR—the call letters stood for Falling Star Radio—and staggered his schedule with his friend's so that they wouldn't be on the air at the same time.

Dissatisfied with AM, the pirates turned their attention to the other broadcast band. After the usual adventures in tinkering and junk-picking, yet another station was on the air. They named it WXMN, an homage to Major Armstrong and his original experimental FM station, W2XMN.

"The reaction was instantaneous," Weiner later wrote. "We gave out the phone number to see if people were listening, and we soon discovered that our 50-watt transmitter covered the whole city of Yonkers and beyond. We got calls from listeners as far away as New Jersey and upstate New York. . . . The response for one day's broadcast was much larger than an entire month on 1620 KHz."[12]

The FM transmitter had a habit of overheating, and one night it caught fire in the middle of a broadcast. When the station returned to the air, it did so with another FM operation in tow, the memorably named WSEX. Before long, Michael Schaitman, a friend in the Bronx, had set up a fifth station, WBRX. Its signal was weaker and its programming less vigorous, but the transmitter did warm up Schaitman's apartment on those cold New York nights.

Without meaning to, Weiner had launched an entire network. It referred to itself alternately as the American Radio Broadcasting System and the Falling Star Network, and though the Bronx station soon closed its doors, the others grew and thrived, with thirty to fifty people either hosting shows or volunteering in some other capacity. Naturally, the government soon noticed all this activity.

By "the government," I don't just mean the FCC. G-men started tailing the kids, and the Westchester County Police Department assigned some men to investigate them. Exasperated, Weiner and Ferraro decided to see whether they could get on the air *without* breaking the law. They traveled to Washington and met with Nicholas Johnson, figuring that, as the closest the FCC had to a New Left commissioner, he might help them. Johnson was sympathetic, but his hands were tied.

A month later, the government demonstrated just how powerless Johnson was. On the morning of August 12, 1971, a federal marshal dragged Weiner from his bed and arrested him for broadcasting without a license, while officers shut down the other stations across town. The raids received some media attention—Pacifica was particularly supportive, with Weiner and others making their case over WBAI— but the ride was over. Weiner and Ferraro were each sentenced to a year's probation, and none of the Falling Star stations would ever return to the air.

But that didn't mean unlicensed broadcasting itself was dead. (Indeed, Ferraro and Weiner would soon return to piracy—it was they who launched the offshore Radio New York International.) Even as the feds closed in on the Yonkers network, another tribe of broadcasters was taking to the airwaves of Bakersfield, California. One of them was named Jim Simmons.

Simmons had grown up in Ridgecrest, a small town in the California desert. The airwaves there were almost completely dark; in the daytime you catch could only two stations, and at night you *might* pick up a signal from Oklahoma City or the Great Salt Lake. With so few options available, the local broadcasters tried to be everything to everybody: middle-of-the-road music in the mornings, teenybopper stuff in the afternoons, hard rock at night. As the 1960s waned, Simmons got a job at one of those desert outlets, KLOA, where he DJed on evenings and weekends and played pretty much what he wanted. It was AM radio, but when it did its rock shows, it looked to FM freeform for its cues. "As 1969 turned into 1970," Simmons recalls, "tight playlists weren't that dominant."[13]

In 1970, Simmons crossed the Sierras to start classes at Bakersfield College, in the heart of the Great Central Valley. A year before, Bakersfield's favorite son, the great Merle Haggard, had dominated the country charts with a song about a town in Oklahoma:

> We don't smoke marijuana in Muskogee
> We don't take our trips on LSD
> We don't burn our draft cards down on Main Street
> We like living right and being free

That may well have been how they lived further east, in Muskogee, Oklahoma, U.S.A. But marijuana, acid, and draft resistance had arrived in Bakersfield, to the discomfort of some of the older generation but to the hedonistic delight of Simmons and his friends at the community college. And what better way to broadcast the gospel of sex, drugs, and rock 'n' roll—and what the hell, maybe some Haggard, too—than radio?

So Simmons and some others set up a campus station. That wasn't unusual, of course—except that they didn't bother to get a license. The college gave them a small space, some friendly pros at the local legal stations gave them some surplus parts, the kids hooked up a transmitter, and suddenly a new station—KBC—was on the air. By year's end, about twenty-five people were involved in the project, and some Bakersfield businesses were thinking about coming aboard as sponsors. The programming was mostly music, mixed and matched in an unformatted combination: usually rock, but some jazz and country, too; and, after an unexpected fight, some rhythm and blues. (Some black students had picketed outside the studio in spring 1971, demanding that the primarily white programmers give them "access" to the station. The puzzled broadcasters eventually managed to explain to the militants that they already *had* access: virtually anyone who wanted a show could have one. The marchers, tuned to the confrontational politics of the day, had evidently taken to the streets without first simply applying for airtime.)

The station eventually got a license and became a formal part of the college, complete with official funding and a spot in the school curriculum; it stayed afloat until the 1990s. Simmons, meanwhile, moved out of town, transferring to San Diego State and quickly growing disillusioned with his new classmates' serious, "professional" approach to student broadcasting. He got into concert promotion, earned his degree, made his way around the state, and kept finding himself back in Bakersfield. It was there, in 1975, that he started hearing about a weird FM outlet called "Channel One, KLOS," a station with no format, no commercials, just lots of good music. Intrigued, Simmons made a few calls and eventually figured out what his friends had been listening to. The all-night DJ on KERN—an independently owned, very eclectic, very popular rock station—had been operating an unlicensed outlet out of his house as a hobby; he called it Channel One. When no one was around to run it, he would rig up his transmitter to rebroadcast whatever was on KLOS, a rock powerhouse in Los Angeles. Careless listeners were assuming that the two outfits were the same—hence, "Channel One, KLOS."

By then, Simmons had decided to stay in Bakersfield. He got in touch with the mysterious Channel One DJ, whose on-air name was Phil Drake, and before he knew it he was living on Drake's floor and doing a morning show under the pseudonym Head ("Channel One gives you Head in the morning"). More people tuned in, and more started volunteering; the station was soon operating twenty-four hours a day. After Head finished his morning show, a folk music fan called The Moonshadow would come on the air; then came The Emperor of Wyoming and his obscure space rock; then came a lady called Suite Irene; then came a man dubbed Hot Rod. The station had an enormous music library (as a professional DJ, Drake had been accumulating promotional records for years) and, according to its morning man, soon had an enormous audience as well. "It really became a big thing in the town," Simmons recalls. "You couldn't go anywhere where you didn't hear it. In the car next to you when you were stopped at a red light, people talking about it in the mall when you passed them by—you could just tell. . . . I had the impression that *everybody* listened." The signal covered the whole city, plus some outlying areas.

The carousel soon stopped. Before the year was out, the town's two legal rock stations found that they were losing listeners and ad revenue to Channel One. (Channel One didn't run any commercials, but that didn't keep its rivals from losing ad money. Advertisers knew the audience they were after wasn't listening to the licensed stations as much as before, and they knew better than to keep spending the same amount for airtime as though nothing had changed.) The stations complained to the FCC, and a bunch of DJs soon found themselves trying to sneak the transmitter down Drake's back stairs while the government knocked on his front door. They didn't make it.

There were other illicit stations in the 1970s, too, scattered here and yon. Weiner and Ferraro, now relocated to northern Maine, even held a pirate conference there in 1972. One of the more unusual unlicensed outlets was KBSA, run by—of all things—the Fairfield, California, chapter of the Explorer Scouts. (The Explorers are a co-ed wing of the Boy Scouts, aimed at older teenagers.)

KBSA was on the air from 1973 to 1976; it used both an FM transmitter, which *may* have been weak enough to avoid breaking the law, and an AM transmitter, which deployed about one hundred watts of power, blanketed the whole town, and definitely *wasn't* legal. With time, it also began broadcasting—legally—over the local cable company's community information channel. The station covered local sports (high school games, the Police Athletic League), played popular music, sponsored dances, and even ran a few commercials, though rarely in exchange for money: in a typical barter, a man installed an acoustic ceiling in the studio for some ad time.

An audience gradually grew. Once, graced with thirteen extra copies of a Supertramp album—all right, so they didn't exactly break with the musical mainstream—the DJs decided to give the records to anyone who'd show up. Imagine their surprise after they announced this over the air, when the plaza outside was so packed with people that hardly anyone could move.

All this was done nonclandestinely, with the blessing and support of Fairfield's civic institutions. After all, the station was sponsored by the Boy Scouts. How could it be up to no good? At one point, it received a relatively friendly visit from an amused FCC agent. "You boys have a really good sound," he told them. "Why don't you go legal?"[14]

Then there was "Mark the Peg-legged Brass Pig," who ran an AM station with three friends in Virginia from 1976 to 1979, then switched over to FM for a few more years. Its programming was uninspired, or so Mark claims today ("we played pretty much the same dreck that most college stations were playing at the time"), but the technical quality was well above average for a hobby operation.[15] I note his stations because he is one of the few unlicensed operators whose career spans both the early experiments of the 1970s and the modern micro movement: in 1996, he returned to radio, building a pirate station called the Anime Music Network. (The Brass Pig is a Japanophile, and *anime* is

Japanese film animation.) His programming reflected both his interest in the East and his distaste for the state of the West, and, as he discovered how far his signal was reaching, his delight in his work grew:

> Something in my chemistry changed. That evil grin I had thought I'd lost years ago slowly came back. The sinister mad scientist was at work again in the back of my head. I knew it was time for another "cleansing." The air waves were saturated with putrid signals modulated by acid rock, RAP, and other asundry unpleasant outpourings of a sick society. My collection of fine Japanese music CDs had grown to immense proportions, and I was dying to start sending these positive signals to counter-balance against the evil signals out there, to "appease the gods."

So it went until the end of the year, when a storm destroyed his setup and, for personal reasons, he decided not to rebuild it.

And more: Radio Free Ithaca, playing underground rock in upstate New York in the early 1980s; WHGC, a short-lived gospel outlet based in a Virginia church; a horde of stations in Florida; another horde in central Indiana, one of which even rented a billboard. Stations in the Midwest: in Cleveland, Chicago, Milwaukee. Stations on the coasts, from Los Angeles to Maine.

The biggest cluster of pirates was in New York City; the most famous were two teenagers, John Calabro and Perry Cavalieri, who ran WCPR[16] in Brooklyn's Marborough housing project. They started their station in response to AOR's fossilizing effect on rock radio: "We were always music fans," Calabro later recalled, "but sometime in the mid-1970s we stopped being thrilled with it. It was boring."[17] So they took matters into their own hands, bought a transmitter from another pirate, and started playing the music they wanted to hear. They also brought talk radio back to their borough. "Brooklyn, which is bigger than most cities, had no local programming," Calabro complained. "There were national talk shows—we could tune to Larry King on sixteen separate places on the dial—but there were no local talk shows."[18]

"Local" is a relative term, of course. Hardly a micro station, the Brooklyn operation could be heard, one journalist reports, "throughout New England, into the Midwest, and south to Virginia and the Carolinas."[19] They later shifted to FM and, still later, to shortwave.[20]

They also inspired a lot of imitators, in the New York region if nowhere else. In 1982, the British weekly *The Economist* reported that "at least 20" pirates were active "around New York," plus "enough in New England to support what is called the Pirate Radio Network."[21] The New Yorkers' "Free Radio Campaign" claimed to have one hundred affiliates. Yet hardly any of those broadcasters built a serious audience. Many of the stations noted by *The Economist* could be heard only on shortwave. And even on the AM and FM bands, few unlicensed outlets lasted long, and almost all of them conducted their business clandestinely. When the yippie tabloid *Overthrow* ran a piece about pirate broadcasting in 1985, the pseudonymous author ("Comrade Jim") simply assumed that pirates would transmit from the shadows. The article alluded briefly to Britain's old offshore operations, but its real inspirations, it seemed, were Third World guerrillas ("The world's most famous Radio Pirate was Fidel Castro, who operated Radio Rebelde . . .").[22]

But it was also in 1985, in Fresno, California, that low-power, local broadcasting—*microbroadcasting*, as some would soon start to call it—started creeping into the sunshine. A black man named Walter Dunn (or, as he called himself on the air, the Black Rose) started operating Zoom Black Magic Radio from a 1944 Arjo trailer parked just outside his home. He'd actually started the station on a dare, but it rapidly evolved into something bigger: as the only black-oriented station in Fresno, it quickly found a following, broadcasting grassroots music, militant talk, and ads for black businesses. Soon Dunn wasn't just a pirate but an evangelist for the nascent cause, preaching the virtues of low-power radio.

One of the outlets he helped inspire was WTRA, based in the rundown housing projects of Springfield, Illinois. And it was with WTRA and its founder—M'banna Kantako, *née* DeWayne Readus—that the modern microbroadcasting movement begins. Dunn begat Kantako, and Kantako begat hundreds more.

9

Micro Radio: Every Man a DJ

When I talk to people, they tell me that they feel us inside of them. It's not just that they listen to us on the radio. They feel us inside.

—M'banna Kantako

A SMALL GROUP of cameras gathered in a courtyard at the John Hay Homes, waiting for the tall black blind man to speak. A younger fellow—dressed, like the speaker, in black T-shirt, black pants, and black beret—guided him to the microphones. The blind man's name was De-Wayne Readus, and he planned to get arrested that day.

"It's a beautiful day for freedom, ain't it?" he said. "Let me begin by extending a welcome to our friends, our colleagues, and members of the press. Welcome to the bottom of the American dream. Or as we call it out here in the projects, the American nightmare."

Readus began softly and slowly, speaking with more volume and intensity as he continued. His impending arrest, he announced, was no cause for fear. It was a victory—"for creativity over destruction, for imagination over regimentation. . . . Let us remember the story of this victory, so we can pass it on to our children as a humble inspiration to them to carry on the struggle for freedom. Somebody tell them of the day that it took an Afro-Saxon from Washington and five white policemen to shut down a one-watt radio station being operated by an unarmed blind man. Somebody tell them how the pulse of WTRA's one watt of truth has overpowered the 50,000 megawatts of establishment propaganda for over 16 months."

He spoke for four minutes, relating his station's proudest moments: how it gave a voice to the victims of police brutality, taught young people radio skills, and gave the black people of Springfield, Illinois, a taste of liberty. He took a few questions from reporters. And then he switched on his transmitter and waited for the police to come.

And waited. And waited.

Finally he entered an apartment, a cameraman from the press conference right behind him, and placed a call to the cops.

"Yeah, this is DeWayne Readus, and I would like a car sent to 333 North 12th Street." A pause. "Well, I've just committed an act of civil disobedience, and I want to be arrested." Another, briefer pause. "I violated an FCC, ah, citation. You can check it, just turn your radio on—107.1." After another pause, Readus recited his phone number, then fell silent again. In the background, a Tracy Chapman song blared.

"Yeah," Readus muttered into the receiver. "Sure." He turned from the phone. "They put me on hold," he said, and burst out laughing.

"Hey, David!" a reporter cackled. "Tell 'em he's having a hard time getting arrested!"

Readus was still speaking into the phone. "You can't arrest me?" he was saying. "The FCC has to arrest me?"

Off camera, someone was cracking up completely. "I didn't know the FCC *had* policemen," a voice said.

Someone piped up. "Since this is a federal violation, maybe we should go down to the federal building." So they piled into a car and headed to the feds' local outpost.

No FCC agents were in.

"It sure is hard to get arrested in America, isn't it?" a reporter shouted.

"Yeah," Readus replied. "When you *want* to get arrested."[1]

Readus knew a few things about arrests. A childhood bout with glaucoma had started him on the road to blindness, but it took some cops to finish the job. It had happened in 1983, while Readus was DJing at a party. A brawl broke out and the police arrived, in theory to stop the melee, in practice to add to it. When they were through beating the disc jockey, he couldn't see a thing.

The experience helped radicalize Readus, and two years later he joined some other residents of the John Hay Homes—plus the cherubic and bearded Mike Townsend, a professor at Sangamon State who resembled nothing so much as a militant Santa—in organizing the Tenants' Rights Association. The TRA first fought a planned expansion to the local expressway, then convinced the Springfield School Department to add a new bus stop. (Before, many kids from the projects had to cross a dangerous intersection to get to school.) It then moved deeper into politics, getting involved in a battle over the city government's structure.

In 1985, some civil rights activists sued Springfield under the Voting Rights Act, demanding that it abandon its commission form of government, a centralized system with little room for neighborhood input—and, hence, little room for the low-income blacks concentrated in John Hay and similar housing projects. The TRA supported the suit, then cried foul when the plaintiffs settled with the city. Springfield had agreed to some concessions—it would adopt a ward-based system, with ten locally elected aldermen—but for Readus and others, this was only a baby step toward community control. And indeed, the John Hay activists quickly found themselves at odds with the first representative to be elected from their ward, partly over trade with South Africa and partly over the police. The alderman had proposed creating a civilian review board to hear complaints about brutality, but the association deemed his plan too weak; it wanted a board with more teeth.

Few of these nuances made their way into the local press, which cared little for the TRA. Sick of the slanted coverage, the activists decided to create some media of their own. Townsend suggested that they publish a newspaper. Readus, aware that much of the group's constituency was illiterate, had a better idea. "I'm blind," he told Townsend; "let's do radio. I don't get off on print that much."[2]

The TRA couldn't afford to navigate the FCC's expensive application process, so it decided not to apply for a license. Readus had heard of the Black Rose's station in Fresno, and he didn't see why he couldn't do the same thing. Besides, he didn't really think the FCC had the right to tell people whether or not they could be on the air.

So he bought some equipment from a company called Panaxis,[3] and, on November 25, 1987, his half-watt operation—christened WTRA, after the group that birthed it—went on the air. The signal didn't reach much further than the boundary of the John Hay Homes, but that was all right: that was the only audience it wanted. Readus took the helm as "deprogramming director," and for eighteen months, the authorities let the station broadcast its rap, reggae, radical rhetoric, and bread-and-butter commentary on local issues. The first programs were relatively low key: Readus's wife Dia or their kids would start playing music after dinner, and then Readus would take over around 10. Soon listeners were joining the station themselves—kids especially—and producing shows of their own.

With time, WTRA became a thorn in the police department's side. In January 1989, some Springfield cops beat a local boxing coach and his son. Readus interviewed the victims in their hospital beds, then broadcast the tape to an outraged audience. A couple of months later, Readus was there after a domestic dispute turned into a hostage crisis, with around a hundred heavily armed officers on the scene. After three days of tension, covered live on WTRA, someone started shooting; three people from the projects were killed. In the days that followed, Readus continued to investigate the standoff and the shootings, and concluded that the police were engaged in a coverup. By overreacting to the initial dispute, Readus argued, the police had paved the way for the tragedy; they may as well have killed the victims themselves.

In fact, Readus suggested, that might be just what they had done.

In that atmosphere, Readus began inviting victims of police brutality onto the station to tell their stories. The local constabulary ran to the FCC, alleging that a listener had complained to them about on-air profanity. The feds ordered the station to shut down. The broadcasters turned off the transmitter and considered their options. After two weeks, they were back on the air.

The FCC retaliated by levying a $750 fine. To this day, Readus has refused to pay it. Aware that the man probably doesn't have $750 to pay, the commission left him alone, ignoring him for the next ten years. This led to that embarrassing moment in the Hay Homes courtyard when no one was willing to arrest Readus, but it also let his station thrive. It pumped up its power, eventually reaching a level of thirteen watts. It changed its name several times—first to Zoom Black Magic Liberation Radio, then to Black Liberation Radio, then to African Liberation Radio, then to Human Rights Radio. Readus changed his name, too, to M'banna Kantako ("Resisting Warrior").

But its central concerns have stayed the same. It still speaks to Springfield's dispossessed, and it still keeps close tabs on the cops. Kantako now keeps a police scanner at home and broadcasts its contents between shows. (Sometimes he mixes the scanner reports with a tape of barnyard hogs squealing. Once he played a full ninety minutes of the hogs, after introducing it as a "secretly recorded meeting at the Springfield police station.") M'banna claims his broadcasts have reduced police violence against blacks, and while it's hard to draw a direct cause-and-effect relationship between the two, there's anecdotal evidence to support his stance. On October 13, 1990, journalists Luis Rodríguez and Tony Prince dropped by Kantako's apartment to do a show about police brutality. According to Rodríguez, two cops immediately accosted the pair as they left the station, ordering them "to spread our legs and place our hands against a wall." Apparently angry about the show they'd just heard, the officers harassed the pair for around twenty minutes—and then, "Suddenly, residents of the project began pouring out of their apartments. It turned out Kantako was broadcasting an account of what the police were doing as his wife . . . relayed details from the porch."[4] The cops let the reporters go.

Dia and the couple's homeschooled children started to read books and newspapers over the air, often editorializing along the way, and M'banna continued to deliver his fiery commentaries on the news, denouncing racism, police brutality, drugs, the war on drugs, and injustices both distant and close to home. Music, too, remained a part of the stew, though M'banna barred records he deemed too sexist or materialistic. Not as many kids helped at the station as before: many who'd once been part of the project had been harassed by the police or at school. Kantako himself was nearly killed when someone fired a .357 Magnum slug into his home.

Not even the death of the John Hay Homes silenced the station. In February 1997, the Department of Housing and Urban Development took a wrecking ball to the projects. When they kicked M'banna and some others out of an apartment they were using for youth programs, Kantako recorded the eviction and later played it on the station. It was 4:45 in the morning, but a midget who lived nearby came by to make sure everything was all right. "So that's the power of it," Kantako later exclaimed. "I mean here's a midget coming into these projects that are now empty except for me and my family. He thought the eviction was happening right then. If he was listening to the program he would have to think there are hundreds of police and everything over here, but he came at 4:45 in the morning."[5]

Human Rights Radio continued to broadcast from the Kantakos' apartment until February 28, the night before their building came down. Then they packed up the transmitter and moved it to his new home. The community was a little more dispersed after the Homes died, but it was still there, and still suffering; and Kantako and his transmitter were still there to give it a voice.

A decade after Kantako's attempt to get arrested went awry, the

gendarmes finally arrived, shutting down his transmitter and confiscating his equipment in September 2000. They claimed the station had
started interfering with air traffic control signals, a charge that may
have been true (we'll take a closer look at the air-traffic issue later on).
In October, Kantako went back on the air, the problem apparently
fixed—and broadcast a tape of the preceding month's raid. In December, the feds shut him down again. At press time, he's transmitting once
more, waiting for the government's next move.

The Springfield station received a flurry of attention in 1989 and 1990,
with stories in major newspapers, on NPR, even in *Playboy* and on MTV.
Around that time, Kantako and Townsend started thinking about starting a network of micro-powered operations. They made a video showing how to set up a station of your own, and encouraged others to follow them onto the air. With time, this blossomed into a movement. By
1997, there were by some counts as many as a thousand micro stations
around the country.

Why did micro radio take off so suddenly, when for decades it had
rarely been more than a hobby? One could make a narrowly technical
argument: good broadcast equipment was getting cheaper; therefore,
more people went on the air. But there was more at work:

1. Consolidation swept commercial radio in the 1990s, for reasons
   we'll examine later. As a result, station formats became even
   more narrow, more risk averse, and more obsessed with demographics. Career broadcasters started losing their jobs, to be replaced by computer programs and satellite feeds. In some markets, you simply couldn't do anything interesting on the air if
   you wanted to work at a licensed station.
2. The community radio movement hit its growing pains in the '80s
   and '90s. It had started relying on Washington for money right
   before an unfriendly administration came to town. In response,
   as we've seen, many stations turned to professional consultants
   and commercial underwriters for help. In the past, disgruntled
   DJs might have started new outlets of their own, but times had
   changed. The Class D option had been closed. The price of existing FM licenses had skyrocketed. And would-be broadcasters
   faced increasingly intense competition for increasingly rare noncommercial frequencies, with the religious chains particularly

eager to expand. If you were interested in reviving the old style of community radio, piracy was often your only viable option.

This was eventually proclaimed by no less a source than Lorenzo Milam. "Now NPR and the FCC and PBS and the commercial broadcasters have finally, and at last, perverted the Communications Act of 1934," he wrote, "so that there is no way in the world—outside of you and me handing over a check for $20,000,000 to some existing broadcaster—for us to get on the air, legally, in any of the top 100 markets. Thus I highly recommend going illegal."[6]

3. There was a surge in other sorts of do-it-yourself media, from xeroxed zines to the so-called cassette underground, a network —many networks—of musicians who record their work at home and trade it by mail (and, after the invention of MP3s, by e-mail).

4. Would-be pirates had more role models. For a few days in 1987, Allen Weiner and some disgruntled broadcasters transmitted freeform rock 'n' roll over Radio New York International, an offshore station aboard the good ship *Sarah*. The Coast Guard quickly raided and destroyed it, without any statutory authority to do so, but it got a lot of attention in the meantime: the press loved it (*Rolling Stone* named it the best radio station of the year), and it became a bright symbol to fans fed up with the state of rock radio. It also reminded Americans just what pirate radio was, and it surely prompted some people to think about starting pirate stations of their own. M'banna Kantako's example had the same effect, especially since he was doing radio so *cheaply*.[7]

Of all the people Kantako inspired, the best known was a Berkeley leftist named Stephen Paul Dunifer. As a teen in the 1960s, Dunifer had been involved at the fringes of the Free Speech Movement; his first job, a couple of years later, was as an engineer at a TV station. By the '90s, he was devoting his time to political causes, one of which involved his hometown's famous People's Park. The authorities wanted fewer public concerts in the park, and had started seizing amplifiers from any concert stage that failed to meet all the city's labyrinthine rules. In response, Dunifer suggested installing a radio transmitter on stage, with power low enough to fall below the FCC's regulatory radar. The audience would tune their radios to the appropriate frequency, the amps would be unnecessary, and the cops wouldn't be able to do a damned thing. The plan worked, and Dunifer—aware not just of Kantako's station, but of Japan's Mini FM movement—started thinking about other uses for an FM transmitter.

When the Gulf War began, in 1991, Dunifer became disgusted with the mainstream media's overwhelming bias in favor of President Bush's foreign policy. KPFA presented some dissenting voices, of course, but Pacifica was already starting to rot, and Dunifer knew it. He didn't think he could be sure it would still be there when the next war came along.

So he started a new station. Free Radio Berkeley held its first experimental broadcast at a Rainbow Family gathering in April 1992. (The Rainbow Family is a loose association of hippies and other counterculture types.) Dunifer returned to his workshop to build a better transmitter, then hauled it out in December, broadcasting in front of KPFA to drive home the point that Pacifica was losing its way.

Two months later, Free Radio Berkeley was ready for a regular schedule. It initially transmitted weekly from Dunifer's house, but, after a close call with the FCC, he started broadcasting from the Berkeley hills instead—always wary, always moving, with Dunifer's accomplices carrying his equipment in their backpacks. Gradually, the station's schedule expanded, airing the familiar community-radio sampler of music and left-wing politics plus a smattering of surprises, such as the occasional militiaman. One source of volunteers was KPFA, which started purging its radical elements just as Free Radio Berkeley started to receive national attention.

As Dunifer was starting his station, two more activists, Richard Edmondson and Jo Swanson, were founding San Francisco Liberation Radio across the Bay. Edmondson had only recently left the ranks of the homeless—or "semi-homeless," as he prefers to say, since he still could sleep in whatever run-down car, camper, or van he was driving at the time. For four years, from 1986 to 1990, he roamed the country with his German shepherd; for two more years, he lived on the streets of San Francisco. It was there that he discovered Food Not Bombs, a group that regularly clashed with the cops for feeding homeless people without a permit. And it was there, in 1992, that he met Stephen Dunifer, at a radio workshop at the San Francisco Art Institute.

Dunifer's presentation was thick with technical jargon, and many found it more frustrating than illuminating. "I hadn't gotten much out of the workshop," Edmondson later wrote, "and I thought the same was pretty much true for others. The suspicion was confirmed a week or so later when only a fraction of those who had been present turned up for a second workshop—at Dunifer's workspace in Berkeley. Then a third workshop, at which only a fraction of those turned out, came and went, until pretty soon, out of those who had been at the original workshop at the institute, there was pretty much only me—turning up at Dunifer's door and calling him on the phone, trying to make myself as useful as possible without being too much of a nuisance."[8] Meanwhile, Edmondson and other members of Food Not Bombs started syndicating a radio show to community stations.

In May 1993, with Dunifer's help, the now-housed Edmondson and his housemate Swanson were on the air. They initially based their station where Edmondson used to live—in the back of his VW van—and transmitted clandestinely from the hills. On September 22, 1993, that changed. Around 9:30 that evening, FCC agent David Doon traced the illegal signal to the Volkswagen and knocked on the door. Edmondson refused to show Doon any identification, refused to let him look in the vehicle, and drove away. He figured that was the end of it, only to discover the local police had blocked off the entire northbound lane of Webster Street. The officers ordered him to stop and to leave the van with his hands in plain sight, as though he might pull an Uzi from his wagon and mow the coppers down. It gradually became clear that the police had no idea who Edmondson was or why they had been called out to stop him. Cops continued to arrive, and at least twenty were there when Doon finally reappeared, checked Edmondson's ID, and allowed the broadcaster to go on his way.

The event frightened Edmondson, but it also brought the station a lot of positive publicity. He may even have gained a few listeners: some of the officers, upset that Doon had wasted their time, asked Richard about his broadcasting schedule. "After that," Swanson later explained, "we realized that we had nothing to lose so we decided to broadcast out of our own apartment, and that made things a lot easier."[9] Like its sister station in Berkeley, San Francisco Liberation Radio benefited from the exodus from KPFA, with one purged Pacifica programmer—former Panther Kiilu Nyasha, host of *Freedom Is a Constant Struggle*—becoming (in effect) a co-owner of the operation. The station soon became a resource for San Francisco's substantial activist community. (Not that it lacked detractors. One former Pacifica staffer, while admiring

Edmondson's own programs, told me that the station as a whole seemed like "a bad KPFA.")

Meanwhile, like Dunn and Kantako before him, Dunifer was turning into an evangelist, preaching the micro radio gospel to anyone willing to listen. On June 1, 1993, the FCC gave him an unintended boost by fining him $20,000 for unlicensed broadcasting—twenty times the levy the law allowed. (They defended this by arguing that the ordinary penalty was only for "routine" violations.) Dunifer asked the National Lawyers Guild to defend him.

The Lawyers Guild is a venerable radical institution with roots in the Marxist Old Left. Its Committee on Democratic Communications, however, had lately been drifting in a more anarchistic direction.[10] The Guild was already interested in micro radio: Alan Korn, an attorney there, had researched the issue thoroughly while preparing to defend Kantako against the FCC, an effort that ended when M'banna decided not to meet the commission in court. (That, he feared, would imply that he accepted its right to rule the air.) Now Dunifer was offering to be a test case instead.

The FCC delayed action for months, and Free Radio Berkeley kept broadcasting in the meantime. The commission then filed in district court for an injunction to shut the station down, prompting the biggest boost the free radio movement had received to date. On January 20, 1995, Judge Claudia Wilken refused to grant the injunction, citing the possibility that the ban on micro radio was unconstitutional. Dunifer was free to keep broadcasting until she made her final ruling. Wilken did ultimately side with the government, but she didn't do so until June 1998, giving Free Radio Berkeley more than three years to grow, to build support, and to inspire others to go on the air.

The FCC was outraged. ("This opens up such a can of worms," its attorney David Silberman told Wilken. "You're giving carte blanche for this group of people to operate a radio station without a license.")[11] The National Association of Broadcasters was angry, too. But the David-and-Goliath story drew in the nation's journalists. And if the story they wrote and rewrote—the tale of Stephen Paul Dunifer, lone-wolf foe of the FCC—sometimes implied that the larger micro movement didn't exist, it also inspired many readers to join that movement themselves.

I was one of those journalists, writing about the case in the October 1995 issue of *Reason*. Like many newcomers to the issue, I spent much of my time trying to figure out whether there was any truth to the charge that micro stations were more likely to interfere with other broadcasters' signals. Dunifer's attorney, Luke Hiken, was emphatic: they weren't. "The only people who've complained are the FCC themselves," he told me. "They've driven up right next to the transmitters and reported that they're receiving unlicensed broadcasts on someone else's frequency."[12]

The FCC, needless to say, told a different story, insisting that it had received several complaints. But had it? A year before, *The Conspiracy*— the local Lawyers Guild's newsletter—had filed a request under the Freedom of Information Act for the origins, dates, and details of stations' complaints against Dunifer's broadcasts. In its reply, the commission explained that "several informal inquiries or complaints were received from local broadcast engineer and consultant sources who either saw articles in the local newspapers, heard the broadcasts themselves, saw one of Mr. Dunifer's flyers, had read Mr. Dunifer's internet postings, or had seen or heard about the Commission's May 1993 monetary forfeiture action issued against Mr. Dunifer." Furthermore, "these contacts were made by telephone or in person, no written records of the inquiries were made, and the individuals involved expressly requested confidentiality."[13] In other words, as of 1994, all the alleged complaints related to the undisputed fact that Dunifer was making unlicensed broadcasts, and not to any instances of interference. And no records of those purported communications existed.

Had there been problems since October? I spoke with Silberman and with Beverly Baker, the then-head of the FCC's Compliance and Information Bureau; both cited a complaint by KFOG, a rock station in San Francisco. A telephone conversation with KFOG's program director drew a blank; he suggested I speak with the legal department of the station's parent corporation, Susquehanna, in York, Pennsylvania. There, one lawyer passed me on to another lawyer, who directed me to yet another lawyer, who said he wasn't the person I should be speaking with.

The complaint's origin eventually emerged: a letter dated May 2, 1995, sent from Susquehanna senior vice president Charles T. Morgan to the FCC's general counsel (and future chairman), William Kennard. The letter—sent from Pennsylvania, not San Francisco—was apparently a product of federal prodding. "The existence," Morgan wrote,

> of Free Radio Berkeley and other so called "Pirate Radio" operators in the San Francisco Bay area was a point of discussion at an FCC panel

at the recent NAB convention in Las Vegas. Ms. Beverly Baker . . . was
a member of that panel and stated that to her knowledge "the FCC had
not received any complaints concerning these illegal operations."
After this panel discussion, I discussed this matter with members of
the Commission's staff who suggested that I direct this letter to you.[14]

The bulk of Morgan's complaints, like those cited in the FCC's earlier response, concerned the station's legal status, not interference. Indeed, he came up with only two listener protests, just one of which
involved KFOG. For his part, Dunifer declared that no one had complained to *him* about interference—and if someone did, he'd immediately shut his transmitter down long enough to fix the problem.

Eventually, I realized that the essential issue wasn't whether this
particular pirate was stepping on someone else's airwaves. Dunifer
probably wasn't, but not every microcaster was as careful. The important fact was that low-watt broadcasters were no more likely than anyone else to cause interference. Indeed, *unlicensed* broadcasters were no
more likely than anyone else to cause interference. Legal stations can be
sloppy sometimes, too.

And the FCC isn't necessarily the best way to stop interference,
whether or not the offender has a license.

Consider Radio Maranatha, a Christian pirate on the west side of
Cleveland. Maranatha was founded by Angel Dones, who with his wife
published a weekly paper, *Nuevos Horizontes,* for the city's Hispanic
communities. Dones decided that the Spanish-speaking community
wasn't properly served by Cleveland's existing stations, so he set up
one of his own, at 89.7 FM.

Alas—there already was a station at 89.7: WKSU, an NPR affiliate
based in nearby Kent. Dones knew about the other outlet, but he figured his signal wouldn't interfere with it because it was in a different
town. Kent was only thirty-eight miles away, however, and WKSU had
a large audience in Cleveland. So in January 1998, when Radio Maranatha started broadcasting, listeners started complaining to WKSU, and
WKSU started complaining to the FCC.

It looked like a clear-cut case of interference. Yet the commission
was slow to act, allegedly because of all the protocols its agents had to
follow. "Our attorney said that they're very fastidious," recalls John
Perry, the general manager of the Kent station. "They come in and they
have to tape record so many instances, and do power readings and fre-

quency readings, because when they do finally want to move, they want to have an open-and-shut case. They don't want it to be arguable."[15] Still, when WKSU, acting on its own, got some friendly engineers to take readings and accumulate the information the FCC needed, they finished well before the government was ready to move.

In the meantime, claims Perry, Dones pushed his power up from twenty watts to four hundred, "essentially wiping us out in probably a good third to a half of Cleveland metro area." Dones strongly denies this. (His exact words: "That's a lie.")[16] Either way, the feds still wouldn't act. "We had had our attorneys file a complaint with the commission," Perry complains. "We had contacted our congressional delegation and lobbyists, National Public Radio—everybody had been placing calls to the FCC. Listeners were writing letters. They were very, very much aware of the existence of the pirate." After a couple months of frustration, WKSU decided it might be better off bypassing the commission altogether. So it prepared to file a lawsuit instead—to sue Radio Maranatha for interfering with its signal and consequently causing a dip in its income. (Fewer listeners means fewer pledges, and Perry says some underwriters were starting to pull out, too.)

In other words, the station returned to the approach Congress had rejected seventy years before: to treat interference as a tort.

WKSU was hardly opposed to federal regulation of the airwaves. Indeed, it hoped the threat of the lawsuit would finally prompt the FCC to act. The station's attorney approached the FCC and said it had three days to enforce the law. If it didn't do so within that time, the Kent station would apply for a temporary restraining order from the Cuyahoga County courts, thus transferring jurisdiction from Washington to Ohio.

Almost instantly, the FCC made its move, and in March Maranatha left the air. According to Dones, he had reached an agreement with the Kent station just a day before the feds arrived: he would move to a different frequency, and it would withdraw the suit. If that's true, that means that both stations could still be broadcasting today if the FCC had stayed out of the dispute.

Clearly, there's a gulf between the government's interest in enforcing its licensing scheme and stations' interest in enforcing the clarity of their signals. If interference is the question, the FCC isn't the best answer.

•

When Judge Wilken finally ruled against Free Radio Berkeley, she did so on narrow technical grounds. Dunifer, she decided, did not have standing to challenge the constitutionality of the FCC's rules, because he had not applied for a waiver to those regulations. It was a bizarre decision. The FCC had raised the waiver issue in its arguments, and at least one unlicensed station—Excellent Radio, in Grover Beach, California—had tried, unsuccessfully, to apply for one. But in all its history, the commission had only twice waived the relevant regulations. One case was in Alaska, the one state where low-power radio was allowed anyway. The other involved an isolated southwestern Indian reservation. Hardly the stuff of which precedents are made.

Nonetheless, the court ordered Free Radio Berkeley to cease broadcasting, and after an emergency meeting the station shut itself down. Many other operations, including San Francisco Liberation Radio, followed suit. Wilken also enjoined Dunifer from "doing any act, whether direct or indirect, to cause unlicensed radio transmissions or to enable such radio transmissions to occur."[17]

But in the three years before Wilken's ruling, the number of pirates had exploded. Many believed, falsely, that Dunifer's grace period applied to them as well. Dunifer began giving workshops on how to start a micro radio station; he also started selling transmitter kits. (The latter activity gave him a bad reputation in some quarters: sometimes Dunifer took forever to mail out the kits, they didn't always work when they arrived, the assembly instructions weren't very clear, and Dunifer wasn't always helpful—indeed, he could be downright rude—when his customers called him for assistance.) Nor was Dunifer the cause's only missionary. The movement had spread across the country and over the northern and southern borders, with several people taking on evangelical roles. There was, for example, a Santa Cruz radical named Tom Schreiner, who helped about a dozen stations go on the air in both the United States and Mexico. Schreiner had no technical background: a high school dropout from the Fresno projects, he'd spent some time working as a carpenter, gotten into Berkeley without a high school diploma, and eventually become an archeologist. Now in his forties, the longtime fan of the Black Rose had become similarly excited by Black Liberation Radio and by Dunifer's early experiments in Berkeley.

In 1994, Schreiner tried and failed to put a station on the air in Santa Cruz. A year later, feeling that the political climate was changing, he helped a different group launch Radio Zapata in nearby Salinas. Many more stations followed, from Radio Watson in Watsonville, California, to several Zapatista outlets in Chiapas. His own city proved more amenable to unlicensed radio a year later, when Free Radio Santa Cruz went on the air; it gathered enough of a following for the city council to endorse it four years later. And in 1996, Schreiner helped organize an international microbroadcasting conference in the Bay Area.

"I'm not interested in making micro radio legal," he says. "Frankly, I think it's better if it's not. I'm interested in radio as an instrument of struggle."[18] The idea was to help people in a town or neighborhood start a station, giving whatever tips, technical assistance, and—sometimes—money that they needed. (Schreiner financed the first eight or nine stations he built, going far into debt in the process. Few paid him back.) Then it was up to the broadcasters to build an institution that was a real part of its community. If they succeeded, then the community would defend the station. If they didn't succeed—well, then maybe the next group he helped would.

These were working-class stations, often run by and for farmworkers. Radio Zapata, Schreiner says, was operated almost entirely by East Salinas's strawberry pickers, plus "some local leadership in the neighborhood that's just as poor as they are." It played music from southern Mexico, it had call-in shows, and it engaged itself in local issues—helping organize a rent strike, for example. It also offered detailed analysis of (and debate over) larger concerns, such as the North American Free Trade Agreement. And all of it was in Spanish.

Radio Watson was launched by El Comité por Derechos Humanos, a secular offshoot of a Watsonville liberation theology group. El Comité already had some radio experience. One member, Olga Diaz, hosted a weekly show on Salinas's Radio Bilingüe affiliate, and she frequently interviewed her Comité cohorts on the air; another member had worked for ten years at a community station in Veracruz, Mexico. With Schreiner's help and funds, the group got Radio Watson running. Soon young people were getting involved, mostly community-college students with part-time jobs around town. "And they," comments the Comité's Frank Bardacke, "sort of took us over."[19] He says that proudly, not bitterly: with the young people behind it, the station attracted a lot of local participation and support. It governed itself democratically and supported itself with car washes, tamale sales, and a garage sale, plus dues from its DJs ($2 a month if you're employed, $1 if not) and the occasional rent party.

Radio Watson played a lot of Mexican music, though not the kind you'd hear on the area's legal stations; Watson's listeners preferred Mexican rock and folk. Grade-school kids did performances in its studio. It covered the rebellion in Chiapas—El Comité strongly supported the Zapatistas—and did live hookups with a correspondent there. It had a sports hour, featuring call-ins and commentaries on soccer matches both in Mexico and in the local youth league. A doctor gave on-air medical advice. There was a poetry program. There were shows on labor issues, by and for the pickers and packinghouse workers. Several people who got their start at Radio Watson later moved on to careers in "legitimate" broadcasting.

As you'd expect, some of the outlets Schreiner helped start were suppressed, not just by the FCC but by angry local authorities. (One— in Hollister, California—was raided by cops who claimed it was a meth lab. They didn't find any methamphetamine or any tools with which to make the drug, but they did seize all its broadcast equipment.) Other stations remained invisible outside their communities, shunning the political limelight.

By now, Schreiner believes, micro radio simply can't be killed. The technical obstacles keep falling, he explains, and more and more people are spreading the word.

One increasingly important medium for spreading such information— though not, one suspects, among migrant farmworkers—was the Internet, which boasted (and boasts) several sites devoted to free broadcasting. The most important: the Free Radio Network,[20] Pirate/Free Radio,[21] and Radio 4 All.[22] The last, interestingly, was a benign byproduct of Pacifica's civil war. Lyn Gerry had assembled a website called Freepacifica, filled with press clips and internal documents. Radio 4 All was its front porch, a site you went through on the way to the meat. She started adding links to other free radio projects, most of which were pirate stations; the micro-related traffic began to increase; and before long, she and her partner, Shawn Ewald, had added a page just for news of the micro movement. Then they launched an e-mail list devoted to the same topic. It's hard to describe just how important these were for radio activists, many of whom were just starting to interact over the Internet. Gerry and Ewald's website and list were places where pirates found out about other stations, where unlicensed engineers traded technical tips, where reporters went for a thumbnail sketch of the movement.

In the East, members of Radio Mutiny, a.k.a. West Philly Pirate Radio, did their first Radio Tour from January to March 1998. Mutiny, founded in 1996, was run by a collection of squatters, gardeners, hackers, and poets, from a black South African expatriate reporter to a health care worker called the Condom Lady who fought AIDS by broadcasting info on safer sex and safer drug use. The station had already gathered a lot of media attention, not just for its programs but for a series of public stunts, such as daring the FCC to shut it down as it broadcast in front of the Liberty Bell. The Radio Tours were its way of spreading the word, as one Mutineer, "Pete triDish," explained,

> We met with brave upstarts of diverse interests and generations, including forest activists, cable access stations, art galleries, labor organizers, black liberationists, a youth rights group, housing activists, college students, riot grrrls, catholic workers and techno enthusiasts. Some amongst these were already masters of their own frequency. At every stop, we set up and demonstrated a small transmitter in a café, a bookstore, a classroom, a community center or any venue that would have such rogues as us. . . . We marveled at the knowledge and ingenuity of other pirates whose paths we crossed, and brought tidings of new technique and innovation from station to station.[23]

TriDish—his given name is Dylan Wrynn, but "it's not easy going through life named after a hippie rock star"[24]—is a carpenter in his twenties, with dark-rimmed glasses, short-cropped hair, and a Castroesque black beard.[25] He was joined on the tour by several more pseudonymous Mutineers: the Mystery Kickboxer, Jenna Cide, and Winston Churchill.

The tour was quickly followed by the East Coast Microbroadcasting Conference, hosted by Radio Mutiny in a West Philadelphia church and elementary school in April 1998. Almost simultaneously, the western wing of the movement held a conference cum protest outside the NAB's annual gathering in Las Vegas. Some regional convocations followed, as well as a wider-ranging Grassroots Media Conference in Austin.

Mutiny, alas, didn't last much longer: the FCC busted it on June 22, and it was undergoing too much internal discord to reconstitute itself. The FCC's chief enforcer, Richard Lee, attended the bust, which happened to take place while the station was shut off. Undeterred, Lee switched the transmitter on—thus violating his own agency's rules—and announced that anyone tuned in was listening to an illegal radio station. And then he switched it off again, for good. (Lee also posed for a picture in front of Radio Mutiny's flag and helped himself to some prophylactics the Condom Lady had left as a present for the FCC.)

TriDish nonetheless went on a second Radio Tour in February and March 1999, along with Joan d'Arc of the Constructive Interference Collective in Memphis, Anne Tennah of Free Radio Gainesville, and a Brooklyn pirate dubbed Bubba Deluxe. Between the two long trips were several mini-tours that dropped by just one or two towns.

Another hub of the micro movement was Boston's Allston neighborhood, where a journalist named Stephen Provizer launched a public-access station called (naturally) Radio Free Allston. The outlet didn't have much of a direct impact outside Massachusetts, but its example was often touted to show how much one unlicensed station could accomplish. Provizer drew support from a remarkably wide range of Bostonians—not just activists and fans of independent music, but conservatives, moderates, and apolitical types, including immigrants from Vietnam, Haiti, Cape Verde, Brazil, and even farther-flung nations. The result was a station so impressive that even the Boston City Council endorsed it.

The Allston station finally disbanded in October 1997, following a visit from the FCC. But at least one of its principal figures—Provizer—remains active in the micro radio movement, both on his own and through his group, the Citizens' Media Corps. In 2000, he helped start a new station on the AM band.

One more force spreading the micro radio gospel was the ever-present inspiration of M'banna Kantako. In 1990, following his lead, Napoleon Williams and his girlfriend, Mildred Jones, set up a second Black Liberation Radio station, in Decatur, Illinois. Kantako soon retreated from the national scene, preferring to focus his work on Springfield, but other militant blacks, many of them associated with the anarchist group Black Autonomy, independently launched their own Kantako-inspired outlets, in Kansas City, in Richmond, and in Chattanooga.

The Chattanooga outlet was founded by a former Black Panther named Lorenzo Ervin. Ervin is the sort of figure one might timidly describe as *controversial*: in 1969, at a time when Panther leaders around the country were dying at the hands of the police, he decided to hijack an airplane to Cuba, which promptly deported him to Czechoslovakia.

He then made his way to Germany, where American agents drugged him and dragged him back to the United States, where he served nearly fifteen years in prison.

Disillusioned with Marxism, Ervin turned to anarchism. He also turned to radio, getting involved with the prison's carrier-current station and, after his release, with WRFG in Atlanta. Upon returning to Chattanooga, Ervin heard about Kantako's project and decided to start his own station, known alternately as Black Liberation Radio/Chattanooga and as 88.5 FM Chattanooga Free Radio. Most of Lorenzo's volunteers were more interested in playing records than in talking about local and global issues, but he still made time for politics, at times taking his microphone into the city's parks and streets and inviting passersby to share their thoughts. (People were less intimidated there, he found, so the discussions were "more frank" than he'd get on a call-in show.)[26] A white Chattanoogan described Ervin's outlet to me as "Lorenzo's hack radio that nobody listens to"; a black Chattanoogan, on the other hand, reported that *everybody* listened to it."

BLR/Chattanooga went off the air in 1998, as other projects and problems vied for Ervin's attention. That same year, some unpleasant information emerged about Decatur's Black Liberation Radio station, still run by Napoleon Williams.

For eight years, Williams's troubles with the government had been a rallying point for the microbroadcasting movement. The problem here wasn't the FCC: the commission had fined Williams $17,500 during his first year on the air, but it didn't send in any troops after he failed to pay them. The problem was the local authorities. Williams had a history of legal problems, including a prison sentence for armed robbery and subsequent allegations of theft, child abuse, and domestic assault; he and his wife were involved in an ongoing battle with the county Department of Children and Family Services for custody of their daughters. Until 1998, most activists assumed that these were simply trumped-up charges. Williams was constantly critical of both the police and the social welfare authorities, and they, in turn, subjected him to constant harassment. On January 9, 1997, for instance, the local cops raided Williams's home and seized his broadcast equipment, accusing him of "eavesdropping"—a felony charge based, apparently, on his taping and airing a pair of telephone calls. (That particular charge rankled Judge Scott Diamond when it landed in his court. "Linda Tripp gets probation for taping over 100 hours and then send an Afro-American man to jail for two phone calls?" he asked.[27] Williams, who had faced six months in prison, instead received thirty months probation and a fine.)

But on December 22, 1998, Dharma Bilotta-Dailey and Tracy Jake Siska began circulating a paper called "Black Liberation Radio: An Independent Investigation." The pair had conducted their investigation at the invitation of Napoleon himself, who had long urged outsiders to investigate for themselves whether the authorities were persecuting him or protecting the public. They had arrived openly biased in the broadcasters' favor, and they did a lot of work on Black Liberation Radio's behalf even as they investigated the charges against the station's operators. But as the evidence stacked up, they changed their minds.

Among the duo's conclusions:

- "Napoleon has claimed that the accusations of child abuse, and subsequent taking of his two children, revolve around a 1990 allegation made by Napoleon's stepdaughter. We learned through the internal records of the Illinois Department of Children and Family Services that at least three separate incidents of sexual abuse have been reported to DCFS in Illinois. All incidents were prior to the station going on the air." They make for gruesome reading, and I will spare you the details. Suffice it to say this: "Napoleon's known record in Illinois for sexual abuse against young children goes back as far as his residency in Illinois. It involves multiple children in unrelated incidents that span four years. These are unrelated victims and witnesses. Interviews with them were taken by different children's services workers. Separate police reports were made. We do not believe that all of these children with all of these parents and backgrounds could be making these stories up, or are the dupes of child protective services workers. Their workers did not know Napoleon when the first charges of abuse were made because Napoleon had just moved to Decatur from St. Louis. Napoleon had not started his station yet, and was not a target for local officials."[28]
- "A 1990 record mentions that Napoleon had violated a protection from abuse order that had been given to his ex-wife. In general, the purpose of a protection order is to protect a woman from a man with a history of violence against her. . . . On December

27, 1991 Napoleon literally broke the door down of Mildred's friend's apartment. He then proceeded to attack Mildred, smashing her head against the wall several times, and injuring her arm. Neighbors called the police. . . . In later police reports Napoleon confessed to the beating of Mildred." The pair later reconciled, and Mildred refused to testify against Napoleon in court. Yet, "References made by two of Napoleon's partners are enough for us to conclude that violence is a habit for Napoleon."[29]

- "Though it is difficult to refute or assert the verity of any particular claim of theft, we note that Napoleon's history of reported theft goes back at least eleven years prior to BLR going on the air."[30] It's therefore difficult to claim that the station caused his troubles.

Siska and Bilotta-Dailey didn't trade their loyalty to Napoleon for loyalty to the local authorities: the "eavesdropping" charge was still pretty egregious, and they weren't impressed with Mildred Jones's probation officers, who had sent Mildred "to prison for not completing her GED on time, despite illness, pregnancy and the need to nurse [a] three month old infant. The probation officers did not allow the GED teacher to testify in her probation hearing—something that the teacher regularly does—and instead misrepresented the teacher's statements."[31] But if the Decatur power structure did some terrible things, then so did Napoleon Williams.

This was a blow to the micro movement, sparking rifts that still persist today. (Lorenzo Ervin sharply questioned the Decatur report and broke off ties with virtually everyone who felt otherwise.) It didn't make a difference on a policy level: there are villains in every segment of society, and Napoleon Williams no more discredited the idea of Black Liberation Radio than Huey Meaux discredited the idea of Pacifica. But Napoleon and Mildred were a cause célèbre, regarded by many as heroes. When the truth came out, it hurt. Williams, a friend of Siska's concluded, was "a grifter who had latched onto a movement for his own gain."[32]

Some crooks and con men were bound enter the micro radio universe. The most tragic case wasn't in Decatur but in Los Angeles, where a widely loved activist's efforts to build a low-power station ended up killing him. Born in Tulsa, Michael Taylor was a former drug dealer and crack addict who had sobered up, gotten radicalized, and started working at Pacifica's KPFK, where he impressed a lot of his colleagues and listeners as a smart, caring, and passionately committed man. Squeezed out during the Pacifica purges—unlike several other black hosts, he wasn't fired, but he balked when management told him it would have to review all his programs before they aired—Taylor had decided to start a micro station instead, a Kantako-like outlet he'd call Los Angeles Liberation Radio.

Some of the people who joined the project were there for the right reasons. Bob Marston, for instance, gave technical help to several L.A. pirates, simply because he believes in the free radio cause. But some of the others were crooked, the sort of people who always seem to creep in when something is outlawed. In April 1996, Taylor was kidnapped, tortured, and shot. One of his partners was sentenced to death for his role in the murder (even though Taylor strongly opposed the death penalty). Two others were sent to jail.

The trio hadn't shared Taylor's vision for the station: they wanted to run commercials, and, unlike the coalition-minded Taylor, they wanted to run only black programming. When he broke with them, they insisted he give them the radio equipment he'd bought, and when he refused, they killed him. Los Angeles Liberation Radio was never born.

Fortunately, such stories were rare. Far more common were projects like Excellent Radio, operated from a storefront studio in downtown Grover Beach, at the heart of California's midstate Five Cities Area. In many ways, the Grover Beach station resembled San Marcos's Kind Radio. It had a lot of local supporters, including members of the local government. It covered local issues intensely, including live broadcasts of city council meetings. The rest of its schedule was as lively and diverse as its talk shows, mixing musical genres with no regard for commercial custom. It even shared Kind's roots in the marijuana subculture: the station's founder, Charley Goodman, owned a head shop next door.

But just as every town is different, so is every micro radio station. The Five Cities Area has a long history of bohemian mysticism, dating back to the days when the town of Halcyon was a stronghold of Theosophy. For years, the dunes have drawn free spirits to the region, and they've left a rich alternative culture behind, to lurk, sometimes invisibly, between the strip malls and beach shops and expressways. The avant-garde composer-pianist Henry Cowell lived there, not far from the Theosophists' Temple of People. So did Ella Young, a gun-running mystic from Ireland; and Gavin Arthur, astrologer and author and nephew of the twenty-first president; and Meyer Baba, the guru; and John Cage, the composer. It was this *other* Grover Beach that conjured an illicit signal into the ether, a station where the region's submerged voices could finally be heard, sometimes speaking directly into the microphone, sometimes buzzing in the background. (When the broadcasters built their studio, they decided not to soundproof it, letting the ambience of the street spill into the room and over the air.) Over the years, Goodman had become an amateur archivist, collecting and studying remnants of the beaches' bohemian lore. From this he developed a spiritual optimism that would suffuse his station.

Free Radio Berkeley served its fetal time as a PA system in People's Park; Kind Radio grew from the *Hays County Guardian*. Excellent Radio began as an art show and was inspired by two TV sets nestled in a Cambodian pagoda. In 1995, some of Goodman's friends performed an original opera, *The Father of Lies*. One of the props was the aforementioned pagoda; within it were two video screens, one displaying a moving mouth, the other a pair of eyes. The contraption made Goodman think about television's role in society. TV, he felt, kept people alienated from each other. We needed a different kind of media, he decided: media that would bring people together.

Goodman had already set aside part of his head shop as the Excellent Center for Art and Culture. He had also heard stories about M'banna Kantako's station in Springfield. Low-power radio seemed to be the medium he'd been looking for, and it soon inspired a new exhibit for the Excellent Center, *The Father of Lies vs. the Mother of Invention*. The father of lies was TV; the mother of invention was microbroadcasting.

The more Goodman investigated the topic, the more convinced he became that Grover Beach needed a station like Kantako's. "I'd thought I'd just do a pictorial show about this," he recalls. "Then I thought, *Jesus Christ, if this guy with no money and no eyes can do this, what kind of pussy am I if I don't do the same damn thing?*"[33] He already had some experience—he'd DJed for a decade at a nearby NPR outpost—and Stephen Dunifer lived only a few hours to the north. The transmitter he ordered from Free Radio Berkeley didn't work, but fortune soon intervened: while Goodman was waiting for Dunifer to repair his product, an engineer at the NPR station lent him one of its backup transmitters. Excellent Radio held its first broadcast almost immediately afterward.

The station matured quickly. Only two weeks after its debut, a storm knocked down all the region's radio towers—except Goodman's. Charley monitored his scanner closely, passing along storm news and emergency announcements to his listeners. The NPR station soon asked for its backup transmitter back, quieting Excellent Radio until the re-paired Dunifer kit arrived. But for a short time, it had been the only op-eration on the air. "It was a good example," Goodman says, "of how quickly you could become important."

Goodman asked the city council whether he could broadcast its meetings. After a few months, he got the go-ahead. The city attorney understood that the station had no license, but that, he felt, was a mat-ter between it and the FCC. California's open meetings act, on the other hand, guaranteed it the right to cover the council.

The station family continued to grow. Its volunteers ranged from skate punks to retirees, from white hippies to Spanish-speaking *cumbia* DJs. There was an afternoon kids' show, *Treasure Ivan*, hosted by '60s tunesmith Ivan Ulz, onetime composer for the Byrds, the Four Fresh-men, and other ancient pop groups. There was a swing show, a ska show, and a weekly helping of "pure pop for now people." One pair of programmers started interviewing the stars of the World Wrestling Fed-eration. And a sixtyish teacher-turned-Green named Annie Steele, al-ready locally famous for fighting the pesticides she blamed for local ill-nesses, hosted an evening talk show called *Pollutions—Solutions*. Local officials used to revile Steele as a crank, and, as she's the first to admit, they weren't without good reason. "I do my homework now," she told the *Santa Maria Times*. "When I first started, I didn't know what the homework was."[34] Over the years, as she learned more and made more allies, she graduated from crank to gadfly, and from gadfly to full-fledged force. After she joined Excellent Radio, her show became a local institution, the place where—for example—members of the Planning Department would come to talk with their constituents about the con-tamination of the nearby Nipomo Dunes.

Then there was Rudy, host of a tremendously popular Saturday-night reggae, rap, and R&B party, *A Taste of Soul*. Rudy was a former gangbanger who'd gone straight; his show had a big following among young people and, damn the stereotypes, among some of the local cops, who saw Rudy as a good influence. (Excellent Radio maintained cordial relations with the police, who faxed it the same press releases they sent

to all the other local media. The station even had a retired highway patrolman on its staff.)

The federal cops, naturally, were a different matter. The station
eventually received the inevitable letter from the FCC, based on a year-
old complaint that it was interfering with the search-and-rescue radio
service. The truth, Goodman later reported, turned out to be much more
mundane:

> We found it was about radio phones within this one block residential
> area where they are certainly not going to be doing much Search and
> Rescue. We might have broken into the communications of some-
> body's mobile communicator or something. So, we sent back east for a
> particular filter that would take care of this and we went off the air
> after we did the last city council meeting to show that we were more
> than willing to comply like any other radio station. We put in the filter
> which cleaned up the problem and then we went back on the air. . . .
> We've been broadcasting ever since.[35]

The phrase "ever since" is unfortunately out of date. One day after
Judge Wilken issued her ruling against Dunifer, Excellent Radio closed
its doors, announcing it would wait for a formal change in the law before returning to the air. Now dormant, the studio still seemed somehow alive, with the accumulated stock of a few years' activity still dec-
orating its walls: signs, fliers, placards, notes, a Ricky Skaggs bumper
sticker, posters of Malcolm X and Martin Luther King, a painting of a
cat, and, in the hall outside, Homer Simpson rendered either as a small
statue or a large doll.

In the meantime, echoes of Excellent Radio continued to rever-
berate through the beaches. Mark Kent, cohost of *The Surfin' Show*,
had already parlayed his program into a syndicated commercial-
radio gig; when Goodman stopped, Kent kept going. The former
highway cop moved his jazz show to NPR. And the Excellent crew
helped launch three more micro stations—now also discontinued,
alas—before the mother studio turned silent, all in nearby Santa
Maria. Two were in churches, and one was based in a halfway house
for juvenile delinquents. The kids went on the air on Friday and Saturday nights, under the house's supervision and with the judicial authorities' unofficial support.

These weren't simply traces of a dormant radio station. They were signs of transformed lives. Before Kent joined the station, he was a surfer working in his dad's auto body shop. Now he had a fledgling career as a broadcaster. And he could still surf. Hell, he had to. It was part of his job.

The biggest hotbed of unlicensed radio wasn't in California. It was in Florida, in Miami, Tampa, Fort Lauderdale, and various points in between—a pirate sector that evolved with little contact with other American microcasters. It was a good landscape for low-power broadcasting: flat and spacious, with few hills or skyscrapers to block a signal's progress. The Florida scene emerged in the mid-'80s, before M'banna Kantako and Stephen Dunifer discovered piracy; it grew out of the same sort of amateur tinkering that had produced the Falling Star Network in Yonkers and WMAS at the Western Military Academy. But the Florida stations caught on in ways those earlier experiments didn't: the technology fell into the hands of dancehall DJs, who started to broadcast their mixes, and immigrants, especially from Haiti and Jamaica, who found that micro radio was virtually the only way they could talk to one another on the air. By the 1990s, there were stations devoted to the biker subculture, to right-wing and left-wing dissent, to Christianity, to reggae, to immigrant Greeks. One of the most intriguing operations was Miami's Beach Radio, described by the reporter Sarah Ferguson in *Vibe* magazine:

> Beach Radio . . . started broadcasting an eclectic mix of hip hop, reggae, jazz, jungle, house, and talk from a South Beach penthouse.
>
> Beach repaired to a former crackhouse that now feels like Moon Doggie's surf shack: walls covered in tags and reggae posters, an old longboard stashed in one corner. DJs range from Luke, a Hilfiger model and grandson of Errol Flynn who plays conscious reggae, to Brother Mike, a blind guy who brings in stacks of oldies printed in braille. During the Saturday night hip hop show, hosted by a local MC named Rolup, it's not unusual to find 30 kids throwing down freestyles. Beyond music, Beach operates like a virtual community center, from helping residents campaign against high-rise development to promoting a campaign to free a whale from the Miami Seaquarium. Neisen Kasdin, the mayor of South Beach, is an occasional caller to one of the morning shows.[36]

The Florida scene could be pretty raucous. Not all the broadcasters were as careful about interference as they should have been, and some ended up jamming other pirates' signals along with those of licensed operations. Some of the stations were aware of the national micro movement, but many weren't. Willie Brown, Sr., started WLUV ("The Love Station") in Homestead, a poor, rural town at the edge of the Everglades, in 1985, after hearing about another Florida pirate. From then until 1998, when the FCC shut him down, he never contacted any microcasters outside the state, and none of them contacted—or even, apparently, were aware of—him. Most of his listeners didn't even realize their favorite station was illegal. Willie is an active member of the Homestead community, particularly its Christian and black subsections; his station played classic gospel music with some contemporary material mixed in. It also featured locally oriented talk, including interviews with candidates and, more regularly, a constant stream of announcements.

I visited Brown in 1999.[37] His wall is covered with citations from civic organizations, churches, and bodies of government, honoring him for his lifetime of activism. (Among other things, he helped found the local African-American Heritage Festival and the Martin Luther King Day Parade. On a less symbolic level, he's worked to bring jobs and homes to town, to beautify the streets, and to start an eye clinic.) He drove me around town that afternoon, introducing me to his former listeners. They were still loyal. Ask them about "Brother Brown" and they'll tell you how his station kept them abreast of events around the county, how it played Christian music they couldn't hear anywhere else, how it kept them company during the day. One retiree said how much she preferred it to the soap operas that share her afternoons now.

Not every Florida pirate was so benign. There is a substantial underworld in southern Florida, and unlicensed radio, as we've noted, sometimes appeals to people engaged in other unlawful activities. On September 1, 1999, for instance, police discovered a warehouse full of stolen goods, including a Range Rover, several hundred airbags, many other auto parts, some counterfeit vehicle identification stickers, some gold jewelry, and a handgun. The cops say the loot was linked to a station they'd helped the FCC bust in Hollywood, Florida, the day before. According to Cheryl Stopnick, a spokeswoman for the Broward County Sheriff's Office, the operators had been "using the airwaves to direct the criminal activities of their associates."[38] Assuming that's accurate, it's still hard to tell how widespread this sort of criminal connection is, though the FCC, naturally, plays it up as much as it can.

Even with such thieves at work, it's possible that southern Florida's loose tribe of hip-hop pirates—a network closely aligned with the city's dance clubs, with whom they share many DJs—has prevented more crime than it has inspired. In 1993, DJs Albert "Uncle Al" Moss and Tyrone "Tiny Tim" English, of Bass 91.9 FM, were widely credited with keeping the city's black community calm during the potentially explosive trial of William Lozano, a Hispanic police officer who shot and killed a black biker. The station was cofounded by Calvin Mills, a local record producer, and was based in Liberty City, a desperately poor ghetto. Unlike the Black Liberation stations, it maintained friendly relations with the city cops, participating in their Jammin' with the Man program. The local press was kind to them, too: the *Miami Herald* wrote that the DJs "do their best to take on the responsibilities [of licensed stations]. There's no on-air profanity. They play no sexually explicit lyrics and they stress the importance of staying in school."[39]

The same spirit was at work in another Liberty City outlet, Hot 97.7, the station that made a civic leader out of Brindley Marshall, a.k.a. Bo the Lover. In a past life, Marshall had been a gangster (in 1984, he even smuggled a gun into a courtroom) and had spent five years in prison. Upon his release, he turned his life around, returning to a pastime he'd originally taken up in his early teens: DJing. He quickly became one of the most popular disc jockeys on the club/party circuit.[40] A charismatic man in his thirties, Bo first went on the air in 1996. At first he ran a micro station, but by the time the FCC got him, he was transmitting at two thousand watts, covering all of Miami and then some.

Liberty City is the poorest, most run-down part of Dade County. Jobs are scarce, litter covers each corner, drug abuse is rampant, and crime is high. The Pure Funk Playhouse—the warehouse where the station had been based, which still serves as headquarters for Bo's DJing business—is only a few blocks from the dumpster where a little girl was killed in the crossfire between rival gangs. The Playhouse is painted yellow and red, with big black letters advertising the presence of "Pure Funk DJ's" inside. The outer walls also announce "Hot 97.7" to passersby, a sign that the pirates weren't trying to hide their activities from the law.

In fact, for a while, the local police set up a camera in an abandoned bank across the street, to surveil the young blacks who'd hang out in front of the Playhouse all day long. "They were sure we were fronting for something," says Bo. "They kept sending undercover cops over here, trying to buy crack."[41] It didn't take Bo long to figure out that the would-be buyers weren't real crackheads. They just weren't rude enough. Real addicts don't wait for you to finish talking with someone else before they ask you for some cocaine, Bo explains. They interrupt you. They demand the drugs. And you have to shoo them away.

Which they did. Unlike some of Miami's pirate stations, Hot 97.7 would never, say, broadcast where to score some coke, or where someone had spotted some cops. They always told pushers to stay off their corner, and, after that initial period of mistrust, the local police decided that the people in the warehouse weren't merely real DJs, but real allies in keeping kids away from drug abuse and violence. Liberty City's gangs are a far cry from the gently spacy potheads of San Marcos, Texas. Bo wanted nothing to do with them.

His disdain for the gangs was contagious. I hate to throw around clichés like "positive role model," but it became obvious as I watched Bo with the kids who hung out at the Playhouse after school—including other former gangsters who'd followed Bo's lead in cleaning up their lives—that he was exactly that. Miami Police Sergeant Frank Dean, the beat cop on Bo's block, praised Marshall's influence, attested that he "keeps these kids employed," and contrasted his station with the ones associated with criminals.[42] He wouldn't condone broadcasting without a license (naturally), but he had nothing but kind words for Bo's project.

In a neighborhood where there just isn't much to do, Hot 97.7 gave people a creative outlet. It also broadcast community announcements, and not just the bland local-calendar kind. (When a kid ran away from home, the police told his parents that they'd have to wait a day before they started searching. So Mom and Dad went to Bo's radio station, the call went out over the air, and by the end of the day the runaway had been found.) It also aired some talk shows. Kat, a teen mother turned community activist, hosted a weekly program called *Underground Teen Talk*, in which service providers and others took teenagers' calls about pregnancy, HIV, and related issues.

Above all, Hot 97.7 was *popular*. This wasn't unusual for Miami's outlaw stations, though there are those who'd prefer to deny it. "Let me find a way to say this tactfully," a DJ at one licensed station told *Vibe*.

"Miami has got Venezuelans and Colombians and Haitians and Cubans and a whole lot of people who just got off the boat from these repressive regimes, and now they think they're in America, the land of the free, and they think you can do whatever they want. [But] they're a bunch of little rookies. Qualitywise, they all suck."[43]

Someone forgot to tell the listeners. In other parts of the country, record companies were wondering why some of their releases were selling well in Miami without any local airplay. Then they found out that a lot of stations *were* playing them—it's just that those stations weren't licensed. (According to *Vibe*, Big Pun's album *Capital Punishment* topped Miami's Soundscan charts weeks before any of the legal stations were playing it.) After that, they routinely sent their new releases to the pirates.

As some licensed operations asked the FCC to shut the pirates down, other mainstream stations started copying their illicit competitors. So in 1996, when a Liberty City pirate called The Bomb started making waves, WEDR started a show called *The Bomb* and hired a former pirate DJ to host it. And in early 1998, when some fully licensed businessmen launched Tampa's WILD 98.7 FM, their disc jockeys claimed to be kids broadcasting illegally from a boat in Tampa Bay. Even after the hoax was exposed, some listeners still thought they were real pirates—just unaccountably lame ones.

From Alabama to Oregon, from Utah to Rhode Island, in bedrooms and churches, in schools and reservations, new stations emerged. The pirates ranged from Panthers to Promise Keepers, from teens to retirees. The Grid, in Cleveland, transmitted dance music from a local gay nightclub. Free Radio 1055, just north of Cincinnati, mixed contemporary Christian music with more secular pop. KBLT, in Los Angeles, featured underground rock; its DJs included punk godfathers Keith Morris (of the Circle Jerks) and Mike Watt (of fIREHOSE and the Minutemen). When L.A. rapper Ice Cube had trouble getting his music on mainstream radio, he started a pirate station, with a little help from the Black Rose. "He'd go to different places, set up his gear in a garage, and people would find the station," producer Bryan Turner told the *Toronto Sun*; "then he'd get shut down and move somewhere else."[44]

In 1994, Pearl Jam paid fellow Seattle rocker James Lane (of Tchkung!, among other bands) to build a micro station mobile enough to bring on tour. After some initial problems—Lane ordered a Dunifer kit, which took over three months to arrive, consisted of "a box of parts and some handwritten instructions," and eventually had to be rebuilt almost from scratch—the band had a transmitter in hand.[45] "After showing Eddie how small I could actually make the thing," Lane recalls, "it suddenly dawned on us that we could put the thing in a van and do the whole tour punk-rock style."[46] And so they did, dubbing themselves Monkey Wrench Radio and broadcasting their concerts. After the tour, Lane moved the station to a storage closet in Seattle and renamed it F.U.C.C., broadcasting "anything that's independent or noncorporate" (and some stuff that isn't) at 89.1 FM.[47] Pearl Jam, meanwhile, sent Dunifer some complimentary concert tickets.

Lane operated F.U.C.C. under a variety of pseudonyms ("Felch Dunderhead," "Popeye Khan"); more than fifty volunteers joined the station. "I really admire the people that are spinning," Lane remarked in 1997. "Most of them aren't 'professional' DJs—they're more like audiophile musicologists who have thousands of records and can never hear their favorite stuff on mainstream corporate radio." They had a hard time building an audience, though: the station had to move constantly to avoid the FCC's snoops, often to neighborhoods where its 69.5-watt transmitter couldn't reach its former listeners.

Still, it fared better than Seattle Liberation Radio, a left-wing project that suffered serious technical difficulties. "We've decided that the Dunifer kits are not the way to go," one member of the SLR collective told me, his voice dry with understatement. "The equipment just doesn't work." They never did acquire a consistently working transmitter (though they briefly managed to send a signal down a single block), and Lane rebuffed them when they proposed a merger. ("What I like to focus on is the music," he explained, "and not the politics behind it.") At least one Liberationist got a show on F.U.C.C., but most of the others wrote off Lane as a guy who wouldn't return their calls. By 1999, though, after both F.U.C.C. and Seattle Liberation Radio had expired, veterans of both joined a fresh project called Free Seattle Radio. Meanwhile, the Pearl Jam/F.U.C.C. transmitter fell into the hands of Black Ball Radio, a radical experiment in listener-programmed broadcasting. Its contributors send in music, newscasts, and promos via e-mail, as MP3s. The station then broadcasts them, both over Pearl Jam's old transmitter and over the World Wide Web.

Elsewhere in Seattle, a reggae pirate set up shop in the North End, a militiaman put together a project called Neither Left Nor Right, and several short-lived alternative-rock stations emerged and dissolved. In L.A., in the congressional elections of 1998, Maria Armoudian of the Green Party set up a micro station at a billboard in the North Hills, promoting her platform to anyone tuned to 1500 AM. The Pennsylvania branch of the Industrial Workers of the World, banned from leafleting a Job Corps site in person, borrowed some equipment from Radio Mutiny and broadcast its message instead. Several temporary stations pop up each year at Burning Man, the annual counterculture festival in the Nevada desert.

Walt Gardzki started a station in Philadelphia that plays nothing but haiku, read by a computer-generated voice over an electronic beat. There's a retirement home in Texas where a resident runs a station, playing long-forgotten hits for his housemates.[48] Elsewhere in Texas, a Lutheran Church in Austin used an FM transmitter for school announcements, unaware that it was breaking the law until a friendly engineer told it so.

The Reverend Edwin Valentin preached Pentecostalism and played sacred music over a 90-watt transmitter in Detroit. Not far away, in suburban Berkley, Michigan, a teenage rocker played music of a more secular sort. KMAD, at Jersey City State College, sounded like a legal station: it had a faculty adviser and followed almost all the FCC's regulations—but not the one about getting a license. In the San Juan Islands, just south of British Columbia, some ingenious engineers planned to set up seven or so transmitters and link them via the Internet, allowing them to reach all the islands—a rather large coverage area—without interfering with the bigger stations. Then the FCC shut down another San Juan microcaster, scaring the network-to-be into dropping its plans.

In Apache Junction, Arizona, KISS 89 FM belonged to the local chamber of commerce, had a business license and a state tax ID, covered local politics, and broadcast church services and high school sports. In another part of the state, Radio Caroline (named for the more famous British pirate) featured news and information for the gay community.

There are Hispanic stations, Haitian stations, high school stations, even Hasidic stations. Stations in the Dunifer mold have appeared around the country, from Asheville to Iowa City, from Gainesville to Houston, from Memphis to the west side of Chicago. Other outlets have expressed the militia/patriot outlook, from 88.3 Braveheart in northwestern Pennsylvania to North Valley Radio in western Washington state. Some stations emerge for just a day or two, to broadcast at an annual festival or fair, and then disappear for a year.

Live drama. In-jokes. In-depth news. Sermons in Spanish. Small-town bulletins. Big-band music. Poetry readings. Planning-board hearings. They've all been broadcast on micro radio, and so has much, much more.

And yes, some less savory sorts of radio have turned up in the microbroadcasting world as well. I'm not referring to the fascist or Leninist pirates, whose briefs on behalf of the totalitarian fringe can at least boast of being unavailable in most other parts of the broadcast band. I'm referring to lousy habits imported from mainstream radio. Just as some legal stations have automated as much as possible, replacing disc jockeys with software and satellite feeds, some pirates have adopted a practice that's a little less high-tech but no less lazy. A press account of Radio Free Springfield—that's the Springfield in Missouri, not Kantako's Springfield—describes a DJ announcing that he has a class to attend, so he's "gonna have to go on shuffle play for a couple of hours."[49] That is, he loaded some discs into his CD changer and let it play the tracks in random order. That might produce a serendipitous segue or two, but it really isn't good radio.

At least Radio Free Springfield intended to expand—to build a better studio, bring more programmers aboard, and make itself a community resource. But what about the pirate Muzak station a radio buff caught in Seattle's Lake Hills neighborhood? "Pirate Muzak"—OK, so the incongruity is enjoyable. I'm a little less charmed by another signal my Seattle acquaintance discovered: "There is a station now on 102.1 MHz in the south end of Belltown who was occasionally identifying as 'KFIR—The Tree!' but now broadcasts nothing but NOAA Weather Radio 24 hours a day."[50] If listeners want to hear automated DJs and weather reports, they hardly want for stations to listen to.

One study has suggested that *most* pirate programming fits this profile. An 1994 article in *Journalism Quarterly* argued that the programs on unlicensed stations do not differ significantly from those on licensed outlets, except for being skewed toward rock and comedy—that is, toward material preferred by the young.[51] But while the article's data may look formidable, they aren't really relevant. For one thing, most of the broadcasts surveyed were by shortwave pirates, not locally based micro stations. What's more, the study excluded broadcasts made after 1992, limiting it to a time when the micro movement was only beginning to swell.

A better approach would be to survey those stations that established, or tried to establish, a permanent public presence in their communities. From Kind Radio to the Grid, these stations *exist* to present programs you can't hear elsewhere. And even those pirate outfits that play more familiar material still tend to spout rather radical critiques of mainstream broadcasting. Consider this bubbly prospectus from Boston's EBRadio:

> The station is locally-based and the music format of the station is unique, by today's standards. Why? Because of all the "Mixes, Varieties, Lites, and Classic" boring formats. Each one of them becoming more and more irritating and fragmented. . . .
>
> On EBRadio, you'll hear quite the "opposite" of most radio stations, for example: James Taylor, America, Redd Rascal, Brian Setzer, Duncan Sheik, Private Lighting, Stevie Wonder, New England, XTC and even the Christian band DOXA. The station is not afraid to play album cuts that no one else plays by groups such as Steely Dan, Doobies, Angel, Beatles, Redd Rascals, XTC, Earth, Wind, and Fire, Alice Cooper, Jonathan Richmond [sic] and Sweet. I've even heard the Brady Bunch, the Partridge Family, Patrick Hernandez, LaFlavour, Voyage and well, never mind![52]

It's hard to think of Stevie Wonder and the Beatles as an alternative to the mainstream. Those are, after all, two of the most popular recording artists of recent history, and several other acts listed don't lag far behind. Yet by putting its musical enthusiasms before rigid formatting, by broadcasting without joining the licensed broadcasting profession, and by focusing on its own neighborhood (its signal doesn't stretch past its block), even EBRadio is an alternative to standard radio, with its harsh hierarchies and its strict line between producer and consumer.

Besides, the very existence of "mainstream" pirates is a sign that something's deeply wrong with commercial radio. A case in point: Stephen Franco's WDIS, in Oxon Hill, a suburb of Washington, D.C. In 1994, the discount mart manager started broadcasting rap, lowbrow comedy, and sales announcements over his store's loudspeakers. In 1996, encouraged by his customers' response, he started broadcasting over the FM band as well. Over the next two years, he ran an unlicensed station that, however free-spirited and locally rooted it may have been, never strayed far from "normal" broadcasting. When the FCC finally busted him, Franco told the *Washington Post* that he wasn't trying to rock the boat: "If someone would let me into radio, I'd be there tomorrow. I'd show up half an hour early, every day."[53] But he *hasn't* been able to get a job at someone else's radio station, and the government's red tape has kept him from starting his own outlet—except illegally.

Franco's adventure reflects both his entrepreneurial spirit and his love for radio. The fact that he had to go pirate speaks ill, not of him, but of the industry and the laws that protect it.

On October 4 and 5, 1998, dozens of unlicensed broadcasters congregated in Washington, D.C., to protest the FCC's stranglehold on the broadcast band and to call for decriminalizing micro radio.

The event began with a series of workshops at the Latin American Youth Center, in the Mount Pleasant section of town; the sessions ranged from classes on building transmitters to a friendly debate over whether commercial and noncommercial pirates should make common cause. At day's end the activists repaired to La Casa, a neighborhood church, and mixed with a local audience at a neighborhood cabaret. Rappers rapped, poets recited, and musicians played music of all kinds: Latin American, Eastern European, bluegrass. More than two hundred people turned out for the show, filling the small temple and spilling into the block outside. Others listened to it on Radio Free Mount Pleasant, a station built for the occasion.

The next day, between fifty and a hundred activists marched on the FCC and NAB buildings, hauling an elaborate series of puppets. In the lead: a giant Pinocchio marionette, complete with expanding nose, named "Kennardio" after FCC chairman William Kennard. Behind Kennardio, pulling his strings: a giant ape with a TV set in place of its head, labeled "National Association of Broadcasters." Behind that beast, pulling *its* strings: a giant green pyramid covered with corporate logos, representing the well-heeled powers behind both the commission and the association. Several costumed marchers posed as the FCC's "nerd patrol," complete with "triangulation backpacks"; one of those packs contained an FM transmitter, allowing the marchers to broadcast interviews, chants, and a few verses of the C. W. McCall hit "Convoy" to the motorists and office workers they passed.

The marchers stopped in front of the FCC building, where they continued their unlicensed broadcast in plain sight of the commission's enforcers, then progressed to the NAB building, where a protester deftly lowered the lobby's flag and raised a Jolly Roger.

That would be a grand image with which to end this chapter. But the day was only half over. After the theft of the broadcasters' banner, the police dispersed the march; a sixteen-year-old girl was nearly arrested for allegedly stealing the flag (which she did not have), and a man was briefly booked for interfering when the police handcuffed the young woman. The FCC had tolerated, even enjoyed, the demonstration, with cheerfully bewildered staffers smiling and waving from their office windows. The NAB was far less good-natured.

For the day concluded, not with a march or a petty theft, but with microbroadcasters lobbying their representatives on the Hill. Two years ago, that would have seemed futile, but now . . . who could be sure? There were intriguing rumblings in the political class, the press, and even the FCC, sparking a combustible combination of paranoia and hope. The atmosphere seemed to be changing. For the first time in years, it seemed plausible—maybe—to hope for a legal micro radio service.

And for an afternoon, the NAB didn't even have a flag.

10

The FCC's Wars

We're from the government, and we're here to help you.

—old joke

IT IS 6:30 in the morning, November 19, 1997. A harsh pounding wakes Leslie Douglas Brewer, the beefy, hairy owner of a Tampa electronics store. Outside, a SWAT team has massed, along with dozens of local police, Customs agents, and federal marshals. A helicopter hovers above the Brewers' suburban home. Below, the cops are heavily armed and ready to shoot.

Upon letting the police in, Doug and his wife are ordered to the floor, guns held to their heads, as the screaming invaders handcuff them. Cops run through the house, confiscating anything that looks like radio equipment. Others keep close watch on the Brewers, tailing them constantly, following them even into the bathroom. Some train their weapons on the family cat. It will be twelve hours before the Brewers are allowed to leave their home.

Not far away, in Seminole Heights, cops are arresting Kelly Benjamin, a.k.a. Kelly Kombat, seizing yet more equipment, plus some marijuana and paraphernalia they claim to have found during their search. They release him later that day on a $1,000 bond. And in Lutz, another Tampa suburb, fifty-three-year-old Lonnie Kobres is startled awake around quarter to seven by a police helicopter, noisy and bright, shining its glaring spotlight through his bedroom window. "It was a mini-Waco," the conservative broadcaster later told a reporter. "We looked out, and there were wall-to-wall police cars, men in black carrying assault rifles. Some were running towards the house with one of those battering ram things. If we hadn't opened the door, there'd have been no more door."[1]

Kobres, too, would lose equipment in the raid. He would also be charged with criminal conduct, quickly found guilty in a federal court, and sentenced to six months' house arrest, during which he would be forced to wear an electronic monitoring device. He would also receive three years' probation and a $7,500 fine.

Brewer, Benjamin, and Kobres were all pirate broadcasters, each with a radically different style. The first called himself the Tampa Party Pirate; his core audience was the west Florida biker community. The second recorded dense sound collages; his listeners hailed from an artier counterculture. The third preached a right-wing, "constitutionalist" sort of libertarianism; his audience was populist, patriotic, and not a little paranoid.

On November 19, all three found themselves facing the wrong end of the government's guns, for no crime worse than exercising unlicensed freedom of speech. If Kobres's crowd took this as a sign that their paranoia was justified, I think you can forgive them for that.

American radio is very capitalist, in the crude sense of the word: the industry is a busy bazaar, rife with deal making, speculation, and hustlers trying to get rich quick. It is also very socialist, in the crude sense of the word: it has long relied on the government to protect its biggest players, to shore up their profits, and to ensure that the competition doesn't get too unruly.

And so, when the NAB held its annual Radio Show in Seattle in October 1998, the floor was abuzz with the sound of entrepreneurship. Salesfolk hawked prefabricated jingles, syndicated shows, new technologies, and more, creating a capitalistic din. Upstairs, experts lectured broadcasters on how best to get government off their backs, leading seminars with such titles as "Employment Law and Protected Groups" and "Running Successful Contests, Promotions and Casino Spots—Without Being Fined by the FCC."

Except on Thursday afternoon, when the talk turned to how best to get government *onto* certain broadcasters' backs, lest their competition hurt the bottom line. Up in Room 609, the conventioneers noted with pleasure the dragnet that had captured the Tampa trio, among many others, a year before. The crackdown had actually began a couple of months before the Florida busts, with a raid on former doo-wop singer Sal Anthony's station in Howell, New Jersey; between then and October, dozens of operations had felt the federal boot.[2] In Seattle, in Room 609, the assembled broadcasters urged the FCC to crack down even harder. And please, *please,* to forget this notion that Chairman William Kennard had been tossing around, this idea of actually creating a legal micro radio service.

It was an attorney, John Fiorini, who made the NAB's case against legalized microbroadcasting that day. It would create too many more stations for the government to regulate, he argued, declaring that the FCC was stretched thin as it was. What's more, the new stations might block the shift to digital radio, a technology that will allow broadcasters to send CD-quality signals to drivers, office workers, and other listeners in no position to notice the difference.

Above all, Fiorini declared, "It simply cannot be done in the AM and FM bands without causing grave interference to existing stations."[3] This wasn't true, though I've little doubt that the audience believed it. Wading through the crowds at the Seattle convention, I caught more carelessly swinging elbows, arms, and bags than I would in any ordinary crowd. *These broadcasters can't even share a room without ramming into each other,* I realized. *No wonder they don't think they could share an electromagnetic spectrum.*

It was an odd afternoon. Then again, it was an odd year. With the FCC simultaneously suppressing unlicensed radio and mulling a legal low-power service, the politics of microbroadcasting had grown hopelessly confused. Even more maddeningly, the FCC initially denied a new crackdown was under way at all. When I called John Winston of the Compliance and Information Bureau in December 1997, he told me there'd been "no recent increase" in enforcement. "We've always taken the same approach to pirate broadcasting since the 1930s. We're doing no more than what we would ordinarily do."[4] The crackdown, he claimed, was a mirage: in the wake of an article about Doug Brewer in the *Wall Street Journal,* the press had simply paid more attention to normal enforcement efforts.

Well, I replied, I've been keeping pretty close tabs on this stuff for a while, and I started getting the impression of a crackdown several months before the *Journal* piece. The pirate world was abuzz about it. Stations that had operated with impunity for ages suddenly found themselves targeted. And the microcasters at WDOA, in Worcester, Massachusetts, had heard the word from the horse's mouth: the agents who visited them had told them that the FCC had changed its priorities, on the orders of new chief Kennard.

Winston was unmoved. Nothing had changed, he repeated. There was no clampdown. As for the testimony from Worcester—well, he gave "no credence" to that. Meanwhile, I was having trouble giving credence to Winston: not long after our conversation, I spoke with Vincent Kajunski, the FCC's New England district director, and he confirmed the substance of the Worcester agents' reported remarks. The following April, compliance and information chief Richard Lee would settle the matter: appearing on a panel at the East Coast Microbroadcasting Conference, he discussed the new crackdown without trying to pretend it wasn't under way.[5]

The FCC wasn't limiting itself to enforcing its own laws. As the federal crackdown intensified, many micro stations found themselves facing zoning challenges. In 1998, some evidence emerged that suggested that a deliberate federal campaign was behind this. Thomas B. Hooper, the director of the Bloomfield, Connecticut, planning and zoning department, reported that the FCC approached him to ask whether Prayze FM, a black-oriented Christian micro station, was violating any zoning laws. The commission then encouraged him to crack down on the station on those grounds. In that case, the city refused, and Hooper instead told the people at Prayze what had happened.[6]

The FCC was particularly active in Florida—not just because there were so many pirates there, but because the FCC's chief cop in the region, Ralph Barlow, was especially bent on wiping out piracy. The Floridians proved more resilient than expected. Speaking at that same NAB convention in Seattle, Richard Lee confessed that Miami was confounding his agency. "When we went down to Miami before," he reported,

> it was our expectation that we would close them all down. What we found down there was that they have their own underground frequency coordinating committee working down there. The first day, when we showed up at site one, they started making phone calls to sites two, three, and on up to 30 and 40. When you get down to Friday, the stations have moved or they've got off the air, and we have to start from scratch again.[7]

Further Florida dragnets proved just as ineffective.

No one at the NAB was pretending a crackdown wasn't under way. Indeed, the group had practically taken responsibility for it. On September 5, 1997, NAB president Edward Fritts issued a statement praising the FCC for its recent turn. "We are delighted," he announced, "that federal authorities have stepped up enforcement against pirate radio stations. The NAB Radio Board in June asked for the FCC to focus more attention on the growing number of unlicensed stations. We commend the Commission for sending a strong message to broadcast bandits that their illegal activities will not be tolerated."[8] (Three months later, NAB rep Dennis Wharton declined to comment on Winston's there's-no-crackdown stance. "In the last several months, there have been a number of enforcement actions taken by the FCC," he said instead. "And we support those actions.")[9]

Convening in Las Vegas in 1997, the NAB had sponsored a special panel on pirate radio, much like the session in Seattle a year later. The conversation was not cheery. Beverly Baker of the FCC warned darkly that "some of them are connected to the militia movement" and hinted of connections between "some of the ones in Florida" and the drug trade. Jack Goodman, introduced as "the NAB's point man on pirate radio," denounced the whole movement as "crooks."[10] The association was declaring war.

There was one note the NAB hit again and again: *microbroadcasting causes planes to fall from the sky.* It was a strange charge: the FCC had alleged only a handful of cases in which pirate stations were supposed to have interfered with air traffic communications, far fewer than the number of licenced signals that had caused such interference. And there was good reason to doubt even those slight claims. In 1998, Dharma Bilotta-Dailey and Tracy Jake Siska filed a Freedom of Information Act request with the Federal Aviation Administration, asking for "any paperwork that related to cases of air traffic communications interference by radio stations, licensed or unlicensed," for "the period between January 1, 1990 and May 15, 1998."[11] The agency came up with a total of *one* unlicensed outlet that had caused such troubles, a Sacramento station that immediately and voluntarily shut itself down when it was told about the problem. Even this report was suspicious, Bilotta-Dailey notes, because "it doesn't have all of the documentation that should accompany a serious interference complaint."[12]

Meanwhile, the documents revealed that several *licensed* stations had interfered with air traffic signals, and not all of them were as cooperative as the Sacramento pirates. Some had kept it up for years; according to a 1995 FAA report, the agency's Sandia Crest site had suffered interference from nearby stations since 1967. Another 1995 report revealed that FM interference at Florida's North Perry Airport had been a problem since 1976, if not earlier, and might have been responsible for a mid-air collision in 1990.

And what about the other events the FCC had alleged—pirates in places like West Palm Beach and Puerto Rico who'd supposedly cut in on airports' radios? "I'm at a loss to tell you why they [the FAA] do not have anything in their records about those cases," the FCC's Joe Casey told Siska and Bilotta-Dailey.[13]

Furthermore, if micro radio *were* likely to lead to such troubles, that would be an argument for legalization, not repression. After all, if a station's cutting in on your signal, you want to know how to get ahold of it to tell it to stop. You want it to have a public phone number. You don't want it to be unduly afraid of showing its face.

I asked FCC rep Winston about the air traffic question, shortly after his agency busted two Florida pirates that had allegedly interfered with a nearby airport's communications. How many other cases like that had there been? He gave a vague reply: "Several." Where? "In Virginia. And other places." Well, when was the Virginia case? "About four years ago." Further inquiry revealed that this incident involved, not a micro station, but deliberate, malicious interference. Winston would not say more than that because the case was "still under investigation"—which was odd, since he also said it had already gone to trial.

Perhaps aware that this argument wasn't working, the spokesman shifted tacks. The worst problem with the pirates, he declared, is that they aren't part of the Emergency Alert System; thus, their listeners would not quickly hear about a natural disaster or a war. Of course, if micro radio were legal, it could easily plug into the EAS. More to the point: by Winston's logic, the government should ban *anything* that doesn't involve listening to an EAS-linked station, from canoeing to violin playing to sex.

The fact that the FCC was spouting such palpable nonsense should have relaxed the radio industry: at least the commission was still in their pocket. Furthermore, the courts were ruling pretty consistently in the FCC's favor. When Claudia Wilken finally issued her opinion regarding Free Radio Berkeley, other judges around the country started following her lead.

Just a few days after Wilken's decision, for instance, Judge Patrick Conmy in North Dakota ruled against Roy Neset, a farmer in the tiny town of Tioga. If ever there was a station that defied the rationales for FCC regulation, this was it. Tioga can hardly be said to suffer from spectrum scarcity, and Neset's operation wasn't likely to interfere with any other signals. There *were no* other FM stations in Tioga. The only legal station in town was a country outlet on the AM band. There was, however, some bad blood between Neset and David Guttormson, the country station's owner and manager, who quickly called in the FCC. Judge Conmy adopted Wilken's opinion wholesale, without even hearing from Neset's law team. In essence, he used the Berkeley decision as a rubber stamp. The Dunifer case was starting to emerge as a precedent.

More bad news for the pirates soon followed in the case of Prayze FM, the black Connecticut station. Prayze had played gospel music and allowed the area's churches to use its airwaves. One of those local temples, the Maranatha Pentecostal Church, was scarcely able to pay its bills before Prayze went on the air. With the exposure the station gave it, Maranatha's membership quadrupled, its revenue doubled, and it soon had to move into a larger building. With the extra money it was taking in, it was able to take in homeless boys, start new charities, and give more counseling to the poor. Its grateful pastor, David Knight, declares that Prayze was "*directly* responsible for the spiritual and financial revival of Maranatha Pentecostal."[14]

On February 27, 1998, Prayze's attorneys had asked Judge Warren Eginton for a temporary restraining order against the FCC. Their station's case—an unusual one, in that they were suing the commission rather than the other way around—was pending, and they wanted to ensure that the government wasn't going to raid the premises in the weeks before the case began.

Eginton refused, in part because the government's attorneys assured him that they were not planning any such invasion. When Prayze's lawyers brought up the heavy-handed Tampa raids, government counsel Alan Soloway gave this interesting explanation for the events: "The Tampa, Florida case involved individuals who were urging the armed resistance to the United States, and in fact possessed weapons in the station at the time that the warrant was effectuated," so "there was a very real threat to agents of the FCC, agents of the Federal Bureau of Investigation, and other law enforcement personnel that effectuated that warrant of arrest. That situation is not present here."[15]

That's true: it wasn't. But it wasn't present in Florida, either.

In any event, many in the micro movement were excited about this case: the judge might not have issued the restraining order, but he nonetheless seemed very sympathetic to the broadcasters. "All First Amendment issues I think are important," he explained. "I think the balance would favor Prayze. Certainly, the likelihood of success I think is very great for Prayze here. I know the Government may disagree with me on that and that's not a judgment that can be made until the record is fully unfolded here. But it does seem to me that where you've got evidence of a media operation trying to perform, certainly you should favor this type especially of media operations."[16]

But in October, Judge Wilken's influence reached Connecticut. Eginton told Prayze it could broadcast for another month while it applied for a waiver from the FCC, and in November, with no waiver evident (of course), the courts ordered the station off the air. Prayze's lawyers appealed the decision. So, for that matter, did Dunifer's and Neset's. None, as yet, has gotten anywhere.[17]

In other words, the FCC suffered a couple of small legal blows, but its power to shut down unlicensed stations remained essentially unchanged. And that was good news for the NAB. Right?

Well, yes. But something else was worrying the NAB. Chairman Kennard certainly opposed unlicensed broadcasting—the crackdown had come on his watch, after all—but he didn't seem displeased with the larger notion of opening the airwaves to low-power radio. A new microbroadcasting service might counteract the recent trend toward consolidation, he reasoned. It might also increase the number of black-owned stations, an issue dear to Kennard, the commission's first African American chair.

Three petitions had been filed with the commission, each calling in its own way for legal microbroadcasting. They ranged from former low-power-TV entrepreneur Rodger Skinner's proposal, which would have allowed stations of anywhere from twenty to three thousand watts,[18] to the plan offered by Nickolaus Leggett, Judith Leggett, and Don Schellhardt, which initially granted just one watt to its licensees. (Schellhardt and the Leggetts weren't very familiar with radio technology when they first wrote their petition, and when they realized just how little power one watt is, they revised their request upward.) In between was the Community Radio Coalition, a diverse group of petitioners that included Jeremy Lansman, who'd evidently had second thoughts about the Class D service he had helped abolish. On top of that, the National Lawyers Guild had filed comments with the FCC that amounted to a full-fledged counterproposal, and another fellow, Harold McCombs, had petitioned for an "event broadcasting" service. His idea wasn't to let new full-time stations on the air but to let sports arenas, concert halls, airports, and the like do special broadcasts at set-aside times. Kennard told the FCC's Office of Engineering and Technology to digest all the petitions, take in comments from all comers, and come up with a proposal for a new service.

This was another blow to the NAB, which would have preferred it if the task had fallen to the Mass Media Bureau, the segment of the commission most dominated by broadcast interests. The Office of Engineering and Technology, by contrast, is run by engineers, and if it sometimes tends to be overly enamored of centralized management of the spectrum, it's also less beholden to companies seeking protection against competition.

On top of that—as though the NAB didn't have enough worries already—the press was catching hold of the microbroadcasting story, with reports appearing everywhere from *USA Today* to National Public Radio. NPR management filed comments opposing any new micro radio service, which is exactly what you'd expect from the institution that had driven the destruction of the Class Ds. But its reporters seemed much more sympathetic to the idea, to judge from the stories they filed. Indeed, most of the media's reports ranged from neutral to positive. And the neutral stories tended to leave the same residue as the positive ones: even if the pirates themselves came off as a little nutty, the idea of unlicensed broadcasting spread to people who might not have thought of going on the air before.

So the NAB seemed to be losing both the PR battle and its grip on the FCC. It was time, it decided, for a counterattack.

The backlash took off, or tried to, in April 1998, as the deadline for public comments on the micro radio petitions grew near. The FCC later extended the deadline, but not before a deluge of urgent faxes and e-mails descended on station managers across the country. One, issued by Jim du Bois of the Minnesota Broadcasters Association, succinctly stated the industry's rhetorical strategy: "You should avoid arguments suggesting that the proposed new service would create more competition; rather, you should emphasize the interference and regulatory problems microbroadcasting would certainly generate."[19] In other words, try not to sound self-interested, even if it's the fear of competition that's foremost on your mind.

Despite du Bois's advice, broadcasters flooded the FCC with warnings that new competition would destroy their stations. The established industry couldn't help sounding protectionist. It's in its nature.

Even when the National Hockey League revived Harold Mc-Combs's call for an event-broadcasting service (though not the particular details McCombs had proposed), the NAB threw a fit. From a common-sense point of view, it's hard to see why: all the NHL wanted the government to do was to let promoters set up antennas inside indoor arenas and transmit radio signals to the fans in the seats. So if you're going to your first game, and you're not sure why the ref just made a call, a channel might explain the relevant rules. Or if you don't speak English, a channel might transmit info in your native language. Maybe you'd like to hear some play-by-play coverage, as though you were watching the game at home. Maybe you're blind or hard of hearing and could use some extra info about what's happening on the rink. The NHL proposal would have allowed arenas to provide any of those services, along with pre-game entertainment, emergency announcements, ads for the concession stand, and more.

But the very idea of someone new using the airwaves seemed to scare the broadcast industry. The NHL first suggested its idea in April 1998, in its comments on the low-power petitions, and a year later made a formal proposal of its own. The NAB's response was quick and venomous.

Among the highlights:

- There's no need to broadcast information about the rules the referees are enforcing, because "information for the novice fan on game rules and play may be delivered through a better-edited and lower-priced printed game program."
- There's no need to cover games in other languages, because the league "could implement multi-language announcing through its public address announcers, similar to that used in international competitions." And, again, "important notices and game play information could be delivered through secondary language printed game programs."
- "For a relatively small financial investment, local, regional, and

national sports teams could also want licenses for their indoor facilities through the proposed service. Consequently, large high school gymnasiums, municipal hockey rinks, collegiate athletic facilities, NFL domed stadiums as well as indoor tennis pavilions would all be eligible for a license under the NHL's proposal. The low cost of indoor broadcast equipment combined with the vast number of eligible indoor sport facilities could lead to thousands of licenses that would require FCC policing."[20] In other words, some people might take a cheap, convenient technology and adapt it to offer services that other people might want.

Evidently, the members of the NAB don't want to compete even with a station that can't be heard outside a single hockey rink.

All this came after years of public policy dedicated to the assumption that bigger is better—that to survive, radio must become a tight clan of consolidated chains offering formulaic formats. A series of buyouts had swept through the industry, with the number of station owners shrinking by more than seven hundred in less than two years, leaving three companies in control of over a thousand stations nationwide. The trend was even more pronounced in the nation's largest markets, where it became common for a handful of companies to own almost all the commercial outlets in town. This being American radio, the wave of mergers reflected a combination of crude capitalism and crude socialism: people were making a lot of money, but in a way shaped by the state, which had eased restrictions on combinations while making it steadily harder for startup stations to challenge the chains.

This began as a desperate effort to stave off financial disaster. As the 1990s began, more than half the radio stations in America were losing money. Many were going dark—the industry's poetic term for leaving the air. The conventional wisdom blamed this on Docket 80–90, a Reagan-era rule change that had, over the loud protests of the big broadcasters, loosened the restrictions on how many operations could coexist in one market, opening the FM dial to 689 new outlets.[21] Between that and other, relatively small reforms, the number of commercial FM stations jumped from 3,800 in 1983 to 6,077 in 1991.

With so many stations competing for advertisers, the price of airtime fell, and so, therefore, did broadcasters' profits. Stations were dying, the argument went, because they couldn't handle all the competition; the solution was to license fewer stations and to let existing owners consolidate their holdings.

So the FCC reversed itself. Rather than allow more stations to enter a market, it would allow existing station owners to own more stations within a market. (The notion of allowing *both* was never on the table: few at the FCC are enamored with laissez faire.) In 1992, the commission legalized "duopolies"—that is, it allowed owners to control more than one station in the same city. Further changes to the rules followed, culminating in the Telecommunications Act of 1996, passed with bipartisan support,[22] which among other things allowed companies to own an unlimited number of stations nationwide and as many as eight in certain markets.

The chains began forcing advertisers into must-buy deals, whereby to get a plum spot for a commercial on a popular station, an advertiser must also buy time on one of the company's other outlets as well. Between that, increased automation, and the booming national economy, profits quickly rebounded, with revenues steadily increasing from 1992 on.

At the same time, paradoxically, listenership fell through the floor. According to the analysts at *Duncan's American Radio*, a leading industry newsletter, the percentage of people who actually listen to the radio has been steadily declining since 1989. There was a slight uptick in the early 1990s, thanks largely, they suspect, to the boom in talk radio. But that soon reversed, and by the decade's end listenership had hit a low unseen since 1981. The *Duncan's* analysts attribute the decline to the trend toward extremely segmented formats, the converse loss of several once-thriving niche formats, the decline in locally oriented programming, the increase in the number of commercials per hour, and the simple fact that, when two rival stations share an owner, they devote less effort to promoting themselves.[23]

It can't be long before the admen start to figure out that they're paying more to reach fewer people, and start either demanding lower prices or taking their business elsewhere.

That wasn't the extent of the industry's problems. Besides micro radio, which sounded like Docket 80–90 all over again, there were the simultaneous challenges of Web radio, which we'll examine later, and the Direct Audio Radio Service.

As this book goes to press, a company called Sirius[24] is about to start broadcasting one hundred channels of music, news, sports, and talk from three Loral satellites. Its programming will range from familiar formats (soft rock, hip hop, "smooth jazz," "modern country") to more specialized fare. There will be one channel for *cumbia*, one for *meringue*, one for *boleros* ("the great, timeless Latin standards of song from the '30s–'60s"). Jazz—real jazz, not that "smooth" impostor—will inhabit a channel or two; so will opera, club music, and Tex-Mex. Alternative rock will occupy two channels, one more alternative than the other; blues, reggae, and classic country will have territories, too. There will be a children's channel, a gospel channel, a "world beat" channel. Plus ten channels of news, ten of sports, ten in Spanish, and many more. You'll be able to pick up these signals—all of them—anywhere in the country. Without static.

And without commercials. For a $200 startup fee, customers will acquire a small satellite dish[25] and a card that allows their car radios to receive the signals, and then they'll pay a subscription fee of $9.95 a month. Sirius will thus accrue its profits by selling programming directly to its audiences, rather than by selling audiences to advertisers.

This has been a long time coming. The FCC started the process of allocating satellite radio licenses back in 1990, but it didn't actually get around to awarding them until 1997. Even now, it's devoted such a small portion of the band to the new service that it has awarded licenses to only two companies. (The other is XM Satellite Radio,[26] which will offer up to a hundred varied channels of its own, including five for Spanish speakers, three for Christians, and one for C-Span junkies.[27] XM's program director, incidentally, is AOR godfather Lee Abrams.) But even with such a limited, oligopolistic scope, the new service will be a serious challenge to traditional terrestrial stations, which fought hard against allowing any direct-satellite radio at all. In 1994, the NAB released a report, ominously titled *The Truth about Satellite Radio*, arguing that competition from the heavens would put the industry into an economic "free fall." And that, it warned, would have "devastating effects" on local radio and the "community service" it provides.[28]

The satellite companies replied that audiences would still listen to local stations for weather reports, local news, and other regionally specific information; the satellites would be a supplement, not a replacement, for the existing industry. What they didn't mention was just how little localism remains on the outlets they'll be "supplementing," for all the latter's caterwauling about threats to local radio.

One of the NAB's favorite lines has been that a micro radio service would merely "duplicate" existing programming. The lobby should watch what it says. If duplication were its worry, the FCC might as well wipe out the NAB's outlets, let the satellites deliver their nation-wide variety packs, and give the entire AM and FM bands to the micro stations.

In this atmosphere, the great radio chains—the empires of the air— will have to change radically or die. American radio isn't just standing at a crossroads. It's standing there with a ton of bricks falling toward its head.

Despite the NAB's objections, on January 28, 1999, the FCC went ahead and issued a Notice of Proposed Rulemaking on micro radio. In plain English, that means it drafted a proposal for a micro radio service and asked for public comments on it. All three Democratic commissioners voted for the Notice, with one Republican joining them and one casting the lone dissenting vote.

The NAB's friends on the Hill were quick to protest. Almost imme-diately, the chair of the House Telecommunications Subcommittee— Billy Tauzin (R–Louisiana), whose campaign coffers were awash with broadcasters' donations and whose own daughter worked for the NAB—asked Kennard to dump the proposal. "The policy, political, economic and budgetary ramifications of this undertaking are poten-tially staggering," he wrote to the commissioner, adding that Kennard should not "proceed" without first "consulting with Congress."[29] A day later, Tauzin reiterated his position in a speech before the NAB, arguing that the FCC had no power to create a micro radio service without con-gressional authorization (which wasn't true) and, amusingly for a con-servative Republican, that the new stations might eat into the audience for public radio.

Not everyone in Congress sided with the NAB. Representative David Bonior (D–Michigan) wrote a letter, cosigned by twenty-seven other legislators, endorsing a legal micro radio service. The letter stopped short of endorsing unlicensed broadcasting, but several con-gressfolk, such as Lois Capps (D–California), separately spoke kindly of some existing pirate stations (in Capps's case, Excellent Radio).

But only two names on the letter belonged to Republicans: Lincoln Diaz-Balart and Ileana Ros-Lehtinen, both from Florida and both pre-sumably aware that a lot of their constituents listen to pirate radio. A number of actual microbroadcasters were Republicans, of course, as were some prominent pro-micro activists—Don Schellhardt, for example, who after filing one of the original petitions to the FCC started organizing a group of "moderate" micro boosters called the Amherst Alliance. But among elected Republicans, the dominant attitude was that of Arizona's Senator John McCain, who said would-be microcasters ought to get "a Web page or a leased access cable channel" instead.[30] Or—worse yet—Conrad Burns of Montana, chair of the Senate Communications Committee, who argued against opening the airwaves thusly: "I've had all the diversity I can stand."[31]

The funny thing is, the proposal that inspired all this apoplexy wasn't all that radical. Kennard's original plan would have created three new classes of stations, one operating at a maximum power of a thousand watts, one at no more than a hundred watts, and one—perhaps—at one to ten watts. (The last category was more a tentative suggestion than a concrete proposal.) But only the first would be a "primary" service. The others, as "secondary" services, could be bumped by any new station that comes along.

This was especially problematic for the last remnants of the Class D service—a handful of outlets that had, despite their secondary status, survived. Now they could conceivably be pushed off the air by a wave of thousand-watt interlopers, even though the old Class Ds would have a much stronger claim to the title "micro radio." (The plan would have allowed businesses to own as many as five of the new stations. What was "micro" about that?)

All this raised the question of whether the proposal was not just too strict but, in some ways, too lax. There is nothing wrong with thousand-watt stations in themselves, or with owning more than one broadcast outlet. But it seems odd to refer to a chain of five stations, each transmitting a thousand watts of power, as a microbroadcaster. If the FCC is going to relegalize low-power FM by creating a special micro radio service, that service should license only micro radio stations. Right?

Some in the micro radio community filed comments with the FCC, hoping to nudge it toward a more digestible proposal. Others simply rejected the plan outright. Stephen Dunifer denounced it as a "bogus" scheme "designed to invoke the splitting of the movement to reclaim the airwaves."[32] Lyn Gerry worried that it would turn micro radio into a "mini-NAB."[33] The National Lawyers Guild filed comments urging that the new service be entirely noncommercial; in this, they were joined by two more pro-micro groups, the Prometheus Radio Project and the Micro Empowerment Coalition. (Privately, some of these activists admitted that they'd just as soon have a certain percentage of the new licenses reserved for noncommercial broadcasters. But they worried that if they didn't ask for everything, they'll end up with nothing.)

The fight for legal low-power radio was fought not just in Washington but in town halls around the country. The most impressive grassroots movement was in Michigan, where Tom Ness, editor of a Ferndale music-and-politics paper called *Jam Rag*, had launched the Michigan Music Is World Class Campaign in 1996. The group got its start, Ness reports, "as an attempt to figure out why the local music community/ economy was withering"; it "quickly came to the unanimous conclusion that lack of airplay was by far the main factor."[34] In 1997, its activists circulated through the state, getting people to sign an open letter to stations encouraging them to play more local music. "We got hundreds of signatures," Ness recalls. "Frankly, it had very little effect on the stations—but elected officials took it very seriously. Seeing it was a popular cause (and the 'right' thing to do), eventually about four dozen state senators and representatives signed on. We also went out of our way to approach community leaders of any kind, their prestige helping to bring in further signatures."[35]

With time, as they realized they weren't making much of an impact on the existing radio industry, the activists got interested in making it easier to start stations of their own. The new cause drew support from businesses with an interest in the local music scene—studios, clubs, CD stores—as well as civic groups, churches, and even local governments: more than forty city councils in Michigan (including Detroit's) passed resolutions, many of them unanimously, calling for the legalization of micro radio.[36]

Back in D.C., the National Association of Broadcasters adopted a tactic of delay, constantly asking the FCC to extend the deadline for comments on its proposal and—when the much-delayed due date finally passed on August 2, 1999—asking it to extend the deadline for replies to the comments already filed. In Congress, Tauzin actually started talking about cutting off funds for the FCC if it didn't drop the plan. He soon drew back from the battle, after musicians in Louisiana began to complain that their senator was working against his constituents' interests. But the NAB gives money to many politicians, and the other anti-micro voices in Congress did not slacken.

In November 1999, the saga took another strange turn. As the FCC folded its Compliance and Information Bureau into a larger Enforcement Bureau, outgoing compliance chief Richard Lee filed a whistle-blower complaint with the U.S. Office of Special Counsel, charging Kennard with illegal activity. The dispute centered around Billie Meyer, the wealthy owner of a NASCAR racetrack in Ennis, Texas, who had broadcast live races and commercials with unlicensed AM, FM, and TV transmitters. In April 1999, the FCC shut down Meyer's broadcast facilities. Meyer responded by contacting his congressman, Republican Joe Barton, a regular recipient of Meyer's campaign contributions. Barton in turn contacted Kennard, who called Lee at home and, according to Lee's complaint, "directed me to contact the manager of the CIB Dallas field office . . . and tell the manager to contact Mr. Meyer immediately by telephone and tell Mr. Meyer that he could resume the unlicensed operations without FCC intervention. Further Chairman Kennard stated that the Dallas Office was to take no further action against Mr. Meyer and he (Chairman Kennard) would take full responsibility."[37] Lee reluctantly did so, and Kennard set to work getting Meyer a special experimental license.

All this, Lee's complaint concluded, violates "sections of the Communications Act, various FCC rules and regulations, and the Administrative Procedures Act; and their actions also constitute gross mismanagement, an abuse of authority, and could have posed a danger to the public safety. In addition, I believe their actions violated government ethics rules."[38]

Kennard replied that what he'd done, while unusual, was not unprecedented, then authorized an internal investigation of the matter. Whether or not he was guilty of lawbreaking (and for the record, the investigation found no wrongdoing), the affair reveals a lot about how Washington really works: sometimes, as Michael Kinsley has written, the scandal isn't what's illegal but what's legal. If equal enforcement of the law can be abrogated just because one scofflaw is tight with his congressman, the FCC's rhetoric about acting in "the public interest" is an even darker joke than we suspected. One high-ranking enforcer at the FCC told me that if he were making exceptions for unlicensed stations, he'd let Doug Brewer slip by, not Billie Meyer. "Brewer has several other licenses with the FCC," the official commented. "He certainly should've gotten some sort of 'chairman's waiver,' if that's what they're calling it."[39] Instead, he got a SWAT raid.

But the story's even more complicated than that. The story of Lee's complaint was leaked to the press not by Lee himself but by Senator McCain's office; and at that point, McCain was one of the loudest critics of Kennard's micro radio plan. Lee's motives seem more pure, but he too was upset at Kennard: he had not been named head of the new Enforcement Bureau. Washington's wheels turn within wheels. . . .

The FCC finally announced its plan on January 20, 2000. It was a more modest proposal than the one it had floated a year before. Gone were the thousand-watt stations. Gone, at least initially, were the five-station chains.[40] Gone, in fact, was any sort of business-based micro-broadcasting: this was an entirely noncommercial service. This was due partly to lobbying by leftist foes of commercial radio, partly to lobbying by existing commercial stations that didn't want to compete for advertisers, and mostly to the fact that, under pre-existing law, new commercial stations had to be awarded by auction, but noncommercial stations didn't. Since one of the main reasons for micro radio was to get frequencies into the hands of people who weren't rich, auctioning them off didn't seem prudent.

Gone also was legal urban micro radio on more than a piddling scale. The plan freed up many new frequencies in the countryside, but very few in big cities: just one in Philadelphia, for example, and none at all in Chicago, New York, and Los Angeles. (In such places, the feds felt the dial was already full—which no doubt surprised all the pirates who'd operated there for years.) The one upside to this is that the FCC already knew, more or less, where the stations it was allowing would fit, thus saving applicants the costly services of lawyers and engineers.

The commission also refused to license anyone known to have broadcast illicitly since February 26, 1999, unless they "ceased engaging in the unlicensed operation . . . within twenty-four hours of being advised by the Commission to do so."[41] Needless to say, that angered the pirate activists—the very people who put micro radio on the Washington agenda—though most everyone realized that former pirates could probably still slip onto the air. They just couldn't be part of the group to which the station was licensed.

The plan contained other limits: the stations still weren't a full-fledged primary service, for example. Despite that, it was an amazing triumph. One of the motliest rebellions of the late twentieth century had taken on one of Washington's richest, best-connected lobbies, forcing the Federal Communications Commission to open another crack in the airwaves. That, at least, was a triumph worth savoring.

Not that anyone got to savor it for long. The plan faced an immediate array of challenges: the NAB sued to stop it,[42] and Representative Michael Oxley (R–Ohio) proposed a bill to repeal it. (Oxley hoped to take over Tauzin's Telecommunications Subcommittee, and with the Louisianan stepping back from the micro radio fight, the NAB took advantage of the rivalry.) When it began to look like Oxley's measure might not pass, Representative John Dingell (D–Michigan) amended it to keep the FCC's plan in place but install new restrictions on it, theoretically to reduce interference. Though neutrally worded, the actual effect would be to bar about 80 percent of the new stations from going on the air. National Public Radio lobbied House Democrats to back the revised bill, and it passed by a vote of 274-110.[43]

Representative Judd Gregg (R–New Hampshire) then introduced an anti-micro bill in the Senate. Its chief foe was John McCain, who had been rethinking his opposition to micro radio. McCain proposed a compromise bill, which allowed lower-power radio to exist but also gave larger stations the right to sue any newcomers that caused harmful interference, with the loser paying the winner's legal bills. That might not be a bad idea in the abstract, but McCain's proposal contained some odd features. The burden of proof would be on the defendant, not the plaintiff. The low-power stations would not have the equal ability to sue stations that interfered with *them*. And "interference" would be defined by the National Academy of Sciences, a superficially sensible suggestion that actually made no sense at all. Scientists may be qualified to measure interference, but that doesn't mean they should be the ones to decide how much interference is too much. That's a political decision.

McCain's bill, opposed by most micro radio activists as well as the NAB, went nowhere, and neither did a second version that excised such troublesome measures as the invocation of the National Academy of Sciences. It nonetheless posed trouble for Gregg's rival measure, since the latter had to pass through McCain's Commerce, Science and Transportation Committee before it could reach the Senate floor. Senator Rod Grams (R–Minnesota) introduced a slightly more moderate measure— it was modeled on Dingell's proposal to eviscerate Kennard's plan rather than Oxley's proposal to kill it entirely—but this, too, was blocked by McCain.

Frustrated, the bill's backers decided to bypass McCain's committee altogether and attach their legislation to the appropriations bill for fiscal year 2001. President Clinton initially came to the defense of his FCC chairman's plan, threatening a veto if it—along with various other measures—was not stripped from the appropriations package. When the measure reached his desk, though, the lame-duck president signed it. And the man about to replace him, George W. Bush, had never displayed any enthusiasm for low-power radio.

The plan wasn't completely dead. A few new frequencies still opened in some rural areas: even as Congress passed the NAB's bill, the FCC released a list of 255 applicants who were eligible for low-power licenses under the newly restrictive rules. Meanwhile some court challenges to the ban on micro radio were still pending. And one of John McCain's staffers announced that reversing the Grams rider would be one of the senator's top priorities for 2001. "It would be somewhat negligent to give up completely now," Pete triDish wrote to fellow activists, "since there are a few more cards to play over the next months. But overall, I think we can all at this point say with assurance that even Kennard was completely deluded about his ability to make even the most modest changes in favor of democratic reform of the media."[44]

With such bleak sentiments in the air, it may seem utopian to call for far-reaching radio reforms. Still, there's much that the FCC could do—or, rather, stop doing—to allow lively radio to flourish. Forget the Kennard plan. Suppose a more radical reform, a full-fledged revolution, were possible. What should it look like?

It would lower entry barriers. It would remove the fees and paperwork that would-be broadcasters now must endure. It would also reform the FCC's expensive technical specifications, which were enacted to prevent interference with other signals. On the surface, that sounds sensible, but it's actually inefficient: it would make much more sense just to hold broadcasters liable for any substantial interference they may cause and then, that incentive in place, let them figure out how they're going to avoid stepping on other signals' toes. Among other benefits, this would fuel technical innovation, as low-budget engineers strive to build cheaper equipment that nonetheless gets the job done. The present system, by contrast, locks archaic technologies into place.

It would allow frequencies to subdivide. Suppose a station can be heard over, say, a hundred square miles. That same area could be served by several stations on the same frequency, if they divided the region into smaller coverage areas with appropriate buffers between them. But under present law, while one can sell a signal, one cannot sell a piece of that signal.

That's not exactly accurate: technically, the spectrum is government property, and you can't sell a signal you don't own. But one can, with relatively little trouble, sell a license to broadcast over a particular frequency. What one can't do is subdivide a frequency and sell off a chunk of it.

So if our hypothetical station (let's call it KBIG) decides to sell itself outright to a chain (let's call it KRAP), it can. But if it wants to reduce its wattage and let an entrepreneur or civic group take over part of its previous coverage area, it will somehow have to guarantee to the buyers that the FCC will allow them to transmit to the space it has emptied. There is, of course, no way to do this; and even if there were, the application process for the new station would still be drawn out and expensive. The risk for the buyers would be too high.

When a giant falls or falters, smaller outlets ought to be able to rush in and take pieces of the electromagnetic ground where he once stood. Instead, the law says he has to sell all his ethereal territory at once, meaning that only another giant can afford to buy it. So the law encourages consolidation, which in turn encourages centralized, automated, prefabricated programming.

It would allow stations to broadcast closer to each other. To avoid interference, there must be buffers between broadcasters. That is why there are no stations at 101.2 FM—the FCC won't risk interfering with the outlets at 101.1 and 101.3. (Similarly, if a station is transmitting at 101.3, you must be a substantial physical distance away before you can be licensed to transmit at 101.1 or 101.5.)

No one disputes the need for such buffers. But the current rules are based on the technical standards of the 1950s. It's now possible for far more stations to fit onto the spectrum without interfering with one another. The FCC is already pragmatic enough to allow stations some leeway in bargaining with each other to set the actual boundaries of their coverage areas. It should let them actually sell interference easements, allowing both established and new broadcasters to set up shop at a closer frequency if they pay for the privilege.

It would open up new spectrum. Anyone who keeps up with trends in both broadcasting and point-to-point communications soon notes a strange contradiction. The broadcasters believe the ether is almost completely filled. The phone companies believe it's actually expanding: as new technologies make it easier to squeeze more signals onto the spectrum, for all practical purposes we get more of it.

This doesn't just reflect the fact that broadcast stations cannot compress or split up their frequencies. It reflects the fact that they are limited to two artificial reservations, the AM and FM bands. But if the FCC would open more of the ether to broadcasting, manufacturers could sell *downconverters*: small devices that would attach to or sit near a radio and convert signals sent over other sections of the spectrum. The Philips Clevercast, used for converting data broadcast from satellites, works on such a principle. So, for that matter, does DirecTV, which allows a TV set built to receive UHF and VHF signals pick up broadcasts made in the SHF band. But if you want to bring down the price of the converter, you'll need a highly integrated device without a high parts cost, and in order for companies to invest in developing such a machine, you'll need a regulatory regime that allows the product to be put to the use for which it was devised. In the pithy words of Bennett Kobb, author of the widely used *SpectrumGuide: Radio Frequency Allocations in the United States*, "Manufacturers will make just about any gizmo if they see a mass market." Until then, Kobb notes, "We're using a 60-year-old technology with FM, and it's creating an artificial scarcity, when we could accommodate for all practical purposes an unlimited class of stations."[45]

Real reform, in short, means radical deregulation—*real* deregulation, not the halfway measures we've been fed since the Nixon years.

The government has loosened a lot of the rules governing telecommunications over the past three decades, often to good effect. The court-ordered breakup of AT&T may not have rid the phone market of monopoly, but it inspired far more competition than existed before, to consumers' initial confusion but ultimate benefit. Reagan's FCC removed many of the "public interest" requirements faced by radio and TV broadcasters, including the Fairness Doctrine. And the FCC removed many legal barriers to cable and satellite TV in the 1970s and 1980s. Most notably, it began licensing satellite earth stations that were far smaller and cheaper than those previously allowed. The result was more diversity on the air.[46]

Yet there is a difference between loosening and liberation. Consider the Cable Communications Policy Act of 1984, which undid some regulations but imposed several new ones as well. Most notably, it codified the creation of franchise monopolies, arrangements in which local governments protect cable companies against would-be competitors. As the sociologist Thomas Streeter has written,

> Cable was able to grow, not so much because regulations were simply eliminated, but because, beginning in the early 1970s, cable's status among the policy community was changed from industry threat to industry component; haltingly, sometimes awkwardly, but nonetheless systematically, those with influence surrounding the FCC came to bring cable into the fold and to consider cable's survival and health part of the legitimate goals of industrial system management. The result was not a radical change in industry structure toward entrepreneurialism but rather a series of incremental adjustments within the existing oligopolistic, center-periphery, advertising-supported system of electronic media. Cable has not revolutionized the basic corporate liberal structure of television; it has been integrated within it.[47]

Sure enough, today's cable channels are generally owned by the same financial empires that dominate other media. There's far more variety and competition on TV than in the days when most towns had only three televisual options, but cable still hasn't reached its real potential. The technology has changed radically, but the social arrangements that surround it have not.

So the FCC is still a captive of the industries it regulates. It has its share of internal fissures and splits, which occasionally allow proposals like Docket 80–90 or low-power FM to move forward. But in general, it has eased the restrictions that chafe the most powerful companies while tightening the rules that protect their privileges. Consider the Telecommunications Act of 1996. It removed a host of barriers to chain ownership of radio stations; most hailed or jeered it as the most far-reaching deregulation yet. Yet it introduced new rules even as it cleared away old ones, imposing whole new bureaucracies—the Telecommunications Development Fund, the National Education Technology Funding Corporation—and introducing strict controls on electronic speech.[48] The result was a body of law so complex that one analyst complained, "If the devil's in the details, then we must be in hell."[49]

Real reform ultimately means abolishing the FCC. It means allowing those who use a piece of spectrum to have title to it, limited by other users' right not to suffer interference. But the title would apply only to the spectrum the broadcaster is using: if new technologies allow others to squeeze onto a nearby frequency without interfering, they shouldn't have to ask the first user's permission. (Similarly, if a station does not broadcast constantly for twenty-four hours a day, seven days a week, there's no reason another broadcaster should not simply take over the remaining hours of the day or week, as long as the second operation does not misrepresent itself as the first.)

Under real deregulation, the government would stop hoarding spectrum for future uses and throw it open to the public—auctioning it off, distributing it by lot, or simply allowing new users to homestead it.[50] The feds would stop "zoning" the spectrum: those with title to pieces of the ether would have the flexibility to use it as they please, for broadcasting or cellular phones or anything else. (The present system, in which Washington reserves most sections of the spectrum for specific uses only, has led to a massive misallocation of the airwaves, discouraging innovation and locking old technologies in place.) If the specter of private monopoly emerges—and it probably won't, considering how much room there is on the spectrum, how much more is being made available by new technologies, and the simple fact that the existing telecom monopolies depend on government protection for their power—but if it does, shouldn't antitrust law be enough to keep it in check? Why turn to the industry-captured FCC?

Some unlicensed stations went off the air as the fight over legal low-power radio unfolded, hoping it would improve their chances of getting licensed. Others actually returned to broadcasting: Free Radio Berkeley may have officially disbanded, but The Activists Formerly Known As Free Radio Berkeley are still around. Late in 1998, Dunifer suggested that the micro movement should mimic the tactics of the radical green group Earth First! Several of his compatriots apparently took his suggestion literally, and decided to operate a radio station while sitting in a Willard Park tree. Their makeshift operation—set atop well-balanced platforms and christened Tree Radio Berkeley—went on the air on November 23, transmitting news and music 'round the clock in a style much like Dunifer's early broadcasts from the Berkeley hills. Listeners dropped by with supplies—water, pizza, batteries, tapes—and another micro station, SPURT, set up a simulcast in another tree, about fifty feet away. (SPURT stands for Solar Powered Urban Radio Transmissions. Since they were solar powered, tree-based broadcasting was a natural next step for them.)

The DJs, who called themselves Sparrow and The Birdman of Berkeley, came down on December 4, signing off with Janis Joplin's "Bye Bye Baby." Some more activists picked up the ball, starting Berkeley Liberation Radio at Free Radio Berkeley's old frequency. The new outlet arrived in the summer of 1999, just as the battle between Pacifica management and KPFA was at its height. Along with San Francisco Liberation Radio, it gave airtime to the protesting staffers, sometimes transmitting live from the encampment outside the locked station— much like Free Radio Berkeley's maiden broadcast in 1995. Still more veterans of Dunifer's station started broadcasting from flea markets, as Flea Radio Berkeley.

In a sane world, the government would let such projects proliferate in peace. It sure makes more sense then storming a man's home and pointing a gun at his cat.

11

CB, the Internet, and Beyond

Pig-Pen, this here's the Rubber Duck
We just ain't a-gonna pay no toll
So we crashed the gate doing 98
I says: Let them truckers roll
—C. W. McCall

IMAGINE THIS. THE FCC gives a slice of spectrum to the general public. It's easy to get a license to use it, and even easier to go on the air without one. This special band becomes a weird melting pot, a place where point-to-point chatter mixes with primitive broadcasts; a place dominated by blue-collar workers, small businesses, and hobbyists, building a lively subculture; a place almost entirely free of state and corporate control.

The place already exists. It's called the Citizens Band. And before you blithely assume that microbroadcasting alone will usher in a radio utopia, you should think a bit about what happened to CB.

In 1993, the writer I. R. Ybarra bought a CB radio, planning to use it to talk with a friend who lived nearby. Things didn't work out that way. "You couldn't get a word in edgewise," Ybarra reports:

> "Aaaaooohp!!" The belcher blats into his microphone several more times, whistles, and puts on loud-modulating echoing recording of the Woody Woodpecker trademark "A hoo hoo a-HOO hoo!" at fast speed.
>
> Then another male voice calls: "HEY Cleo! Got yer ears on? Hey, CLEO! Cleo, got yer ears on? Cleo, got yer ears on? Hey Cleo?"

Put a beat behind it, maybe, and it might not be so bad. But it ain't Bertolt Brecht's dream of "the finest possible communication apparatus in public life," either.

"Last fall," Ybarra continues, "I spent several afternoons or evenings with the walkie-talkies turned on to listen to the types of transmissions these people were making, and one fact looms tall: I did not hear a single substantive conversation. Not once." At one point, the writer "listened in reeling amazement as a man with some kind of Deep-South accent got on and repeated what I think was the word 'five' what I would estimate to be at least a thousand times. . . .

"What's the story here?" Ybarra concludes. "Is this what people revert to when the controls are off? Good god."[1]

Good God, indeed. What happened to the Citizens Band?

CB radio was born in 1945, the product of an electromagnetic peace dividend. World War II had just ended, freeing some military frequencies for civilian use. Daniel Noble, vice president of Motorola, suggested that some of this spectrum should be reserved for private communication. Policemen and big boats already used two-way radios. Noble proposed making them more widely available. Small businesses could adopt them, he explained: they'd be useful for delivery trucks, fishermen, valets, even doctors. The FCC agreed, and reserved some shortwave space for a service along those lines. In 1949, it made the arrangement permanent.

And almost nothing happened. CB had been planted in infertile soil, an ultra-high-frequency zone open to only the most expensive and sophisticated radios. This started to change only in 1958, when the FCC siphoned twenty-three channels from the amateur band and offered them "for personal use by any individual."[2] Operators could use up to four watts of power, which on this band gave them a legal range of about fifteen to thirty miles. The commissioners expected the revamped service to be a place for "substantive and useful messages related either to the business activities or personal convenience of private citizens."[3] The displaced hams warned that it would turn into a giant party line instead. The amateurs proved more prescient than the regulators: within a year the feds were battling "improper" use of the Citizens Band, at one point even trying to bar speaking in "hobby-type expressions."[4]

The harder the authorities fought, the unrulier the CBers became. The FCC imposed a license application fee, hoping that would squeeze out the riffraff. In response, people simply neglected to get licensed. Tens of thousands joined the band each year, mostly blue-collar sorts that the government never expected to use the service. The regulators lacked the resources to enforce their edicts. Eventually, they threw up their hands and accepted the fact that the Citizens Band had been overrun with actual citizens.

In the '70s, of course, CB became a fad, a topic for trucker movies and country songs. Even Betty Ford joined in, signing on as "First Momma." By 1975, the government was getting two hundred thousand license applications a month. In 1976, it took in 4.8 million. And that's just the people who bothered to apply: no more than half the country's CB users were licensed at all. In 1976, an overwhelmed FCC stopped trying to charge for licenses. Even that didn't deter the pirates. It still took the feds a few months to process that permit, and they obviously weren't serious about enforcing the rules. So why bother applying?

There was a vibrant CB culture even before the '70s blitz, a working-class world with its own customs, institutions, and even language, a stew brewed from Arkahoma dialect, ham jargon, and police code. The new CB fad threw those old communities into disarray. According to the historians Carolyn Marvin and Quentin Schultze, the impact was lethal:

> In the early 1970s, handles like Plumber, Crowbar, Janitor, and Slim Jim characteristically referred to the occupations of their owners and evidenced the blue-collar majority among users. Handles evoking a middle-class leisure-oriented lifestyle, like Beachcomber, Sky Pilot, and Tennis Bum, began to appear with the rush of novices to the band.
>
> These new operators were nomadic travelers who had mastered the jargon and etiquette for successful operation, but lacked a CB identity built on a particular locality or group. The mass popularity of CB . . . disrupted local-channel groups for which CB had been a focus of everyday shared experience, personal interests, and social occasions.[5]

The immigrants, they conclude, were unassimilable, immune to the informally enforced customs that had allowed earlier Citizens Band communities to flourish.

There are those who dispute this unhappy account. The newcomers simply built a different kind of community, CB's defenders declare—more anonymous and more mobile, but still very real. At least one nomadic band managed to maintain a stable on-air society: the truck drivers. In 1973, independent truckers used their CBs to coordinate highway blockades around the country, protesting the new speed limits imposed during the oil crisis. The scattered trucks became a free-floating rebel network linked by radio, the American equivalent of Radio Alice's wireless protest networks.

This species of CB had a pronounced anti-authoritarian streak, hostile to highway cops and the FCC. Truckers and other drivers used their radios to issue Smokey reports, warning of speed cops lying in wait. The more pragmatic policemen—those out to save lives, as opposed to those out to raise revenue—welcomed the practice. It did, after all, make people slow down. And when a truly reckless driver was loose, few CB hounds shied from alerting the police along with each other.

It's not hard to leap from there to a defense of '70s CB. In this view, the million-man chatterbox was really a cowboy community of the highways, answering one another's distress calls and evading the patrolman's gaze. Hard-core enthusiasts still maintained a less fleeting subculture, based not on evading speed traps or sticking it to The Man but on friendship and conviviality. They met at regional festivals, their families in tow, and often traveled in *convoys*, groups of radio-equipped cars and trucks moving en masse. Many kept CB sets in their homes as well as their cars; a few got rid of their phones, reasoning that they never called anyone long distance and could always reach their local friends and relatives with their radios. Most came from unprivileged backgrounds. (When three sociologists surveyed participants at two "breakers"—carnival-like conventions organized by CB clubs—they found that 90 percent of those who were employed had working-class or lower-middle-class jobs.)[6] Contrary to the claims of Marvin and Schultze, this world did not die in the '70s. It grew, swelling along with the larger CB fad, adapting to the new circumstances. At first.

But each month brought more newcomers, and there was only so much bandwidth available. The FCC added another seventeen CB channels to the original twenty-three, but that still wasn't enough. Conversations piled atop conversations. Citizen signals interfered with TV broadcasts. Informal sanctions began to lose their power; people felt freer to act like jerks. And still the din swelled. "Normally, only about half the transmissions one hears on a given channel are intelligible," complained one journalist; "the rest sound like the speaker was shaving with an electric razor while munching granola."[7] Something had to give, and that something turned out to be CB itself. By the 1980s, the Citizens Band was a virtual ghost town. It was an old Yogi Berra paradox, played out in real life: *Nobody ever goes there anymore. It's too crowded.*

By the time Ybarra bought those walkie-talkies, it was over. Such tools were still useful under certain circumstances (like a worksite), and the truckers, of course, had never stopped talking. But the larger CB world was decimated, just eddies of babble swirling in an empty sea.[8]

CB collapsed from a fatal combination: spectrum was scarce, and there was no reliable means of excluding people from it. It was a *tragedy of the commons*, the ecologist Garrett Hardin's term for what happens to a resource everyone can use but no one is responsible for. Open to all and stewarded by none, the Citizens Band was quickly overgrazed.

It's instructive to compare CB to early amateur radio, which faced similar constraints yet managed to thrive. The parallels are striking, down to the news stories each medium generated. The Progressive Era press alternately glorified the hams and reviled them. One moment they were brave inventor-heroes, nobly scanning for distress signals at sea. The next they were dangerous pranksters, butting in where mere amateurs weren't welcome. The CB subculture produced the same mixed reaction. Were these people rugged frontiersmen, helping stranded motorists and bringing a sense of community to the road? Or were they irresponsible hoaxers, speeders, and scofflaws, producing nothing but—to quote *Newsweek*—"a plague of citizen's-band messages that are clogging the airwaves and posing a virtually insuperable problem of control"?[9]

The amateurs, as we've seen, organized complicated covenants to keep troublemakers in line. The CB world developed a similarly rich system of informal norms.[10] Even after the population boom of the '70s, some groups managed to congregate on channels of their own. (As late as 1977, the president of the American CB Radio Association told reporters about a channel in Oregon that had been "taken over by about 20 lesbians who work as tree planters.")[11] But most of those arrangements failed to hold—though they proved far more resilient than the rules the state tried to impose from above.

So why did they finally fail where the amateurs' efforts had succeeded? Because the hams had much more spectrum to work with, and thus much less to fight over; and because their controls became legally enforceable, more or less, while the CB norms did not.

By now the point is moot: the Internet offers the anonymous chat-rooms that CB once provided, without the problems of scarcity and interference (albeit at a greater expense). And cellular phones now offer mobile communications to the masses (albeit in a much less communal form). Indeed, it was cell phones, arguably, that sealed the Citizens Band's fate. With CB boundaries proving unenforceable, consumers adopted a new technology that didn't pose that problem.

That doesn't leave much on the Citizens Band, now that the '70s stampede is over. "Hey, CLEO! Got yer ears on?" "A hoo hoo a-HOO hoo!" "Five, five, five, five, five." As Ybarra asked: Is this what people revert to when the controls are off? If micro radio were legal, would the airwaves be swamped with *this*?

The pessimists can point to plenty of evidence. Look at the worst dregs of the Internet, at the pointless chatroom babble and mountains of stupid spam. Look at public access TV, where good independent filmmaking and quirky local shows rub shoulders with *The Coprophiliacs' Crusade* and *The Aryan Power Hour*. Look at talk radio: sometimes a paragon of democratic media, but sometimes a wasteland of bigots and blowhards. Radio is only as good as the people broadcasting. What happens if, after the walls come down, no one turns out to have anything to say? What if all the creative pirates I've profiled are anomalies, sure to be crowded out quickly by crap?

One might reply that the professional mediamakers have produced their fair share of garbage, too, and that for all the shoddy stuff on public access and the Net, they've also aired a lot of good material that otherwise would never have been seen. One consequence of great diversity is that whatever you like may seem to be drowning in a sea of slop. What's important is for the good stuff to be out there, and for people to know how to find it. And, as important, how to create it themselves.

There are two more causes for hope, both related to the Internet. One is the possibility of near-infinite bandwidth, of a world in which it won't matter how much garbage is out there because there will always be room for the programs you prefer. The other is networked micro radio, a system that selects the best that microcasters have to offer and leaves the worst stranded in their ten-watt lots.

Infinite bandwidth is a common prediction in futurist circles. (For some of us, that's a reason to be skeptical.) The scenario goes like this. Cable and phone companies are investing millions in fiber-optic wires that can carry far more data than the Internet can currently withstand, and advances in wireless technology may make even those systems obsolete. Spectrum will multiply until scarcity essentially disappears. Television, telephones, radio, and the Web will merge into a giant network, in which every consumer can also be a producer. Our networked computers will be cheap and often portable, with as many channels to choose from as there are books and magazines to read today.

George Gilder, the right-wing futurist, expounded this view in his 1990 book *Life after Television*. For Gilder, network TV was a temporary aberration, a centralized structure made necessary by the technical limitations of its time. "The expense and complexity of the tubes used in television systems meant that most of the processing of signals would have to be done at the station," he argues, while the receiver "had to be relatively simple." The result was "a top-down system—in electronic terms, a 'master-slave' architecture. A few broadcast centers would originate programs for millions of passive receivers, or 'dumb terminals.' Spectrum scarcity would force TV to adopt a centralized system, limited to relatively few channels, with no two-way communication."[12]

Technology has changed this, the argument concludes. Smart microchips will replace dumb vacuum tubes. Spectrum scarcity will give way to spectrum abundance. There will be no need to centralize intelligence in broadcast studios; there will be no need to conserve the ether. Television, a "totalitarian" medium in which a few giant businesses produce three or six or five hundred channels geared to the lowest common denominator, will fall. A new, more participatory network will emerge: Every Man a TV Station.

And, by extension, Every Man a Radio Station. Gilder doesn't write about radio, but it isn't hard to extend his analysis that way. Already, many stations simulcast their signals over the Net, making their shows available to anyone with a computer, a modem, and some audio software. Some "radio" stations exist only on the Net, a form of unlicensed broadcasting that is entirely legal. Several are devoted to freeform, or to forms of music that are scarce on the ordinary dial. (KNAC, an L.A. station for heavy metal fans who didn't like their music watered down, left the FM dial in 1995. In 1998, it resurfaced on the Internet, webcasting to online aficionados.)

At this point, such projects can be fairly expensive. Webcasting itself is getting steadily cheaper, but bandwidth is still pretty pricy: it costs a lot to let even fifty listeners tune to a netcast at once. Some futurists promise that this will soon change, once the techies perfect "multicasting." Current webcasts send every listener a private stream of data, creating severe congestion problems. Multicasting sends just one data stream to everyone, eliminating the trouble. Some primitive multicast systems are already operating, though some argue that they're ill matched to the way most people use the Net.

Still, the hopeful scenario has it that ordinary people will soon be able to broadcast with the reach of direct-satellite radio for little more than it costs to run a micro radio station. A Gilderian utopia—right?

Maybe. The problem with Gilder's vision is that it turns so totally on technology. Technical change is important, obviously. But all the software in the world can't overcome sufficiently steep political barriers. Technology doesn't just alter social relations: it is itself a product of social relations. The history of telecommunications isn't a tale of unconstrained invention, of one industrial product begetting another with inexorable evolutionary logic. It is a series of human choices, a long litany of technologies that powerful interests have advanced at the expense of others. We've already seen how RCA's clout led regulators to push television while holding back FM. For years, similarly, the FCC blocked cable TV, even though it arguably lacked the statutory authority to do so. It also kept cellular phones off the market for more than a decade.

Never forget this. *It is deregulation that is allowing new tech to enter the marketplace, not new tech that is allowing deregulation.* From direct-satellite radio to cheap micro transmitters, new technologies have had to bide their time, ready to be used but blocked by Washington. The government didn't pass its micro radio plan because it was technically possible. It passed it because thousands of Americans were defying the law, just like the hams who ignored the Radio Act of 1912 and carved out space not only for amateurs but for broadcasters. Or the hobbyists who built proletarian chatrooms in the Citizens Band. Or the nerdy revolutionaries who turned a military communication system into the anarchistic Internet we know today.

Nothing about mass media should be taken as given. An alternate America might never have banned amateur broadcasting, allowing Gilder's pluralist vision to take hold seventy years ahead of schedule. Another, completely bound to established interests, might have blocked *any* technology that threatened the industry leaders' market share, even if some of those established companies could have profited from the innovation. In another, it might not have mattered what the government did, because the people simply wouldn't feel like using the machines at their disposal. The point isn't that technical restraints aren't significant. It's that they cannot be considered outside the important influences of politics and culture.

So it makes sense to ask what can be done *now*, under the constraints we already face, before concerning ourselves with any Internet technologies that might arrive later—or, for that matter, with the political reforms that need to be won.

Enter networked micro radio. Some stations are using the Net, not to broadcast to a mass audience, but to share shows with one another. The A-Infos Radio Project, a collective of online anarchists, has set up a website through which micro stations, legal community stations, and independent producers can upload and download news reports, full-length documentaries, and other shows in MP3 form. On any given week, the menu might include a strike report from Flint, a travelogue from Barbados, a history of American Buddhism, a newscast delivered in Spanish, and dozens more options.

In 1999, some Seattle activists embraced this idea as they prepared to protest a meeting of the World Trade Organization. For several years, much of the city's alternative media—print and video as well as radio—had been joined in a loose association known variously as the Independent Media Coalition and the Independent Media Cabal. Now dubbed the Independent Media Center, they set up a website offering audio, video, and text coverage of the anti-WTO protests and the heavy-handed police response, while simultaneously broadcasting on a temporary micro station. The protests ended, but the Seattle IMC did not. And in other cities around the world, inspired imitators created dozens more IMCs of their own. One appeared, for example, in Washington, D.C., to cover April 2000's protests against the World Bank and the International Monetary Fund:

> When Mobilization Radio, the low-watt station that covered the protest, announced that the FCC were at the door to shut them down, three hundred demonstrators arrived on the scene in minutes. "What happened next was probably unprecedented in the history of microradio," wrote Joe Tuba, for the IMC. Apparently taken aback by the crowd, the police, FBI, FCC and assorted other intelligence left the scene without making arrests or grabbing equipment. "The crowd im-

mediately took the street in celebration . . . and the station was disas-
sembled and carried out as the participants left the building and re-
gained anonymity as members of the crowd."[13]

Each IMC is completely autonomous—and some, granted, have done
higher-quality work than others. No matter: one can take what is valuable, retransmit it, and leave the rest to rot. To the extent that one is re-
transmitting audio files, this is something utterly new: radio with the
flexibility of e-mail.

This marks a sea change. Satellites have been a centralizing force
within community radio, taking power from local volunteers and encouraging stations to rely on federal funds and institutionally produced
programs. The Internet, cheaper and more dispersed, has had the opposite effect. As the Net's speed and bandwidth increase, it's becoming
easier for independents to distribute their programs as quickly and as
far as their better-endowed competitors on satellite. The result: a true
network, headless and decentralized, shifting its boundaries each moment. Call it *molecular* radio: a web of atom-sized stations, bound by the
Net into a larger confederation. And you don't even need a computer to
listen to it.

Netcasting has also been converging with two other technologies, creating something very different from traditional radio. One of those
technologies is the MP3 file, and the various means that have emerged
to transfer such digitally stored sound online. The second is the software that mainstream radio uses to plan its playlists.

Increasingly, program directors have been using computers to
choose the records their stations will play. The most popular such program is Selector, made by Radio Computing Services. Once a catalog of
the music library has been entered—not a terribly onerous task, since
the typical station has a library of only five hundred to a thousand
songs, the vast majority of which are rarely played—the director gives
Selector a series of instructions and the program produces a playlist.
Those parameters might be broad genre restrictions ("no rap"), general
patterns ("two upbeat songs, followed by one ballad, then repeat"), or
more narrow rules ("no more than three songs with female vocalists per
hour"). Selector then chooses which songs will be played, and in what
order, for the next twenty-four hours, seven days, or whatever horizon
the programmer prefers.

Invented by Andrew Economos in 1979, Selector has spawned several offspring. One is SelectorReach, which combines Selector's data with information from the local Arbitron ratings. ("Filters include age, gender, ethnicity and preference," declares the company website, "all of which can be selected individually. For example, you can see black women age 25–34 . . .")[14] Another spinoff, Master Control NT, doesn't just choose which songs to play. It actually plays them, along with all the appropriate ads, promos, and prerecorded DJ bits. Welcome to the completely automated radio station.

For decades, consultants have been trying to figure out the formula that will generate the perfect series of songs for a station's audience. Now there's a tool that will turn those preferences into a playlist. But what happens if the listeners have access to that same program—and to a much larger library of music on the Web? What if a website let listeners select their own parameters and then followed them to the letter, with no commercial interruptions and no DJ schtick? Some users might choose a familiar generic format ("play young country" or "play classic rock"). Some might combine a couple of formats ("play young country *and* classic rock"). Some might get ridiculously specific ("I like old-school hip-hop, mid-tempo ska, country music from before 1970, and Miles Davis's *Kind of Blue*"). It would be a relatively simple matter for the site to track which songs are being played and to pay the appropriate parties a licensing fee, funded perhaps by user subscriptions and perhaps by other means.

Already, crude versions of this are beginning to appear. RealJukebox will shuffle all kinds of digitally stored music: you can load on tracks from your own CDs, and you can pull in MP3s from around the Net. Napster and its imitators have allowed much larger music libraries to grow online, where any user can rip a song from a CD and put it up for anyone else to download. Meanwhile, Click Radio, Sonicnet, and other companies let Web surfers create their own "stations," picking the genres they want their computers to play. MongoMusic allows listeners to specify not just their favorite genres and eras, but the tempo, beat, and even mood they prefer. "As I write this," one journalist wrote in late 2000, "it's bleak and rainy outside, putting me in the mood for languorous, lugubrious songs. I open Radio Mongo at MongoMusic and request ultraslow, medium-heavy indie rock songs, and the moody Tortoise track that opens my set perfectly suits my melancholy. More dolorous tracks follow. Later, wanting to cheer up a bit, I make the weight one point lighter and the tempo one point faster. A delicious track by the gritty-girlie pop-punk band Clare Quilty comes on. . . . After 15 minutes of playing around on MongoMusic, I've created a station that surprises and delights me with the songs it plays." The reporter, incidentally, finds this kind of alarming. "The music may be speaking right to me," she explains, "but it's alienating being a niche market of one."[15]

Were it not for one legal barrier, such sites could track listeners' preferences even more closely. The Digital Millennium Copyright Act of 1998 burdens Internet stations with a host of restrictions aimed at making it harder for listeners to predict when any particular song will be played. The idea is to keep them from copying the tune without paying for it. It's unclear just how much this would restrict a customized radio station—or, for that matter, why such "piracy" is any different from simply taping songs off the radio. The music industry is scared, though, and the legal battles are already under way.

Customized radio won't mean the death of traditional broadcasting. It will mean changes, though, for modern radio's research-driven style. As access to the Net becomes cheaper—and more portable—it will be harder for old-fashioned stations to draw listeners away from online services, especially as they simultaneously face competition from direct-satellite radio and from microbroadcasters. Traditional radio stations will be able to do one thing, though, that an automated, Web-based system can't. Like the old freeform stations, they can hire skilled hosts who know their music and understand how to put disparate songs together in creative sets that no scheduling engine could conceive.

Then program directors could stop playing super-DJ and take on the larger visionary role of shaping their stations' personalities, of figuring out the boundaries of what they will play and finding the right staff to play it. And if the old outlets don't do that, surely some websites and micro stations will.

Customized Internet audio streams are in many ways the opposite of molecular radio. One is private, the other shared; one is automated, the other participatory. But between them, they're a substantial challenge to the broadcast business and its accumulated habits.

I stopped by Kind Radio again in 1999, about a year before the government shut it down. By this time, Kind was starting to seem less like a solitary station and more like a node in a vibrant Hill Country network. That evening, Neva Humble—yes, that's a pseudonym—was hosting *Humble Time*, a showcase for Texas songwriters. From the speaker came a series of wonderful acoustic songs, far better than the bland slop that most country stations play. This was the only syndicated show on Kind: at that point, eight stations regularly broadcast it, two of them unlicensed and the others perfectly legal.

Every week, Neva and her husband Ace record an open-mike session at a hundred-year-old country store in Freiheit, a tiny town about midway from Austin to San Antonio. From the four-hour tape they edit a one-hour program, put it on a CD, and send it to participating stations. On Kind Radio, Neva had *two* hours to fill, so hosting the show required more than just playing the disc. She had to edit out the ads (Kind still banned commercials), then fill up the second hour with favorite tracks from past programs. The task was even trickier the night I visited, since one of the CD players was acting up. To fill the dead-air gap between tracks, Neva had to turn on the microphone and give a play-by-play account of her struggle to cue the next song. The listeners didn't seem to mind: she has a great radio voice and, I gathered from the frequent phone calls, several devoted male fans. (I could hear only her side of the conversations, but it wasn't hard to figure out what some callers were saying. "Aw," she told one. "You're just saying that because I'm a girl.")

Most of the songs that night were country or blues, though the showcase is open to all genres of music. Some jazz acts have performed there, for instance, including the Austin pianist who wrote Stevie Ray Vaughn's hit "Cold Shot." A few stars and semi-stars have played the showcase—Ray Wylie Hubbard, for one—but most of the performers don't even have recording contracts. By and large, they come from Austin, San Antonio, and the vast rural space in between: from small towns like Wimberley, Fredericksburg, and Canyon Lake. Occasionally, they travel longer distances. One week, a Canadian happened to be in town while the show was in session and decided to perform. They say he was pretty good.

Even after Kind was killed, *Humble Time* kept going. The people behind it continued their other creative projects, too. Ace still played in Fools in Love, a local rock/funk/reggae band. By day, he made his living running a recording studio, the Sonic Deli, out of the house he shares with Neva. The studio has thus far resisted the temptation to start its own label, but Ace is thinking about publishing music on the Internet.

Thanks to the Net, *Humble Time* had acquired a small following around the world. For the most part, though, it is invisible outside central Texas. The most interesting cultural activity often takes place in such corners and crevices, far from the mass media's eye. But the people who create that culture are rarely afraid to use the bigger media's tools—radio, CDs, the Internet—to fashion their garage-based art.

In the jargon of the day, they're a part of the New Media, an ill-defined term for talk radio, desktop publishing, the World Wide Web, and every other self-directed or participatory medium that has flourished in recent years. Not everyone in the old media likes the new. "The new media cater to and are built up by people who used to sit on bar stools and complain to each other," the reporter Gwen Ifill, then of NBC, complained in 1994. "Now they can dial an 800 number and complain for free."[16]

Ifill speaks for a lot of her colleagues. She's also more right than she realizes. The "new" media are descended from the original media of taverns, bars, and cafés; of songs and rumors, graffiti and wallposters, broadsheets and fliers. In 1646, an Ifillesque preacher warned the English Parliament that alehouses were "the meeting places of malignants and sectaries."[17] Naturally, the government periodically cracked down on unlicensed taverns.

We still have bars, and we still trade information there. But the mass media have overshadowed the older order of taverns and fliers, creating the illusion that their standardized product, handed down from the high castles of Hollywood and Manhattan, has a legitimacy lacked by our less distant means of interaction.

They are wrong. They may be professionals and the tavern folk mere amateurs, but the advantages of professionalism have been oversold. Fifty years ago, the mass media might have seemed ready to overwhelm our more immediate, more human world, our ancient networks of conversations and rumors. Today, it is we who threaten to overwhelm the mass media, invading the airwaves and computer screens that the elite once reserved for itself. It's reached the point where the news and culture industries are marketing some of their wares as "independent" even when they're not. Record companies start small subsidiaries, packaging their releases like an indie label's efforts. Big-budget studios advertise their blockbusters as independent films. Mainstream magazines ape zine styles.

None of which will still the flood of truly independent art, reporting, and commentary, of the cultural renaissance whose most exciting face is the micro radio movement. And don't worry too much about the Citizens Band, or the worst excesses of cable access, talk radio, and the Net. If there's also been an explosion of drivel, smut, and paranoia, so be it: at least it's *our* drivel, smut, and paranoia. These voices come unvarnished.

Notes

NOTES TO CHAPTER 1

1. Kind definitely reduced crime on Joe Ptak's block. With a twenty-four-hour radio station in the area, there was always at least one person awake to keep an eye out for burglars.

2. Apparently, that was the name of a band. But it also reflected the tone of the show.

3. Personal interview, June 19, 1998.

4. Quoted in Rebecca Thatcher, "Runoffs Saturday in San Marcos," *Austin American-Statesman*, May 29, 1998, p. B1.

5. Quoted in Roger Croteau, "San Marcos' KIND Marks First Anniversary," *San Antonio Express-News*, March 26, 1998, p. B1.

6. Personal interview, June 19, 1998.

7. This conversation took place in my apartment in October 1998.

8. Andrew Nelson Lytle, "The Hand Tit," in Twelve Southerners, *I'll Take My Stand: The South and the Agrarian Tradition*, New York: Harper and Brothers, 1930, p. 244. For an extension of this argument in a somewhat different cultural context, see Hakim Bey, *Immediatism*, San Francisco: AK Press, 1994 [1992].

9. DJ Tashtego, "Community Struggle and the Sweet Mystery of Radio," in Ron Sakolsky and Stephen Dunifer (eds.), *Seizing the Airwaves: A Free Radio Handbook*, San Francisco: AK Press, 1998, p. 139.

NOTES TO CHAPTER 2

1. Clinton B. DeSoto's *200 Meters and Down: The Story of Amateur Radio* (West Hartford, Conn.: American Radio Relay League, 1936) asserts that the Hudson River station was founded in 1911. Another source—"The First Radio Club in America," *Radio Broadcast*, January 1923—says 1913.

2. Richard Hofstadter, *The Age of Reform: From Bryan to F.D.R.*, New York: Knopf, 1955, p. 5.

3. Quoted in Robert Wiebe, *Businessmen and Reform: A Study of the Progressive Movement*, Cambridge, Mass.: Harvard University Press, 1962, p. 18.

4. "The Ham," *Wireless Age*, December 1919, p. 37. Early ham magazines are filled with descriptions of jerry-rigged radios. For some especially intriguing

examples of the amateurs' ingenuity, including a fellow who combined a radio transmitter with a bicycle, see Michael Brian Schiffer, *The Portable Radio in American Life*, Tucson: University of Arizona Press, 1991, pp. 39–42.

5. Quoted in Sally Gregory Kohlstedt, *The Formation of the American Scientific Community: The American Association for the Advancement of Science, 1848–1960*, Champaigne: University of Illinois Press, 1976, p. 8.

6. Quoted in Mark Siegel, *Hugo Gernsback, Father of Modern Science Fiction*, San Bernardino, Calif.: Borgo Press, 1988, p. 19.

7. Paul A. Carter, *The Creation of Tomorrow: Fifty Years of Magazine Science Fiction*, New York: Columbia University Press, 1977, p. 5.

8. Gernsback's admirers have striven hard to present his stranger predictions as accurate forecasts. Thus, Lee de Forest, introducing a reprint of *Ralph 124C 41+* in 1950, could claim, "His 'Menograph,' or thought recorder, is today crudely realized in our lie-detector." Er, not quite.

9. Hugo Gernsback, *Ralph 124C 41+: A Romance of the Year 2660*, second edition, Lincoln, Neb.: Bison Books, 2000 [1925], p. 9. [First edition serialized in *Modern Electrics* in 1911.]

10. DeSoto, p. 26.

11. Ibid.

12. Quoted in Susan J. Douglas, *Inventing American Broadcasting, 1899–1922*, Baltimore: Johns Hopkins University Press, 1987, p. 210.

13. "The 'Wireless' Devotees of Chicago," *Electrical World*, July 21, 1910, p. 139.

14. Quoted in Douglas, p. 230.

15. Ibid., p. 234.

16. DeSoto, p. 35.

17. Oral History Research Office, "Music in the Air . . . and Voices on the Crystal Set," *American Heritage*, August 1955, p. 76.

18. Michele Hilmes, *Radio Voices: American Broadcasting, 1922–1952*, Minneapolis: University of Minnesota Press, 1997, p. 39.

19. Quoted in Asa Briggs, "The Pleasure Telephone: A Chapter in the Prehistory of Media," in Ithiel de Sola Pool (ed.), *The Social Impact of the Telephone*, Cambridge, Mass.: MIT Press, 1977, p. 44.

20. "Marconi on Radio-Pictures," *Wireless Age*, September 1920, p. 8.

21. Bertolt Brecht, *Brecht on Theatre: The Development of an Aesthetic*, edited and translated by John Willett, New York: Hill and Wang, 1964, p. 52.

22. Robert F. Gowen, "The 'Ham' What Am," *Radio Broadcast*, February 1923, p. 305.

23. One college station—9XM, transmitting from the University of Wisconsin at Madison—kept beaming its signals, thanks to a special arrangement with the military. Renamed WHA in 1921, it still broadcasts today.

24. Douglas, p. 298.

25. J. Andrew White, "Amateur Radio a Necessity," *Wireless Age*, April 1921, p. 10.

26. Julian K. Henney, "A Summer on the Great Lakes: IV—People and Visits," *Wireless Age*, October 1919, p. 22.

27. I don't mean to exaggerate the antistatism of the 1920s. As Robert Nisbet has written, "In national projects of reclamation, in agriculture, in educational assistance to the states and cities, in social work for the indigent, and in investigations of central-planning possibilities, the federal government often came closer in the twenties to the Wilson War State than to anything that had preceded it in American history" (Robert Nisbet, *The Present Age: Progress and Anarchy in Modern America*, New York: Harper and Row, 1988, p. 49). But it was still a substantial retreat from Wilson's total state, even when federal power was advancing: it was the age of Prohibition, but also of bootlegging and speakeasies.

28. WWJ was first on the air, but as an amateur station, 8MK. KDKA was the first licensed commercial broadcast station.

29. Among the amateur stations that went commercial was Doc Herrold's operation. It had, of course, gone off the air during World War I, but it eventually returned; on December 9, 1921, it was given the commercial call letters KQW. Herrold later sold the operation to a local church, which hired and then fired him as chief engineer. The station's license eventually fell into the hands of the Columbia Broadcasting System, which changed the outlet's name to KCBS and moved it to San Francisco. It remains there to this day.

30. Oral History Research Office, p. 67.

31. Susan Smulyan, *Selling Radio: The Commercialization of American Broadcasting, 1920–1934*, Washington: Smithsonian Institution, 1994, p. 23.

32. "Hot Hoot Owl Stuff," *Wireless Age*, May 1924, p. 40.

33. Smulyan, p. 23.

34. Ronald H. Coase, "The Federal Communications Commission," *Journal of Law and Economics* 2 (October 1959), pp. 1–40.

35. Erik Barnouw, *A Tower in Babel*, New York: Oxford University Press, 1966, p. 92.

36. Jonathan W. Emord, *Freedom, Technology, and the First Amendment*, San Francisco: Pacific Research Institute, 1991, p. 146.

37. Quoted in ibid., p. 147.

38. Quoted in ibid., p. 150.

39. Thomas Hazlett, "The Rationality of U.S. Regulation of the Broadcast Spectrum," *Journal of Law and Economics* 33 (April 1990), p. 141.

40. The Federal Radio Commission was originally slated to exist for only a year. Congress reauthorized it for another twelve months in 1928 and indefinitely in 1929.

41. Quoted in Emord, p. 154.

42. Quoted in Robert McChesney, *Telecommunications, Mass Media, and Democracy: The Battle for the Control of U.S. Broadcasting, 1928–1935*, New York: Oxford University Press, 1994, p. 126.

43. Clarence Dill, "A Traffic Cop for the Air," *Review of Reviews*, February 1927, pp. 183–184.

44. Senator Dill maintained oddly cordial relations with the industry he habitually attacked, leading some to suspect he was more a Conscious Agent than a Useful Idiot.

45. Some scholars also compare it to fee-simple ownership in land, but there are some significant differences. It's hard to argue, for instance, that a radio station's rights are violated if its transmissions are jammed by a rival signal that doesn't reach beyond the jammer's own property. For an elaboration of this point, see Tom Bell, "The Common Law in Cyberspace," *Michigan Law Review* 97 (1999).

46. Oral History Research Office, p. 75.

47. Though on a global level, something like it took place. Notes Hazlett: "decades later, international divisions of spectrum rights were achieved via national homesteading" (Hazlett, p. 172, n. 137).

48. McChesney, p. 27.

49. Quoted in ibid.

50. "Some Problems in the Broadcasting of Religion," *Radio Broadcast*, November 1923.

51. McChesney, p. 208.

52. Eugene Leach, "Tuning Out Education: The Cooperation Doctrine in Radio, 1922–38," 1983 (at www.current.org/coop/index.html).

53. By the time the 1930s were well under way, the most visible broadcast reformers were concerning themselves with such burning issues as—I am not making this up—whether children's radio serials were "too exciting." For a lucid discussion of that debate, see Mark I. West, *Children, Culture, and Controversy*, Hamden, Conn.: Archon Books, 1988, pp. 31–42.

54. All quotes are from "Interplanetary Radio Signals?" *Wireless Age*, March 1920, pp. 11–15. The Tesla reference is from Douglas, p. 305.

55. "Mars Still Silent to Marconi and the Earth," *Wireless Age*, August 1922, p. 26.

56. Mark Twain, *Life on the Mississippi*, New York: Penguin Books, 1984 [1883], p. 95.

NOTES TO CHAPTER 3

1. Wallace Hamilton, quoted in Matthew Lasar, *Pacifica Radio: The Rise of an Alternative Network*, Philadelphia: Temple University Press, 1999, pp. 17–18.

2. Henry Lee Roy Finch, quoted in ibid., p. 6.

3. John Whiting, "The Lengthening Shadow: Lewis Hill and the Origins of Listener-Sponsored Broadcasting in America," *Dolphin* #23, 1992.

4. "Radio Station at Beattyville Goes on Ether," *Courier-Journal*, October 18, 1940.

5. Ruth Foxx, "Educational Radio's First Rural Station," *Public Telecommunications Review*, September–October 1979, p. 20.

6. Charles A. Siepmann, *Radio's Second Chance*, Boston: Little, Brown, 1946, p. 17.

7. Lewis Hill, "The Theory of Listener-Sponsored Radio," in Eleanor McKinney (ed.), *The Exacting Ear: The Story of Listener-Sponsored Radio, and an Anthology of Programs from KPFA, KPFK, and WBAI*, New York: Pantheon, 1966, p. 21.

8. That is why, though I am opposed to such regulations, I sometimes find it hard to sympathize with broadcasters mildly injured by "public interest" infringements on their freedom of speech. An old cliché comes to mind, the one about sauce and geese and ganders.

9. Quoted in Tom Lewis, *Empire of the Air: The Men Who Made Radio*, New York: HarperCollins, 1991, p. 254.

10. He posthumously won all his FM lawsuits, to the considerable financial benefit of his widow, Marion.

11. It was, in fact, larger than the band previously set aside for FM. In this way, even as the FCC crippled the first generation of FM broadcasters, it inadvertently made room for far more stations, and therefore more experiments, the next time around.

12. John Whiting, "Pacifica Radio: An American Oasis," *British American*, September 1990.

13. John Whiting, "Pacifica in Vincula," *Radical Poetics*, January 1996.

14. The name "Pacifica" itself referred to pacifism, and not, as some have inaccurately assumed, to the nearby Pacific Ocean.

15. Paul Goodman, *Drawing the Line: The Political Essays of Paul Goodman*, edited by Taylor Stoehr, New York: Free Life Editions, 1977, p. 204.

16. The first *explicitly* anarchist broadcasts were probably the radio messages transmitted in 1921 by the anti-Bolshevik rebels of Kronstadt, Russia. Or—since the Kronstadt uprising was not exclusively anarchist—Radio CNT-FAI, the voice of the libertarian forces in the Spanish Civil War.

Then there was this close call in the Yugoslav town of Fiume, during the brief period in which, led by the poet-magician (and future fascist) Gabriele d'Annunzio, the city adopted an essentially anarchist system of "government" devoted to music, public festivals, and little or no actual governing:

> Guglielmo Marconi, visiting Fiume on his yacht Electra, was met at the landing by Gabriele d'Annunzio, the latter's legionnaires, the city authorities and a great throng of cheering citizens, who later massed

themselves in front of the Commander's palace and vociferously insisted that the visitor deliver an address.

Senator Marconi complied, and, speaking from the central balcony of the palace, announced his decision of donating to Fiume a powerful radio station capable of transmitting news great distances, so that the world might learn of what was going on in Fiume. The announcement was greeted with a tremendous demonstration.

"Marconi Pledges Radio Station to Fiume," *Wireless Age*, November 1920, p. 8.

The short-lived Republic of Fiume soon fell, and I have seen no reports of it establishing a radio service before the end of its revolutionary experiment. But who knows? Maybe, for a month or two, a primitive Radio Free Fiume managed to transmit some playful sedition across the continent . . .

17. Lasar, p. 71.

18. Hill, pp. 21–22.

19. Ibid., p. 25.

20. Eleanor McKinney, "About Pacifica Radio," in McKinney, p. 13.

21. *FCC v. Sanders Brothers Radio Station*, 309 U.S. 470; 60 S. Ct. 693; 1940 U.S. LEXIS 1247; 84 L. Ed.

22. Siepmann, p. 241.

23. Merlin H. Aylesworth, "Radio Is Doomed," *Look*, April 26, 1949, p. 66.

24. Quoted in Michael C. Keith, *Voices in the Purple Haze: Underground Radio and the Sixties*, Westport, Conn.: Praeger, 1997, p. 25.

25. Gilbert A. Williams, *Legendary Pioneers of Black Radio*, Westport, Conn.: Praeger, 1998, p. 8.

26. Quoted in ibid.

27. Quoted in William Barlow, *Voice Over: The Making of Black Radio*, Philadelphia: Temple University Press, 1999, p. 106. KVET, an otherwise white station, was owned by future Texas governor John Connally.

28. Quoted in ibid., p. 134.

29. Personal communication, September 3, 1997.

30. Ibid.

31. Lorenzo Milam, *Sex and Broadcasting: A Handbook on Starting a Radio Station for the Community*, fourth edition, San Diego: Mho and Mho Works, 1988, p. 147. [First edition published in 1971.]

32. Richard Fatherley, *Radio's Revolution and The World's Happiest Broadcasters* (audiotape), 1998.

33. Such systems could get aggravatingly complex. In 1958, for example, WAMM, in Flint, Michigan, "was beginning every half hour with a '6-T formula.' First in the hour was a WAMM Tune Tip, a new record. Next was one of the WAMM Tip Top Tunes, from the top-60 list. Third a WAMM All-Time Tune (million seller) was heard, followed next by another Tip Top Tune. Fifth came another All Time Tune, and sixth another Tip Top Tune" (David R. MacFarland,

. *The Development of the Top 40 Radio Format*, New York: Arno Press, 1979, pp. 263–264).

34. Sam Smith, "The Canaries of Studio A, and Other Tales of Washington Radio," *Washington History* 7:2 (Fall–Winter 1995–96).

35. Quoted in MacFarland, p. 269. This self-image—the radio entrepreneur as heroic capitalist buccaneer—owes a lot to Ayn Rand, a pop philosopher whose paeans to unfettered markets were a strong influence on McLendon. A hard-core free-marketeer, McLendon also supported civil rights for blacks and gays, was pro-choice, and opposed the Vietnam War.

36. Quoted in Ronald Garay, *Gordon McLendon: The Maverick of Radio*, New York: Greenwood Press, 1991, p. 160. Emphasis in the original.

37. My discussion of the *Billboard* surveys draws on MacFarland, pp. 288–295.

38. Bill Stewart, quoted in ibid., p. 367.

39. Ed McKenzie, quoted in Bill Simon, "Jocks Not Playing Disks They Prefer," *Billboard*, November 11, 1957, p. 38.

40. Quoted in Kerry Segrave, *Payola in the Music Industry: A History, 1880–1991*, Jefferson, N.C.: McFarland, 1994, pp. 121–122. Note how the report blames the DJs for the limited playlist, when in fact such lists were imposed by management.

41. Representative Oren Harris (D–Arkansas), quoted in ibid., p. 148.

42. The National Association of Radio Announcers, a federation of black disc jockeys, remained vibrant for a little longer, but was splintered in the Black Power ferment of the late '60s and soon went under.

43. For more on payola's intersection with organized crime, see Fredric Dannen, *Hit Men: Power Brokers and Fast Money Inside the Music Business*, second edition, New York: Vintage Books, 1991. [First edition published in 1990.] Dannen never makes a convincing case that payola itself should be illegal, but he does a good job of showing the other illicit activities with which payolists are often involved.

44. Cousin Bruce Morrow and Laura Baudo, *Cousin Brucie!: My Life in Rock 'n' Roll Radio*, New York: Beech Tree Books, 1987, pp. 166–167.

45. Ibid., p. 167.

46. Lorenzo Milam, *The Cripple Liberation Front Marching Band Blues*, San Diego: Mho and Mho Works, 1984, pp. 15–16.

47. Ibid., p. 17.

48. Quoted in Denzil Walter, "News Letter," *Washington Teamster*, October 4, 1963.

49. Personal interview, August 27, 1997.

50. All quotes from Lasar, pp. 147–149.

51. Lasar comments: "A plutocracy that spoke in the language of democracy, a business that spoke in the name of pacifist/anarchism, the Pacifica

Foundation had been designed for a political economy that did not exist: a stateless society of anarcho-syndicalist cooperatives. In the absence of a pacifist political presence, Hill and his friends reached out to their one surviving ally: liberalism, the liberalism of academics like Frank Freeman [a loud opponent of KPFA's marijuana program], the ACLU, the Ford Foundation, and the FCC. . . . But in their zeal for financial and political support, the first Pacificans failed to create an institutional structure that would transmit the original Pacifica idea to future generations" (ibid., p. 157).

52. Quoted in ibid., p. 163. Lasar stresses that, contrary to legend, it was Hill's health, not the station warfare, that most likely led him to suicide. Indeed, he had attempted to kill himself once before, in mid-1956, a time of relative peace at the station but not in Hill's aching spine.

53. Milam, *The Cripple Liberation Front Marching Band Blues*, p. 126.

54. Ibid., p. 127.

55. Michael Bader, personal interview, September 24, 1997. All subsequent Bader quotes come from this interview, unless otherwise noted.

56. Milam, *The Cripple Liberation Front Marching Band Blues*, p. 135.

57. Personal communication, October 26, 1997.

58. Lorenzo Milam, *The Radio Papers: From KRAB to KCHU, Essays on the Art and Practice of Radio Transmission*, San Diego: Mho and Mho Works, 1986, p. 69.

59. Quoted, or probably just paraphrased, in Milam, *The Cripple Liberation Front Marching Band Blues*, pp. 135–136.

60. Personal communication, October 27, 1997.

NOTES TO CHAPTER 4

1. Lorenzo Milam, "The Real Honest True Deregulation of Broadcasting," *Whole Earth Review* 68 (Fall 1990), pp. 130–131. He adds, sourly, "Later these stations and their followers devolved into lecture halls for social and political minorities."

2. Personal interview, August 27, 1997. All subsequent Yurdin quotes come from this interview, unless otherwise noted.

3. The network also set up a repeater station, KPFB, in 1955. This extended the range of KPFA's signal but offered no original programming.

4. Quoted in Eleanor McKinney, "About Pacifica Radio," in McKinney (ed.), *The Exacting Ear*, p. 16.

5. *WBAI Folio*, January 10–24, 1960.

6. Steve Post, *Playing in the FM Band: A Personal Account of Free Radio*, New York: Viking, 1974, p. 68.

7. Marshall McLuhan, *Understanding Media: The Extensions of Man*, New York: Signet, 1964, p. 265. Shepherd, by the way, was also a ham radio buff.

8. Bob Bergstresser, personal communication, April 12, 1999. He adds: "yes, I know Allen thinks of himself as an intellectual."

9. Top Forty godfather Todd Storz was also a talk radio pioneer.

10. Quoted in Christopher Koch, "Pacifica," 1968 (at www.radio4all.org/fp/koch.txt).

11. Ibid.

12. Post, pp. 80–81.

13. Gerald Jonas, "By the Dawn's Early (Bah!) Light," *New York Times*, March 26, 1967.

14. Personal communication, October 1, 1997.

15. Post, p. 38. A similar hoax had taken place on KPFK's *Radio Free Oz* in 1967.

16. Paul V. Dallas, *Dallas in Wonderland: The Pacifica Approach to Free Radio*, privately published, Los Angeles, 1967, p. 49.

17. Quoted in Frederick Wiebel, Jr., "Firesign Theatre" (at geocities.com/SunsetStrip/Alley/2928/disfire1.htm).

18. Quoted in ibid.

19. Personal interview, April 1, 1999. All subsequent Mussell quotes come from this interview. Mussell, incidentally, first got into radio as a pirate, building and operating an unlicensed transmitter in 1957, at age six.

20. "Echo Poem," from Firesign Theatre, *Dear Friends* (LP), Columbia Records, 1972. Originally broadcast on KPFK in 1970 or 1971.

21. To my taste, the best are *How Can You Be in Two Places at Once When You're Not Anywhere at All* (1969); *Don't Crush That Dwarf, Hand Me the Pliers* (1970); *I Think We're All Bozos on This Bus* (1971); and *"Everything You Know Is Wrong!"* (1974).

22. Quoted in Wiebel.

23. *Broadcasting*, April 23, 1962, p. 94.

24. FCC Docket No. 15615, Exhibit 2: "Biography of Jeremy D. Lansman."

25. Ibid.

26. Milam, *Sex and Broadcasting*, p. 126.

27. KRAB *Program Listing* #49a.

28. KRAB *Program Listing* #36.

29. Tad Cook, personal interview, May 23, 1997.

30. KRAB *Program Listing* #46.

31. KRAB *Program Listing* #42.

32. Lorenzo Milam, letter to Haley, Bader & Potts; undated, but filed on May 28, 1964.

33. Andrew Haley, letter to Lorenzo Milam, July 20, 1964.

34. Quoted in Hugh Carter Donahue, "The Fairness Doctrine Is Shackling Broadcast," *Technology Review*, November–December 1986. There have been several attempts to demonstrate that the Fairness Doctrine really did foster

open speech; the most extensive I've seen is Pat Aufderheide's "After the Fairness Doctrine: Controversial Broadcast Programming and the Public Interest," *Journal of Communication* 40:3 (Summer 1990). By now, though, it's clear that the repeal of the Fairness Doctrine actually precipitated a renaissance of opinionated, controversial speech, in the form of the talk radio boom.

35. Personal interview, August 27, 1997.

36. Emmett Watson, "Viewing the 'Media,'" *Seattle Post-Intelligencer*, February 1, 1965, p. 17.

37. John J. Eckhart, "A KRAB Is a Radio Station," *Catholic Northwest-Progress*, January 29, 1965.

38. Richard F. Shepard, "Latin Programs Ended in Seattle; 45 Other Languages Still Thrive over U.S. Stations," *New York Times*, July 13, 1963.

39. The station did run commercials on one program: WOR's *Jean Shepherd Show* was rebroadcast with the ads intact, on the grounds that they were "an integral part of the talk." (The host, after all, took time to make fun of them.) Shepherd returned the favor: on at least two of his shows, he read excerpts from KRAB's program guide, referring to the station as "Radio Sorehead." In Shepherd's personal lexicon, "sorehead" was a compliment.

40. Quoted in Stan Stapp, "KRAB, a Fresh Concept in Radio," *Seattle—North Central Outlook*, May 9, 1963.

41. Ibid.

42. Lorenzo Milam, "Where Would Christianity Be Today if Jesus Had Had a Professional Fund-Raiser as a Disciple?" KRAB *Program Listing* #48.

43. KRAB *Program Listing* #23.

44. KRAB *Program Listing* #24.

45. Milam, *Sex and Broadcasting*, pp. 56–57.

46. Post, p. 131.

47. Lorenzo Milam, letter to Michael Bader, November 5, 1965.

48. "Program Investigations," FCC Docket No. 15615, Exhibit No. 7.

49. Andrew Haley, letter to Lorenzo Milam, January 12, 1964.

50. Jeremy Lansman, letter to Michael Bader, November 3, 1964.

51. Robert K. Sanford, "Segregated Parochial School Here Outstrips Growth of Church with Which It Is Affiliated," *St. Louis Post-Dispatch*, March 27, 1966.

52. Jay Sand, *The Radio Waves Unnameable*, November 26, 1995 (at www.wbaifree.org/fass).

53. Quoted in ibid.

54. Donahue has claimed that he approached other stations before going to KMPX and that "he had not heard Miller's show before he talked with Crosby," though he'd "been told about it" (Susan Krieger, *Hip Capitalism*, Beverly Hills: Sage, 1979, p. 33). That account seems rather unlikely, and at least one of Donahue's contemporaries—the Detroit DJ Dave Dixon—has disputed it:

"Tom Donahue is a blowhard. His claims are crap! He and his friends were smoking dope and listening to Larry Miller, who brought the sound from Detroit to San Francisco" (quoted in Keith, *Voices in the Purple Haze*, p. 24). Of course, Dixon's views may be distorted by civic pride: few others have described Miller's folk-music shows in the Motor City as full-fledged freeform.

55. Quoted in Krieger, p. 79.

56. Post, p. 178.

57. Wes "Scoop" Nisker, *If You Don't Like the News . . . Go Out and Make Some of Your Own*, Berkeley: Ten Speed Press, 1994, p. 53.

58. Personal interview, September 17, 1997.

NOTES TO CHAPTER 5

1. Nicholas Johnson, ". . . And at the FCC, a Crackdown on Lyrics," *DC Gazette*, April 26, 1971, p. 15.

2. Tom Thomas, personal interview, June 11, 1997. All subsequent Thomas quotes come from this interview, unless otherwise noted.

3. "Flow" was a big word at KDNA. "It was considered a very high art form to be able to reach across genres and place and time and find things that connected," Thomas reports. "People who could do that went to the head of the class."

4. There was a low-level exchange of tapes with other community stations, as well as programs from the BBC, the Canadian Broadcasting Corporation, and the Library of Congress. The station had some more esoteric foreign sources, too, such as Radio Finland.

5. Elizabeth Gips, personal communication, November 12, 1997.

6. Milam, *The Radio Papers*, p. 81.

7. Personal interview, August 15, 1997.

8. Technically, they got $900,000 for it, but they also arranged a consultancy agreement with the buyer, Cecil Heftel, for another $200,000.

9. A few years after St. Louis's KDNA stopped broadcasting, some Hispanics in Granger, Washington, revived the call letters. Their station received some early assistance from KRAB's Jack Straw Foundation, completing the circle.

10. Quoted in Keith, p. 41.

11. Personal interview, September 17, 1999.

12. Danny Schechter, *The More You Watch, the Less You Know: News Wars/ (sub)Merged Hopes/Media Adventures*, New York: Seven Stories Press, 1997, p. 90.

13. Nisker, p. 53.

14. Dan Carlisle, quoted in Keith, p. 183.

15. Lorenzo Milam, memo to staff of KCHU, undated.

16. Krieger, p. 48.

17. After leaving Los Angeles, Yurdin reprised his Kapusta Kid character for a few months at San Diego's KPRI. His show there featured a horde of regular guests, most of them drawn from the city's underground newspaper; one was a high school kid named Cameron Crowe, who would go on to write *Fast Times at Ridgemont High* and *Almost Famous*.

18. Jan Reid, *The Improbable Rise of Redneck Rock*, New York: Da Capo Press, 1974, p. 70.

19. Ibid.

20. Ibid., p. 71.

21. Personal interview, June 21, 1998. All subsequent Chamkis quotes come from this interview.

22. *Musical Trot* continued to air on KPFT until 1995, making it the longest-running program in the station's history.

23. Nicole Mones, personal communication, October 11, 1999.

24. Steve McVicker, "Wasted Days, Wasted Lives (Part 1)," *Houston Press*, February 22, 1996.

25. Personal interview, September 17, 1997.

26. Joe Nick Patoski, "Sex, Drugs, and Rock and Roll," *Texas Monthly*, May 1996.

27. Personal communication, October 11, 1999.

28. Personal interview, August 12, 1999.

29. Personal interview, August 6, 1997.

30. Personal interview, April 9, 1999. All subsequent Uncle Sherman quotes come from this interview.

31. Personal interview, August 15, 1997.

32. Later simply called *The Planet*, after the original financiers pulled out and the show turned to *High Times* publisher Tom Forcade for support.

33. Personal interview, October 8, 1997.

34. In 1989, a former FAT disc jockey, Sully Roddy, landed a job doing a roots-music show called *All Kinds of Country*. The program included a fair amount of comedy, but the funniest thing about it was who aired it: KSAN, which had given up freeform in favor of a heavily formatted pop-country sound ten years before. (Roddy later moved the show to a series of other stations.) A few years later, another KFAT veteran, Felton Pruitt, started a syndicated show called *FAT Music*. His slogan: "Fewer hits, more often."

35. Quoted in Keith, p. 136.

36. Quoted in ibid., p. 126.

37. Jim Ladd, *Radio Waves: Life and Revolution on the FM Dial*, New York: St. Martin's, 1991, pp. 284–285.

38. John Parikhal, quoted in Jeremy Schlosberg, "Format Monotony," *Mediaweek*, September 9, 1991, pp. 27–28.

39. Schechter, p. 105.

40. Ladd, p. 280.

41. The other station Tom Donahue launched in Los Angeles—KPPC—evolved, after a fashion, into KROQ, the only commercial outlet in the L.A. market to embrace punk rock.

42. The seeds of the new Afro-freeform were planted in 1966, when George "Hound Dog" Lorenz, a white R&B jock, bought Buffalo's WBLK-FM and hired an all-black staff. The music was limited to R&B, but the jocks revived the old black radio style, and the station had an impressive array of public affairs shows (including a Black Muslim hour). In 1967, New York's WLIB-FM adopted what the historian William Barlow calls "a free-form jazz format" (Barlow, *Voice Over*, p. 233). And there were a few others: KAGB, in Los Angeles; WGPR, in Detroit; WHUR, in Washington, D.C. All except the L.A. station were commercial successes. But each either fell prey to bad circumstances—when Lorenz died, for instance, a conglomerate bought his Buffalo operation and mainstreamed its format—or slowly drifted away from their founding principles. The general trend was to drop most of the talk shows, reduce the DJs' autonomy, and adopt a slick, pop-heavy format called "urban contemporary." For more on black freeform, see Barlow, pp. 230–241.

43. As we'll see, the FCC did loosen its grip a bit in the 1980s, issuing far more licenses than before. The chief effect was not a return to freeform, but the opposite: an increase in niche formats. The arrival of Internet radio in the 1990s, a medium with no regulatory entry barriers that also poses fewer technological costs, led to an influx of both freeform and niche stations—not a surprising combination, since freeform itself is a niche. But Net radio, of course, is a new beast altogether.

44. Freedman also spent some time at the University of Michigan's WCBN, which readers with a knack for keeping track of call letters will recall was my college station. It too favors freeform.

45. This had precursors outside radio, too. DJs had started mixing records in the London discos of the 1960s, paving the way for the "northern soul" club scene and, eventually, for house music. (See Bill Brewster and Frank Broughton, *Last Night a DJ Saved My Life: The History of the Disc Jockey*, New York: Grove Press, 2000 [1999].) And in Jamaica, with its mobile sound systems, "a record stopped being a finished thing. Instead, in the studio, it became a matrix of sonic possibilities, the raw material for endless 'dubs.' . . . And when a record was played through a sound system, with a deejay toasting [rapping] over the top, it was no longer a complete piece of music but had become a tool of composition for a grander performance" (ibid, p. 109).

46. Quoted in Milam, *Sex and Broadcasting*, p. 327.

47. Personal interview, April 8, 1997. All subsequent Jaisun quotes come from this interview.

48. Personal interview, May 27, 1997.

49. When KRAB finally went under, *Live Elsewhere* moved to the University of Washington's student outlet, then known as KCMU. Several KRAB shows survived in this fashion, finding new stations to take them in.

50. Personal interview, May 29, 1997.

51. Personal communication, October 12, 1999.

52. Personal interview, February 26, 1999.

53. The station is licensed in the city of Everett but is actually located in a suburb, Lynnwood.

54. In 1974, shortly before Milam moved to Dallas, he and Lansman petitioned the FCC to examine—among other issues—whether churches were broadcasting commercial material on the explicitly noncommercial section of the FM band. When news of this reached the Christian broadcasting community, it mutated into one of America's most resilient urban legends: that the atheist activist Madalyn Murray-O'Hair was trying to abolish Christian radio. Letters continue to flood the FCC to this day, urging it not to adopt a petition it actually rejected more than two decades earlier. For more on this episode, see *The Petition against God: The Full Story of the Lansman-Milam Petition*, Dallas: Christ the Light Works, 1975, which contains the original petition, several responses to it, and a satiric introduction written by Milam and attributed to "Pastor A. W. Allworthy."

55. Milam, *The Radio Papers*, p. 115.

56. Personal interview, August 27, 1997.

57. Colin Pringle, "The Troubles We Had at the Hippie Radio Station" (at www.halcyon.com/colinp/radio.htm).

58. Milam, *The Radio Papers*, p. 123.

59. In the 1990s, this mutated into an online journal, *The Review of Arts, Literature, Philosophy, and the Humanities,* or *RALPH* (at www.ralphmag.org).

NOTES TO CHAPTER 6

1. See Ralph Engelman, *Public Radio and Television in America: A Political History*, Thousand Oaks, Calif.: Sage, 1996, p. 127.

2. Glenn Garvin, "How Do I Loathe NPR? Let Me Count the Ways," *Liberty*, August 1993, p. 45.

3. Hirschman's place in Pacifica history is difficult to describe. She was no friend to station democracy (at KPFK, she was nicknamed "the Czar"), but she also hearkened back, in some ways, to the broadcasting vision of Lewis Hill (who, come to think of it, wasn't always a great friend to station democracy either).

On resigning from KPFK, she wrote,

Years ago we were proud to be an "elitist" station. Our whole concept of "elite" cut across the lines of age, race, and class. We saw our audience as being those who were responsive to ideas—political, artistic, visionary.

Now the word "elite" is distinctly unfashionable. Today we are concerned over whether we are reaching "the people." Interestingly, "the people" we seem to have in mind appear to be less intelligent than our former listeners."

Quoted in Ron Ridenour, "Making Waves at Pacifica Radio: KPFK," *Seven Days*, March 28, 1977.

4. That said, its biggest audience-booster was probably Hirschman's decision to play NPR's *Morning Edition* twice in a row each day. Hirschman has since changed her surname to Seymour, as a fundraising gimmick.

5. Milam, *Sex and Broadcasting*, p. 233.

6. Richard Kostelanetz, *Radio Writings*, Union City, N.J.: Further State(s) of the Art, 1995, p. 167.

7. My narrative ignores the other great question about the Corporation for Public Broadcasting: whether it is morally proper to force people to fund speech with which they disagree. This is not because I think the question is unimportant—indeed, I myself find the CPB objectionable on those grounds—but because it has not, alas, been a significant issue either in the government's decision to launch the corporation or in stations' decisions to take or refuse its money.

8. Thus, at one point in the CPB's early years, it gave KRAB a one-time, $7,500 award. The same year, the station received larger grants from local sources.

9. Quoted in Milam, *Sex and Broadcasting*, pp. 273, 275.

10. Morgan Miller, personal interview, August 10, 1997.

11. Quoted in Richard Mahler, "Community Radio: Its Day in the Sun," *Public Telecommunications Review*, March–April 1979, p. 70.

12. Personal interview, July 26, 1997. All subsequent Phaneuf quotes come from this interview.

13. Milam, *The Radio Papers*, p. 104.

14. Personal interview, August 27, 1997.

15. If you'd like to sort out the competing claims for yourself, see Michael C. Keith, *Signals in the Air: Native Broadcasting in America*, Westport, Conn.: Praeger, 1995, pp. 21–22.

16. David Armstrong, *A Trumpet to Arms: Alternative Media in America*, Los Angeles: J. P. Tarcher, 1981, p. 215.

17. Sam Smith, "Magna Cum Probation: Falling from Grace at Harvard U," *Progressive Review*, April 1999, p. 10.

18. Ibid., p. 12.

19. Quoted in Guy Raz, "Radio Free Georgetown," *Washington City Paper*, January 29–February 4, 1999. The angry manager, Ken Sleeman, went on to run an unlicensed low-power station out of his house in Rockville,

Maryland, and to give technical assistance to a micro station in D.C.'s Mount Pleasant neighborhood.

20. WGTB was revived in 1996 as a carrier-current station. Its schedule contains no political programs, although the rock music it plays is fairly adventurous by commercial standards.

21. Milam, *Sex and Broadcasting*, pp. 120–121.

22. The CPB offers two more programs, its Station Development Grants and Program Acquisition Grants, to plug small stations into the public radio satellite system and help them meet the CPB's funding standards.

23. Jon Bekken, "Community Radio at the Crossroads: Federal Policy and the Professionalization of a Grassroots Medium," in Sakolsky and Dunifer, p. 33. See also Jon Bekken, "The End of the CPB?" *Radio Resistor's Bulletin*, March 1995.

24. Quoted in Edd Routt, James McGrath, and Fredric A. Weiss, *The Radio Format Conundrum*, New York: Hastings House, 1978, pp. 277–278.

25. Personal interview, April 17, 1997.

26. The NFCB also supported a new rule requiring stations to broadcast a minimum number of hours per day—more fallout, one suspects, from the St. Louis battle.

27. Federal Communications Commission, Second Report and Order, In the Matter of Changes in the Rules Relating to Noncommercial Educational FM Broadcast Stations, 69 F.C.C. 2d 240, 246 (1978).

28. Petition of the Intercollegiate Broadcast System to the FCC, Docket 20735, filed June 26, 1972.

29. David Josephson, personal communication, April 2, 1997.

30. More precisely, it announced a freeze on new Class D licenses. The freeze later became permanent.

31. The new rules did not apply in Alaska, which organizes its FM spectrum differently.

32. See Scott M. Martin, "Educational FM Radio—The Failure of Reform," *Federal Communications Law Journal* 34 (Summer 1982), p. 431.

33. Quoted in Mahler, p. 75.

34. I stole both of those examples from William Barlow, "Community Radio in the U.S.: The Struggle for a Democratic Medium," *Media, Culture and Society* 10:1 (1988), pp. 81, 96–98.

35. The conflict arguably dated to the federation's birth, but something really shifted in the late 1980s.

36. *Community Radio News*, August 1994, p. 1.

37. Cathy Melio, personal interview, January 8, 1997.

38. Bekken, "Community Radio at the Crossroads," p. 34.

39. Jay Teutenberg, "KOPN-FM, Columbia, Missouri, Community Radio," *Radio Resistor's Bulletin*, December 1993.

40. Ibid.

41. Don Jacobson, "Experience Talks about the HSP," *Radio Resistor's Bulletin*, December 1994.

42. "Mission statements" themselves tend to be nonsense, but the process of sorting out a station's purpose can be valuable.

43. Personal interview, December 12, 1996.

44. Personal interview, February 10, 1997. All subsequent Scott quotes come from this interview, unless otherwise noted.

45. Harvey Wheeler, personal communication, February 12, 1997.

46. *A Vision for Pacifica Radio: Creating a Network for the 21st Century*, April 1997 (at www.pacifica.org/board/docs/avision.html).

47. Letter to Belinda Griswold, December 12, 1996.

48. Playing the Gingrich bogeyman card was rather disingenuous. As one former KPFK worker told me, "Newt Gingrich is not a threat. Pacifica was poised to profit greatly off of Newt Gingrich. All you had to do was be there and basically say, 'We criticized Gingrich.' And the money would come in."

49. *A Vision for Pacifica Radio*.

50. Letter to Belinda Griswold, December 12, 1996.

51. *A Vision for Pacifica Radio*.

52. Personal interview, December 12, 1996.

53. Whiting, "Pacifica in Vincula."

54. Pat Scott, "Pacifica: We Want to Be Effective, Not Bust Our Union" (letter), *Current*, July 8, 1996.

55. Jacqueline Conciatore, "Workers Charge Pacifica with Union Busting," *Current*, June 17, 1996.

56. At featurestory.com/about.html.

57. "Feature Stories News: Is It Pacifica or Is It Fox?" February 24, 2000 (at savepacifica.net/strike/fsn.html).

58. Minutes, Pacifica Program Directors' Meeting, Albuquerque, New Mexico, February 27, 1995.

59. Pacifica Administrative Council, National Program Process Agreement, June 1993.

60. Interviewed by Peggy Norton, "Independent Radio's Problems and Prospects," *Z*, March 1994.

61. Larry Bensky, remarks prepared for Pacifica National Board, February 28, 1999. Because of a time limit, Bensky was unable to complete his presentation; he later circulated the full version via e-mail.

62. Ibid. Bensky, incidentally, is another broadcaster who's worked in both community radio and commercial freeform: before coming to KPFA in the early '70s, he was news director at KSAN.

63. Armando J. Arvizu, Corporation for Public Broadcasting, Office of

Inspector General: Compliance Audit of Pacifica Foundation, Berkeley, California, Audit Report No. 97-01, April 9, 1997.

64. Corporation for Public Broadcasting Board, finding in response to the inspector general's audit, May 19, 1997.

65. Robert Coonrod, letter to Patricia Scott, September 14, 1998.

66. Quoted in John Sommers, post to Freepacifica e-mail list, June 27, 1999.

67. Pacifica Foundation, "Pacifica Foundation Fundraising Policies," press release, May 23, 1999.

68. Matthew Lasar, "Pacifica and Conditional Grant Seeking," press release, May 25, 1999.

69. Michael Palmer, e-mail to Mary Frances Berry, July 9, 1999.

70. Pete Bramson, statement at press conference, Berkeley, California, July 28, 1999.

71. Quoted by Mimi Rosenberg, interview on *Flashpoints*, KPFA, August 25, 1999.

72. Quoted in Judith Coburn, "There's Something about Mary," *Salon*, October 12, 1999.

73. Some early speculation had it that the signal was coming from Los Angeles, which was not true. Pacifica's apologists seized on this and some other false rumors as evidence that the dissidents were playing loose with the facts, as though there were any comparison between some inaccurate rumors among the protesters and the foundation's pattern of deliberate dissembling.

74. David Giovannoni, Report to the Pacifica Board, February 25, 2000.

NOTES TO CHAPTER 7

1. Collective A/Traverso, "Radio Alice—Free Radio," in Sylvere Lotringer and Christian Marazzi (eds.), *Semiotext(e) Italy: Autonomia*, New York: Semiotext(e), 1980, p. 132.

2. Quoted in Peter M. Lewis, "Community Radio: The Montreal Conference and After," *Media, Culture and Society* 6:2 (April 1984), p. 144.

3. Quoted in Judith Malina, "Nonviolence in Bologna," in *Semiotext(e) Italy*, p. 126.

4. In an incestuous twist, Radio Atlanta broadcast from the *Mi Amigo*—the same ship used, until 1962, by the Swedish pirate Radio Nord.

5. Quoted in Alan Travis, "Big Guns Missed Radio Caroline," *Guardian*, June 6, 1998, p. 7.

6. When the *London Times* asked BBC officials for their reaction to the survey, they replied that "Radio Scotland's transmissions were very close to the Light Programme [BBC] wave length, and that sometimes confused listeners." In modern lingo, this is called *spin*. The historian Donald Browne notes, "Since Radio Scotland identified itself several times an hour, the confu-

sion should have been minimal." Don R. Browne, "The BBC and the Pirates: A Phase in the Life of a Prolonged Monopoly," *Journalism Quarterly* (Spring 1971), p. 93, n. 25.

7. Quoted in Paul Harris, *When Pirates Ruled the Waves*, London: Impulse, 1968, p. 43.

8. Erwin S. Strauss, "When Pirates Ruled the Waves (A Review)," *Reason*, February 1971, p. 11.

9. Indeed, some bombs attributed to the left were actually planted by fascists, who wanted to provoke a crackdown. Historians are still sorting out just who was responsible for which atrocity.

10. Percy Allum, "Terrorism in Italy," *New Society*, March 30, 1978, p. 711.

11. Quoted in Roberto Grandi, "Italy," in Philip T. Rosen (ed.), *International Handbook of Broadcasting Systems*, New York: Greenwood Press, 1988, p. 163.

12. My discussion of this and other left-wing radio stations in 1970s Italy draws on John Downing, *Radical Media: The Political Experience of Alternative Communication*, Boston: South End Press, 1984.

13. The Italian Communist Party had condemned the invasion, but the Florentine branch, evidently more Stalinist than headquarters, supported it.

14. Collective A/Traverso, p. 133.

15. John Downing, *The Media Machine*, London: Pluto Press, 1980, p. 205.

16. See ibid, p. 204.

17. When America's established broadcasters went on the offensive against micro radio, they pointed to Italy to rally the troops. In a memo faxed to licensed stations around the country on April 23, 1998, *Radio Ink* publisher Eric Rhoads warned that some at the FCC felt "that it is acceptable to allow thousands of new, low power stations. Their belief is that this will give everyone their chance to broadcast their agenda to their local community. Rome, Italy, has hundreds of neighborhood radio stations, so many you cannot drive across town on one frequency without encountering dozens of signals. *Your* market could be flooded with similar interference." Note the odd redefinition of "interference."

18. I've borrowed the phrase "second left" from the historians George Ross and Laura Frader, who distinguished the *autogestionnaire* tendency from the "first left" of the Trotskyist and Maoist sects and the "third left" of mainstream social democracy. See George Ross and Laura Frader, "The May Generation: From Mao to Mitterand," *Socialist Review* 18:4 (October–December 1988).

19. Quoted in Marc Raboy, "Media and Politics in Socialist France," *Media, Culture and Society* 5:3/4 (July–October 1983), pp. 303–320.

20. "Radio-Freeing Europe," *Reason*, January 1984, p. 20.

21. Quoted in Sandy McCroskey, "Radio X-Periment in Amsterdam: Veteran Air Pirates Seize Cable License," *Overthrow*, Spring 1986, p. 7. For more on the Dutch squatters and their media, see ADILKNO, *Cracking the Movement:*

Squatting beyond the Media, translated by Laura Martz, New York: Autonomedia, 1994. [Dutch edition published in 1990.]

22. West German broadcasting was long hobbled by the nation's newspaper interests, which lobbied fiercely to keep the airwaves free of anyone who might compete for ad revenue.

23. Quoted in "Micro Radio Legalized in Japan," *National Lawyers Guild Committee on Democratic Communications Newsletter,* July 1995, p. 3.

24. Quoted in Aki Okabe, "It All Started in Kobe" (at www.igc.org/ ohdakefoundation/npo/kobe.htm).

25. Some Indians in southern Ontario and Quebec have recently returned to unlicensed broadcasting, declaring that they owe their allegiance to the sovereign First Nations, not to the government of Canada, and that the latter thus has no right to regulate them.

26. Paulette Jiles, "Community Radio in Big Trout Lake," appendix to Milam, *Sex and Broadcasting,* p. 283.

27. Paulette Jiles, *North Spirit: Sojourns among the Cree and Ojibway,* St. Paul, Minn.: Hungry Mind, 1995, p. 29.

28. As Lorenzo Milam wrote with admiration, "think of . . . any of those rich booby state educational broadcast organizations going out to the boonies, setting up a tiny station for the people, and then having the 'broadcast-animator' *work himself out of a job!*" Milam, *Sex and Broadcasting,* p. 280.

29. Both quotations from Arturo E. Bregaglio and Sergio Tagle, "The New Wave: The Emergence of Low-Power Radio in Argentina," in Bruce Girard (ed.), *A Passion for Radio: Radio Waves and Community,* Montreal: Black Rose Books, 1992, pp. 182–183.

30. And also, less fortunately, to revamp the old Third Programme to make it more responsive to lowest-common-denominator tastes. Thus the crown jewel of the BBC—the service whose quality almost justified the state monopoly—was watered down beyond recognition. And no autonomous outfit like the early Pacifica was permitted to pick up the slack.

31. A. Presenter, "Localism or Parochialism: The Dilemma of Local Radio," *Raven* 32 (Winter 1995), p. 332.

32. Simon Reynolds, "Rave and Jungle on UK Pirate Radio," June 1998 (at furious.com/perfect/simonreynolds.html).

33. Quoted in Alex Benady, "The Outlaws of the Airwaves," *Independent,* July 7, 1998.

34. By some accounts, it is France's *only* profitable private network.

35. Jean-Paul Lafrance and Jean Paul Simon, "France: Broadcasting in Turmoil," in Nick Jankowski, Ole Prehn, and James Stappers (eds.), *The People's Voice: Local Radio and Television in Europe,* London: John Libbey, 1992, pp. 177–178.

36. A more independent community station, Radio Bamakan, came to Mali

in 1991. Unlike Kayes, Bamakan did not arrive with state support. Indeed, when it first began broadcasting, it was unlicensed, and the government tried to shut it down. It is now fully legal, as is a private commercial station that followed it onto the air.

37. Wijayananda Jayaweera and Louie Tabing, "Villages Find Their Voice," *UNESCO Courier*, February 1997, p. 34.

38. Carlos A. Arnaldo, "By the People, for the People," *UNESCO Courier*, February 1997, p. 33.

39. Ibid, p. 34.

40. Evelyn Foy, "A Difficult Birth for C.R. in Sri Lanka," *InteRadio* 2:3 (1991).

41. MJR David, "Mahaweli Community Radio," in Girard, pp. 138–139.

42. Genuflecting briefly to social justice concerns, the Social Democrats argued that only wealthy groups would be able to afford to participate in the *när-radio* system. This prediction proved completely false, in part because many groups opted to share studio space with one another.

43. Typically, the CBC provides the bare necessities—a small console, a tape recorder, some microphones, a couple of CD players and/or turntables—and asks the locals to provide the studio space.

NOTES TO CHAPTER 8

1. One person who didn't care for how the feds treated McIntire's outfit was Lorenzo Milam. "After all," he wrote, "they are experimenting, as we all ought, with controversial radio: their one failing is that they refuse to believe—religious militants are such dolts—that there are other points of view that deserve airing." Milam, *Sex and Broadcasting*, p. 64.

2. If river-based stations count as "offshore," you might also include WUMS—the call letters stood for "We're Unknown Mysterious Station"—which the journalist Andrew Yoder says "operated irregularly from the banks of the Ohio River from 1924 until 1948." Andrew Yoder, "The History of Unlicensed Radio," *Electronics Now*, June 1, 1999.

3. Post to Broadcast e-mail list, May 26, 1998.

4. Chuck Forsberg, personal communication, November 12, 1998.

5. Chuck Forsberg, "Radio Free Moscow, 1960–1961" (at psg.com/~caf/rfm.html).

6. Quoted in The Hound, "Dave Rabbit," in Neil Strauss with Dave Mandl (eds.), *Radiotext(e)*, New York: Semiotext(e), 1993, p. 50.

7. Allan H. Weiner with Anita Louise McCormick, *Access to the Airwaves: My Fight for Free Radio*, Port Townsend, Wash.: Loompanics, 1997, p. 12. My discussion of Weiner's career draws heavily on this memoir, an engaging piece of Americana that I recommend highly.

8. Such signals are legal under the FCC's Part 15 regulations, which allow people to make very-low-powered transmissions without a license, provided they do not interfere with other signals. Part 15 exists to permit devices such as garage openers, which should give you an idea of how short such transmitters' range is.

9. Ibid., p. 47.

10. Ibid.

11. Quoted in Lawrence Soley, *Free Radio: Electronic Civil Disobedience*, Boulder: Westview Press, 1998, p. 55.

12. Weiner, p. 60.

13. Personal interview, November 3, 1998. All subsequent Simmons quotes come from this interview.

14. Bob Bickford, "More Notes about KBSA-FM," 1987/1995/1997 (at daft.com/~rab/kbsa.html).

15. All quotes about Mark's stations are from his website (at members .tripod.com/~AMN92).

16. Later called WFAT, and still later WHOT.

17. Quoted in Soley, p. 58.

18. Quoted in ibid.

19. Andrew Yoder, "FM Microcasting: It's a Neighborhood Thing," *Hobby Broadcasting*, Spring 1998, p. 17.

20. Their shift from FM to shortwave came in 1989, after a run-in with the FCC—and, coincidentally, just as the modern micro movement was starting to emerge. They were also involved, briefly, with Allan Weiner's Radio New York International.

21. "Pirate Joe and the Kilocycle Kops," *Economist*, American edition, April 24, 1982, p. 57.

22. Comrade Jim, "Underground Broadcasting," *Overthrow*, April–May 1985, p. 16. The yippies' interest in pirate radio goes at least as far back as 1971, when Abbie Hoffman, aware that not every town had a *Radio Unnameable* of its own, included some guerrilla-broadcasting tips in his *Steal This Book*.

NOTES TO CHAPTER 9

1. *Low Power Empowerment*, Paper Tiger Television, November 4, 1991.

2. Quoted in Soley, p. 72.

3. The TRA paid for the equipment, which cost $600, with a grant it had received from the Catholic Church's Campaign for Human Development. The Campaign revoked its support when it found out it had funded an unlicensed radio station, but by that time Readus had already spent the money.

4. Luis J. Rodríguez, "Rappin' in the Hood," *Nation*, August 12–19, 1991, p. 194.

5. M'banna Kantako, quoted in Jerry Landay, "We're Part of the Restoration Process of Our People," in Sakolsky and Dunifer, p. 98.

6. Conference materials, Grassroots Radio Conference I, 1996.

7. Another inspiration: the cult film *Pump Up the Volume* (1990), starring Christian Slater as a teenage pirate fighting a corrupt high school and the FCC.

8. Richard Edmondson, *Rising Up: Class Warfare in America from the Streets to the Airwaves*, San Francisco: Librad Press, 2000, pp. 12–13.

9. "Radio Activists Speak Out!" in Sakolsky and Dunifer, p. 91.

10. For evidence of this, examine an article Committee leaders Peter Franck and Alan Korn wrote in 1995, declaring that media activists "cannot rely on the power of the state to get it right. This is because powerful institutions contain the built-in contradictions of centralization and bureaucracy" (Peter Franck and Alan Korn, "A Question for the CDC and the Guild," *National Lawyers Guild Committee on Democratic Communications Newsletter*, July 1995, p. 6).

11. Quoted in Elaine Herscher, "Judge Refuses FCC Plea to Bar Free Radio Berkeley," *San Francisco Chronicle*, January 21, 1995, p. A17. An eyewitness later told me that when Wilken announced her ruling, Silverman's head "nearly exploded."

12. Personal interview, May 1995.

13. Beverly Baker, letter to Betsy Johnsen, October 14, 1994.

14. Charles T. Morgan, letter to William Kennard, May 2, 1995.

15. Personal interview, May 18, 1998. All subsequent Perry quotes come from this interview.

16. Personal interview, November 2, 1999.

17. Order Granting Plaintiff's Motion for Summary Judgment and Granting Permanent Injunction, *United States v. Stephen Paul Dunifer*, p. 18, June 16, 1998.

18. Personal interview, September 23, 1999. All subsequent Schreiner quotes come from this interview.

19. Personal interview, September 23, 1999. All subsequent Bardacke quotes come from this interview.

20. At www.frn.net.

21. At pirateradio.about.com/entertainment/pirateradio.

22. At www.radio4all.org.

23. Pete triDish, "Radio Mutiny on Tour!" *Hobby Broadcasting*, Summer 1998, pp. 32–33.

24. Personal communication, August 3, 1999.

25. "I try to keep a good sense of humor about these writers who are more interested in describing my beard than in the issues." Pete triDish, post to MRN e-mail list, October 27, 2000.

26. Lorenzo Ervin, seminar at East Coast Microbroadcasting Conference, April 1998.

27. Quoted in Dan Fields, "Napoleon Williams Receives Probation," *Decatur Herald-Review*, December 18, 1998.

28. Dharma Bilotta-Dailey and Tracy Jake Siska, "Black Liberation Radio: An Independent Investigation," privately circulated, December 1998.

29. Ibid.

30. Ibid.

31. Ibid.

32. Tracy Jake Siska, personal interview, November 11, 2000.

33. Personal interview, November 13, 1998. All subsequent Goodman quotes come from this interview, unless otherwise noted.

34. Eric Firpo, "From Day Care Provider to Toxic Avenger," *Santa Maria Times*, March 29, 1996, p. 16.

35. Quoted in Stephen Dunifer, "Refabricating Community," in Dunifer and Sakolsky, p. 156.

36. Sarah Ferguson, "Radio Free Florida," *Vibe*, November 1998.

37. I was joined on my trip by my colleague Michael Lynch, who subsequently wrote a fine article about both WLUV in Homestead and Hot 97.7 in Miami. Those seeking a more in-depth discussion of those stations should read his piece: "Dead Air," *Reason*, August–September 1999.

38. Personal communication, March 23, 2000. As of that date, the case had not yet gone to trial.

39. Tony Pugh, "BASS-FM Gets a Warm Reception," *Miami Herald*, June 6, 1993, p. B5. The record is far from clear, but the station may have been named for an earlier BASS-FM—also a pirate outlet—founded by the rapper Luther Campbell in 1989.

40. Michael Lynch and I mentioned his name in several places around town—in a grocery store, a school, etc.—and someone always knew who he was.

41. Personal interview, April 26, 1999.

42. Personal interview, April 26, 1999. Dean also confirmed Bo's story about the police surveillance.

43. Kid Curry, quoted in Ferguson.

44. Quoted in Errol Nazareth, "Hip-Hop His #1 Priority, Canadian Makes U.S. Rap Label a Success," *Toronto Sun*, April 18, 1999, p. S6.

45. Personal communication, September 7, 1999.

46. Ibid.

47. Personal interview, April 26, 1997. All subsequent Lane quotes come from this interview.

48. Forgive my vagueness, but he isn't seeking publicity and I don't want to alert the FCC.

49. Quoted in Scott Jacoby, "Pumping Up the Volume," *Ozarks*, June 1998. Nor is the Springfield DJ the only microcaster to engage in that practice. I've heard anecdotal accounts of the same thing happening at other unlicenced out-

lets, and I've seen a press account describing it at yet another station (Rona Kobell, "Warrant Wrenches Radio Rebel off the Air," *Pittsburgh Post-Gazette*, November 8, 1998, p. B1).

50. Personal (anonymous) communication, July 18, 1997. That "The Tree" moniker is actually kind of witty: it's a parody of one of Seattle's legal stations, "The Mountain."

51. Steve Jones, "Unlicensed Broadcasting: Content and Conformity," *Journalism Quarterly* (Summer 1994).

52. From the EBRadio website (at home.flash.net/~ebradio).

53. Quoted in Marc Fisher, "Radio Free Oxon Hill," *Washington Post*, August 14, 1998, p. D7.

NOTES TO CHAPTER 10

1. Quoted in Sarah Foster, "SWAT Teams vs. Airwaves 'Pirates': Do Unlicensed Radio Stations Pose a Danger to the Public?" *WorldNetDaily*, December 18, 1997.

2. Anthony eventually acquired a licensed station. In 1998, he bought WCNJ in Hazlet, New Jersey, and shifted it to a "Solid Gold" oldies format.

3. John Fiorini, at "Pirate Radio and Microradio" workshop, NAB Radio Show, October 15, 1998.

4. Personal interview with John Winston, December 8, 1997. All subsequent Winston quotes come from this interview.

5. Shortly after my interviews with Winston and Kajunski, I e-mailed Kennard. "Different FCC officers give me different answers to this question," I wrote, "so I thought I'd just go to the top: Has the FCC made enforcement against pirate radio more of a priority in the last few months, or has it not?" Four days later, he replied: "The FCC's enforcement policy has been consistent during the past few months." Which initially sounds like a denial, but seems more delphic the more you think about it. (William Kennard, personal communication, December 14, 1997.)

6. There were also several cases of FCC agents pressuring landlords to evict their microcasting tenants.

7. Richard D. Lee, at "Pirate Radio and Microradio" workshop, NAB Radio Show, October 15, 1998.

8. Edward Fritts, press release, September 5, 1997.

9. Personal interview, December 8, 1997.

10. Beverly Baker and Jack Goodman, at NAB conference, April 1997.

11. Tracy Jake Siska and Dharma Bilotta-Dailey, "FCC's Interference Argument Grounded," *Extra!*, January–February 1999.

12. Dharma Bilotta-Dailey, post to MRN e-mail list, September 26, 1998.

13. Siska and Bilotta-Dailey, "FCC's Interference Argument Grounded."

14. Affidavit of Pastor David Knight, *Prayze FM and Mark Blake v. Federal Communications Commission*, June 24, 1998, p. 2. Emphasis in original.

15. Issuance of a Temporary Restraining Order before the Honorable Warren W. Eginton, *Prayze FM and Mark Blake v. Federal Communications Commission*, February 27, 1998, pp. 11–12.

16. Ibid., p. 3.

17. For a while, the hot court case involved several programmers from Steal This Radio, which in 1998 sued the FCC for violating its rights of free speech. Like the Prayze case, this took the unusual form of a microbroadcaster bringing the government to court, rather than the other way around; like the Prayze case, it raised a lot of hopes but ultimately lost.

18. Skinner wrote to Stephen Dunifer early on, hoping for support from the pirate camp. After Dunifer and most other microcasters rejected his petition, Skinner turned to denouncing unlicensed radio altogether.

19. Jim du Bois, memo to station managers, April 27, 1998.

20. Comments of the National Association of Broadcasters, In the Matter of Petition for Rule Making to Create an Indoor Sports and Entertainment Radio Service, RM-9682, submitted August 9, 1999, pp. 3–4, 6.

21. Thank FCC chairman Mark Fowler, a genuine believer in free markets, for that one. Only a few years before, by contrast, the NAB had easily beaten back a proposal by the House Communications Subcommittee chair, Representative Lionell Van Deerlin (D–California), to reallocate UHF channels 67, 68, and 69 to FM, making room for as many as 450 new low-power stations in each urban market.

22. The bill passed 414–16 in the House and 91–5 in the Senate, with President Clinton's support.

23. J. T. Anderton and Thom Moon, "Distant Early Warning: Another APR Decline" (at duncanradio.com/comments.html).

24. Formerly known as CD Radio.

25. Or, thanks to various corporate partnerships, they can buy a new car with a special antenna that renders the dish unnecessary.

26. Formerly known as the American Mobile Radio Corporation.

27. Some of those channels will include commercials; others will not.

28. Quoted in Brooks Boliek, "Broadcasters Trying to Shoot Down Satellite Radio," *Hollywood Reporter*, December 29, 1994.

29. Representative Billy Tauzin, letter to William Kennard, February 11, 1999.

30. Speech before the National Association of Broadcasters, April 20, 1999.

31. Quoted in "Republican Opposition against Microradio Mounts at NAB Show," *Public Broadcasting Report*, April 23, 1999.

32. Post to MRN e-mail list, February 13, 1999.

33. Post to MRN e-mail list, February 1, 1999.

34. Personal communication, September 27, 1999.

35. Post to MRN e-mail list, March 19, 1999.

36. Towns in other states passed similar resolutions, but no other state saw the kind of organized grassroots effort that swept through Michigan.

37. Richard D. Lee, Disclosure of Information Form, November 2, 1999.

38. Ibid.

39. Personal (anonymous) interview, November 1999.

40. After two years, organizations would be allowed to own five low-power licenses. After four years, the cap would jump to ten.

41. Federal Communications Commission, Report and Order, MM Docket 9925, In the Matter of Creation of a Low Power Radio Service. Adopted January 20, 2000; released January 27, 2000.

42. Another suit was filed by pirates upset that the plan was so narrow. In an amusing twist, the court combined the two challenges.

43. NPR was joined by the International Association of Audio Information Services, representing 135 of the country's 150 Reading Services for the Blind, which argued that low-power radio would interfere with its members' programs (readings of newspapers, transit information, and the like, usually transmitted via FM stations' subcarrier frequencies). Defenders of the FCC's plan pointed out that it already included permanent protection for the reading services.

44. Post to MRN e-mail list, December 15, 2000.

45. Personal interview, February 17, 1999.

46. Jimmy Carter's FCC also began to authorize low-power TV stations and found space for more VHF channels.

47. Thomas Streeter, *Selling the Air: A Critique of the Policy of Commercial Broadcasting in the United States,* Chicago: University of Chicago Press, 1996, p. 175.

48. The speech regulations—the Communications Decency Act, a subset of the larger Telecom Act—were later ruled unconstitutional.

49. Susan A. Lynner, "FCC Opts for Federal Framework over State Discretion in Local Competition Proposal," *Telecommunications Regulatory Update,* April 25, 1996, p. 3.

50. The usual argument against homesteading is that it would unleash an unruly land rush, as the pent up demand for unused spectrum pushes a wave of air-hungry entrepreneurs onto the dial, spreading chaos and stepping on each others' toes. But even if this were true, it would be a problem only for the initial disbursement of spectrum rights—so there'd still be room for homesteading in the long run.

NOTES TO CHAPTER 11

1. I. R. Ybarra, "CB Radio Revisited and the Information Superhighway," *Alternative Press Review,* Spring–Summer 1995, pp. 20–21.

2. Quoted in Carolyn Marvin and Quentin J. Schultze, "The First Thirty Years," *Journal of Communication* (Summer 1977), p. 108. It shouldn't be surprising that the FCC would take those channels from the hams, the least powerful incumbents on the spectrum.

3. Quoted in ibid., p. 109.

4. Quoted in ibid.

5. Ibid., pp. 115–116.

6. Harold R. Kerbo, Karrie Marshall, and Philip Holley, "Reestablishing 'Germeinschaft'?: An Examination of the CB Radio Fad," *Urban Life* 7:3 (October 1978).

7. Quoted in Erwin G. Krasnow and Lawrence D. Longley, *The Politics of Broadcast Regulation*, second edition, New York: St. Martin's, 1978, p. 167. [First edition published in 1973.]

8. That said, there may yet be some life in that old CB corpse, despite Ybarra's report. A Texas group called Red Asphalt Nomad has brought an avant-garde sensibility to CB Channel 23, mixing Smokey reports and open conversations with tape loops, police scanners, white noise, and music. Sometimes they aimlessly drive en masse, trading poetic comments about the landscape—combining the convoy with the *dérive*.

9. "Blabbermouths," *Newsweek*, September 10, 1973, p. 53. Other press accounts noted the use of CB radios among prostitutes, burglars, and other lawbreakers.

10. At the height of the CB fad, Hollywood produced a movie that showed those controls in action, down to a vigilante group that smashed offenders' transmitters. The film was Jonathan Demme's *Citizens Band* (1977), sometimes known as *Handle with Care*. Viewers can decide for themselves how much of this was based on real practices and how much sprang entirely from the screenwriter's imagination.

11. Quoted in Krasnow and Longley, p. 165.

12. George Gilder, *Life after Television*, New York: Norton, 1992 [1990], pp. 40–41.

13. Laura Flanders, "Move Over, Pacifica! Here Come IndyMedia," *CounterPunch*, April 15–30, 2000.

14. At rcsworks.com/products/selector/selreach.htm.

15. Michelle Goldberg, "Mood Radio," *Noise*, November 2000.

16. Quoted in John H. Fund, "The Power of Talk," *Forbes MediaCritic*, Spring 1995, p. 55.

17. Quoted in Christopher Hill, *The World Turned Upside Down: Radical Ideas during the English Revolution*, New York: Penguin Books, 1975 [1972], p. 198.

Index

313

About the Author

JESSE WALKER is an associate editor of *Reason* magazine. His articles have appeared in many publications, including the *New York Times*, *L.A. Weekly*, *Salon*, the *New Republic*, the *All-Music Guide*, *Radio World*, and Z. He lives in Los Angeles.